Understanding the Social World

To Julia Ellen Schutt

SAGE was founded in 1965 by Sara Miller McCune to support the dissemination of usable knowledge by publishing innovative and high-quality research and teaching content. Today, we publish over 900 journals, including those of more than 400 learned societies, more than 800 new books per year, and a growing range of library products including archives, data, case studies, reports, and video. SAGE remains majority-owned by our founder, and after Sara's lifetime will become owned by a charitable trust that secures our continued independence.

Los Angeles | London | New Delhi | Singapore | Washington DC

Understanding the Social World

Research Methods for the 21st Century

Russell K. Schutt
University of Massachusetts Boston

Los Angeles | London | New Delhi
Singapore | Washington DC

Los Angeles | London | New Delhi
Singapore | Washington DC

FOR INFORMATION:

SAGE Publications, Inc.
2455 Teller Road
Thousand Oaks, California 91320
E-mail: order@sagepub.com

SAGE Publications Ltd.
1 Oliver's Yard
55 City Road
London EC1Y 1SP
United Kingdom

SAGE Publications India Pvt. Ltd.
B 1/I 1 Mohan Cooperative Industrial Area
Mathura Road, New Delhi 110 044
India

SAGE Publications Asia-Pacific Pte. Ltd.
3 Church Street
#10-04 Samsung Hub
Singapore 049483

Publisher: Jerry Westby
Associate Editor: Jessica Miller
eLearning Editor: Nicole Mangona
Editorial Assistant: Laura Kirkhuff
eLearning Editor: Nicole Mangona
Production Editor: David C. Felts
Copy Editor: Amy Marks
Typesetter: C&M Digitals (P) Ltd.
Proofreader: Christine Dahlin
Indexer: Maria Sosnowski
Cover Designer: Gail Buschman
Marketing Manager: Amy Lammers

Printed in the United States of America.

Library of Congress Cataloging-in-Publication Data

Names: Schutt, Russell K., author.
Title: Understanding the social world : research methods for the 21st century / Russell K. Schutt.
Description: Thousand Oaks, California : SAGE, [2017] | Includes bibliographical references and index.
Identifiers: LCCN 2015040054 | ISBN 978-1-5063-0601-8 (pbk. : alk. paper)
Subjects: LCSH: Social sciences—Research—Methodology.
Classification: LCC H62 .S3497 2017 | DDC 300.72/1—dc23 LC record available at http://lccn.loc.gov/2015040054

This book is printed on acid-free paper.

16 17 18 19 20 10 9 8 7 6 5 4 3 2 1

Brief Contents

On the Study Site

edge.sagepub.com/schuttusw

Detailed Contents

©iStockphoto.com/joste_dj

Chapter 3. Research Ethics 31

Section II. Fundamentals of Social Research

©iStockphoto.com/KM6064

Chapter 4. Conceptualization and Measurement 44

© Can Stock Photo Inc. / Paha_L

©iStockphoto.com/ThomasVogel

Section III. Basic Social Research Designs

© Can Stock Photo Inc. / Paha_L

Chapter 9. Unobtrusive Methods 137

©iStockphoto.com/sanjeri

Chapter 8. Qualitative Methods 119

©iStockphoto.com/Juanmonino

Chapter 10. Evaluation and Mixed-Methods Research 157

Section IV. Analysis and Reporting of Social Research

Roz Woodward/Photodisc/Thinkstock

Chapter 11. Quantitative Data Analysis 171

©iStockphoto.com/Yuri_Arcurs

On the Study Site

edge.sagepub.com/schuttusw

About the Author

Russell K. Schutt, Ph.D., is Professor and Chair of Sociology at the University of Massachusetts Boston and Lecturer on Sociology in the Department of Psychiatry (Massachusetts Mental Health Center, Beth Israel Deaconess Medical Center) at the Harvard Medical School. He completed his B.A., M.A., and Ph.D. degrees at the University of Illinois at Chicago and was a postdoctoral fellow in the Sociology of Social Control Training Program at Yale University. In addition to *Investigating the Social World: The Process and Practice of Research*, now in its eighth edition, and adaptations of that text—*Making Sense of the Social World* (with Dan Chambliss), *Research Methods in Psychology* (with Paul G. Nestor), *The Practice of Research in Criminology and Criminal Justice* and *Fundamentals of Research in Criminology and Criminal Justice* (with Ronet Bachman), *The Practice of Research in Social Work* and *Fundamentals of Social Work Research* (with Ray Engel), and *Research Methods in Education* (with Joseph Check)—he is the author of *Homelessness, Housing, and Mental Illness* and coeditor of *Social Neuroscience: Brain, Mind, and Society* (both with Harvard University Press) and author of *Organization in a Changing Environment* (SUNY), coauthor of *Responding to the Homeless: Policy and Practice* (Plenum), and coeditor of *The Organizational Response to Social Problems* (JAI). He has authored and coauthored 50 peer-reviewed journal articles as well as many book chapters and research reports on mental health, homelessness, service preferences and satisfaction, organizations, law, and teaching research methods. His research has included a mixed-methods investigation of a public health coordinated care program, a study of community health workers and recruitment for cancer clinical trials, a mixed-methods study of a youth violence reduction program, a randomized trial of a peer support program for homeless dually diagnosed veterans, and a randomized evaluation of housing alternatives for homeless persons diagnosed with severe mental illness, with funding from the National Cancer Institute, the Veterans Health Administration, the National Institute of Mental Health, the John E. Fetzer Institute, and state agencies. His current scholarly foci are the impact of the social environment on cognitive and community functioning, the meaning of housing and service preferences, and the value of alternative organizational and occupational structures for service delivery. His prior research has also included investigation of social factors in legal decisions and admission practices and of influences on job and service satisfaction. Details are available at http://rschutt.wikispaces.umb.edu.

Preface

The social world in the 21st century presents new problems for society and new challenges for researchers, but it also offers many opportunities for progress and understanding. Rapid advances in information technology; growing global trade and communication; and intersecting social, environmental, and economic transformations require innovative social research methods to describe an increasingly complex reality and to identify its diverse sources.

You are already part of this transformative process, both in your expectations for the social world and in the ways you interact with it. From Facebook to WhatsApp, from Uber to Google, the way you interact with the social world and the way you obtain information from it differs in many ways from those in the last century. *Understanding the Social World: Research Methods for the 21st Century* is a new type of research methods textbook for this new environment. It reflects the research requirements of a social world shaped by Big Data and social media, Instagram and avatars, blogs and tweets; and it confronts the research difficulties created by cell phones, privacy concerns, linguistic diversity, and multicultural neighborhoods.

What most distinguishes *Understanding* from *Investigating the Social World*, the more comprehensive text on which this book is based, and from other texts is its brevity, its focus on the methods most relevant to the 21st-century social world, and its engagement with the most pressing issues in this social world. At the same time, no core social science methods are overlooked and no key research standards are slighted; the emphasis is on engaging material that connects with your experiences and relates to the social theories you are learning, while not neglecting basic concepts or enduring standards. *Understanding the Social World* is fast-paced and visually sleek, so that it can take you across disciplinary and national boundaries and past conflicts, with an emphasis on mixed methods, ethical practices, and practical application.

Each of the major elements and methods in social research are represented in *Understanding the Social World*: inductive and deductive reasoning, contributing to social theory and reviewing research literature, qualitative and quantitative approaches, measurement validity and reliability, ethical standards and procedures, as well as experiments, surveys, qualitative methods, unobtrusive methods, evaluation research, and mixed methods. Basic techniques in both quantitative and qualitative data analysis are presented and guidelines for research reporting are reviewed. Each chapter uses research examples from the 21st century and provides features that enhance engagement, including **Research in the News** and **Careers and Research**. Ethics in research is the focus of an early chapter and then a section of each research design chapter. End-of-chapter materials provide summaries for review, questions for discussion, and exercises for practice.

Many research studies used for examples are available on the student study site in their original SAGE journal article format, with questions that encourage further exploration. The study site also offers quizzes, flashcards, interactive exercises, links to relevant resources on the Internet, and extra appendices.

❖ Teaching and Learning Goals

The first goal of this book is to introduce you to the social science research methods that shape the content of your courses, the programs of government agencies, the sales strategies of businesses, and the news of the day. Each chapter integrates instruction in research methods with investigation of interesting aspects of today's social world, such as social networking; intimate partner violence; crime and police practices; responding to disasters; and political preferences. You will learn in each chapter how learning the methods of social research can help you to answer questions about the social world.

The other key goal of this book is to give you the critical skills necessary to evaluate research. Just "doing research" is not enough. Just reading that some conclusions are "based on a research study" is not sufficient. You must learn to ask many questions before deciding that research-based conclusions are appropriate. What did the researchers set out to investigate? How were people selected for study? What information was collected, and how was it analyzed? Throughout this book, you will learn what questions to ask when critiquing a research study and how to evaluate the answers. You can begin to sharpen your critical teeth on the illustrative studies throughout the book.

This book also provides you the foundation for doing research. Substantive examples will help you see how methods are used in practice. Exercises at the end of each chapter give you ways to try different methods alone or in a group. Research methods cannot be learned by rote and applied mechanically. Thus, you will learn the benefits and liabilities of each major approach to research and why employing a combination of them is often preferable. You will learn how to conduct limited research projects throughout the book, and by the time you finish it you will be ready to be a full participant in large research projects and to study more advanced research methods.

❖ Organization of the Book

Understanding the Social World is organized in four sections that reflect the process of conducting and critiquing research: developing a research question with a foundation in the research literature and social theory and attention to ethical procedures; determining the fundamental elements of conceptualization and measurement, sampling, and procedures for testing cause-effect relations, when appropriate; choosing a basic research design; and analyzing data and reporting findings. The three chapters in the first section, "Foundations for Social Research," introduce the why and how of research in general. Chapter 1 shows how research has helped us understand the impact of social networking and changes in social ties. It also introduces some alternative approaches to social research, with a particular emphasis on the contrast between quantitative and qualitative research approaches. Chapter 2 illustrates the basic stages of research with a series of experiments on the police response to intimate partner violence, it emphasizes the role of theory in guiding research, and it describes the major strategies and goals for research projects. Chapter 3 highlights issues of research ethics by reviewing classic studies and contemporary debates and by introducing the institutional review boards that examine the ethics of proposed research.

The three chapters in the second section, "Fundamentals of Social Research," discuss how to evaluate the way researchers develop their concepts and design their measures (Chapter 4), draw their samples (Chapter 5), and justify their statements about causal connections (Chapter 6). As you learn about these processes, you will also read about research on poverty, trust, gangs, homelessness, and violence. Chapter 6 also serves as a bridge to the next section by introducing experimental methods, a basic research design that focuses attention on tests about cause-effect relationships.

"Basic Social Research Designs," the third section, presents the primary designs used by researchers to collect data about the social world (in addition to experiments): survey research, qualitative methods, unobtrusive methods, and evaluation research. Each chapter presents several different approaches to these basic research designs, so that part of what you will learn is how to select the best possible design for a research question (and how to critique researchers' choices to rely on a particular design). Chapter 7, on survey methods, reviews multiple variable features that shape the success of survey designs, while Chapter 8, on qualitative methods, reviews the logic of qualitative research as well as the different types of participant observation methods and the strategies of intensive interviewing and focus groups. Chapter 9, on unobtrusive methods, presents five different approaches that are all "unobtrusive" but that require very different techniques: unobtrusive measures, secondary data analysis, Big Data analysis, historical and comparative methods, and content analysis. Chapter 10 concludes this section with a review of the methods used in evaluation research and the logic behind the mixed-methods approaches that are increasingly used in evaluation research and many other research projects.

The final section, "Analyzing and Reporting of Social Research," presents the processes required for successful completion of a research project. Chapter 11 gives you a hands-on introduction to analyzing quantitative data, with interesting statistical examples you can carry out on the web (see also Appendix D). This chapter will also show you exactly what to look for when evaluating basic statistics in research reports. Chapter 12 introduces some of the rapidly developing approaches to analyzing qualitative data, ranging from conversation analysis and institutional ethnography to visual sociology. You will also learn about the method of participatory action research, which engages research participants in both the design and the analysis of research projects, as well as about using computer programs for analyzing qualitative data. Chapter 13 finishes up with an overview of the process of writing and organizing journal articles and research reports and a discussion of ethical problems related to social research and reporting.

❖ Distinctive Features

Understanding the Social World breaks new ground with newly popular research methods, enhanced tools for learning in the text and online, and contemporary, fascinating research findings. Other innovations in approach, coverage, and organization are:

- *Up-to-date coverage of research methods.* Research methods continue to develop and new challenges must be overcome as our social world continues to change. This text reflects increased attention to visual methods, expanded use of web surveys, growing reliance on smartphones, and use of social media. Some researchers have begun to explore the Internet with qualitative techniques, so there is expanded coverage of web surveys and related issues and sections on Internet-based forms of qualitative research. The chapter on mixed methods and the sections on Big Data and institutional ethnography also reflect recent developments in research.

- *Examples of social research as it occurs in real-world settings.* The leading examples that introduce research in each chapter are current and plentiful. Fascinating examples of research on social ties, domestic violence, crime, and other social issues demonstrate that the exigencies and complexities of real life shape the application of research methods.

- *Web-based instructional aids.* The book's study site includes interactive exercises that link directly to original research articles, published by SAGE, on each major research topic. It is important to spend enough time with these exercises to become comfortable with the basic research concepts presented. The interactive exercises allow you to learn about research on a range of interesting topics as you practice using the language of research.

- *Careers and Research.* Each chapter highlights the career of a researcher—a former student like you—who has used the methods discussed. What better incentive to study hard and master these methods!

- *Research in the News.* Timely examples of research affecting today's social world are highlighted in each chapter. Additional examples are available on my blog, Researching the Social World, http://investigatingthesocialworld .com/2014/09/28/welcome-to-the-investigating-the-social-world-8th-edition-blog-site/. Maybe you'll be inspired to discuss with other students the ways that research methods help us to understand the social world.

It is a privilege to be able to share with so many students the results of excellent social science investigations of the social world. If *Understanding the Social World* communicates the excitement of social research and the importance of evaluating carefully the methods we use in that research, then I have succeeded in representing fairly what social scientists do. If this book conveys accurately the latest developments in research methods, it demonstrates that social scientists are themselves committed to evaluating and improving their own methods of investigation. I think it is fair to say that we practice what we preach.

Now you're the judge. I hope that you and your instructor enjoy learning how to understand the social world and perhaps do some investigating along the way. And I hope you find that the knowledge and (dare I say it?) enthusiasm you develop for social research in this course will serve you well throughout your education, in your career, and in your community.

❖ A Note About Statistical Analysis

All you need to carry out the statistical analyses in Chapter 11 and the corresponding exercises is access to the Web. Data sets and interactive programs are available for analyses at the University of California, Berkeley, website (http://sda.berkeley.edu/archive.htm) and at the National Opinion Research Center site (www.norc.uchicago.edu/GSS+Website/).

❖ Ancillaries

⑤SAGE edge™

edge.sagepub.com/schuttusw

SAGE edge offers a robust online environment featuring an impressive array of tools and resources for review, study, and further exploration, keeping both instructors and students on the cutting edge of teaching and learning. SAGE edge content is open access and available on demand. Learning and teaching has never been easier!

SAGE edge for students provides a personalized approach to help students accomplish their coursework goals in an easy-to-use learning environment.

- Mobile-friendly **eFlashcards** strengthen understanding of key terms and concepts

- Mobile-friendly practice **quizzes** allow for independent assessment by students of their mastery of course material

- A customized online **action plan** includes tips and feedback on progress through the course and materials, which allows students to individualize their learning experience

- **Learning objectives** reinforce the most important material

- **Video and multimedia links** which appeal to students with different leaning styles

- EXCLUSIVE! Access to full-text **SAGE journal articles** that have been carefully selected to support and expand on the concepts presented in each chapter

SAGE edge for instructors supports teaching by making it easy to integrate quality content and create a rich learning environment for students.

- **Test banks** provide a diverse range of pre-written options as well as the opportunity to edit any question and/or insert personalized questions to effectively assess students' progress and understanding

- Editable, chapter-specific **PowerPoint® slides** offer complete flexibility for creating a multimedia presentation for the course

- EXCLUSIVE! Access to full-text **SAGE journal articles** that have been carefully selected to support and expand on the concepts presented in each chapter to encourage students to think critically

- **Video and multimedia links** includes original SAGE videos and Researcher Interview videos

- **Lecture notes** summarize key concepts by chapter to ease preparation for lectures and class discussions

- **Chapter-specific discussion questions** to help launch classroom interaction by prompting students to engage with the material and by reinforcing important content

Acknowledgments

My thanks first to Jerry Westby, publisher and acquisitions editor extraordinaire for SAGE Publications. Jerry's consistent support and exceptional vision have made it possible for this project to flourish, and his good cheer and collegiality have even made it all rather fun. Associate editor Jessica Miller also contributed her outstanding talents to the success of this text and to the quality of the Careers and Research highlights. Book production was managed with great expertise and good cheer by David Felts, while the remarkable Amy Marks proved herself to be one of publishing's most conscientious and effective copy editors. Nicole Mangona artfully managed development of book ancillaries, and Amy Lammers developed an ambitious marketing strategy. I am grateful to work with such talented staff at what has become the world's best publisher in social science.

My thanks also to Philip Brenner for suggestions for the survey methods chapter and to Ronet Bachman and Chuck Lubbers for helping to secure Careers and Research vignettes. I also am indebted to the first-rate social scientists whom Jerry Westby recruited to critique my proposal and early chapter drafts. Their thoughtful suggestions and cogent insights have helped improve every chapter. They are:

Edward E. Ackerley, University of Arizona and Northern Arizona University

Francisco J. Alatorre, New Mexico State University

Jacqueline Bergdahl, Wright State University

Tricia C. Bruce, Maryville College

Christine C. Fay, Elms College

Donna Goyer, California State University San Marcos

Eric Grulke, Northern Arizona University

Kellie J. Hagewen, College of Southern Nevada

Amy Holzgang, Cerritos College

Kim Humphrey, Northern Arizona University

Fanying Kong, Bellevue University

Ashleigh Kysar-Moon, Purdue University

Chuck Lubbers, University of South Dakota

Allan McBride, University of Southern Mississippi

Ashley B. Mikulyuk, University of Portland

Mladen Mrdalj, Northeastern University

Heather Macpherson Parrott, Long Island University-Post

Katelyn J. Rozenbroek, University of Miami

Baffour K. Takyi, University of Akron

Darcie Vandegrift, Drake University

I am also grateful for the expert and timely assistance of Brittne Lunnis, the University of Massachusetts Boston Ph.D. student who served as my SAGE assistant for this book. I could not have completed this work in a timely fashion without her enthusiasm and commitment. Brittne also tailored materials from my other SAGE methods texts for the student study site and the instructors' resource site.

The interactive exercises on the website began with a series of exercises that I developed in a project at the University of Massachusetts Boston. They were expanded for the second edition of *Investigating the Social World* by Tom Linneman and a team of graduate students he directed at the University of Washington—Mark Edwards, Lorella Palazzo, and Tim Wadsworth—and tested by Gary Hytrek and Gi-Wook Shin at the University of California, Los Angeles. My format changes in the exercises for the third edition were tested by my daughter, Julia Schutt. Diane Bates and Matthew Archibald helped revise material for instructors, and Judith Richlin-Klonsky revised some examples in Chapter 9 for the third edition. Kate Russell developed a new set of exercises and made many other contributions for the seventh edition, as did Whitney Gecker for the eighth edition. Brittne Lunnis has now tailored them for *Understanding the Social World*.

I continue to be indebted to the many students I have had the opportunity to teach and mentor, at both the undergraduate and graduate levels. In many respects, this book could not have come to fruition without the ongoing teaching experiences we have shared.

I also share a profound debt to the many social scientists and service professionals with whom I have collaborated in social science research projects.

No scholarly book project can succeed without good library resources, and for these I continue to incur a profound debt to the excellent librarians at the University of Massachusetts Boston and to Harvard University's library staff and their extraordinary collection.

Again, most important, I thank my wife, Elizabeth, for her love and support and our daughter, Julia, for the joy she brings to our lives and the good she has done in the social world.

Science, Society, and Social Research

Online social networking services added a new dimension to the social world in the early years of the 21st century. Mark Zuckerberg started Facebook in 2004 as a service for college students like himself, but by August 2015, Facebook had grown to be a global service with 1.49 billion users—more than one of every six people in the world and four out of every five persons in the United States (Internet World Statistics 2012; Statista 2015; Statistic Brain 2013; U.S. Census Bureau 2013). When we talk about our social world, social media must be part of the conversation.

Do social media enhance social relations, or do they diminish our engagement with others? That's where social researchers begin, with questions about the social world and a desire to find answers to them. Keith N. Hampton, Lauren Sessions Goulet, Lee Rainie, and Kristen Purcell (2011) analyzed the responses received in a survey about social networks and Facebook and reported that 79% of U.S. adults ages 18 to 22 use the Internet and 59% use social networking services, but this usage complements their other social ties, rather than displacing them.

This chapter gives special attention to questions about Internet use, social networking services, and social ties, but its goal is to illustrate the value of social research and introduce the methods of social research in relation to a compelling contemporary issue. We cannot avoid asking questions about our complex social world, or our position in it. In fact, the more that you begin to "think like a social scientist," the more such questions will come to mind—and that's a good thing! But it is through learning how answers to questions about the social world can be improved with systematic methods of investigation that we can move beyond first impressions and gut reactions. The use of research methods to investigate questions about the social world results in knowledge that can be more important, more trustworthy, and more useful than reliance just on personal opinions and individual experiences. You will also learn about the challenges that researchers confront. By the chapter's end, you should know what is "scientific" in social science and appreciate how the methods of science can help us understand the problems of society.

❖ The Value of Social Research

As you begin this book, you might wonder whether learning about social research methods is worth the effort. It is if you would like to do as well as possible in your other social science courses; if you want to maximize your career opportunities; and if you care about the community you live in, the schools your children may attend, and the direction of the nation. In courses ranging from the sociology of gender to the politics of communication, you will read about social research results and so need to know how to assess the quality of the evidence produced. Almost any organization for which you might work, from a government agency or a nonprofit organization to a private employer, conducts or at least uses social research methods to evaluate programs, identify client needs, or assess customer satisfaction. If you plan to work as a program director, social service worker, or in almost any other capacity, your ability to understand social research will help you to evaluate information and make decisions; of course, it is also a necessary foundation for graduate school. And there can be even more direct benefits if you take advantage of one of the many job opportunities in social science research at one of the hundreds of organizations that evaluate and help to advance social policy, such as the RAND Corporation,

Photo 1.1 Researchers are taking a close look at the effect of social media on social relations. What effect do you think they have?

the National Opinion Research Center (NORC), the Institute for Social Research (ISR), Mathematica, and ABT Associates (Prewitt, Schwandt, & Straf 2012:28). As you will see in the "Careers and Research" vignettes throughout *Understanding the Social World*, there are many opportunities to enhance your job prospects if you understand social research methods.

The U.S. federal government spent about $1.3 billion on social science research (including psychology and economics) in fiscal year 2011, and federal statistical agencies and programs had a total budget exceeding $6.5 billion in fiscal 2012 (Prewitt et al. 2012:31-32). In the United Kingdom, social science research expenditures from all sources at universities amounted to £851 million ($1.3 billion) in 2010–2011 (Bastow, Dunleavy, & Tinkler 2014:11). Social science research has identified influences on voting, variation in civic engagement, and the role of social factors in physical and mental health (AAU 2013). The results have included programs that have helped to increase voter turnout, reduce violence in communities, lessen smoking and hence rates of lung cancer, improve the health and well-being of infants, and lower rates of domestic violence. From wellness visits by teen mothers to community-based policing, social science research has helped to improve social welfare (Abrams 2007:2-4; NIH n.d.). By learning the methods used in this type of research, you can begin to evaluate its quality and help to shape its impact. Are you ready to proceed?

AUDIO LINK
Social Media

SAGE JOURNAL ARTICLE
Social Activity and Older Demographics

❖ Avoiding Errors in Reasoning About the Social World

How can we improve our reasoning about the social world? How do social research methods help us to avoid errors rooted in personal experiences? First, let's identify the different processes involved in learning about the social world and the types of errors that can result as we reason about the social world.

When we learn about the social world, we engage in one or more of four processes: (1) "*observing*" through our five senses (seeing, hearing, feeling, tasting, or smelling); (2) *generalizing* from what we have observed to other times, places, or people; (3) *reasoning* about the connections between different things that we have observed; and (4) *reevaluating* our understanding of the social world on the basis of these processes. It is easy to make mistakes with each of them.

My favorite example of the errors in reasoning that occur in the nonscientific, unreflective discourse about the social world that we hear on a daily basis comes from a letter to famous advice columnist Ann Landers. The letter was written by someone who had just moved with her two cats from the city to a house in the country. In the city, she had not let her cats outside and felt guilty about confining them. When they arrived in the country, she threw her back door open. Her two cats cautiously went to the door and looked outside for a while, then returned to the living room and lay down. Her conclusion was that people shouldn't feel guilty about keeping their cats indoors. Even when they have the chance, cats don't really want to play outside, she reasoned.

Do you see this person's errors in her approach to

- *Observing?* She observed the cats at the outside door only once.

- *Generalizing?* She observed only two cats, both of which previously were confined indoors.

- *Reasoning?* She assumed that others feel guilty about keeping their cats indoors and that cats are motivated by feelings about opportunities to play.

- *Reevaluating?* She was quick to conclude that she had no need to change her approach to the cats.

©iStockphoto.com/w-ings

Photo 1.2 What could the woman with the cats have done to avoid the four errors in reasoning?

You don't have to be a scientist or use sophisticated research techniques to avoid these four errors in reasoning, but the methods of social science are designed to reduce greatly the risk of making them. **Science** relies on logical and systematic methods to answer questions. Science does this in a way that allows others to inspect and evaluate its methods. In this way, scientific research develops a body of knowledge that is continually refined, as beliefs are rejected or confirmed on the basis of testing empirical evidence. **Social science** relies on scientific methods to investigate individuals, societies, and social processes. Although the activities involved in social science methods—asking questions, observing social groups, or counting people—are similar to things we do in our everyday lives, social scientists develop, refine, apply, and report their understanding of the social world more systematically, or "scientifically," than does Joanna Q. Public.

Observing

One common mistake in learning about the social world is **selective observation**—choosing to look only at things that are in line with our preferences or beliefs. When we are inclined to criticize individuals or institutions, it is all too easy to notice their every failure. For example, if we are convinced in advance that all heavy Internet users are antisocial, we can find many confirming instances. But what about elderly people who serve as Internet pen pals for grade-school children? Couples who maintain their relationship when working in faraway cities? If we acknowledge only the instances that confirm our predispositions, we are victims of our own selective observation.

Our observations can also simply be inaccurate. If, after a quick glance around the computer lab, you think there are 14 students present, when there are actually 17, you have made an **inaccurate observation**. If you hear a speaker say that "for the oppressed, the flogging never really stops," when what she said was, "For the obsessed, the blogging never really stops" (Hafner 2004), you have made an inaccurate observation.

Such errors occur often in casual conversation and in everyday observation of the world around us. In fact, our perceptions do not provide a direct window onto the world around us, for what we think we have sensed is not necessarily what we have seen (or heard, smelled, felt, or tasted). Even when our senses are functioning fully, our minds have to interpret what we have sensed (Humphrey 1992). The optical illusion in Photo 1.3, which comes from a JCPenney billboard that could be seen as either a teakettle or a saluting Adolf Hitler, should help you realize that perceptions involve interpretations. Different observers may perceive the same situation differently because they interpret it differently (so JCPenney quickly took down the billboard after complaints).

ENCYCLOPEDIA LINK
Generalizability Theory

Social science methods can reduce the risk of selective or inaccurate observation by requiring that we measure and sample phenomena systematically. For example, what role did social media play in the popular uprisings in the Middle East that started after 2008? It's easy to make up a "story" based on some messages sent by participants, but did this really involve lots of people? A group of researchers from Social Flow, the Web Ecology Project, and Microsoft Research (Lotan et al. 2011) investigated this issue using social research methods. They sampled 168,663 tweets posted January 12–19, 2011, mentioning keywords related to Tunisia, and 230,270 tweets posted January 24–29, 2011, mentioning keywords related to Egypt. They then identified those tweets that were retweeted most often and the distinct Twitter users within these tweets. Exhibit 1.1 shows how one tweet was retweeted frequently and so contributed to the news of popular support for the Egyptian protests.

Science: A set of logical, systematic, documented methods for investigating nature and natural processes; the knowledge produced by these investigations.

Social science: The use of scientific methods to investigate individuals, societies, and social processes; the knowledge produced by these investigations.

Selective observation: Choosing to look only at things that are in line with our preferences or beliefs.

Inaccurate observation: An observation based on faulty perceptions of empirical reality.

Overgeneralization: Concluding unjustifiably that what is true for some cases is true for all cases.

Generalizing

Overgeneralization occurs when we conclude that what we have observed or what we know to be true for some cases is true for all or most cases (Exhibit 1.2). We are always drawing conclusions about people and society from our own interactions, but sometimes we forget that our experiences are limited. The social world is, after all, a complex place. We can interact with just a small fraction of individuals in the social world, and we may do so in a limited span of time. Thanks to the Internet, social media, and the practice of "blogging," we can easily find many examples of overgeneralization in people's thoughts about the social world. Here's one posted by a frequent blogger who was called for jury duty (http://busblog.tonypierce.com/2005/06/yesterday-i-had-to-go-to-jury-duty-to.html, posted on June 17, 2005):

yesterday i had to go to jury duty to perform my civil duty. *unlike most people* i enjoy jury duty because i find the whole legal process fascinating, especially when its unfolding right in front of you and you get to help decide yay or nay.

Do you know what the majority of people think about jury duty? According to a Harris Poll, 75% of Americans consider jury service to be a privilege (Grey 2005), so the blogger's generalization about "most people" is not correct. Do you ever find yourself making a quick overgeneralization like that?

Social science research methods can reduce the likelihood of overgeneralization by using systematic procedures to select individuals, groups, events, messages, and the like to study that are representative of the individuals, groups, events, messages, and the like to which we want to generalize. In the study of the role of social media in the Arab Spring events highlighted in Exhibit 1.1, the researchers

Photo 1.3 An optical illusion: What do you see?

■ EXHIBIT 1.1   **Retweets of Quote in Support of Egypt Protesters by Other Journalists Over Time**

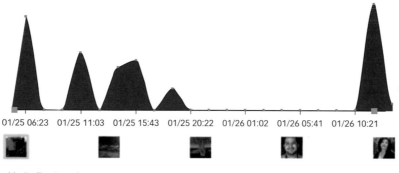

adamakary (Mainstream Media Employee)

Police guard in tahrir tells me, I'm just following orders, doing my job. Otherwise, I'd be with the protesters #jan25 #egypt

Source: Lotan et al. 2011:1394.

■ EXHIBIT 1.2   **The Difference Between Selective Observation and Overgeneralization**

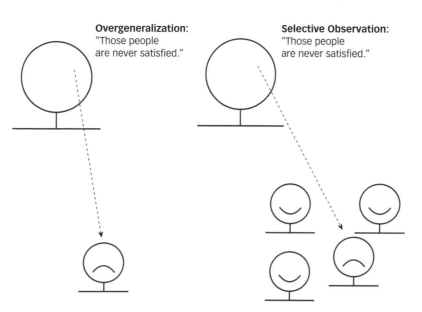

explain carefully how they selected tweets to study and why they chose to sample only from 10% of the most popular tweets; they also caution that this means their analysis does not represent all the types of tweets sent during this period.

Reasoning

When we jump to conclusions or argue on the basis of invalid assumptions, we are using **illogical reasoning**. It is not always so easy to spot illogical reasoning. For example, more than 74% of American households now use the Internet (File & Ryan 2014). Would it be reasonable to propose that the 26% who don't participate in the "information revolution" avoid it simply because they don't want to participate? In fact, many low-income households lack the financial resources to buy a computer or pay for an Internet connection, and so they use the Internet much less frequently; that's probably not because they don't want to use it (Rainie & Horrigan 2005:63). Conversely, an unquestioned assumption that everyone wants to connect to the Internet may overlook some important considerations; for example, 17% of nonusers of the Internet said in 2002 that the Internet has made the world a worse place, so they may not use it because they don't like what they believe to be its effects (UCLA Center for Communication Policy 2003:78). Logic that seems impeccable to one person can seem twisted to another.

To avoid illogical reasoning, social researchers use explicit criteria for describing events and identifying causes and for determining whether these criteria are met in a particular instance.

Reevaluating

Resistance to change, the reluctance to reevaluate our ideas in light of new information, may occur for several reasons:

- *Ego-based and institutional commitments.* We all learn to greet with some skepticism the claims by leaders of companies, schools, agencies, and so on, that people in their organization are happy, that revenues are growing, and that services are being delivered in the best possible way. We know how tempting it is to make statements about the social world that conform to our own needs or the needs of our employers, rather than to the observable facts. It can also be difficult to admit that we were wrong, once we have staked out a position on an issue. Barry Wellman recounts a call from a reporter after the death of what he believed were four "cyber addicts" (Boase, Horrigan, Wellman, & Rainie 2006:1). The reporter just wanted a quote from a computer-use expert, such as Wellman, that would affirm his belief. But the interview didn't last long:

Illogical reasoning: Jumping to conclusions or arguing on the basis of invalid assumptions.

Resistance to change: The reluctance to reevaluate our ideas in light of new information.

The reporter lost interest when Wellman pointed out that other causes might be involved, that "addicts" were a low percentage of users, and that no one worries about "neighboring addicts" who chat daily in their front yards. (Boase et al. 2006:1)

RESEARCH

In the News

WHY DOESN'T THE INTERNET REACH EVERYONE?

In a recent survey, social psychologist Ethan Kross found that young people who spent more time on Facebook felt less good about their own lives. He concluded that the problem was that the rosy self-portraits they saw on Facebook made users feel deficient by comparison.

So when we investigate the social world, it's a good idea to inquire about our participants' online social worlds as well as their face-to-face contacts. We also can use postings to social media sites as another source of data about the social world.

For Further Thought ?

1. People have always tried to manage their images in the social world. Do social media allow us to take this impression management to a whole new level?

2. What are the consequences for our everyday lives?

3. What does this mean for the research methods we use to study the social world?

News source: Burge, Kathleen. 2014. "Overblown Facebook Personas Can Leave Friends Deflated." *Boston Globe*, September 30.

- *Excessive devotion to tradition.* Some degree of devotion to tradition is necessary for the predictable functioning of society. Social life can be richer and more meaningful if it is allowed to flow along the paths charted by those who have preceded us. But too much devotion to tradition can stifle adaptation to and understanding of changing circumstances.

- *Uncritical agreement with authority.* If we do not have the courage to evaluate critically the ideas of those in positions of authority, we will have little basis for complaint if they exercise their authority over us in ways we don't like. And, if we do not allow new discoveries to challenge our beliefs, our understanding of the social world will remain limited. Do you see some of the challenges social science faces?

Because they require that we base our beliefs on evidence that can be examined and critiqued by others, scientific methods lessen the tendency to develop answers about the social world from ego-based or institutional commitments, excessive devotion to tradition, or unquestioning respect for authority. For example, when Alice Marwick and danah boyd investigated what adults usually refer to as "bullying" on social media, they found that teens themselves often instead used the term *drama* as a way of distancing themselves from the concept of bullying. According to the researchers, "'drama' connotes something immature, petty, and ridiculous," even though the communications themselves may be quite hurtful. Marwick and boyd did not accept without question either the adult concept of bullying or the teen concept of drama as the appropriate way to think about the gossip, jokes, and arguments on social media. Instead, they examined these communications critically and so were able "to recognize teens' own defenses against the realities of aggression, gossip, and bullying in networked publics" (Marwick & boyd 2011:23).

❖ Types of Social Research

Whatever the motives, there are four types of social research projects. This section illustrates each type with examples from the large body of research about various aspects of social ties.

Descriptive research: Research in which social phenomena are defined and described.

Descriptive Research

Defining and describing social phenomena of interest is a part of almost any research investigation, but **descriptive research** is often the primary focus of the first research about some issue. For example, Miller McPherson, Lynn Smith-Lovin, and Matthew E. Brashears (2006) designed social research to answer the descriptive question: What is the level of particular types of social ties in America? Measurement (the topic of Chapter 4) and sampling (Chapter 5) are central concerns in descriptive research. Survey research (Chapter 7) is often used for descriptive purposes. Some unobtrusive research also has a descriptive purpose (Chapter 9).

■ EXHIBIT 1.3   **The Value of Facebook**

Percentage of Facebook users who say that in the past year Facebook has become more important to them and who say they are spending more time on Facebook compared with last year

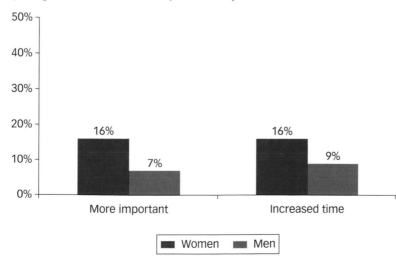

Source: Pew Research Center's Internet & American Life Project Omnibus Survey, conducted December 13 to 16, 2012, on landline and cell phones. *N* for male Facebook users = 233. *N* for female Facebook users = 292.

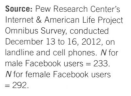

Example: Comings and goings on Facebook? Lee Rainie, director of the Pew Internet Project, and his colleagues Aaron Smith and Maeve Duggan (2013) sought to describe the frequency with which Americans stopped using Facebook and the reasons they did so. To investigate this issue, they surveyed 1,006 American adults by phone and asked them such questions as "Do you ever use Facebook?" and "Have you ever voluntarily taken a break from using Facebook for a period of several weeks or more?"

They found that two thirds of American adults who use the Internet also use Facebook and that most (61%) say they have voluntarily taken a break from using Facebook at some time for at least several weeks (Rainie et al. 2013:2). They also asked about the importance of Facebook to users and found that the importance attached to Facebook by women had grown more in the previous year than it had for men (see Exhibit 1.3).

Exploratory Research

Exploratory research seeks to find out how people get along in the setting under question, what meanings they give to their actions, and what issues concern them. The goal is to learn "What is going on here?" and to investigate social phenomena without explicit expectations. Exploratory research frequently involves qualitative methods, which are the focus of Chapters 8 and 12.

Example: How does cyberbullying occur and how do victims cope? University of Washington social researchers Katie Davis, David P. Randall, Anthony Ambrose, and Mania Orand (2015) were concerned by the prevalence of bullying among adolescents and wondered how youth responded when they were victimized by online harassment. They identified an opportunity to explore this issue through an analysis of 1,096 comments made in response to a blog post by singer/songwriter Amanda Palmer about the suicide of 15-year-old Amanda Todd after a topless picture of her that circulated online led to years of cyberbullying. Davis and her colleagues found that the primary reasons given for having been bullied were physical appearance, sexual orientation, and pursuing nonmainstream interests. Popular coping strategies included seeking social support, finding a creative outlet, ignoring or blocking the bully, as well as self-talk and taking the perspective of the bully in order to understand his or her motivations.

Exploratory research: Seeks to find out how people get along in the setting under question, what meanings they give to their actions, and what issues concern them.

Explanatory research: Seeks to identify causes and effects of social phenomena and to predict how one phenomenon will change or vary in response to variation in some other phenomenon.

Explanatory Research

Explanatory research seeks to identify the causes and effects of social phenomena and to predict how one phenomenon will change or vary in response to variation in some other phenomenon. Internet researchers adopted explanation as a goal when they began to ask such questions as "Does the Internet increase, decrease, or supplement social capital?" (Wellman, Haase, Witte, & Hampton 2001). Chapter 6 focuses on the meaning of causation and how to identify causal effects with experimental methods; Chapter 7 addresses this issue in relation to survey methods.

CAREERS
and Research

JESSICA LEBLANC, RESEARCH ASSISTANT

Jessica LeBlanc majored in sociology at the University of New Hampshire, but she didn't really know what kind of career it would lead to. Then she took an undergraduate statistics course and found she really enjoyed it. She took additional methods courses—survey research and an individual research project course—and really liked those also.

By the time she graduated, LeBlanc knew she wanted a job in social research. She looked online for research positions in marketing, health care, and other areas. She noticed an opening at a university-based research center and thought their work sounded fascinating. As a research assistant, LeBlanc designed survey questions, transcribed focus group audiotapes, programmed web surveys, and managed incoming data. She also conducted interviews, programmed computer-assisted telephone surveys, and helped conduct focus groups.

The knowledge that LeBlanc gained in her methods courses about research designs, statistics, question construction, and survey procedures prepared her well for her position. Her advice to aspiring researchers: Pay attention in your first methods class!

Example: What effect does Internet use have on social relations? Jeffrey Boase, John B. Horrigan, Barry Wellman, and Lee Rainie (2006), sociologists at the University of Toronto at the time (Boase and Wellman) and researchers at the Pew Internet Project (Horrigan and Rainie), sought to understand how the Internet is affecting community life in general and the maintenance of social ties in particular. For this purpose, they analyzed data from two phone surveys, conducted in 2004 and 2005, of 4,401 Americans. Boase and his coauthors (2006) found that the Internet and e-mail help people maintain dispersed social networks and do not conflict with the maintenance of social ties in the local community involving personal or phone contact.

Evaluation Research

Evaluation research examines programs, policies, or other efforts to affect social patterns, whether by government agencies, private nonprofits, or for-profit businesses. Evaluation can include elements of descriptive, exploratory, and explanatory research. The focus of evaluation research on programs, policies, and other conscious efforts to create change raises some issues that are not relevant in other types of research (Lewis-Beck, Bryman, & Liao 2004:337). Chapter 10 reviews the basics of evaluation research.

Photo 1.4 Upstream Healthy Living Centre

JOURNAL LINK
Wi-Fi Use

Example: Does a socially oriented intervention improve health and well-being among older people? Colin Greaves and Lou Farbus (2006) evaluated the impact on depression, social isolation, and physical health of a community-based intervention by the Upstream Healthy Living Centre in Devon, England. Upstream provides trained mentors who visit elderly people in their homes frequently to work on creative, exercise, and/or cultural activities ranging from computer activities, painting, and creative writing to Tai Chi, group walks, and book clubs. Activities emphasize social interaction in groups and creative stimulation. Greaves and Farbus conducted qualitative interviews with diverse program participants and some program mentors and administered a quantitative survey to most participants at program entry and then after 6 and 12 months of participation. Both the qualitative and quantitative data provided evidence of improvements in health status and social engagement as a result of program participation. Depression scores improved and perceived social support increased after 12 months, with mixed results on some other measures but many positive comments about program benefits.

❖ Quantitative and/or Qualitative Methods

Did you notice the difference between the types of data used in the studies about the Internet? The primary data used in the descriptive survey about Facebook use were counts of the number of people who had particular numbers of social ties and particular kinds of social ties, as well as their age, education, and other characteristics (Rainie et al. 2013). These data were numerical, so we say that this study used **quantitative methods**. In contrast, Keith Hampton and Neeti Gupta (2008) observed Wi-Fi users in public spaces. Because the researchers recorded their actual observations and did not attempt to quantify what they were studying, we say that Hampton and Gupta (2008) used **qualitative methods**.

The distinction between quantitative and qualitative methods involves more than just the type of data collected. Quantitative methods are most often used when the motives for research are explanation, description, or evaluation. Quantitative researchers are often guided by a positivist philosophy. **Positivism** asserts that a well-designed test of a specific prediction—for example, the prediction that social ties decrease among those who use the Internet more—can move us closer to understanding actual social processes. Research guided by positivism

Evaluation research: Research that describes or identifies the impact of social policies and programs.

Quantitative methods: Methods such as surveys and experiments that record variation in terms of amounts. Data that are treated as quantitative are either numbers or attributes that can be ordered by magnitude.

Qualitative methods: Methods such as participant observation, intensive interviewing, and focus groups that are designed to capture social life as participants experience it rather than in categories predetermined by the researcher. These methods rely on written or spoken words or observations that do not often have a direct numerical interpretation and typically involve exploratory research questions, an orientation to social context and human subjectivity, and the meanings attached by participants to events and to their lives.

Positivism: The belief, shared by most scientists, that there is a reality that exists quite apart from our own perception of it, that it can be understood through observation, and that it follows general laws.

presumes that our perceptions and understanding of the social world can be distorted by errors like those discussed in this chapter, but scientific methods can help us to see and understand reality more clearly.

Exploration is more often the motive for using qualitative methods, although researchers also use these methods for descriptive, explanatory, and evaluative purposes. Qualitative research is often guided by the philosophy of **constructivism**. Constructivist social scientists believe that social reality is socially constructed and that the goal of social scientists is to understand what meanings people give to reality, not to determine how reality works apart from these constructions. This philosophy rejects the positivist belief that there is a concrete, objective reality that scientific methods help us understand (Lynch & Bogen 1997); instead, constructivists believe that people construct an image of reality based on their own preferences and prejudices and their interactions with others and that this is as true of scientists as it is of everyone else in the social world.

Chapters 2 and 3 highlight several other differences between quantitative and qualitative methods, and Chapters 8 and 12 present qualitative methods in much more detail.

Important as it is, the distinction between quantitative and qualitative orientations or methods shouldn't be overemphasized. Social scientists often combine these methods to enrich their research. For example, Keith Hampton and Barry Wellman (2000) used surveys to generate counts of community network usage and other behaviors in Netville, but they also observed social interaction and recorded spoken comments. In this way, qualitative data about social settings can be used to understand patterns in quantitative data better (Campbell & Russo 1999:141).

The use of multiple methods to study one research question is called **triangulation**. The term suggests that a researcher can get a clearer picture of the social reality being studied by viewing it from several different perspectives. Each will have some liabilities in a specific research application, and all can benefit from a combination of one or more other methods (Brewer & Hunter 1989; Sechrest & Sidani 1995).

The distinction between quantitative and qualitative data is not always sharp. Qualitative data can be converted to quantitative data, for example, when we count the frequency of particular words or phrases in a text or measure the time elapsed between different observed behaviors. Surveys that collect primarily quantitative data may also include questions asking for written responses, and these responses may be used in a qualitative, textual analysis. Qualitative researchers may test explicit explanations of social phenomena using textual or observational data. We consider a *mixed-methods* strategy in more detail in Chapter 10.

❖ Conclusions

I hope this first chapter has given you an idea of what to expect from the rest of the book. The aim is to introduce you to social research methods by describing what social scientists have learned about the social world as well as how they have learned it. The substance of social science is inevitably more interesting than its methods, but the methods become more interesting when they're linked to examples from substantive investigations.

Understanding the Social World is organized into four sections. The first section on Foundations for Social Research includes the introduction in Chapter 1, and then an overview of the research process in Chapter 2 and an introduction to issues in research ethics and an overview of research proposals in Chapter 3. The second section, Fundamentals of Social Research, presents methods for conceptualization and measurement (Chapter 4), sampling (Chapter 5), and causation (Chapter 6) that must be considered in any social research project. The third section, Social Research Designs, introduces the major methods of data collection used by sociologists: survey research (Chapter 7), qualitative methods (Chapter 8), unobtrusive methods ranging from historical and comparative methods to secondary data analysis (Chapter 9), and evaluation and mixed-methods research (Chapter 10). The last section, Analyzing and Reporting, introduces techniques for analyzing quantitative data with statistics (Chapter 11) and analyzing qualitative data with a variety of techniques (Chapter 12), as well as guidelines for evaluating research reports (Chapter 13).

Constructivism: Methodology based on questioning belief in an external reality; emphasizes the importance of exploring the way in which different stakeholders in a social setting construct their beliefs.

Triangulation: The use of multiple methods to study one research question; also used to mean the use of two or more different measures of the same variable.

Each chapter ends with several helpful learning tools. Lists of key terms and chapter highlights will help you review the ideas that have been discussed. Chapter questions and practice exercises will help you apply and deepen your knowledge. A "Careers and Research" example may help you envision future job possibilities, and a "Research in the News" vignette in each chapter will tie research methods to current events.

The study site for this book on the SAGE website provides interactive exercises and quizzes for reviewing key concepts, as well as research articles to review, websites to visit, data to analyze, and short lectures to hear. Check it out at edge.sagepub.com/schuttusw.

Key Terms

Constructivism   10
Descriptive research   7
Evaluation research   9
Explanatory research   8
Exploratory research   8
Illogical reasoning   6

Inaccurate observation   4
Overgeneralization   4
Positivism   9
Qualitative methods   9
Quantitative methods   9
Resistance to change   6

Science   4
Selective observation   4
Social science   4
Triangulation   10

Highlights

- Social research differs from the ordinary process of thinking about our experiences by focusing on broader questions that involve people outside our immediate experience and issues about why things happen, and by using systematic research methods to answer those questions. Four common errors in reasoning are (1) selective or inaccurate observation, (2) overgeneralization, (3) illogical reasoning, and (4) resistance to change. These errors result from the complexity of the social world, subjective processes that affect the reasoning of researchers and those they study, researchers' self-interestedness, and unquestioning acceptance of tradition or of those in positions of authority.

- Social science is the use of logical, systematic, documented methods to investigate individuals, societies, and social processes, as well as the knowledge produced by these investigations.

- Social research can be descriptive, exploratory, explanatory, or evaluative—or some combination of these.

- Quantitative and qualitative methods structure research in different ways and are differentially appropriate for diverse research situations. They may be combined in research projects.

- Positivism is a research philosophy that emphasizes the goal of understanding the real world; this philosophy guides most quantitative researchers.

- Constructivism is a research philosophy that emphasizes the importance of exploring and representing the ways in which different stakeholders in a social setting construct their beliefs. Constructivists interact with research subjects to develop a shared perspective on the issue being studied.

Chapter Questions

The ethical challenges that arise in social research are discussed throughout the book. At the end of each chapter, one of the questions you are asked to consider may be about ethical issues related to that chapter's focus. This critical topic is introduced formally in Chapter 3, but let's begin here with a first question for you to ponder:

1. The chapter refers to research on social isolation. What would *you* do if you were interviewing elderly persons in the community and found that one was very isolated and depressed or even suicidal, apparently as a result of his or her isolation? Do you believe that social researchers have an obligation to take action in a situation like this? What if you discovered a similar problem with a child? What guidelines would you suggest for researchers?

2. Pick a contemporary social issue of interest to you. Describe different approaches to research on this issue that would involve descriptive, exploratory, explanatory, and evaluative approaches.

3. Review the description of quantitative and qualitative approaches. Which approach do you prefer and what is the basis of your preference? Would you prefer to take a mixed-methods approach? Why or why not?

Practice Exercises

1. Review the "Letters to the Editor" section of a local newspaper. Which errors in reasoning do you find? What evidence would be needed to correct these errors?

2. Review "Types of Research" from the Interactive Exercises link on the book's study site. To use these lessons, choose one of the four "Types of Research" exercises from the opening menu.

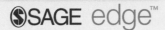

RESEARCHER INTERVIEW LINK
Online Interviews

About 10 questions are presented in each version of the lesson. After reading each question, choose one answer from the list presented. The program will evaluate your answers. If an answer is correct, the program will explain why you were right and go on to the next question. If you have made an error, the program will explain the error to you and give you another chance to respond.

3. Scan the articles on the book's study site for this chapter. Classify the research represented in each article as primarily descriptive, exploratory, explanatory, or evaluative. Describe the evidence for your classification (even if the abstract mentions the type of research, look for other evidence). If more than one type of research is represented in an article, also mention that type.

4. Now read one of the articles in detail and decide whether the approach was quantitative or qualitative (or mixed) and whether the authors were guided primarily by a positivist or a constructivist philosophy. Explain your answer.

STUDENT STUDY SITE

$SAGE edge™

The Process and Problems of Social Research

Learning Objectives

- ❖ Name the three characteristics of a good research question
- ❖ Discuss the role of theory in social research
- ❖ Demonstrate how to search and review the research literature
- ❖ Describe three key social research strategies and when they are best used

- ❖ Name and illustrate the three different longitudinal designs
- ❖ Define the standards of measurement validity, generalizability, causal validity, and authenticity

About 30% of women worldwide who have ever had an intimate partner have experienced intimate partner violence, as have about 23% of those in the United States and other high-income countries (Garcia-Moreno et al. 2013:16-17). As advocates and public officials began to recognize the scope of this problem in the past century, some turned to social researchers for help in identifying effective response strategies. A key concern was whether police should usually arrest men accused of partner abuse when they were called in after an incident, rather than simply issuing a warning, as many police officers were accustomed to doing.

In 1981, the Police Foundation and the Minneapolis Police Department began an experiment to determine whether arresting accused spouse abusers on the spot would deter repeat incidents. The study's results, which were publicized widely, indicated that arrests did have a deterrent effect. Partly as a result, the percentage of urban police departments that made arrest the preferred response to complaints of domestic violence rose from 10% in 1984 to 90% in 1988 (Sherman 1992:14). Researchers in six other cities then conducted similar experiments to determine whether changing the location or other research procedures would result in different outcomes (Sherman 1992; Sherman & Berk 1984).

The Minneapolis Domestic Violence Experiment, the additional research inspired by it, and the controversies arising from it provide examples for our systematic overview of the social research process. Although the original Minneapolis experiment occurred decades ago, that in itself makes an important point about social research: No single study can be considered to provide the definitive answer to a research question, and every study generates additional questions that require more research. Social research is an ongoing process of testing propositions, refining knowledge, exploring new ideas, adapting to changes, and all the while enriching our understanding of the social world.

This chapter shifts from examining *why* social research is conducted to *how* it is carried out—the focus of the rest of the book. The chapter considers how questions for social research are developed, how the existing literature about research questions can be located, and how it should be reviewed. It also looks at how research questions can be connected to social theory and then expressed as testable hypotheses (Exhibit 2.1). Finally, the chapter discusses different social research strategies and standards for social research as a prelude to subsequent chapters. Appendices A and B contain more details related to reviewing the literature.

SAGE JOURNAL ARTICLE
Domestic Violence

■ EXHIBIT 2.1   **Launching a Research Project**

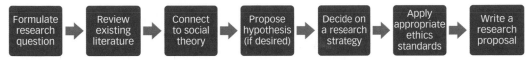

Formulate research question → Review existing literature → Connect to social theory → Propose hypothesis (if desired) → Decide on a research strategy → Apply appropriate ethics standards → Write a research proposal

❖ Social Research Questions

Social research begins with a question about the social world that a researcher seeks to answer through the collection and analysis of firsthand, verifiable, empirical data. It is not a question about who did what to whom, but a question about people in groups, about general social processes, or about tendencies in community change such as the following: What distinguishes Internet users from other persons? How has the level of social inequality changed over time? What influences the likelihood of spouse abuse?

Researchers may decide to focus on a particular **social research question** as a result of reading a research article, because of their personal experiences with the issue, or for any of several reasons. Most research projects focus on questions that arose in previous research. For example, Richard A. Berk, Alec Campbell, Ruth Klap, and Bruce Western (1992) concluded an article on four studies of police responses to spouse abuse by suggesting, "Deterrence may be effective for a substantial segment of the offender population. . . . However, the underlying mechanisms remain obscure" (p. 706). A new study could focus on these mechanisms: What happens to offenders after their arrest that deters some from future abusive acts? Other social research questions may reflect a researcher's personal experiences—"personal troubles"—as C. Wright Mills (1959) put it. Social researchers may also want to help figure out how to lessen the harmful impact of a social problem.

Social research questions should be feasible, socially important, and scientifically relevant (King, Keohane, & Verba 1994). Any study must be possible within the time and resources available, so questions that involve long-term change, a large population, or secretive groups may not be feasible unless substantial funds or special access has been obtained. For research undertakings that are more than a class exercise, the research question should be important to other people and society. A research question meets the criterion of scientific relevance if it focuses on issues that have not been resolved by research already reported in the social science literature.

SAGE JOURNAL ARTICLE
Culture and Theory

Social research question: A question about the social world that is answered through the collection and analysis of firsthand, verifiable, empirical data.

❖ Social Research Foundations

Once they have formulated a research question, and sometimes even before that question has been settled, social researchers search the literature to find other research focused on the same or related research questions and to determine what can be learned from the methods and findings of these previous studies. Conducting a thorough search of the related research literature is also an essential foundation for evaluating the contribution made by a particular research article or research project.

Searching the Literature

The primary goal in searching the literature is to find reports of prior research investigations about the research question of interest. Focus on reports in scholarly journals—*refereed journals* that publish *peer-reviewed articles*—because they have been screened for quality through critique by other social scientists before publication. Most often, editors of refereed journals send articles that authors submit to three or more other social scientists for anonymous review. Based on

Photo 2.1   Social research questions often arise from the observance of social problems. What social problems have you observed that you would like to know more about?

VIDEO LINK ▶
Advice for Researchers

the reviewers' comments, the journal editor then decides whether to accept or reject the article, or to invite the author to "revise and resubmit." This process results in the rejection of articles with major flaws and many improvements in most of the rest. You still have to make your own judgment about article quality, since journals vary in the rigor of their review standards, and, of course, different reviewers may be impressed by different types of articles.

Most articles published in academic journals will be available to you online only if you go through the website of your college or university library. The library pays a fee to companies that provide online journals so that you can retrieve this information without paying anything extra yourself. Since no library can afford to pay for every journal, you may still have to order some of the articles you need through interlibrary loan.

Of course the web offers much useful material, including research reports from government and other sources, sites that describe social programs, and even indexes of the published research literature. Such material may be very useful in preparing, reviewing, and reporting research, but it is not a substitute for searching academic journals for relevant articles.

It can also help to locate reviews of already-published research. Some journals publish articles that review prior research about specific research questions. Such reviews are unlikely to focus on all the specific issues raised by a particular research question, but they can provide a framework for a more focused search of the literature. If you are not familiar with the major concepts, scholars, or research findings pertaining to your research question, you should also consider reading background information in one of the *Annual Review* volumes available for most disciplines (e.g., the *Annual Review of Sociology*) and even the relevant entries in an encyclopedia for the discipline, such as the *Blackwell Encyclopedia of Sociology* or the *International Encyclopedia of the Social and Behavioral Sciences*. These resources may be available online from your college or university library.

Newspaper and magazine articles may raise important issues or summarize social research investigations, but they are not an adequate source for understanding the research literature.

A search of the academic journal literature should include the following steps:

1. *Specify your research question.* Your research question should be neither so broad that hundreds of articles are judged relevant nor so narrow that you miss important literature. "Is informal social control effective?" is probably too broad. "Does informal social control reduce rates of burglary in my town?" is probably too narrow. "Is informal social control more effective than policing in reducing crime rates?" provides about the right level of specificity.

2. *Identify appropriate bibliographic databases to search.* Sociological Abstracts or SocINDEX may meet many of your needs, but if you are studying a question about social factors in illness, you should also search in Medline, the database for searching the medical literature. You may also want to include a search in the online Psychological Abstracts database, PsycINFO, or the version that also contains the full text of articles, PsycARTICLES. Search Criminal Justice Abstracts if your topic is in the area of criminology or criminal justice, or EconLit, if your topic might be addressed in the economic literature. Some combined indexes like Academic Search Complete may be most useful for searches that should span multiple disciplines.

To find articles that refer to a previous publication, such as Sherman and Berk's study of the police response to domestic violence, the Social Science Citation Index (SSCI) will be helpful. SSCI has a unique "citation searching" feature that allows you to look up articles or books and find other articles that have cited these sources.

3. *Create a tentative list of search terms.* List the parts and subparts of your research question and any related issues that you think are important: "informal social control," "policing," "influences on crime rates," and perhaps "community cohesion and crime." List the authors of relevant studies. Specify the most important journals that deal with your topic.

4. *Narrow your search.* The sheer number of references you find can be a problem. For example, searching for "social capital" in May 2015 resulted in 6,754 citations in SocINDEX (with Full Text). Depending on the database you are working with and the purposes of your search, you may want to limit your search to English-language publications, to journal articles rather than conference papers or dissertations (both of which are more difficult to acquire), and to materials published in recent years. If your search yields too many

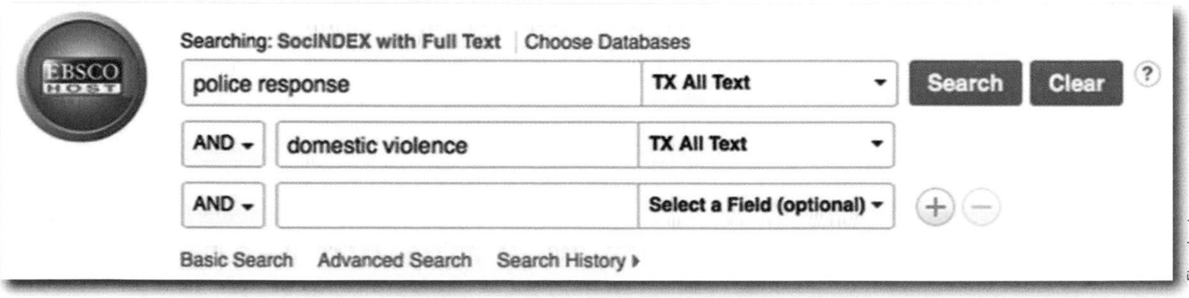

Searching: **SocINDEX with Full Text** | Choose Databases

| police response | TX All Text ▾ | **Search** | **Clear** | ⓘ |

| AND ▾ | domestic violence | TX All Text ▾ |

| AND ▾ | | Select a Field (optional) ▾ | ⊕ ⊖ |

Basic Search   Advanced Search   Search History ▸

Photo 2.2   When starting a search in sociological abstracts, multiple key words can be used to narrow search results. Thinking back to the social problem you identified at the beginning of the chapter, what key words could you use to find more information?

citations, try specifying the search terms more precisely (e.g., "neighborhood social capital"). If you have not found much literature, try using more general or multiple terms (e.g., "social relations" OR "social ties"). Whatever terms you search first, don't consider your search complete until you have tried several different approaches and have seen how many articles you find. Photo 2.2 shows what Sherman and Harris might have entered on their computer if they searched SocINDEX to find research on "domestic violence" and "police response."

5. *Check the results.* Read the titles and abstracts you have found and identify the articles that appear to be most relevant. If possible, click on these article titles and generate a list of their references. See if you find more articles that are relevant to your research question but that you have missed so far. You will be surprised (I always am) at how many important articles your initial online search missed.

6. *Locate the articles.* Whatever database you use, the next step after finding your references is to obtain the articles themselves. You will probably find the full text of many articles available online, but this will be determined by what journals your library subscribes to and the period for which it pays for online access. The most recent issues of some journals may not be available online. If an article that appears to be important for your topic isn't available from your own library, or online, you may be able to request a copy online through your library site or by asking a member of the library staff. Your library may also have the print version.

Reviewing Research

A social science review of the literature describes prior research about one or more related research questions, identifies points of similarity and difference and highlights the strong and weak points in this body of research, and develops general conclusions about the implications of this research and the questions that require further research. Reviewing the literature that you have located is a two-stage process. In the first stage, you must assess each relevant article you have located separately. As a result of this review, you may decide to discard some of the articles as not sufficiently relevant or of adequate quality and you may identify other articles as particularly important. In the second stage of the review process, you should assess the implications of the set of articles (and other materials) you have reviewed for the relevant aspects of your research question and procedures. The result of these two stages should be an integrated review that highlights these implications.

The next two sections illustrate these stages. The first section presents a summary review of a single article found in a search of recent research on the effectiveness of the police response to domestic violence. The second section shows how a single article review can be incorporated within an integrated review of prior research on this research question. This is only an introduction to the process of reviewing the literature. In each subsequent chapter, you will learn how to evaluate more of the specific features of research projects that are discussed in research articles. By the time you finish *Understanding the Social World*, you will be able to write detailed critiques of research articles and then develop persuasive integrated reviews of the body of research about a research question. Appendix A contains a comprehensive set of questions to guide you in your article reviews, but because at this early point in the text you won't be familiar with all the terminology used in those questions, you should wait to practice reviewing articles with the questions in Appendix A until later in the course.

A Single-Article Review

It has been more than three decades since the original Minneapolis experiment by Richard Berk and Larry Sherman on the police response to domestic violence. Although the prevalence of intimate partner violence appears to have declined since then in the United States, the question of how best to respond is still not resolved. One of the complicating factors is the continuation of abuse by the perpetrators after victimized women and their children have been separated from them. April M. Zeoli, Echo A. Ribera, Cris M. Sullivan, and Sheryl Kubiak (2013) from Michigan State University focused on this problem in a research project designed to explore how women respond to abuse by ex-husbands with whom they have had custody disputes.

Zeoli and her colleagues (2013) prepared to investigate this research question by reviewing the literature on intimate partner violence after separation. They found reports that many victimized women were threatened after their abusive relationship was formally ended and that court hearings often led to requirements of joint custody that created opportunities for continued abuse of both mothers and children. However, their literature search identified few studies of how women coped. They decided to contribute to filling this gap in understanding by conducting qualitative interviews with mothers who had been through custody disputes in family court. Their article describes how they made arrangements to review family court records, screened divorce cases for indications of a history of abuse, and then telephoned women to confirm their eligibility and to ask if they would consent to be interviewed. Of 174 women whose telephone numbers they obtained, only 58 (33%) could be contacted and only 23 were ultimately determined to be eligible for the study. As we learn in this way about Zeoli and her colleagues' experience with selecting study participants, we can see that the women they interviewed might not be comparable to those who had moved or changed their phone numbers for other reasons.

Zeoli and her colleagues use quotes from the interviews to illustrate how they classified fathers' harm to children post-divorce (Exhibit 2.2). For example, "neglect" was recorded as the type of harm resulting from a father whose former wife said he "would literally go to work in the morning and come home for five minutes to see . . . that they're still alive and then leave and these children were too little to take care of themselves" (p. 552). Such careful description of procedures allows readers to consider whether they agree with the researchers' decisions and to raise questions about what might have been missed. In their conclusions, the researchers note that they

■ **EXHIBIT 2.2   Fathers' Harm to Children Post-Divorce and Mothers' Strategies to Protect Them (*n* = 10)**

Fathers' harm or likely harm to children	Mothers' strategies to protect children			
	Avoid family court (*n* = 2)	Family court provides no support (*n* = 5)	Family court provides support after extreme harm (*n* = 2)	Family court is supportive(*n* = 2)
Physical harm (*n* = 3)		Kim, Jesy		Vanessa
Emotional abuse precipitating self-injury (*n* = 2)			Jennifer, Meaghan	
Neglect (*n* = 3)	Kathleen	Christina		Meredith
Likely future physical harm (*n* = 4)	Kathleen, Carole	Carole, Karen		Vanessa
Likely kidnapping (*n* = 2)	Carole	Carole		Vanessa

Source: Zeoli et al. (2013:552). With kind permission from Springer Science+Business Media.

didn't examine all abusive tactics used and that their reliance on mothers as informants limited their knowledge about harm suffered by the children. The research thus improves understanding of this aspect of intimate partner violence while also pointing out the limitations of the research design and thus the need for more research.

An Integrated Literature Review

The goal of the second stage of the literature review process is to integrate the results of separate article reviews and develop an overall assessment of the implications of prior research. The integrated literature review should accomplish three goals: (1) summarize prior research, (2) critique prior research, and (3) present pertinent conclusions (Hart 1998:186–187). Let's look at each of these goals in turn:

1. *Summarize prior research.* The summary of prior research should focus on the particular research question of concern, but it may also be necessary to provide some more general background. For example, Victoria Frye, Mary Haviland, and Valli Rajah (2007:398) begin their integrated literature review for a study of "unintended consequences" of the mandatory arrest policy in New York City by describing past research on the intended effect of mandatory arrest on recidivism (rearrest and reassault). After concluding that, "taken together," prior research indicates mandatory arrest does tend to reduce the risk of reassault, they shift to reviewing prior research on unintended consequences of mandatory arrest. They find that prior research indicates that the arrest of women for domestic violence is increasing and that victim characteristics are related to the likelihood of their arrest. This is the key background to their study of unintended consequences. As recommended, their review focuses on articles published in academic peer-reviewed journals and written by credible authors who have been funded by reputable sources (Locke, Silverman, & Spirduso 1998:37–44). Subheadings are often used to distinguish parts of the review relevant to different aspects of a research question, but this is not necessary in the "brief report" by Frye, Haviland, and Rajah.

2. *Critique prior research.* An integrated review should also discuss the strengths and weaknesses of the body of prior research. What issues seem to have been resolved by multiple studies, and what issues remain as points of contention? The major criticism of prior research on "dual arrests" (of women as well as their ex-husbands) by Frye, Haviland, and Rajah is that "it has been studied less" than the effect on male recidivism. When you are ready to check the article review questions in Appendix A, you will find that they will help to ensure that you consider many more possible problems with methodological issues.

3. *Present pertinent conclusions.* Don't leave the reader guessing about the implications of the prior research for your own research question. Present the conclusions you draw from the research you have reviewed and point out any limitations of that research (Fink 2005:190–192; Pyrczak 2005:53–56). The Frye literature noted the inadequacy of prior research but also identified what had been found about the characteristics of female suspects that made them more likely to be arrested. In another investigation of the police response to domestic violence, an integrated literature review by Ray Paternoster and colleagues (1997) concluded that seven prior experiments that had tested the effect of police response had ignored the possibility that "particular kinds of police procedure might inhibit the recurrence of spouse assault" (p. 165); so this was the focus for Paternoster's new research.

❖ Social Theories

The value of a social research project will also be increased if it is connected to social theory. Neither domestic violence nor police policies exist in a vacuum, set apart from the rest of the social world. We can understand behaviors and orientations better if we consider how they reflect broader social patterns. Although everyone has general notions about "how things work," "what people are like," and so on, social scientists draw on more formal sets of general ideas—social theories—to guide their research (Collins 1994). A **theory** is a logically interrelated set of propositions that helps us make sense of many interrelated phenomena. Theory helps social scientists decide which questions are important to ask about the social world and which are just trivial pursuits. Building and evaluating theory is one of the most important objectives of social science.

Lawrence Sherman and Richard Berk's (1984) domestic violence experiment tested predictions derived from two theories: **specific deterrence theory** and **labeling theory**. *Specific deterrence theory* predicts that arresting spouse abusers will lessen their likelihood of reoffending by increasing the costs of reoffending. Crime "doesn't pay" (as much) if the costs of punishment are high (Exhibit 2.3) (Lempert & Sanders 1986:86–87).

■ EXHIBIT 2.3　**Specific Deterrence Theory Prediction**

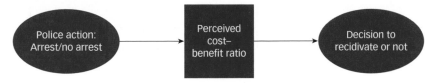

By contrast, *labeling theory* suggests that persons arrested for domestic assault are more likely to reoffend than are those who are not punished. The basic idea is that once an offender is labeled as a deviant by being arrested, and so is treated by other people as deviant, he or she will then be more likely to act in a way that is consistent with the label *deviant* (Becker 1963:9; Scull 1988:678).

As a social researcher, you may work with one of these theories, seeking to extend it, challenge it, or specify it. You may test alternative implications of the two theories against each other. If you're feeling ambitious, you may even seek to combine some aspects of the two perspectives or seek out another. Maybe you'll come up with a different theoretical perspective altogether. In any area of research, developing an understanding of relevant theories will help you ask important questions, consider reasonable alternatives, and choose appropriate research procedures.

> **VIDEO LINK**
> Rational Choice Theory

Theory: A logically interrelated set of propositions about empirical reality.

Specific deterrence theory: Predicts that punishing individuals for crime deters them from further criminal acts, due to their recognition that the costs incurred outweigh the benefits.

Labeling theory: Labels applied to people can result in behaviors and attitudes consistent with the label, with a particular focus on how labeling a person or group of people as deviant can result in their engaging in deviant behavior.

❖ Social Research Strategies

Social research seeks to connect theory with empirical data—the evidence we obtain from the social world. Researchers may make this connection by starting with a social theory and then testing some of its implications with data. This is the process of deductive research; it is most often the strategy used in quantitative methods. Alternatively, researchers may develop a connection between social theory and data by first collecting the data and then developing a theory that explains the patterns in the data (Exhibit 2.4). This inductive research process is often the strategy used in qualitative methods. A research project can draw on both deductive and inductive strategies.

Exhibit 2.5 summarizes how the two theories that guided Sherman and Berk's (1984) research relate to the question of whether to arrest spouse abusers. By helping to make such connections, social theory makes us much more sensitive to the possibilities, and thus helps draw out the implications of the findings.

Explanatory Research

Research designed to evaluate cause-effect relations is explanatory: The goal is to determine why things happen or what the consequences are of some event or characteristic or other action. The process of conducting research designed to test

■ EXHIBIT 2.4　**The Links Between Theory and Data**

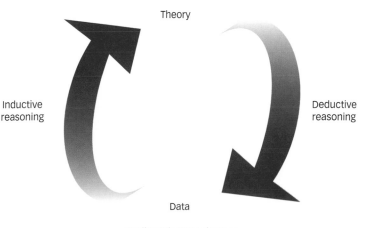

RESEARCH

In the News

MESSAGING AND EMOTIONS

Our social relations are increasingly mediated with technology. Does this distort our ability to relate to others? Consider using text messages to communicate. This truncated form of communication mostly leaves emotion out of the picture and so makes it difficult for message recipients to know how the sender really feels. It also makes it difficult for researchers studying text messages to get the full picture of an interaction that qualitative researchers can otherwise obtain by observing facial expressions and body language and listening to intonations.

But emotions are too important a part of social relations to ignore, so people have become inventive about using punctuation marks and emoticons to make it clear what they "really" mean. This new approach to representing social relations requires new methods of investigation.

For Further Thought ❓

1. Can you develop a plan for measuring some features of punctuation to better interpret the text?
2. Have you found that there has been enough standardization of such punctuation marks that they could be used to represent feelings in a consistent way? How could you validate a measure based on such marks?

News source: Bennett, Jessica. 2015. "When Your Punctuation Says It All (!)." *New York Times*, February 27.

■ **EXHIBIT 2.5**   **Two Social Theories and Their Predictions About the Effect of Arrest for Domestic Assault**

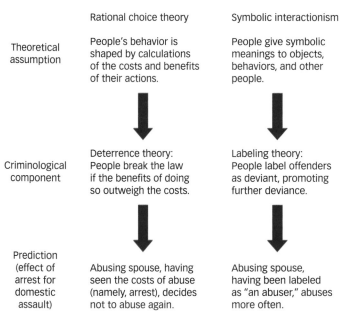

	Rational choice theory	Symbolic interactionism
Theoretical assumption	People's behavior is shaped by calculations of the costs and benefits of their actions.	People give symbolic meanings to objects, behaviors, and other people.
Criminological component	Deterrence theory: People break the law if the benefits of doing so outweigh the costs.	Labeling theory: People label offenders as deviant, promoting further deviance.
Prediction (effect of arrest for domestic assault)	Abusing spouse, having seen the costs of abuse (namely, arrest), decides not to abuse again.	Abusing spouse, having been labeled as "an abuser," abuses more often.

explanations for social phenomena involves moving from theory to data and then back to theory. This process is also termed **deductive research**, because a specific expectation is deduced from a general theoretical premise and then tested with data that have been collected for this purpose.

The deductive process can be characterized with a **research circle** (Exhibit 2.6). We call the specific expectation deduced from the more general theory a **hypothesis**. It is the hypothesis that researchers actually test, not the complete theory itself. A hypothesis proposes a relationship between two or more **variables**—characteristics or properties that can vary.

In deductive research, variation in one variable is proposed to predict, influence, or cause variation in the other. The proposed influence is the **independent variable**; its effect or consequence is the **dependent variable**. After the researchers formulate one or more hypotheses and develop research procedures, they collect data with which to test the hypothesis.

Hypotheses can be worded in several different ways, and identifying the independent and dependent variables is sometimes difficult. When in doubt, try to rephrase the hypothesis as an *if-then* statement: "*If* the independent variable increases (or decreases), *then* the dependent variable increases (or decreases)." Exhibit 2.7 presents several hypotheses with their independent and dependent variables and their if-then equivalents.

Exhibit 2.7 demonstrates another feature of hypotheses: **direction of association**. When researchers hypothesize that one variable increases as the other variable increases, the direction of association is positive (Hypotheses 1 and 4). When one variable decreases as the other variable decreases, the direction of association is also positive (Hypothesis 3). But when one variable increases as the other decreases, or vice versa, the direction of association is negative, or inverse (Hypothesis 2). Hypothesis 5 is a special case, in which the independent variable is qualitative: It cannot be said to increase or decrease. In this case, the concept of direction of association does not apply, and the hypothesis simply states that one category of the independent variable is associated with higher values on the dependent variable.

Explanatory studies and many evaluative studies involve deductive research. In deductive research, the initial statement of expectations for the findings and the design of the research to test these expectations strengthen the confidence we can place in the test. Deductive researchers show their hand or state their expectations in advance and then design a fair test of those expectations. Then, "the chips fall where they may"—in other words, the researcher accepts the resulting data as a more or less objective test of whether the hypothesized associations exist in reality..

Domestic Violence and the Research Circle

The classic Sherman and Berk (1984) study of domestic violence provides our first example of how the research circle works. Sherman and Berk deduced a specific hypothesis from deterrence theory: "Arrest for spouse abuse reduces the risk of repeat offenses." In this hypothesis, police sanction (arrest, separation, or warning) is the independent variable and the risk of repeat offenses is the dependent variable (it is hypothesized to depend on the police sanction).

Sherman and Berk tested their hypothesis by setting up an experiment in which the police responded to the complaints of spouse abuse in one of three ways: (1) arresting the offender, (2) separating the spouses without making an arrest, or (3) simply warning the offender. When the researchers examined their data (police records for the persons in their experiment), they found that of those arrested for assaulting their spouse, only 13% repeated the offense, compared with a 26% recidivism rate for those who were separated from their spouse by the police without any arrest. This pattern in the data, or **empirical generalization**, was consistent with the hypothesis that the researchers deduced from deterrence theory. The theory thus received support from the experiment (Exhibit 2.8).

This was not the end of the story, however. Because of their doubts about the generalizability of their results, Sherman, Berk, and other researchers began to journey around the research circle again, with funding from the National Institute of Justice for **replications** (repetitions) of the experiment in six more cities. These replications used the same basic research approach, but with some changes. Results turned out to be inconsistent—arrest often did not reduce the rate of recidivism—so the initial results were not generalizable to all cities (Sherman & Smith 1992).

Exploratory Research

Research designed to determine how people make sense of their circumstances or to learn how people interact or express themselves is exploratory research. Qualitative research is often exploratory and, hence, inductive. In contrast to deductive research, **inductive research** begins with specific observations or other data, which are then analyzed to develop (induce) a general explanation (a theory) to account for the data. One way to think of this process is in terms of the research circle: Rather than starting at the top of the circle with a theory, the inductive researcher starts at the bottom of the circle with data and then develops the theory. Another way to think of this process is represented in Exhibit 2.9. In deductive research, reasoning from specific premises results in a conclusion that a theory is supported, but in inductive research, the identification of similar empirical patterns results in a generalization about some social process.

Qualitative researchers with an exploratory research design often ask questions such as "What is going on here?" "How do people interpret these experiences?" or "Why do people do what they do?" Rather than testing a hypothesis, the researchers are trying to make sense of some social phenomenon. They may even put off formulating a research question until after they begin to collect data—the idea is to let the question emerge from the situation itself (Brewer & Hunter 1989:54–58).

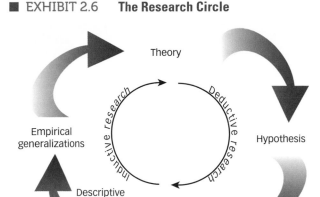

■ EXHIBIT 2.6 **The Research Circle**

Theory

Deductive research

Hypothesis

Data

Descriptive research

Empirical generalizations

Inductive research

Deductive research: The type of research in which a specific expectation is deduced from a general premise and is then tested.

Research circle: A diagram of the elements of the research process, including theories, hypotheses, data collection, and data analysis.

Hypothesis: A tentative statement about empirical reality, involving a relationship between two or more variables.

Example of a hypothesis: The higher the poverty rate in a community, the higher the percentage of community residents who are homeless.

Variable: A characteristic or property that can vary (take on different values or attributes).

Example of a variable: The degree of honesty in verbal statements.

Independent variable: A variable that is hypothesized to cause, or lead to, variation in another variable.

Example of an independent variable: Poverty rate.

Dependent variable: A variable that is hypothesized to vary depending on, or under the influence of, another variable.

Example of a dependent variable: Percentage of community residents who are homeless.

Direction of association: A pattern in a relationship between two variables—the values of variables tend to change consistently in relation to change on the other variable; the direction of association can be either positive or negative.

Empirical generalization: A statement that describes patterns found in data.

Replications: Repetitions of a study using the same research methods to answer the same research question.

Inductive research: The type of research in which general conclusions are drawn from specific data.

■ EXHIBIT 2.7　**Examples of Hypotheses**

Original Hypothesis	Independent Variable	Dependent Variable	*If-Then* Hypothesis	Direction of Association
1. The greater the use of the Internet, the greater the strength of distant family ties.	Level of Internet use	Strength of distant family ties	*If* Internet use is greater, *then* the strength of distant family ties is greater.	+
2. The risk of property theft decreases as income increases.	Income	Risk of property theft	*If* income is higher, *then* the risk of property theft is less.	−
3. If years of education decrease, income decreases.	Years of education	Income	*If* years of education decrease, *then* income decreases.	+
4. Political conservatism increases with income.	Income	Political conservatism	*If* income increases, *then* political conservatism increases.	+
5. Property crime is higher in urban areas than in suburban or rural areas.	Type of community	Rate of property crime	*If* areas are urban, *then* property crime is higher compared with crime in suburban or rural areas.	NA

■ EXHIBIT 2.8　**The Research Circle: Minneapolis Domestic Violence Experiment**

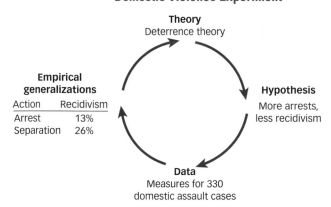

Source: Data from Sherman and Berk (1984:267).

■ EXHIBIT 2.9　**Deductive and Inductive Reasoning**

Deductive

Premise 1:	*All unemployed spouse abusers recidivate.*
Premise 2:	*Joe is an unemployed spouse abuser.*
Conclusion:	**Joe will recidivate.**

Inductive

Evidence 1:	*Joe, an unemployed spouse abuser, recidivated.*
Evidence 2:	*Harold, an unemployed spouse abuser, recidivated.*
Evidence 3:	*George, an employed spouse abuser, didn't recidivate.*
Conclusion:	**All unemployed spouse abusers recidivate.**

Anomalous findings: Unexpected patterns in data.

Serendipitous findings: Unexpected patterns in data, which stimulate new explanations, insights, or theoretical approaches.

Battered Women's Help Seeking

Angela Moe (2007) used exploratory research methods in her study of women's decisions to seek help after abuse experiences. In interviews lasting about 1 hour each with 19 women in a domestic violence shelter, Moe heard what the women had experienced and how they had responded. She then reviewed the interview transcripts carefully and identified major themes that emerged in the comments.

The following quote is from a woman who had decided not to call the police to report her experience of abuse (Moe 2007:686).

> I tried the last time to call the police and he ripped both the phones out of the walls. . . .
>
> That time he sat on my upper body and had his thumbs in my eyes and he was just squeezing.
>
> He was going, "I'll gouge your eyes out. I'll break every bone in your body. Even if they do find you alive, you won't know to tell them who did it to you because you'll be in intensive care for so long you'll forget." (Terri)

What does this suggest to you as a reason that women may not report experiences of abuse to the police?

Explanations developed inductively from qualitative research can feel authentic because they reflect what people said in their own words and provide a sense of how they see the social world. Explanations derived from qualitative research are often richer and more finely textured than they are in quantitative research, but they are likely to be based on fewer cases from a limited area. We cannot assume that the people studied in this setting are like others or that other researchers will develop similar explanations to make sense of what was observed or heard.

Deductive research can lead to an inductive reasoning process when unexpected patterns are found in the data. Such patterns are called **anomalous findings**. When these anomalous findings lead to new explanations, insights, or theoretical approaches, they are called **serendipitous findings**.

The deductive domestic violence research took an inductive turn when researchers began trying to make sense of the differing patterns in the data collected in the different cities. In a replication study of the police response to domestic violence in Florida's Metro-Dade County, Pate and Hamilton (1992) discovered that individuals who were married and employed were deterred from repeat offenses by arrest, but individuals who were unmarried and unemployed were actually *more* likely to commit repeat offenses if they were arrested (Exhibit 2.10). What could explain this empirical pattern? The researchers concluded that people who are employed and married have more of a stake in conformity (they have more to lose as a result of being arrested) and so are more likely to be deterred by the threat of arrest than are those without such a stake in conformity.

Bear in mind that such an explanation formulated after the fact is less certain than an explanation presented before the collection of data and tested in a planned way. Every phenomenon can always be explained in *some* way. Our confidence in the "stake in conformity" interpretation of Pate and Hamilton's results would be strengthened if it were next presented as a hypothesis and then tested with a deductive approach.

Photo 2.3   The deterrent effect that arrest, or threat of arrest, has on individuals varies greatly. What are some ways scientists can study how the effect arrest prevents some individuals from committing crimes?

Descriptive Research

Research is descriptive when its goal is to provide a picture of people, organizations, or other entities; of change over time; or of speech or other texts. Descriptions can be quantitative—such as the distribution of incomes in a population—or qualitative—such as a record of customer-worker interactions in a service agency, but it is intended to represent what, rather than why. Descriptive research does not involve connecting theory and data, but it is still a part of the research circle—it begins with data and proceeds only to the stage of making empirical generalizations based on those data (refer to Exhibit 2.6).

Valid description is important in its own right—and it is a necessary component of all investigations. Before they began an investigation of differences in arrests for domestic violence in states with and without mandatory arrest laws, David Hirschel, Eve Buzawa, April Pattavina, and Don Faggiani (2008) carefully described the characteristics of incidents reported to the police (Exhibit 2.11). Describing the prevalence of intimate partner violence is an important first step for societies and organizations that seek to respond to this problem.

SAGE JOURNAL ARTICLE
Inductive and Deductive Techniques

RESEARCH/SOCIAL IMPACT LINK
Descriptive Research

SAGE JOURNAL ARTICLE
Natural Experiment

❖ Cross-Sectional and Longitudinal Designs

In addition to deciding on the appropriate research strategy—whether descriptive, explanatory, exploratory, or evaluative, researchers must decide whether to collect data at just one or two or more points in time. In **cross-sectional research designs**, all data are collected at one point in time. In **longitudinal research designs**, data are collected at two or more points in time. The research question determines whether cross-sectional or longitudinal data are needed. If the research question concerns only the here and now, there is no need for longitudinal data. Are women paid less than men for comparable work? Cross-sectional data can give us the answer. However, if the research question focuses

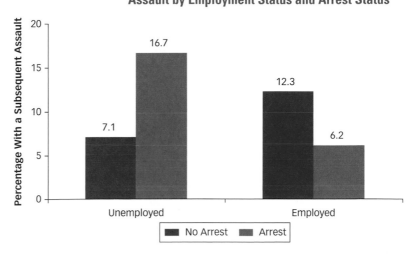

■ **EXHIBIT 2.10**   **Percentage of Suspects With a Subsequent Assault by Employment Status and Arrest Status**

Source: Pate, Antony M, and Edwin E. Hamilton 1992. "Formal and Informal Deterrents to Domestic Violence: The Dade County Spouse Assault Experiment." *American Sociological Review* 57(October):691–697.

■ EXHIBIT 2.11   **Incident, Offender, and Outcome Variables by Victim-Offender Relationship**

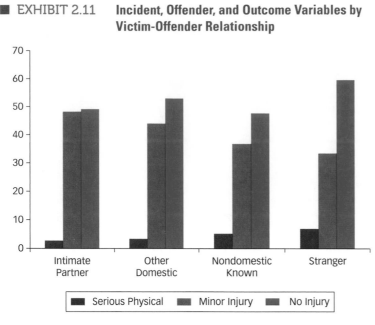

Source: Based on Hirschel et al. (2008).

■ EXHIBIT 2.12   **Relation of Residential Mobility and Faith in Police to Probability of "Giving In"**

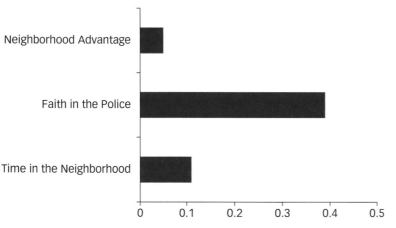

Source: Based on Warner (2014:427).

on change over time or concerns a hypothesis about one change leading to another, then longitudinal data are necessary. How has church membership changed over time? Is implementation of standardized high-stakes testing followed by better student performance? Researchers need data collected over time to answer questions like these.

Cross-Sectional Designs

Barbara Warner (2014) used an ambitious cross-sectional design to improve understanding of informal social control processes in neighborhoods. Drawing on collective efficacy theory, Warner (2014:421) defined the concept of informal social control as the behaviors engaged in by residents to control inappropriate public behaviors, including criminal acts. Her review of the literature on informal social control revealed that factors that increase residents' use of informal social control have been identified (such as social ties), but little research has investigated how people react to these informal social control efforts. Are other residents less likely to commit crimes because of their neighbors? Warner's study involved a survey of residents in 66 neighborhoods in two southern cities that was funded by the National Institute of Justice. Respondents were asked how they would respond to a hypothetical complaint by a neighbor about their behavior (such as playing loud music). Other questions asked about social ties, trust in others, faith in the police, and other behaviors and characteristics.

As indicated in Exhibit 2.12, respondents who had lived in the neighborhood for a longer period of time and had more faith in the police were more likely to say that they would "give in" after a neighbor's complaint than were those who were more mobile and less distrusting of police. Neighborhood economic advantage had little apparent effect by itself. These and other findings help us to understand who is more likely to respond positively to efforts at informal social control.

Longitudinal Designs

In longitudinal research, data are collected at two or more points in time. By measuring the value of cases on an independent variable and a dependent variable at different times, the researcher can determine whether variation in the independent variable precedes variation in the dependent variable. It is more difficult to collect data at two or more points in time than at one time—often it is not even feasible. Nonetheless, the value of longitudinal data is so great that every effort should be made to develop longitudinal research designs when they are appropriate for the research question asked. The following discussion of the three major types of longitudinal designs will give you a sense of the possibilities (Exhibit 2.13).

Cross-sectional research design: A study in which data are collected at only one point in time.

Longitudinal research design: A study in which data are collected that can be ordered in time; also defined as research in which data are collected at two or more points in time.

Repeated Cross-Sectional Designs (Trend Studies)

Studies that use a **repeated cross-sectional design,** also known as trend studies, have become fixtures of the political arena around election time. Particularly in presidential election years, we have all become accustomed to reading weekly, even daily, reports on the percentage of the population that supports each candidate. Similar polls are conducted to track sentiment on many other social issues.

Repeated cross-sectional surveys are conducted as follows:

1. A sample is drawn from a population at Time 1, and data are collected from the sample.

2. As time passes, some people leave the population and others enter it.

3. At Time 2, a different sample is drawn from this population.

Fixed-Sample Panel Designs (Panel Studies)

Panel designs allow us to identify changes in individuals, groups, or whatever we are studying. This is the process for conducting **fixed-sample panel designs**:

1. A sample (called a panel) is drawn from a population at Time 1, and data are collected from the sample.

2. As time passes, some panel members become unavailable for follow-up, and the population changes.

3. At Time 2, data are collected from the same people as at Time 1 (the panel)—except for those people who cannot be located.

■ EXHIBIT 2.13 **Three Types of Longitudinal Design**

Source: Data from Sherman and Berk (1984:267).

Because a panel design follows the same individuals, it is better than a repeated cross-sectional design for testing causal hypotheses. For example, Lee Hulbert-Williams at the University of Wolverhampton and other British social scientists revisited research on the relation between exposure to life events and psychological problems in adults with intellectual disabilities (Hulbert-Williams et al. 2014). Their literature review revealed that this association had frequently been found in cross-sectional research, but that longitudinal research was needed to determine whether the life events preceded an increase in psychological problems. Their study used a fixed-sample (panel) design in which they surveyed 93 residents of a residence for persons with intellectual disabilities and then about 4 years later surveyed the 68 participants from Time 1 who were still available. As they had hypothesized, they found that negative life events preceded greater risk for psychological problems.

Despite their value in establishing time order of effects, panel studies are a challenge to implement successfully. It can be difficult, and very expensive, to keep track of individuals over a long period, and inevitably the proportion of panel members who can be located for follow-up will decline over time. Panel studies often lose more than one quarter of their members through attrition (Miller 1991:170), and those who are lost are often not necessarily like those who remain in the panel. Also, **subject fatigue** becomes a problem if panel members become so used to answering standard survey questions that they start giving stock answers rather than actually thinking about their current feelings or actions—although this does not often occur (Campbell 1992).

Event-Based Designs (Cohort Studies)

In an **event-based design,** often called a cohort study, the follow-up samples (at one or more times) are selected from the same **cohort**—people who all have experienced a similar event or a common starting point. Examples include the following:

- *Birth cohorts*—those who share a common period of birth (those born in the 1940s, 1950s, 1960s, etc.)

- *Seniority cohorts*—those who have worked at the same place for about 5 years, about 10 years, and so on

- *School cohorts*—freshmen, sophomores, juniors, and seniors

An event-based design can be a type of repeated cross-sectional design or a type of panel design. In an event-based repeated cross-sectional design, separate samples are drawn from the same cohort at two or more different times. In an event-based panel design, the same individuals from the same cohort

RESEARCHER INTERVIEW LINK
Research Design

Repeated cross-sectional design (trend study): A type of longitudinal study in which data are collected at two or more points in time from different samples of the same population.

Fixed-sample panel design (panel study): A type of longitudinal study in which data are collected from the same individuals—the panel—at two or more points in time. In another type of panel design, panel members who leave are replaced with new members.

Subject fatigue: Problems caused by panel members growing weary of repeated interviews and dropping out of a study or becoming so used to answering the standard questions in the survey that they start giving stock or thoughtless answers.

Event-based design (cohort study): A type of longitudinal study in which data are collected at two or more points in time from individuals in a cohort.

Cohort: Individuals or groups with a common starting point. Examples include a college's class of 1997, people who graduated from high school in the 1980s, General Motors employees who started work between the years 1990 and 2000, and people who were born in the late 1940s or the 1950s (the baby boom generation).

©iStockphoto.com/narvikk

Photo 2.4 The cohort shown here are veterans of World War II who served in the military between 1939 and 1945. What are some cohorts you belong to?

are studied at two or more different times. Comparing findings between different cohorts can help reveal the importance of the social or cultural context that the different cohorts experienced (Elliott, Holland, & Thomson 2008:230).

❖ Social Research Standards

As research takes us around the research circle, we have to be concerned about whether the connections being made are on target. Do the data obtained really support the theory we think they do? Is the research designed so that it provides a meaningful test of the hypothesis? We have achieved the goal of **validity** when our conclusions about empirical reality are correct. The goal of social science is not to come up with conclusions that people will like or conclusions that suit our own personal preferences. The goal is to figure out how and why the social world—some aspect of it—operates as it does. In *Understanding the Social World,* we are concerned with three standards for validity: (1) **measurement validity**, (2) **generalizability**, and (3) **causal validity** (also known as **internal validity**) (Hammersley 2008:43). Invalid measures, invalid generalizations, and invalid causal inferences will each lead to invalid conclusions. We also focus here on the standard of **authenticity**, a concern with reflecting fairly the perspectives of participants in a setting.

Measurement Validity

A measure is valid when it measures what we think it measures. In other words, a valid procedure for measuring domestic violence is a prerequisite to describing the frequency of domestic violence in families. Measurement validity is our first concern in evaluating the validity of research results because without having measured what we think we measured, we really don't know what we're talking about. Measurement validity is the focus of Chapter 4. Whether measures involve asking people questions, observing people's actions, or reviewing records in a government archive, care must be used in designing or selecting measures and in subsequently evaluating how well they performed. Chapter 4 introduces several different ways to test measurement validity. Researchers cannot just *assume* (or expect us to believe) that measures are valid without any evidence of measurement validity.

Validity: When statements or conclusions about empirical reality are correct.

Measurement validity: When a measure measures what we think it measures.

Generalizability: When a conclusion holds true for the population, group, setting, or event that we say it does, given the conditions that we specify.

Causal validity (internal validity): When a conclusion that A leads to or results in B is correct.

Authenticity: When the understanding of a social process or social setting is one that reflects fairly the various perspectives of participants in that setting.

Sample generalizability: When a conclusion based on a sample, or subset, of a larger population holds true for that population.

Cross-population generalizability (external validity): When findings about one group, population, or setting hold true for other groups, populations, or settings.

Generalizability

The generalizability of a study is the extent to which it can be used to inform us about persons, places, or events that were not studied. Generalizability is the focus of Chapter 5. If every person or community we study were like every other one, generalizations based on observations of a small number would be valid. But that's not the case.

Generalizability has two aspects. **Sample generalizability** refers to the ability to generalize from a sample, or subset, of a larger population to that population itself. This is the most common meaning of generalizability. **Cross-population generalizability** refers to the ability to generalize from findings about one group, population, or setting to other groups, populations, or settings (Exhibit 2.14). Cross-population generalizability can also be referred to as **external validity**. (Some social scientists equate the term *external validity* to *generalizability,* but this book restricts its use to the more limited notion of cross-population generalizability.)

Sample generalizability is a key concern in survey research. Political pollsters may study a sample of likely voters, for example, and then generalize their findings to the entire population of likely voters. No one would be interested in the results of political polls if they represented only the relatively tiny sample that was surveyed rather than the entire population.

Cross-population generalizability occurs to the extent that the results of a study hold true for multiple populations; these populations may not all have been sampled, or they may be represented as subgroups within the sample studied. This was the problem with Sherman and Berk's (1984) results: Persons in Minneapolis who were arrested for domestic violence did not respond in the same way as persons arrested for the same crime in several other cities. The conclusions from Sherman and Berk's (1984) initial research in Minneapolis were not "externally valid."

Causal Validity

Causal validity, also known as *internal validity,* refers to the truthfulness of an assertion that A causes B. It is the focus of Chapter 6. Since much research seeks to determine what causes what, social scientists frequently must be concerned with causal validity. Sherman and Berk (1984) were concerned with the causal effect of arrest on the likelihood of recidivism by people accused of domestic violence, so they designed their experiment so that some accused persons were arrested and others were not and then compared their rates of recidivism.

Chapter 6 will give you much more understanding of how some features of a research design can help us evaluate causal propositions. However, you will also learn that the solutions are neither easy nor perfect: We always have to consider critically the validity of causal statements that we hear or read.

Authenticity

The goal of authenticity is stressed by researchers who focus attention on the subjective dimension of the social world. An authentic understanding of a social process or social setting is one that reflects fairly the various perspectives of participants in that setting (Gubrium & Holstein 1997). Rather than expecting social scientists to be able to provide a valid mirror of reality, those who emphasize the goal of authenticity recognize that what is understood by participants as reality is actually a linguistic and social construction of reality (Kvale 2002:306). For example, Moe (2007) found that the battered women she interviewed "exhibited a great deal of comfort through their honesty and candor" as they produced "a richly detailed and descriptive set of narratives" (p. 683). You will learn more about how authenticity can be achieved in qualitative methods in Chapters 8 and 12.

■ EXHIBIT 2.14   **Sample and Cross-Population Generalizability**

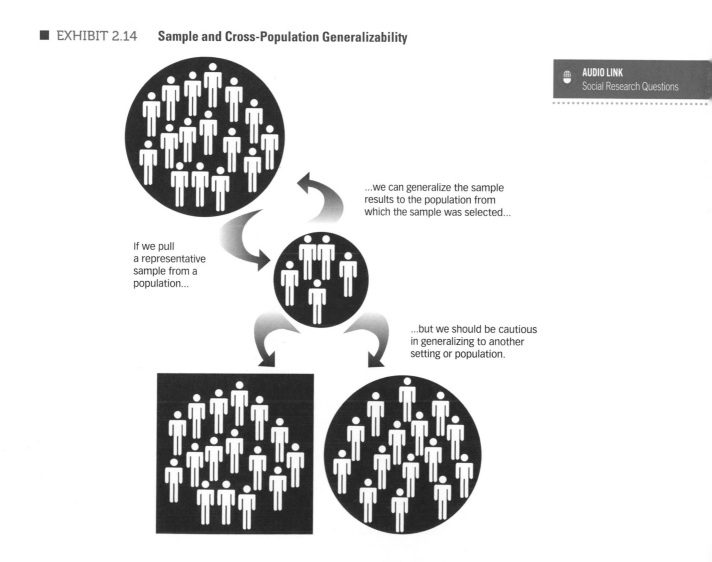

AUDIO LINK
Social Research Questions

...we can generalize the sample results to the population from which the sample was selected...

If we pull a representative sample from a population...

...but we should be cautious in generalizing to another setting or population.

CAREERS
and Research

KRISTIN M. CURTIS, SENIOR RESEARCH PROGRAM COORDINATOR

Kristin Curtis graduated with a master's degree in criminal justice from Rutgers University in Camden in 2010. As a graduate student, she worked on a nationwide research project examining policymaker and practitioner perspectives on sex offender laws, and this experience convinced her that pursuing a career in research was the best fit for her interests and talents. She secured a position as a graduate project assistant at a research institute where she worked on statewide prisoner reentry studies. Curtis has quickly moved up the ranks and in the process has worked on myriad criminal justice projects. Her research assignments require varied methodological approaches including interviews, focus groups, surveys, network analysis, regression models, and geographic information systems (GIS).

One feature of her work that Curtis truly values is the fact that she can participate in other areas of study outside the criminal justice realm. For instance, she has worked on projects that examine the impact of social service organization collaboration on child well-being, financial stability of families, and relationships between children and their caregivers. These projects involve the evaluation of collaborations among social service organizations in multiple counties and employ both qualitative and quantitative research methods. After 8 years, Curtis still enjoys her position as each day presents new challenges and different tasks, including data collection and analysis, finalizing reports, writing grant proposals for potential new projects, and supervising graduate students.

Curtis has advice for students interested in careers conducting research or using research results:

Locate faculty who engage in research in your areas of interest. Even if you are unsure what your primary research areas are, working on a research project allows you to gain exposure to different research methodologies and techniques (i.e., quantitative and qualitative). You might find you enjoy research and pick up conference presentations and academic publications along the way. Remember, college is an opportunity to explore the different career choices in the world, so take advantage of this.

❖ Conclusions

Selecting a worthy research question does not guarantee a worthwhile research project. The next three chapters focus on how particular aspects of the research process help to achieve a worthwhile result. Chapter 4 examines the interrelated processes of conceptualization and measurement, Chapter 5 reviews the sampling strategies that help achieve the goal of generalizability, and Chapter 6 clarifies the meaning of causality and illustrates different methods for achieving causal validity. Most of the remaining chapters then review different approaches to data collection—surveys, participant observation and intensive interviewing, evaluation research, unobtrusive methods—that help, in different ways, to achieve results that are valid.

Of course, social scientists' answers to research questions will never be complete or entirely certain. Interpretations of research results must always take into account the body of related literature and consider a larger theoretical framework. Simply using a large social science toolkit is no guarantee that researchers made the right decisions about which tools to use and how to use them in the investigation of a particular research problem, but you are already learning what to look for in order to evaluate those decisions.

······ Key Terms ··

Anomalous findings   22
Authenticity   26
Causal validity (internal validity)   26
Cohort   25
Cross-population generalizability
     (external validity)   26

Cross-sectional research
     design   23
Deductive research   20
Dependent variable   20
Direction of association   20
Empirical generalization   21

Event-based design
     (cohort study)   25
External validity (cross-population
     generalizability)   28
Fixed-sample panel design
     (panel study)   25

····· **Highlights** ···

- Research questions should be feasible (within the time and resources available), socially important, and scientifically relevant.

- A theory is a logically interrelated set of propositions that helps us make sense of many interrelated phenomena and predict behavior or attitudes that are likely to occur when certain conditions are met.

- Building social theory is a major objective of social research. Relevant theories should be investigated before starting social research projects and they should be used to focus attention on particular research questions and to draw out the implications of research findings.

- Specific deterrence theory predicts that punishing individuals for crime deters them from further criminal acts, due to their recognition that the costs incurred outweigh the benefits.

- Labeling theory predicts that labels applied to people can result in behaviors and attitudes consistent with the label, with a particular focus on how labeling a person or group of people as deviant can result in their engaging in deviant behavior.

- Reviewing peer-reviewed journal articles that report prior research is an essential step in designing new research.

- The type of reasoning in most research can be described as primarily deductive or inductive. Research based on deductive reasoning proceeds from general ideas, deduces specific

expectations from these ideas, and then tests the ideas with empirical data. Research based on inductive reasoning begins with specific data and then develops general ideas or theories to explain patterns in the data.

- It may be possible to explain unanticipated research findings after the fact, but such explanations have less credibility than those that have been tested with data collected for the purpose of the study.

- The scientific process can be represented as circular, with a path from theory to hypotheses, to data, and then to empirical generalizations. Research investigations may begin at different points along the research circle and traverse different portions of it. Deductive research begins at the point of theory, inductive research begins with data but ends with theory, and descriptive research begins with data and ends with empirical generalizatiodns.

- Replications of a study are essential to establishing its generalizability in other situations.

- Longitudinal designs are preferable to cross-sectional designs for establishing the time order of effects.

- The goal of social science research is to achieve valid conclusions that accurately reflect the reality studied. The three dimensions of validity are measurement validity, generalizability, and causal (internal) validity. Qualitative researchers often focus on the goal of authenticity, or reflecting fairly the perspectives of participants in a setting.

····· **Chapter Questions** ·······································

1. Pick a social issue about which you think research is needed. Draft three research questions about this issue. Refine one of the questions and evaluate it in terms of the three criteria for good research questions.

2. If you were to design research about domestic violence, would you prefer an inductive approach or a deductive approach? Explain your preference. What would be the advantages and disadvantages of each approach? Consider in your answer the role of social theory, the value of searching the literature, and the goals of your research.

3. Sherman and Berk's (1984) study of the police response to domestic violence tested predictions derived from specific

deterrence and labeling theories. Propose additional hypotheses about the response to domestic violence that are consistent with one or both of these theories. Which theory seems to you to provide the best framework for understanding domestic violence and how to respond to it? What are the independent and dependent variables in each hypothesis?

4. Researchers often try to figure out how people have changed over time by conducting a cross-sectional survey of people of different ages. The idea is that if people who are in their 60s tend to be happier than people who are in their 20s, it is because people tend to "become happier" as they age. But maybe people who are in their 60s now were just as happy when they were in

their 20s, and people in their 20s now will be just as unhappy when they are in their 60s. (That's called a cohort effect.) We can't be sure unless we conduct a panel or cohort study (survey the same people at different ages). What, in your experience, are the major differences between the generations today in social attitudes and behaviors? Which would you attribute to changes as people age, and which to differences between cohorts in what they have experienced (such as common orientations among baby boomers)? Explain your reasoning.

· · · · · · **Practice Exercises** ·

1. Pair up with one other student and select one of the research articles available for this chapter on the book's study site, at edge.sagepub.com/schuttusw. One of you should evaluate the research article in terms of its research strategy. Be generally negative but not unreasonable in your criticisms. The other student should critique the article in the same way but from a generally positive standpoint, defending its quality. Together, write a summary of the study's strong and weak points, or conduct a debate in class.

2. Research problems posed for explanatory studies must specify variables and hypotheses, which need to be stated properly and need to correctly imply any hypothesized causal relationship. The "Variables and Hypotheses" lessons, found in the Interactive Exercises on the study site, will help you learn how to do this.

   To use these lessons, choose one of the sets of "Variables and Hypotheses" exercises from the opening menu. About 10 hypotheses are presented in the lesson. After reading each hypothesis, name the dependent and independent variables and state the direction (positive or negative) of the relationship between them. In some of these Interactive Exercises, you must write in your own answer, so type carefully. The program will evaluate your answers. If an answer is correct, the program will present its version of the correct answer and go on to the next question. If you have made an error, the program will explain the error to you and give you another chance to respond. If your answer is unrecognizable, the program will instruct you to check your spelling and try again.

3. Return to the article you chose for #1, above. Diagram the process of research that it reports, using the research circle approach in Exhibit 2.6. How well does the process of research in this study seem to match the process symbolized in Exhibit 2.6? How much information is provided about each step in that process?

STUDENT STUDY SITE

⑤SAGE edge™

The Student Study Site, available at **edge.sagepub.com/schuttusw**, includes useful study materials including eFlashcards, videos, audio resources, journal articles, and encyclopedia articles, many of which are represented by the media links throughout the text.

CHAPTER 3

Research Ethics

The desire for recognition, the goal of making a difference, the lust for money, the certainty that we are right, and the difficulty of admitting weakness—none of these human failings disappear during the conduct of social research, nor are they expunged by years of advanced training. Of course, the same could be said about any human endeavor, as the latest headlines on corruption remind us, but perhaps social science bears a particularly heavy burden because its research questions can involve others' lives and beliefs so directly. As a result, social science researchers must maintain high standards of ethical conduct and transparency to assure others that research methods and outcomes are not shaped by personal preference and self-interest. The best protection against biased outcomes and fraudulent conclusions is reliance on social science research methods, openness about procedures, and ongoing dialogue about results.

It is hard to overstate the importance of maintaining ethical standards in research, but it is easy to minimize the difficulty of doing so. Most social scientists and researchers in other fields behave ethically and use research methods honestly as a matter of personal principle and of collective commitment to the goal of scientific discovery. But evidence of dishonesty and outright fraud suggests that it is too common to ignore. A recent report estimates that one scientific paper is retracted every day due to misconduct, and a survey of scientists found that 2% admitted to improper alteration of their data (Marcus & Oransky 2015). Recent public cases make it clear that social science is far from immune to the problem.

In this chapter, you will learn about ethical standards for social science research and the cases that led to codification of these standards. The chapter also covers the specific procedures that colleges and universities use to enforce the standards and the consequences that have ensued when these standards have been violated. By the chapter's end, you should be able to think about social research procedures from the standpoint of the research participants, who deserve as much respect for their well-being as do the social scientists conducting the research. You should also be aware of incentives to violating standards for ethical research and be ready to assess the extent to which the standards have been met in a particular research study.

❖ Historical Background

The development of modern ethical standards for the treatment of research participants began in reaction to discovery of the unethical practices committed in the name of "science" by Nazis before and during World War II. In

1946, after the war, the Nuremberg War Crime Trials exposed horrific medical experiments conducted by Nazi doctors and others and convinced many observers that external standards and enforcement procedures were necessary. It was not until 15 years later, however, that psychologist Stanley Milgram's research on obedience generated a pitched debate about research ethics in the social sciences (Perry 2013:37). Ironically, Milgram's research was motivated in part by his desire to understand why ordinary people went along with the Nazis.

Participants recruited in 1960 from New Haven, Connecticut, for Stanley Milgram's obedience experiments came to a laboratory at Yale University and were asked to administer shocks to other participants who gave "wrong answers" as part of what they believed was a study of learning (see Photo 3.1).

The average level of shock administered by the 40 New Haven adults who volunteered for the experiment was 24.53—a level higher than what the dial indicated was Extreme Intensity Shock and just short of Danger: Severe Shock. Of Milgram's original 40 subjects, 25 (62.5%) complied with the experimenter's demands, all the way to the top of the scale (originally labeled simply as *XXX*). And lest you pass off this result as simply the result of the subjects having thought that the experiment wasn't "real," there is abundant evidence from the subjects' own observed high stress and their subsequent reports that many subjects really believed that the learner was receiving actual, hurtful shocks (Exhibit 3.1).

Are you surprised by the subjects' responses? Do you think the results of this experiment tell us about how people behave in the real world? We return to Milgram's research later in the chapter to illustrate some key issues in research ethics.

As late as 1972, Americans learned from news reports that researchers funded by the U.S. Public Health Service had followed 399 low-income African American men in the Tuskegee Study of Untreated Syphilis in the Negro Male since the 1930s, collecting data to study the "natural" course of the illness and claiming to potential participants that it was providing treatment (Exhibit 3.2). What made this research study, known as the Tuskegee Syphilis Experiment, so shocking was that many participants were not informed of their illness and, even after penicillin was recognized as an effective treatment in 1945, the study participants were not treated (Tuskegee University 2015). Congressional hearings began in 1973, and an out-of-court settlement of $10 million was reached in 1974. President Bill Clinton made an official apology to African American citizens in 1997, for a study "so clearly racist. That can never be allowed to happen again" (CDC 2009; Washington 2006:184).

These and other widely publicized abuses made it clear that formal review procedures were needed to protect research participants. The U.S. government created a National Commission for the Protection of Human Subjects of Biomedical and Behavioral Research, and in 1979 its *Belmont Report* (Department of Health, Education, and Welfare 1979) established three basic ethical principles for the protection of human subjects (Kitchener & Kitchener 2009:7):

- **Respect for persons:** treating persons as autonomous agents and protecting those with diminished autonomy

- **Beneficence:** minimizing possible harms and maximizing benefits

- **Justice:** distributing benefits and risks of research fairly

A Federal Policy for the Protection of Human Subjects was adopted in 1991 and has shaped the course of social science research ever since. Professional associations such as the American Sociological Association (ASA), university review boards, and ethics committees in other organizations may each add to these standards for the treatment of human subjects by their members, employees, and students.

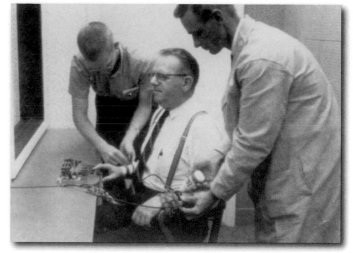

Photo 3.1 The "learner" from Milgram's study was strapped in a chair with electrodes. How many volts do you think you would have administered if you were a participant in this study?

Source: From the film *OBEDIENCE*. Copyright © 1968 by Stanley Milgram, copyright renewed 1993 by Alexandra Milgram and distributed by Alexander Street Press.

■ **EXHIBIT 3.1   Shock Meter**

Source: From the film *OBEDIENCE*. Copyright © 1968 by Stanley Milgram, copyright renewed 1993 by Alexandra Milgram and distributed by Alexander Street Press.

Belmont Report: Guidelines developed by the U.S. National Commission for the Protection of Human Subjects of Biomedical and Behavioral Research in 1979 for the protection of human subjects.

Respect for persons: According to the *Belmont Report,* the ethical principle of treating persons as autonomous agents and protecting those with diminished autonomy in research involving human subjects.

Beneficence: According to the *Belmont Report,* the ethical requirement of minimizing possible harms and maximizing benefits in research involving human subjects.

Justice: According to the *Belmont Report,* the ethical principle of distributing benefits and risks of research fairly in research involving human subjects.

❖ Ethical Principles

Professional associations of social scientists develop codes of ethics that members are expected to adhere to in their research and other activities. For example, the *Code of Ethics* of the American Sociological Association (1999) articulates general principles of competence, integrity, and responsibility as well as respect for the rights, dignity, and diversity of others, including research participants, and being socially responsible and using research to contribute to the public good. The following sections discuss the most important implications of such principles for the conduct of research, including the protection of human participants in research.

Achieving Valid Results

Code of Ethics: Professional codes adopted by professional associations of social scientists for the treatment of human subjects by members, employees, and students and designed to comply with federal policy.

Debriefing: A researcher's informing subjects after an experiment about the experiment's purposes and methods and evaluating subjects' personal reactions to the experiment.

Conflict of interest: When a researcher has a significant financial stake in the design or outcome of his or her own research.

Commitment to achieving valid results is the necessary starting point for ethical research practice. Simply put, social researchers have no business asking people to answer questions, submit to observations, or participate in experimental procedures if they are simply seeking to verify preexisting prejudices or convince others to take action on behalf of their own personal interests. Knowledge is the foundation of human progress as well as the basis for the expectation that social scientists can help people achieve a brighter future. If social scientists set aside their personal predilections in the service of learning a bit more about human behavior, they can honestly represent their research projects as potentially contributing to the advancement of knowledge.

Milgram argued that obedience could fruitfully be studied in the laboratory and that his findings help to explain the lack of opposition to the Nazis in Germany and so could help to prevent such horrific events. Do you believe that our ethical judgments should differ depending on whether we decide that a study provides valid information about important social psychological processes? Should it matter that a 2005 replication of Milgram's experiment (with less severe "shocks") for ABC News supported Milgram's conclusions (Perry 2013:275–279)?

■ EXHIBIT 3.2   Tuskegee Syphilis Experiment Recruitment Letter

Macon County Health Department
ALABAMA STATE BOARD OF HEALTH AND U.S. PUBLICH HEALTH
SERVICE COOPERATING WITH TUSKEGEE INSTITUTE

Dear Sir:

Some time ago you were given a thorough examination and since that time we hope you have gotten a great deal of treatment for bad blood. You will now be given your last chance to get a second examination. This examination is a very special one and after it is finished you will be given a special treatment if it is believed you are in a condition to stand it.

If you want this special examination and treatment you must meet the nurse at _____ on _____ at _____ M. She will bring you to the Tuskegee Institute Hospital for this free treatment. We will be very busy when these examinations and treatments are being given, and will have lots of people to wait on. You will remember that you had to wait for some time when you had your last good examination, and we wish to let you know that because we expect to be so busy it may be necessary for you to remain in the hospital over one night. If this is necessary you will be furnished your meals and a bed, as well the examination and treatment without cost.

REMEMBER THIS IS YOUR LAST CHANCE FOR SPECIAL FREE TREATMENT. BE SURE TO MEET THE NURSE.

Macon County Health Department

This letter is reproduced from an educational website at the University of Illinois's Poynter Center for the Study of Ethics and American Institutions (http://poynter.indiana.edu/sas/lb/facts.html.)

Source: Sharp, Gwen. 2014. "Tuskegee Syphilis Study Recruitment Letter." *The Society Pages.* Retrieved from http://thesocietypages.org/socimages/2014/08/22/tuskegee-syphilis-study-recruitment-letter/

Honesty and Openness

The scientific concern with validity requires, in turn, that scientists be open in disclosing their methods and honest in presenting their findings. In contrast, research distorted by political or personal pressures to find particular outcomes or to achieve the most marketable results is unlikely to be carried out in an honest and open fashion. The act of publication itself is a vital element in maintaining openness and honesty. Others can review and question study procedures and so generate an open dialogue with the researcher.

A recent publication about Milgram's experiment challenges his commitment to the standard of openness and honesty. Gina Perry's (2013) *Behind the Shock Machine: The Untold Story of the Notorious Milgram Psychology Experiments* reveals many misleading statements about participants' postexperiment **debriefing**, about adherence to the treatment protocol, about the extent of participants' apparent distress, and about the extent of support for his favored outcome.

Conflicting interests can create a pressure to avoid being open and honest. **Conflicts of interest** may occur when a researcher has a significant financial stake in the design or outcome of the research. Receiving speaking fees, consulting fees, patents or royalties, and other financial benefits as a result of the way in which a research project is designed or the results that it obtains creates a pressure to distort decisions and findings in one's (financial) favor. Both federal research funding agencies and journal editors require disclosure of possible conflicts of interest so that others can scrutinize the extent to which these conflicts may have lessened researchers' honesty and openness (Fisher & Anushko 2008:96–97).

Professional self-interest also generates conflicts of interest. The pressure to publish research findings in important journals and to receive public and professional recognition for creating important new knowledge motivates many researchers and it can tempt some to alter data or mischaracterize procedures or results so that their findings "look better." This seems to have been behind the problems that led to the retraction of a social science article published in the prestigious journal *Science* in December 2014.

Michael LaCour, a graduate student at UCLA, had conducted a survey funded by the Los Angeles LGBT Center to test the value of using gay canvassers to increase support for legislation that would overturn a same-sex marriage ban. LaCour recruited a senior political scientist at Columbia University to coauthor the *Science* article, in which the claim was made that 10-minute conversations with a gay canvasser could change opponents' minds. But after wide publicity, two University of California, Berkeley, graduate students tried to extend the study and found that there were problems in the data and that the polling firm that LaCour claimed to have used had no record of such a survey. After the apparent fraud was exposed, Dave Fleischer, director of the center that had sponsored the study, remarked that "it really hurts when you trust somebody to be doing an honest assessment of your work and then it turns out that they did not" (Carey & Belluck 2015:A16).

Protecting Research Participants

Several standards concerning the treatment of human subjects are emphasized in federal regulations and the ethical guidelines adopted by many professional social science organizations:

- Research should cause no harm to subjects.

- Participation in research should be voluntary, and therefore subjects must give their informed consent to participate in the research and researchers must disclose their identity.

- Researchers should avoid **deception**, except in limited circumstances.

- Anonymity or confidentiality must be maintained for individual research participants unless it is voluntarily and explicitly waived.

- Researchers should consider the uses of a research project so that its benefits outweigh any foreseeable risks.

Avoid Harming Research Participants

Although this standard may seem straightforward, it can be difficult to interpret in specific cases and harder yet to define in a way agreeable to all social scientists. Does it mean that subjects should not be harmed psychologically as well as physically at all? That they should feel no anxiety or distress whatsoever during the study or only after their involvement ends? Should the possibility of any harm, no matter how remote, deter research?

What about possible harm to the subjects of the famous **prison simulation study** at Stanford University (Haney, Banks, & Zimbardo 1973)? The study was designed to investigate the impact of social position on behavior—specifically, the impact of being either a guard or a prisoner in a prison, a "total institution." The researchers selected apparently stable and mature young male volunteers and asked them to sign a contract to work for 2 weeks as a guard or a prisoner in a simulated prison. Within the first 2 days after the prisoners were incarcerated by the "guards" in a makeshift basement prison, the prisoners began to be passive and disorganized, while the guards became "sadistic"—verbally and physically aggressive (Exhibit 3.3). Five "prisoners" were soon released for depression, uncontrollable crying, fits of rage, and, in one case, a psychosomatic rash. Instead of letting things continue for 2 weeks as planned, Philip Zimbardo and his colleagues terminated the experiment after 6 days to avoid harming the subjects.

Through discussions in special postexperiment encounter sessions, feelings of stress among the participants who played the role of prisoner seemed to be relieved; follow-up during the next year indicated no lasting negative effects on the participants and some benefits in the form of greater insight.

Would you ban such experiments because of the potential for harm to subjects? Are you concerned, like Arthur Miller (1986), that real harm "could result from *not doing* research on destructive obedience" (p. 138) and other troubling human behaviors? How do you think you would have reacted if you were one of the students depicted in Photo 3.2, from the Stanford Prison Experiment?

Potential harm to research participants should also be considered in relation to survey research and observational research. Questions about sensitive personal issues can elicit emotional reactions, including distress. Survey researchers should be prepared to pause or even discontinue questioning and provide a referral to a counselor if a survey includes questions that might elicit such responses.

ENCYCLOPEDIA LINK
Ethical Codes

AUDIO LINK
Milgram's Experiment

JOURNAL LINK
Intensive Rehabilitation Supervision Program

RESEARCH/SOCIAL IMPACT LINK
Research Ethics

Deception: Used in social experiments to create more "realistic" treatments in which the true purpose of the research is not disclosed to participants, often within the confines of a laboratory.

Zimbardo's prison simulation study: Famous prison simulation study at Stanford University by psychologist Philip Zimbardo designed to investigate the impact of social position on behavior—specifically, the impact of being either a guard or a prisoner in a "total institution"; widely cited as demonstrating the likelihood of emergence of sadistic behavior in guards.

■ **EXHIBIT 3.3** **Chart of Guard and Prisoner Behavior**

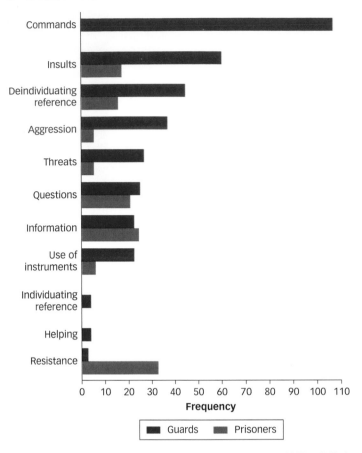

Frequency

■ Guards ■ Prisoners

Source: Adapted from *The Lucifer Effect* by Philip G. Zimbardo. Copyright 2007 by Philip G. Zimbardo, Inc. Used by permission of Random House, Inc., and Random House Group Ltd.

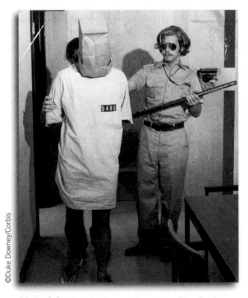

Photo 3.2 In studies such as the Stanford Prison Experiment, do you think the risk to participants outweighs the potential insights that could be gained?

Obtain Informed Consent

The requirement of informed consent is more difficult to define than it first appears. To be informed, consent must be given by persons who are competent to consent, who have consented voluntarily, who are fully informed about the research and know who is conducting the research, and who have comprehended what they have been told (Reynolds 1979). You probably recognize that because of the inability to communicate perfectly, "full disclosure of everything that could possibly affect a given subject's decision to participate is not possible, and therefore cannot be ethically required" (Baumrind 1965:165).

The language of the consent form must be clear and understandable to the research participants and yet sufficiently long and detailed to explain what will actually happen in the research. The consent form in Exhibit 3.4 illustrates a typical approach to these trade-offs.

Experimental researchers whose research design requires some type of subject deception typically withhold some information before the experiment begins, but then debrief subjects at the end in order to maintain something like the full disclosure standard. In a debriefing, the researcher explains to the subjects what happened in the experiment and why, and then responds to their questions. A carefully designed debriefing procedure can help the research participants learn from the experimental research and grapple constructively with feelings elicited by the realization that they were deceived (Sieber 1992:39–41).

The process and even possibility of obtaining informed consent must consider the capacity of prospective participants to give informed consent. Children cannot legally give consent to participate in research; instead, they must in most circumstances be given the opportunity to give or withhold their *assent* to participate in research, usually by a verbal response to an explanation of the research. In addition, a child's legal guardian must give written informed consent to have the child participate in research (Sieber 1992). There are also special protections for other populations who are likely to be vulnerable to coercion—prisoners, pregnant women, persons with mental disabilities, and educationally or economically disadvantaged persons.

Obtaining informed consent also becomes more challenging in collectivist communities in which leaders or the whole group is accustomed to making decisions for individual members. In such settings, usually in non-Western cultures, researchers may have to develop a relationship with the community before individuals can be engaged in research (Bledsoe & Hopson 2009:397–398).

Subject payments create another complication for achieving the goal of informed consent. Although payments to research participants can be a reasonable way to compensate them for their time and effort, payments also serve as an inducement to participate. If the payment is a significant amount in relation to the participants' normal income, it could lead people to participate in a project even though they may harbor reservations about doing so (Fisher & Anushko 2008:104–105).

Avoid Deception in Research, Except in Limited Circumstances

Deception occurs when subjects are misled about research procedures to determine how they would react to the treatment if they were not research subjects. Deception is a critical component of many social psychology experiments, partly because of the difficulty of simulating real-world stresses and dilemmas in a laboratory setting. The goal is to get subjects "to accept as true what is false or to give a false impression" (Korn 1997:4). In Milgram's (1964) experiment, for example, deception seemed necessary because the subjects could not be permitted to administer real electric shocks to the "stooge," yet it would not have made sense to order the subjects to do something that they didn't find to be so troubling. Milgram (1992:187–188) insisted that the deception was absolutely essential, although the experimental records indicate that some participants figured out the deception (Perry 2013:128–129).

RESEARCH/SOCIAL IMPACT LINK
Informed Consent

The results of many other social psychological experiments would be worthless if subjects understood what was really happening to them while the experiment was in progress. For instance, Jane Allyn Piliavin and Irving Piliavin (1972:355–356) staged fake seizures on subway trains to study helpfulness (Korn 1997:3–4). If you were a member of your university's ethics board, would you vote to allow such deceptive practices in research? What about less dramatic instances of deception in laboratory experiments with students like yourself?

Can you see why an ethics board, representing a range of perspectives, is an important tool for making reasonable, ethical research decisions when confronted with such ambiguity? Exhibit 3.5 shows a portion of the complex flowchart developed by the U.S. Department of Health and Human Services (DHHS) to help researchers decide what type of review will be needed for their research plans. Any research involving deception requires formal human subjects review.

Maintain Privacy and Confidentiality

Maintaining privacy and confidentiality is another key ethical standard for protecting research participants, and the researcher's commitment to that standard should be included in the informed consent agreement (Sieber 1992). Procedures to protect each subject's privacy—such as locking records and creating special identifying codes—must be created to minimize the risk of access by unauthorized persons. However, statements about confidentiality should be realistic: Laws allow research records to be subpoenaed and may require reporting of child abuse; a researcher may feel compelled to release information if a health- or life-threatening situation arises and participants need to be alerted. Also, the standard of confidentiality does not apply to observation in public places and information available in public records. To avoid potential problems, social researchers who do not need to contact research participants more than

■ EXHIBIT 3.4 **Consent Form**

University of Massachusetts Boston

Department of Sociology

100 Morrissey Boulevard

Boston, MA 02125-3393

Consent Form for Teen Empowerment Study: Current Organizers

Introduction and Contact Information

I am conducting a study of the Teen Empowerment Program. In order for you to participate, I need to ask for your consent.

The principal researcher is Professor Russell Schutt, Department of Sociology at UMass Boston. I am Whitney Gecker, his research assistant in this project. Please read this form and feel free to ask questions. If you have further questions later, Professor Schutt will discuss them with you. His telephone number is 617-287-6253.

Description of the Project

Teen Empowerment (TE) is an innovative program for youth in Somerville, Massachusetts and several other locations. This research project is a comprehensive evaluation of the Teen Empowerment program in Somerville, MA. It is to learn whether and if so how the TE model is successful. The study will describe the backgrounds, attitudes, experiences and activities of current and past program participants and of youth who applied to the program but did not participate in it. The study will identify the impact of the TE process on individual participants, including their behavior, their feelings about themselves, and their awareness and demonstration of love and forgiveness toward others. It will also examine the effect of TE on participants' relationships with others; on the rate of crime in the community, and on the participants' lives in comparison to the lives of program applicants who were not accepted.

The research procedures involve interviews with current and former youth participants and unsuccessful applicants, as well as observation of group activities. Participation in this study will take approximately one hour. If you decide to participate in this study, you will be asked a series of questions about your attitudes, your experiences in school and work, your relations with family and friends, your health behaviors and experiences of violence. You will also be asked about the Teen Empowerment program and the Somerville community. You will receive a $15 gift certificate for your participation. If you agree, we will also record information that you provided to Teen Empowerment on forms you collected when you applied to the program.

Risks or Discomforts

The primary risk associated with this study is that the investigators may learn information about you that you did not wish to share with them. If you have any concern that you have disclosed information that you do not wish to have known, or if you have any other concerns or feelings as a result of the interview, you may speak with Professor Schutt to discuss this at any point, by calling 617-287-6253, or by communicating by email (Russell.schutt@umb.edu) or regular mail, addressed to Professor Schutt at the University of Massachusetts, 100 Morrissey Blvd., Boston, MA 02125-3393. If you indicate any feelings of distress during the study, the project interviewer will suggest that you speak to a Teen Empowerment staff member and will provide referral information for service agencies in Somerville.

(Continued)

■ EXHIBIT 3.4   **(Continued)**

Confidentiality

Your part in this research is confidential. The final project report will not name the specific individuals who were interviewed nor link comments made in interviews to these individuals. Please note that Massachusetts law requires that information about abuse or neglect must be reported to the Massachusetts Department of Children and Families. If you state that you are abused or neglected, I will inform Professor Schutt, the Principal Investigator, and he will report this information to the Massachusetts Department of Children and Families.

Voluntary Participation

The decision whether or not to take part in this research study is voluntary. If you do decide to take part in this study, you may decline to answer any question and you may terminate participation at any time without consequence. Whatever you decide about participation will not be known to any other current or former Teen Empowerment participants or staff or to anyone else.

Rights

You have the right to ask questions about this research at any time during the study. You can reach Russell Schutt to ask further questions at 617-287-6253. If you have any questions or concerns about your rights as a research participant, you may contact a representative of the Institutional Review Board (IRB), at the University of Massachusetts, Boston, which oversees research involving human participants. The Institutional Review Board may be reached at the following address: IRB, Quinn Administration Building-2-015, University of Massachusetts Boston, 100 Morrissey Boulevard, Boston, MA 02125-3393. You can also contact the Board by telephone or e-mail at (617) 287-5370 or at human.subjects@umb.edu.

I HAVE READ THE CONSENT FORM. MY QUESTIONS HAVE BEEN ANSWERED. MY SIGNATURE ON THIS FORM INDICATES THAT I CONSENT TO PARTICIPATE IN THIS STUDY. I ALSO CERTIFY THAT I AM 18 YEARS OF AGE OR OLDER.

_____   _____
Signature of Participant   Date

_____
Typed/Printed Name of Participant

MY SIGNATURE BELOW INDICATES THAT I CONSENT TO HAVE INFORMATION USED IN THE STUDY THAT I PROVIDED WHEN I APPLIED TO TEEN EMPOWERMENT.

_____   _____
Signature of Participant   Date

_____   _____
Signature of Researcher   Date

_____
Typed/Printed Name of Researcher

Photo 3.3   How might payment for participating in a research study complicate ethical considerations related to social research?

once may ensure that their data are anonymous, so that there are no potential identifiers linking participants to the data about them. Any unique identifier, such as a birthdate or, in some circumstances, place of birth must be omitted in order to ensure anonymity.

There is one exception to some of these constraints: The National Institutes of Health (NIH) can issue a **Certificate of Confidentiality** to protect researchers from being legally required to disclose confidential information. This is intended to help researchers overcome the reluctance of individuals engaged in illegal behavior to sign a consent form or to risk exposure of their illegal activities (Sharma 2009:426). Researchers who are focusing on high-risk populations or behaviors, such as crime, substance abuse, sexual activity, or genetic information, can request such a certificate. Suspicions of child abuse or neglect must still be reported, and in some states, researchers may still be required to report such crimes as elder abuse (Arwood & Panicker 2007).

■ EXHIBIT 3.5   **U.S. Department of Health and Human Services Human Subjects Decision Flowchart 4:
For Tests, Surveys, Interviews, Public Behavior Observation**

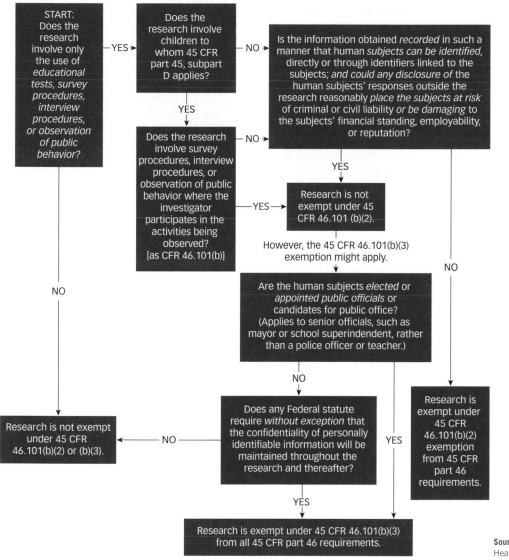

Source: U.S. Department of Health and Human Services.

The **Health Insurance Portability and Accountability Act (HIPAA)** passed by Congress in 1996 created more stringent regulations for the protection of health care data. As implemented by the DHHS in 2000 (revised in 2002), the HIPAA Final Privacy Rule applies to oral, written, and electronic information that "relates to the past, present or future physical or mental health or condition of an individual." The HIPAA rule requires that researchers have valid authorization for any use or disclosure of "protected health information" from a health care provider. Waivers of authorization can be granted in special circumstances (Cava, Cushman, & Goodman 2007).

Certificate of Confidentiality: A certificate issued to a researcher by the National Institutes of Health that ensures the right to protect information obtained about high-risk populations or behaviors—except child abuse or neglect—from legal subpoenas.

Health Insurance Portability and Accountability Act (HIPAA): A congressional act passed in 1996 that creates stringent regulations for the protection of health care data.

Consider Uses of Research So That Benefits Outweigh Risks

Social scientists must also consider the uses to which their research is put. Although many scientists believe that personal values should be left outside the laboratory, some feel that it is proper—even necessary—for scientists to concern themselves with the way their research is used.

The evaluation research by Lawrence Sherman and Richard Berk (1984) on police response to domestic violence provides an interesting cautionary tale about the uses of science. As you recall from Chapter 2, the results of this field experiment indicated that those who were arrested were less likely to subsequently commit violent acts against their partners. Sherman (1993) explicitly cautioned police departments not to adopt mandatory arrest policies based solely on the results of the Minneapolis experiment, but the results were publicized in the mass media and encouraged many jurisdictions to change their policies (Binder & Meeker 1993; Lempert 1989). We now know that the original finding of a deterrent effect of arrest did not hold up in many other cities where the experiment was repeated, so it is not clear that the initial changes in arrest policy were beneficial.

Institutional review board (IRB): A group of organizational and community representatives required by federal law to review the ethical issues in all proposed research that is federally funded, involves human subjects, or has any potential for harm to human subjects.

The potential of withholding a beneficial treatment from some subjects also is a cause for ethical concern. The Sherman and Berk (1984) experiment required the random assignment of subjects to treatment conditions and thus had the potential of causing harm to the victims of domestic violence whose batterers were not arrested. The justification for the study design, however, is quite persuasive: The researchers didn't know before the experiment which response to a domestic violence complaint would be most likely to deter future incidents (Sherman 1992). The experiment provided what seemed at first to be clear evidence about the value of arrest, so it can be argued that the benefits outweighed the risks. Do you agree?

❖ The Institutional Review Board

Federal regulations require that every institution that seeks federal funding for biomedical or behavioral research on human subjects have an **institutional review board (IRB)** that reviews research proposals involving human subjects—including data about living individuals. According to federal regulations [45 CFR 46.102(d)], research is "a systematic investigation . . . designed to develop or

RESEARCH

In the News

IS SAME-SEX MARRIAGE BAD FOR CHILDREN?

"In a federal court in Detroit starting Tuesday, in the first trial of its kind in years, the social science research on family structure and child progress will be openly debated, with expert testimony and cross-examination, offering an unusual public dissection of the methods of sociology and the intersection of science and politics."

This announcement in the *New York Times* focused primarily on the role of a sociologist at the University of Texas, Austin, Mark Regnerus, who published in 2012 findings from a survey that had been funded by $785,000 from private centers that opposed gay marriage. The survey results seemed to indicate that children who had a parent who had ever had a same-sex liaison had worse behavioral and psychological outcomes.

Asserting multiple flaws in the study, Wendy D. Manning, a professor of sociology at Bowling Green State University in Ohio who coauthored a critique of the Regnerus research by the American Sociological Association, said that instead the study simply confirmed other research showing that family stability predicts child well-being: "Every study has shortcomings, but when you pull them all together, the picture is very clear. There is no evidence that children fare worse in same-sex families."

For Further Thought ?

1. Do you believe researchers should be required to reveal the sources of their funding?

2. What are the risks and benefits of conducting research or using research findings to influence public policy?

3. Should IRBs consider whether researchers' personal preferences or their funding sources may bias their research decisions to favor a particular result?

News source: Eckholm, Erik. 2014. "Opponents of Same-Sex Marriage Take Bad-for-Children Argument to Court." *New York Times*, February 22:A16.

contribute to generalizable knowledge," and according to the DHHS [45 CFR 46.102 (f)], a human subject is "a living individual about whom an investigator (whether professional or student) conducting research obtains data through intervention or interaction with the individual or just identifiable private information." The IRB determines whether a planned activity is *research* or involves *human subjects*, but it is monitored by the federal **Office for Protection From Research Risks**.

IRBs at universities and other agencies apply ethical standards that are set by federal regulations but can be expanded or specified by the institution's IRB and involve all research at the institution irrespective of the funding source (Sieber 1992:5, 10). The IRB has the authority to require changes in a research protocol or to refuse to approve a research protocol if it deems human subjects protections inadequate.

To promote adequate review of ethical issues, the regulations require that IRBs include at least five members, with at least one nonscientist and one from outside the institution (Speiglman & Spear 2009:124). The IRB must also include members from both sexes, diverse backgrounds, and multiple professions. When research is reviewed concerning vulnerable populations, such as prisoners, the IRB must include a member having experience with and knowledge about that vulnerable population. Sensitivity to community attitudes and training in human subjects protection procedures is also required (Selwitz, Epley, & Erickson 2013).

> **RESEARCHER INTERVIEW LINK**
> Institutional Review Boards

Every member of an institution with an IRB—including faculty, students, and staff at a college or university—must submit a proposal to their IRB before conducting research with identifiable people that is not solely conducted for educational benefit. The IRB proposal must include research instruments and consent forms, as applicable, as well as enough detail about the research design to convince the IRB members that the potential benefits of the research outweigh any risks (Speiglman & Spear 2009:124). Most IRBs also require that researchers complete a training program about human subjects, usually the Collaborative Institutional Training Initiative (CITI) at the University of Miami (https://www.citiprogram.org). CITI training is divided into topical modules ranging from history, ethical principles, and informed consent to vulnerable populations, Internet-based research, educational research, and records-based research. Each IRB determines which CITI training modules researchers at its institution must complete.

Office for Protection From Research Risks, National Institutes of Health: The office in the U.S. Department of Health and Human Services (DHHS) that provides leadership and supervision about the protection of the rights, welfare, and well-being of subjects involved in research conducted or supported by DHHS, including monitoring IRBs.

Although the IRB is the responsible authority within the institution, many research proposals do not have to be reviewed by the full board (Hicks 2013). Some proposals, including many developed by social scientists, may be exempt from review because they involve very low perceived risk, such as a survey that does not collect information that could be harmful to respondents if it were disclosed or analysis of existing records that are not individually identifiable.

CAREERS
and Research

MANAN NAYAK, SENIOR PROJECT DIRECTOR

After Manan Nayak graduated from the accelerated B.A./M.A. program in applied sociology at the University of Massachusetts Boston, she began her career as a quality assurance analyst for a university-affiliated medical center. Initially, she used her quantitative skills to manage data from multiple clinical trials. In this role, she submitted regular reports to various committees, including the data safety and monitoring committee that ensures each study is scientific and ethically appropriate based on federal regulations. However, it was not until she became a clinical researcher that she appreciated the importance of human subjects boards. As she approached eligible patients for studies, she learned that many patients wanted to participate in the hopes that the data collected could help someone else—despite already dealing with the effects of treatment and multiple demands on their time.

The patients' selflessness motivated Nayak to develop her research career and learn more about ethical and regulatory issues and how to ensure that research teams adhere to strict guidelines. She worked alongside investigators to write applications that clearly state the process the research team will follow, including how participants are identified, what they will be asked to consent to and for how long, as well as how their data will be collected, stored, and distributed. The procedures outlined and approved by the regulatory boards are followed strictly, and any major or minor deviations are reported to the institutional review board immediately, along with a resolution indicating how infractions can be avoided in the future. Bringing to fruition a research study and making a small contribution in understanding how a treatment affects a group of patients and the challenges they face during treatment are the rewards of doing such research. Nayak's advice is to realize, in the excitement of doing social research, the many opportunities available to apply skills you learn in research courses.

Many research proposals that do not meet the criteria for exemption but still pose only minimal risk to human subjects may be given an *expedited* review by IRB representatives (often an IRB administrator and the IRB chair), rather than being sent to a hearing at a meeting of the full IRB. However, the decision of whether a research project is exempt or can have an expedited review must be made by a representative of the IRB (Speiglman & Spear 2009:125–126).

The IRB may also serve as the privacy board that ensures researchers' compliance with HIPAA. In this capacity, the IRB responds to requests for waivers or alterations of the authorization requirement under the privacy rule for uses and disclosures of protected health information in research. Researchers seeking to collect or use existing HIPAA data must provide additional information to the IRB about their plans for using the health information.

❖ Conclusions

The extent to which ethical issues are a problem for researchers and participants in their research varies with the type of research design, but it is always a concern. Survey research creates few risks to research participants, but it does not eliminate the hazards of unethical research procedures or reporting. In fact, researchers from Michigan's Institute for Survey Research interviewed a representative national sample of adults some years ago and found that 68% of those who had participated in a survey were somewhat or very interested in participating in another; the more times respondents had been interviewed, the more willing they were to participate again. Presumably, they would have felt differently if they had been treated unethically (Reynolds 1979:56–57). Conversely, some experimental studies in the social sciences that have put people in uncomfortable or embarrassing situations have generated vociferous complaints and years of debate about ethics, although they may have made major contributions to understanding the social world (Reynolds 1979; Sjoberg 1967).

The evaluation of ethical issues in a research project should be based on a realistic assessment of the overall potential for harm and benefit to research subjects and the researchers' adherence to methodological standards rather than on an apparent inconsistency between any particular aspect of a research plan and a specific ethical guideline. For example, full disclosure of "what is really going on" in an experimental study may be less of a concern if subjects are unlikely to be harmed. Nevertheless, researchers should make every effort to foresee all possible risks and to weigh the possible benefits of the research against these risks. Researchers should consult with individuals with different perspectives to develop a realistic risk-benefit assessment and should try to maximize the benefits to, as well as minimize the risks for, research participants (Sieber 1992:75–108).

SAGE JOURNAL ARTICLE
Driving While Impaired

Key Terms

Belmont Report   33
Beneficence   33
Certificate of Confidentiality   38
Code of Ethics (American
      Sociological Association)   34
Conflict of interest   34
Debriefing   34

Deception   35
Health Insurance
      Portability and Accountability
      Act (HIPAA)   39
Institutional review board (IRB)   40
Justice   33

Office for Protection From
      Research Risks, National
      Institutes of Health   41
Respect for persons   33
Zimbardo's prison
      simulation study   35

Highlights

- Stanley Milgram's obedience experiments led to intensive debate about the extent to which deception could be tolerated in social science research and how harm to subjects should be evaluated.

- Egregious violations of human rights by researchers, including scientists in Nazi Germany and researchers in the Tuskegee syphilis study, led to the adoption of federal ethical standards for research on human subjects.

- The 1979 *Belmont Report* developed by a national commission established three basic ethical standards for the protection

- of human subjects: (1) respect for persons, (2) beneficence, and (3) justice.

- The U.S. Department of Health and Human Services adopted in 1991 the Federal Policy for the Protection of Human Subjects. This policy requires that every institution seeking federal funding for biomedical or behavioral research on human subjects have an institutional review board to exercise oversight.

- Current standards for the protection of human subjects require avoiding harm, obtaining informed consent, avoiding deception except in limited circumstances, maintaining privacy and confidentiality, and ensuring that the benefits of research outweigh foreseeable risks.

- The American Sociological Association's general principles for professional practice urge sociologists to be committed in their work to high levels of competence, to practicing with integrity, and to maintaining responsibility for their actions. They must also respect the rights, dignity, and diversity of others, including research participants, as well as be socially responsible to their communities and use research to contribute to the public good.

- Scientific research should maintain high standards for validity and be conducted and reported in an honest and open fashion.

- Effective debriefing of subjects after an experiment can help reduce the risk of harm resulting from the use of deception in the experiment.

Chapter Questions

1. Milgram's research on obedience to authority has been used to explain the behavior of soldiers charged with intentionally harming civilians during armed conflicts, both on the battlefield and when guarding prisoners of war. Do you think social scientists can use experiments such as Milgram's to learn about ethical behavior in the social world in general? What about in situations of armed conflict? Consider in your answers Perry's discoveries about aspects of Milgram's research that he did not disclose.

2. Should social scientists be permitted to conduct replications of Milgram's obedience experiments? What about Zimbardo's prison simulation? Can you justify such research as permissible within the current ASA ethical standards? If not, do you believe that these standards should be altered to permit Milgram-type research?

Practice Exercises

1. The Collaborative Institutional Training Initiative (CITI) offers an extensive online training course in the basics of human subjects protections issues. Go to the public access CITI site at https://www.citiprogram.org/ and complete the course in social and behavioral research. Write a short summary of what you have learned.

2. The U.S. Department of Health and Human Services maintains extensive resources concerning the protection of human subjects in research. Read several documents that you find on its website, www.hhs.gov/ohrp, and write a short report about them.

3. Read the entire ASA *Code of Ethics* at the website of the ASA Ethics Office, www.asanet.org/images/asa/docs/pdf/CodeofEthics.pdf. Discuss the difference between the aspirational goals and the enforceable rules.

STUDENT STUDY SITE

⑤SAGE edge™

The Student Study Site, available at **edge.sagepub.com/schuttusw**, includes useful study materials including eFlashcards, videos, audio resources, journal articles, and encyclopedia articles, many of which are represented by the media links throughout the text.

CHAPTER 4

Conceptualization and Measurement

The term *poverty* brings to mind a lot of images: children lacking adequate clothing, shacks without running water, dumpster diving for food, long blocks of tenement housing. What images come to your mind? Do they reflect your personal experience, conversations with others, what you have read or pictures you have seen, perhaps even a sociology course? Whatever images appear in your mind, you can readily see that others might see different images and associate the term with different experiences. *Poverty* is likely to mean one thing to a resident of Chicago's Gold Coast and quite another to a peasant farmer in Guatemala. It is therefore important for social researchers to define what they mean by the terms they use and to explain how they have connected these terms to phenomena in the social world.

This chapter begins with examples of the process of **conceptualization**—specifying what we mean by a term, using *poverty*, *youth gangs*, and *trust* as examples. It then reviews the different measurement procedures for such concepts, including questions, observations, and less direct and obtrusive measures, and distinguishes them in terms of "level of measurement." The chapter concludes with an overview of the procedures for assessing measurement quality.

Conceptualization: The process of specifying what we mean by a term. Conceptualization helps translate portions of an abstract theory into specific variables that can be used in testable hypotheses.

Concept: A mental image that summarizes a set of similar observations, feelings, or ideas.

❖ Concepts

We call poverty a **concept**—a mental image that summarizes a set of similar observations, feelings, or ideas. To make that concept useful in research (and even in ordinary discourse), we have to define it. We can't say that only one definition of *poverty* is "correct," or even that one is "better." What we can say is that we need to specify what we mean when we use the term. We also have to be sure that others know what definition we are using. Many concepts are used in everyday discourse without consistent definition, sometimes definitions of concepts are themselves the object of intense debate, and the meanings of concepts may change over time.

Concepts such as poverty require an explicit definition before they are used in research because we cannot be certain that all readers will share a

©iStockphoto.com/ ManoAfrica

Photo 4.1 Though most who see this image would agree that it depicts someone living in poverty, finding a way to measure this objectively is not as straightforward as it might seem.

particular definition. It is especially important to define clearly concepts that are abstract or unfamiliar.

Poverty

Poverty has always been a somewhat controversial concept, because different conceptualizations lead to different estimates of its prevalence and different social policies for responding to it. Most of the statistics that you see about the poverty rate in the United States reflect a 1965 definition developed by Mollie Orshansky at the Social Security Administration (Putnam 1977). She defined poverty with an *absolute* standard that captured the amount of money required to purchase an emergency diet estimated to be nutritionally adequate for about 2 months. The idea is that people are truly poor if they can just barely purchase the food they need and other essential goods. This poverty standard is adjusted for household size and composition (number of children and adults), and the minimal amount of money needed for food is multiplied by three because a 1955 survey indicated that poor families spend about one third of their incomes on food (Orshansky 1977).

Does this sound straightforward? Some observers argue that noncash benefits that low-income people can receive, such as food stamps, housing subsidies, and tax rebates, should be added to cash income before the level of poverty is calculated (Eckholm 2006:A8). Others argue that the persistence of poverty should be considered, so that someone who is poor for no more than a year, for example, is distinguished from someone who is poor for many years (Walker, Tomlinson, & Williams 2010:367–368).

Some social scientists disagree altogether with the absolute standard and have instead urged adoption of a *relative* poverty standard (Exhibit 4.1). They identify the poor as those in the lowest fifth or tenth of the income distribution or as those having some fraction of the average income. The idea behind this relative conception is that poverty should be defined in terms of what is normal in a given society at a particular time. This relative conception of poverty has largely been accepted in Europe (Walker et al. 2010:356). You can see in Exhibit 4.1 that household incomes at the top of the distribution in the United States have increased much more rapidly since about 1980 than those toward the bottom of the income distribution, so a relative standard would lead to the conclusion that poverty has been increasing even though the incomes of the poorest fifth of families have not changed much. Others argue that poverty is as much a matter of how people think about their situation as it is a matter of their actual income and other resources. Although "a car may be a luxury in some poor countries, in a country where most families own cars and public transportation is inadequate, a car is a basic necessity for finding and commuting to work" (Mayrl et al. 2004:10); as a result, families that do not own a car may feel poor, even if their incomes allow them to eat adequately.

Some social scientists prefer a *subjective* definition of poverty as what people think would be the minimal income they need to make ends meet. Of course, many observers have argued that this approach is influenced too much by the different standards that people use to estimate what they "need" (Ruggles 1990:20–23).

Which do you think is a more reasonable approach to defining poverty: some type of absolute standard, a relative standard, or a subjective standard? Be careful here: Conceptualization has consequences! Research using the standard absolute concept of poverty indicated that the percentage of Americans in poverty declined by 1.7% in the 1990s, but use of a relative concept of poverty led to the conclusion that poverty increased by 2.7% (Mayrl et al. 2004:10). No matter which conceptualization we decide to adopt, our understanding of the concept of poverty will be sharpened after we consider the three alternative definitions we have just considered.

RESEARCH/SOCIAL IMPACT LINK
Variables

Youth Gangs

Do you have a clear image in mind when you hear the term *youth gangs*? Although this is quite an ordinary term, social scientists have proposed many different definitions and so far have "failed to reach a consensus" (Howell 2003:75). Exhibit 4.2 lists a few of the many alternative definitions of youth gangs.

What is the basis of this conceptual difficulty? Researcher James Howell (2003:27–28) suggests that defining the term *youth gangs* has been difficult in part because there are so many types of groups termed gangs, and they can change their focus over time. In addition, youth gangs are only one type of social group, and it is important to define *youth gangs* in a way that distinguishes them from these other types of groups, for example, childhood play groups, youth subculture groups, delinquent groups, and adult criminal organizations.

■ EXHIBIT 4.1   **Absolute, Relative, and Subjective Poverty Standards**

Absolute Standard

Subjective Standard

Relative Standard

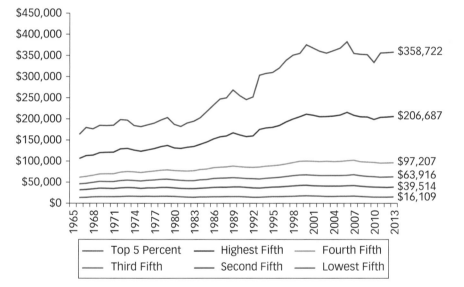

- Top 5 Percent — Highest Fifth — Fourth Fifth
- Third Fifth — Second Fifth — Lowest Fifth

Source: U.S. Census Bureau, Current Population Survey, Annual Social and Economic Supplements. For information on confidentiality protection, sampling error, nonsampling error, and definitions, see www.census.gov/prod/techdoc/cps/cpsmar14.pdf

■ EXHIBIT 4.2   **Alternative Definitions of Youth Gangs**

Gangs are known to engage in traditionally gang-related gambling, drug trafficking, arms trafficking, white collar crime such as counterfeiting, identity theft, and fraud, and non-traditional activity of human trafficking and prostitution. [U.S. National Gang Intelligence Center. 2011. "National Gang Threat Assessment, Emerging Trends," p. 9].
Youth gangs are composed of young people, male or female, and like most street gangs, are either formed for protection or for social and economic reasons. [Blumstein, Alfred. 2002. "Youth, Guns, & Violent Crime." *The Future of Children* 12(2):39].
The term gang tends to designate collectivities that are marginal members of mainstream society, loosely organized, and without a clear, social purpose. [Ball & Curry 1995:227].
[A gang is] an age-graded peer group that exhibits some permanence, engages in criminal activity, and has some symbolic representation of membership. [Decker & Van Winkle 1996:31].

Source: Based on Howell (2003:76).

Trust

Take a look at Photo 4.2. It's a picture used to illustrate the concept of *trust*. Do you see what it is about the picture that represents trust in other people? Have you ever thought about trust when you have left cash on a restaurant table and then walked away? Paxton (2005) defines the concept of trust with examples: "We trust others when we take a chance, yielding them some control over our money, secrets, safety, or other things we value" (p. 40).

Stockbyte/Stockbyte/Thinkstock

Photo 4.2 How well does this picture capture what you think of as "trust"?

In research on regional differences in trust, Brent Simpson (2006:1627) defined general trust as an "expectation of goodwill or benign intent." He found that white Southerners were less trusting than whites in the North. In her research on low-income women, Judith Levine (2015) found that distrust in others emerged after often having been deceived, or otherwise failed by various people and institutions, and then diminished the women's ability to achieve other goals through cooperation with others. Across these different perspectives, the concept of trust seems to be a glue that helps to hold society together.

❖ From Concepts to Indicators

Identifying the concepts we will study and defining their meaning only begins the process of connecting our ideas to concrete observations. **Operationalization** involves connecting concepts to measurement operations. You can think of it as the empirical counterpart of the process of conceptualization. When we operationalize, we identify specific measurements we will take to indicate a concept in the real world.

You learned in Chapter 2 that variables are phenomena that vary. Think of it this way: Usually, the term *variable* is used to refer to some specific aspect of a concept that varies, and for which we then have to select even more concrete **indicators**. The important thing to keep in mind is that we need to define clearly the concepts we use and then develop specific procedures for identifying variation in the variables related to these concepts.

Concepts don't necessarily vary. For example, gender may be an important concept in a study of influences on binge drinking, but it is not a variable in a study of members of a fraternity. When we explain excessive drinking in the fraternity, we might attach great importance to the all-male fraternity subculture. However, because gender does not vary in this setting, we won't be able to study differences in binge drinking between male and female students. So, gender will be a **constant**, not a variable, in this study (unless we expand our sample to include members of both sororities and fraternities, or perhaps the general student population).

Operationalizing the Concept of Race

Race is an important concept in social research and an important focus of many public policy debates. However, what people mean by the concept of race has varied over time and differs between countries, as reflected in changes in questions about race in the decennial U.S. Census (Snipp 2003:565–567). In the 1890 census, *Octoroons* and *Quadroons* were distinguished as different categories of Mulatto, or mixed races. The infamous 1896 U.S. Supreme Court decision *Plessy v. Ferguson* reflected the victory of "Jim Crow" legislation in the South and defined as black any person who had as much as one black ancestor. (Homer Plessy was a Louisiana shoemaker whose skin was white, but he was told he could not ride in the "whites only" section of the train because he had one black ancestor.) By 1920, the U.S. Census reflected this absolute distinction between persons judged black and white by dropping the distinctions involving mixed-race ancestry. In 1930 and 1940, *Mexican* was distinguished, but in 1950 political pressure led to dropping this category as an ethnic minority and instead treating Mexicans as white (Snipp 2003:568–569).

By the late 1950s, the civil rights movement began to influence the concept of race as used by the U.S. Census. In 1960, the census shifted from assessing race on the basis of physical appearance to self-identification (Snipp 2003:569–570). The 1980 U.S. Census introduced a five-category distinction: (1) American Indians and Alaskan Natives, (2) Asians and Pacific Islanders, (3) non-Hispanic blacks, (4) non-Hispanic whites, and (5) Hispanics (Snipp 2003:572–574). In that census, Spanish/Hispanic origin or descent was asked as a question distinct from the question about race (U.S. Census Bureau 1981:3). But after some parents insisted that they should be able to classify their children as multiracial, a federal task force decided to allow respondents to designate themselves as being of more than one race (Snipp 2003:575–576). The resulting question about race reflected these changes as well as increasing distinctions within what had been the Asians and Pacific Islanders category (Exhibit 4.3).

With this new procedure in the 2010 U.S. Census, 36.7% of the country's 50.5 million Latinos classified themselves as "some other race"—neither white nor black; they wrote in such terms as *Mayan, Tejano,* and *mestizo* to indicate their own preferred self-identification, using terms that focused on what social scientists term *ethnic* rather than on racial differences. In that same census, 3% of Americans identified themselves as multiracial (Humes et al. 2011). But this does not represent

Operationalization: The process of specifying the measures that will indicate the value of cases on a variable.

Indicator: The question or other operation used to indicate the value of cases on a variable.

Constant: A number that has a fixed value in a given situation; a characteristic or value that does not change.

a final definition of the concept of race. Some Arab American groups have now also asked for a special category (Vega 2014:A16).

The concept of race also varies internationally, so any research involving persons in or from other countries may need to use a different definition of race. For example, Darryl Fears, former director of the Brazilian American Cultural Institute (in Washington, D.C.), explains how social conventions differ in Brazil: "In this country, if you are not quite white, then you are black." But in Brazil, "If you are not quite black, then you are white" (Fears 2002:A3).

Operationalizing the Concept of Trust

Brent Simpson (2006) combined answers to three questions from a national survey (the General Social Survey) to operationalize the concept of general trust:

Trust Generally speaking, would you say that most people can be trusted (coded 1) or that you can't be too careful in dealing with people (coded 0)?

Helpful Would you say that most of the time people try to be helpful (1) or that they are mostly just looking out for themselves (0)?

Fair Do you think most people would try to take advantage of you if they got a chance (0), or would they try to be fair (1)?

Do these questions, taken together, seem to capture Simpson's conceptualization of general trust as an "expectation of goodwill or benign intent"?

❖ From Observations to Concepts

Qualitative research projects usually take an inductive approach, in which concepts emerge from the process of thinking about what has been observed. So instead of deciding in advance which concepts are important for a study, what these concepts mean, and how they should be measured, qualitative researchers may first record interviews or observations and then identify the important concepts that emerge.

An example here will help you understand the qualitative measurement approach. For several months, Darin Weinberg (2000) observed participants in three drug abuse treatment programs in Southern California. He was puzzled by the drug abuse treatment program participants' apparently contradictory beliefs—that drug abuse is a medical disease marked by "loss of control" but that participation in a therapeutic community can be an effective treatment. He discovered that treatment participants shared an "ecology of addiction" in which they conceived of being "in" the program as a protected environment, whereas being in the community was considered being "out there" in a place where drug use was inevitable:

I'm doin' real, real bad right now. . . . I'm havin' trouble right now staying clean for more than two days. . . . I hate myself for goin' *out* and I don't know if there's anything that can save me anymore. . . . I think I'm gonna die *out there*. (Weinberg 2000:609; *emphases added*)

So Weinberg developed the concepts of *in* and *out* inductively, in the course of the research, and he identified indicators of these concepts at the same time in the observational text. He continued to refine and evaluate the concepts throughout the research.

❖ Measurement Alternatives

The deductive researcher proceeds from defining concepts in the abstract (conceptualizing) to identifying variables to measure, and finally to developing specific measurement procedures. **Measurement** is the "process of linking abstract concepts to empirical indicants" (Carmines & Zeller 1979:10). The goal is to achieve measurement validity, so the measures, or indicators, must actually measure the variables they are intended to measure.

Measurement: The process of linking abstract concepts to empirical indicants. Also, the procedures used to identify the empirical variation in a concept of interest.

■ EXHIBIT 4.3   **The U.S. Census Bureau Ethnicity and Race Questions**

→ **NOTE:** Please answer BOTH Question 8 about Hispanic origin and Question 9 about race. For this census, Hispanic origins are not races.

8. Is Person 1 of Hispanic, Latino, or Spanish origin?

☐ **No,** not of Hispanic, Latino, or Spanish origin
☐ Yes, Mexican, Mexican Am., Chicano
☐ Yes, Puerto Rican
☐ Yes, Cuban
☐ Yes, another Hispanic, Latino, or Spanish origin — *Print origin, for example, Argentinean, Colombian, Dominican, Nicaraguan, Salvadoran, Spaniard, and so on.* 🗹

9. What is Person 1's race? *Mark* ☒ *one or more boxes.*

☐ White
☐ Black, African Am., or Negro
☐ American Indian or Alaska Native — *Print name of enrolled or principal tribe.* 🗹

☐ Asian Indian   ☐ Japanese   ☐ Native Hawaiian
☐ Chinese   ☐ Korean   ☐ Guamanian or Chamorro
☐ Filipino   ☐ Vietnamese   ☐ Samoan
☐ Other Asian — *Print race, for example, Hmong, Laotian, Thai, Pakistani, Cambodian, and so on.* 🗹   ☐ Other Pacific Islander — *Print race, for example, Fijian, Tongan, and so on.* 🗹

☐ Some other race — *Print race.* 🗹

→ If more people were counted in Question 1, continue with Person 2.

Source: U.S. Census Bureau, 2010 Census Questionnaire.

Exhibit 4.4 represents the operationalization process in three studies. The first researcher defines her concept, gang membership, and chooses one variable—self-reported gang membership—to represent it. This variable is then measured with responses to a single question, or indicator: "Do you belong to a gang?" The second researcher defines her concept, poverty, as having two aspects or dimensions: subjective poverty and absolute poverty. Subjective poverty is measured with responses to a survey question: "Would you say you are poor?" Absolute poverty is measured by comparing family income to the poverty threshold. The third researcher decides that her concept, socioeconomic status, is defined by a position on three measured variables: income, education, and occupational prestige.

Social researchers have many options for operationalizing concepts. Measures can be based on activities as diverse as asking people questions, reading judicial opinions, observing social interactions, coding words in books, checking census data tapes, enumerating the contents of trash receptacles, or drawing urine and blood samples. This section introduces the most popular types of measurement—asking questions and making observations—and highlights the value of using measures of different types. Later chapters will introduce other measurement alternatives.

Asking Questions

Asking people questions is the most common and probably the most versatile operation for measuring social variables. This section introduces some options for writing single questions and then examines measurement approaches that rely on multiple questions to measure a concept.

Measuring variables with single questions is very popular. Public opinion polls based on answers to single questions are reported frequently in newspaper articles and on TV newscasts: "Do you favor or oppose U.S. policy . . . ?" "If you had to vote today, for which candidate would you vote?" Social surveys also rely on single questions to measure many variables: "Overall, how satisfied are you with your job?" "How would you rate your current health?"

Single questions can be designed with or without explicit response choices. The question that follows offers explicit response choices and so is termed a **closed-ended (fixed-choice) question** (Presley, Meilman, & Lyerla 1994):

Compared to other campuses with which you are familiar, this campus's use of alcohol is . . . (Mark one)

_____ Greater than at other campuses

_____ Less than at other campuses

_____ About the same as at other campuses

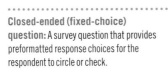

Closed-ended (fixed-choice) question: A survey question that provides preformatted response choices for the respondent to circle or check.

Fixed-choice questions are easy to answer, and their responses are easy to process with computers and to analyze with statistics. However, fixed-response choices can obscure what people really think if the choices do not match the range of possible responses to the question. Many studies show that some respondents will choose response choices that do not apply to them simply to give some sort of answer (Peterson 2000:39).

■ EXHIBIT 4.4   **Concepts, Variables, and Indicators**

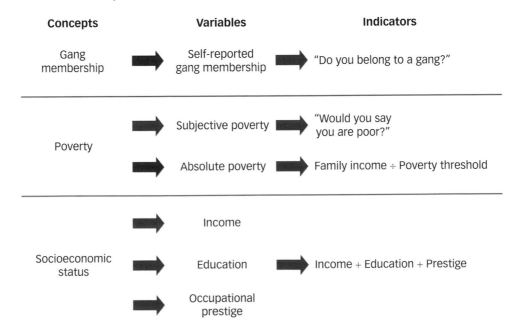

RESEARCH

In the News

DO YOU TWEET WHAT YOU THINK?

Twitter messages are being used increasingly to track public mood and interests, so it is good to know that a new investigation provides some evidence of measurement validity. The Nielsen rating company recruited almost 300 adults in three cities to wear special caps that measured their brain activity while watching TV shows. There was a very strong correlation between the number of tweets, retweets, and replies posted nationally during eight hour-long shows and neurological engagement among the study participants who were watching the shows (but who were not permitted to use Twitter).

For Further Thought **?**

1. Does this validation study convince you that social scientists should take Twitter seriously? What other type of measurement validation research would you suggest?

2. Do you think results would be consistent across demographic groups? What other uses could you think of for such neuroscience-based validation efforts?

News source: Goel, Vindu. 2015. "Study of TV Viewers Backs Twitter's Claims to Be Barometer of Public Mood." *New York Times, March 8.*

Most important, response choices should be **mutually exclusive** and **exhaustive**, so that every respondent can find one and only one choice that applies to him or her (unless the question is of the "Check all that apply" format). To make response choices exhaustive, researchers may need to offer at least one option with room for ambiguity. For example, a questionnaire asking college students to indicate their school status should not use freshman, sophomore, junior, senior, and graduate student as the only response choices. Most campuses also have students in a "special" category, so you might add "Other (please specify)" to the five fixed responses to this question. If respondents do not find a response option that corresponds to their answer to the question, they may skip the question entirely or choose a response option that does not indicate what they are really thinking.

Questions without explicit response choices are termed **open-ended questions**, which respondents answer in their own words. Open-ended questions are most useful when likely answers cannot be predicted. The next question is an open-ended version of the earlier fixed-choice question:

How would you say alcohol use on this campus compares with that on other campuses?

Just like fixed-choice questions, open-ended questions should be reviewed carefully for clarity before they are used.

Making Observations

Observations can be used to measure characteristics of individuals, events, and places. The observations may be the primary form of measurement in a study, or they may supplement measures obtained through questioning. For example, psychologists Dore Butler and Florence Geis (1990) studied unconscious biases and stereotypes that they thought might hinder the advancement of women and minorities in work organizations. In one experiment, they observed discussion groups of male and female students from behind one-way mirrors as group leaders presented identical talks to each group. The trained observers (who were not told what the study was about) rated the number of frowns, furrowed brows, smiles, and nods of approval as the group leaders spoke. Group participants made disapproving expressions, such as frowns, more often when the group leader was a woman than when the leader was a man. To make matters worse, the more the women talked, the less attention they were given. Butler and Geis concluded that there was indeed a basis for discrimination in these unconscious biases.

Combining Measurement Operations

Asking questions, making observations, and other forms of measurement may each include or be supplemented by the others. Interviewers may record observations about those whom they question. Data from employee surveys may be supplemented by information available in company records. Researchers may use insights gleaned from questioning participants to make sense of the social interaction they have observed.

Mutually exclusive: A question's response choices are mutually exclusive when every case can be classified as having only one attribute (or value).

Exhaustive: A question's response choices are exhaustive when they cover all possible responses.

Open-ended question: A survey question to which the respondent replies in his or her own words, either by writing or by talking.

ENCYCLOPEDIA LINK
Triangulation

The available resources and opportunities often determine the choice of a particular measurement method. Responses to questions such as "How socially engaged were you at the party?" or "How many days did you use sick leave last year?" are unlikely to provide information as valid as, respectively, direct observation or company records. However, observations at social gatherings may not answer our questions about why some people do not participate; we may have to ask people. Or, if no record is kept of sick leaves in a company, we may have to ask direct questions.

Triangulation—the use of two or more different measures of the same variable—can strengthen measurement considerably (Brewer & Hunter 1989:17). When we achieve similar results with different measures of the same variable, particularly when they are based on such different methods as survey questions and field-based observations, we can be more confident in the validity of each measure. If results diverge with different measures, it may indicate that one or more of these measures are influenced by more measurement error than we can tolerate. Exhibit 4.5 provides an example: Self-reported frequency of church attendance is higher than observed church attendance (Hadaway et al. 1993). Divergence between measures could also indicate that they operationalize different concepts. An interesting example of this interpretation of divergent results comes from research on crime. Official crime statistics indicate only those crimes that are reported to and recorded by the police; when surveys are used to measure crimes with self-reports of victims, many "personal annoyances" are included as if they were crimes (Levine 1976).

❖ Levels of Measurement

Triangulation: The use of multiple methods to study one research question; also used to mean the use of two or more different measures of the same variable.

Level of measurement: The mathematical precision with which the values of a variable can be expressed. The nominal level of measurement, which is qualitative, has no mathematical interpretation; the ordinal level of measurement is less precise mathematically than the interval/ratio level.

Nominal level of measurement: Variables whose values have no mathematical interpretation; they vary in kind or quality, but not in amount.

Can you name the variables represented in Exhibit 4.5? One variable is "religion"; in the exhibit it is represented by only two attributes, or categories—Protestant and Catholic—but you know that there are many others. One religion is not "more religion" than another; they are different in kind, not amount. Another variable represented in Exhibit 4.5 is "frequency of church attendance." Of course, frequencies *do* differ in amount. Religion and frequency of church attendance differ in their **level of measurement**. Level of measurement has important implications for the type of statistics that can be used with the variable, as you will learn in Chapter 11. There are three basic levels of measurement: (1) nominal, (2) ordinal, and (3) interval/ratio (texts often distinguish interval and ratio as different levels, but practically speaking they can be treated as one). Exhibit 4.6 depicts the differences between these three levels.

Nominal Level of Measurement

The **nominal level of measurement** identifies variables whose values have no mathematical interpretation; they vary in kind or quality but not in amount (they may also be called *categorical* or *qualitative variables*). It is conventional to refer to the values of nominal variables as *attributes* instead of values. *State* (referring to the United States) is one example. The variable has 50 attributes

CAREERS and Research

CAMILA MEJIA, MARKET RESEARCHER

Camila Mejia majored in psychology and earned a graduate degree in clinical psychology at Universidad Pontificia Bolivariana in Colombia. After graduating, she started working in a somewhat unexplored field for psychology in Colombia: market research from a consumer psychology perspective. However, her experience reinforced her belief that we can't understand human behavior without taking account of the social world, and so with this thought in mind and her passion for research, she applied to the master's program in applied sociology at the University of Massachusetts Boston.

After earning her M.A., Mejia returned to Colombia and began a new position in market research for a consumer goods company. Now she conducts social research to provide brands with information that can be used to understand consumer behavior. Her projects use social research methods ranging from ethnography and focus groups to in-depth interviews and surveys. She has been particularly impressed with the ability of ethnographic methods to engage with people in their daily lives in order to understand their buying habits. She is invited into homes to observe usage of consumer goods and accompanies consumers to different stores to observe what they buy, how they interact with brands, and their relationship with the marketplace. Her advice to new students is to seek innovative ways to apply sociology and research methods to understanding the social world.

(or categories or qualities). We might indicate the specific states with numbers, so that California might be represented by the value 1, Oregon with the value 2, and so on, but these numbers do not tell us anything about the difference between the states except that they are different. California is not one unit less of *state* than Oregon is, nor is Oregon twice as much *state*. Nationality, occupation, religious affiliation, and region of the country are also measured at the nominal level. Of course, some people may identify more strongly with their nationality than others, but this comparison involves the variable "strength of identification with nationality," not nationality *per se*.

The attributes we use to measure, or to categorize, cases must be mutually exclusive and exhaustive:

- A variable's attributes or values are mutually exclusive if every case can have only one attribute.

- A variable's attributes or values are exhaustive when every case can be classified into one of the categories.

When a variable's attributes are mutually exclusive and exhaustive, every case corresponds to one, and only one, attribute.

■ **EXHIBIT 4.5**   **The Inadequacy of Self-Reports Regarding Socially Desirable Behavior: Observed Versus Self-Reported Church Attendance**

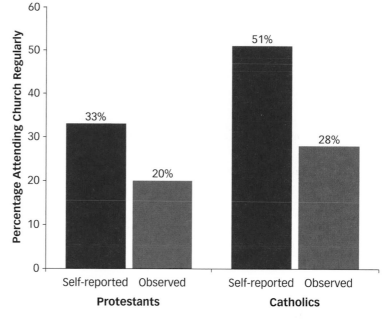

Source: Data from Hadaway, C. Kirk, Penny Long Marker, and Mark Chaves. 1993. "What the Polls Don't Show: A Closer Look at U.S. Church Attendance." *American Sociological Review* 58(6): 741–752.

Ordinal Level of Measurement

At the **ordinal level of measurement**, the numbers assigned to cases specify only the order of the cases, permitting *greater than* and *less than* distinctions. The properties of variables measured at the ordinal level are illustrated in Exhibit 4.6 by the contrast between the levels of conflict in two groups. The first group, symbolized by two people shaking hands, has a low level of conflict. The second group, symbolized by two persons pointing guns at each other, has a high level of conflict. To measure conflict, we would put the groups "in order" by assigning the number 1 to the low-conflict group and the number 2 to the high-conflict group. The numbers thus indicate only the relative position or order of the cases. Although low level of conflict is represented by the number 1, it is not one less unit of conflict than a high level of conflict, which is represented by the number 2.

As with nominal variables, the different values of a variable measured at the ordinal level must be mutually exclusive and exhaustive. They must cover the range of observed values and allow each case to be assigned no more than one value. Often, questions that use an ordinal level of measurement simply ask respondents to rate their response to some question or statement along a continuum of, for example, strength of agreement, level of importance, or relative frequency. Like variables measured at the nominal level, variables measured at the ordinal level in this way classify cases in discrete categories and so are termed **discrete measures**.

Interval/Ratio Level of Measurement

The numbers indicating the values of a variable at the **interval/ratio level of measurement** represent fixed measurement units. The interval/ratio level also involves **continuous measures**: The numbers indicating the values of variables are points on a continuum, not discrete categories. Of course, the numbers also are mutually exclusive and exhaustive, so that every case can be assigned one and only one value.

For example, the following question was used on the National Minority SA/HIV Prevention Initiative Youth Questionnaire to measure number of days during the past 30 days that the respondent drank at least one alcoholic beverage:

During the past 30 days, on how many days did you drink one or more drinks of an alcoholic beverage?

JOURNAL LINK
Nominal Variables

RESEARCHER INTERVIEW LINK
Levels of Measurement

Ordinal level of measurement: A measurement of a variable in which the numbers indicating a variable's values specify only the order of the cases, permitting *greater than* and *less than* distinctions.

Discrete measure: A measure that classifies cases in distinct categories.

Interval/ratio level of measurement: A measurement of a variable in which the numbers indicating a variable's values represent fixed measurement units. They may or may not have an absolute, or fixed, zero point.

Continuous measure: A measure with numbers indicating the values of variables as points on a continuum.

■ EXHIBIT 4.6 **Levels of Measurement**

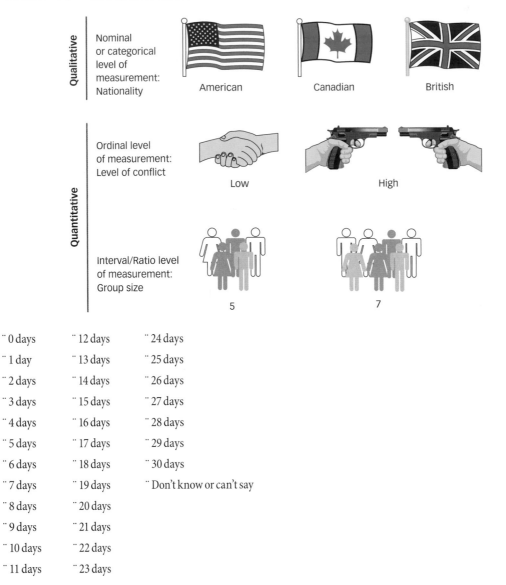

¨ 0 days ¨ 12 days ¨ 24 days

¨ 1 day ¨ 13 days ¨ 25 days

¨ 2 days ¨ 14 days ¨ 26 days

¨ 3 days ¨ 15 days ¨ 27 days

¨ 4 days ¨ 16 days ¨ 28 days

¨ 5 days ¨ 17 days ¨ 29 days

¨ 6 days ¨ 18 days ¨ 30 days

¨ 7 days ¨ 19 days ¨ Don't know or can't say

¨ 8 days ¨ 20 days

¨ 9 days ¨ 21 days

¨ 10 days ¨ 22 days

¨ 11 days ¨ 23 days

We can easily calculate the number of days that separate any response from any other response (except for the missing value of "don't know").

The Special Case of Dichotomies

Dichotomies, variables having only two values, are a special case from the standpoint of levels of measurement. The values or attributes of a variable such as gender clearly vary in kind or quality but not in amount. Thus, the variable is categorical—measured at the nominal level. Yet we can also think of the variable as indicating the presence of the attribute *female* (or *male*) or not. Viewed in this way, there is an inherent order: A female has more of the female attribute (it is present) than a male (the attribute is not present). It's also possible to think of a **dichotomy** as representing an interval level of measurement because there is an equal interval between the two attributes. So what do you answer to the test question, "What is the level of measurement of *gender*?" "Nominal," of course, but you'll find that when a statistical procedure requires that variables be quantitative, a dichotomy can be perfectly acceptable.

Dichotomy: A variable having only two values.

Comparison of Levels of Measurement

Exhibit 4.7 summarizes the types of comparisons that can be made with different levels of measurement, as well as the mathematical operations that are legitimate. Each higher level of measurement allows a more precise mathematical comparison to be made between values measured at that level compared with those measured at lower levels. However, each comparison between cases measured at lower levels can also be made about cases measured at the higher levels. Thus, all three levels of measurement allow researchers to assign different values to different cases. Both quantitative measures allow researchers to rank cases in order.

It is usually a good idea to try to measure variables at the highest level of measurement possible. The more information available, the more ways we have to compare cases. We also have more possibilities for statistical analysis with quantitative than with qualitative variables. Thus, if doing so does not distort the meaning of the concept that is to be measured, measure at the highest level possible. Even if your primary concern is only to compare teenagers with young adults, measure age in years rather than in categories; you can always combine the ages later into categories corresponding to teenager and young adult.

Be aware, however, that other considerations may preclude measurement at a higher level. For example, many people are reluctant to report their exact incomes, even on anonymous questionnaires. So asking respondents to report

Photo 4.3 What potential variables at the nominal level could possibly be used for this group of individuals? What about at the ordinal level?

their income in categories (e.g., less than $10,000, $10,000–$19,999, $20,000–$29,999, . . .) will result in more responses, and thus more valid data, than will asking respondents for their income in dollars.

❖ Units of Analysis

Measures can also differ in the **units of analysis** they represent—that is, the level of social life on which the measure is focused, such as individuals, groups, towns, or nations. In most sociological and psychological studies, the units of analysis are individuals. For example, the researcher may collect survey data from individuals about their feelings of social isolation and their use of alcohol and drugs. The units of analysis may instead be groups of some sort, such as families, schools, work organizations, towns, states, or countries. For example, a researcher may collect data from town and police records on the number of accidents in which a driver was intoxicated and the presence or absence of a server liability law in the town. (These laws make those who serve liquor liable for accidents caused by those to whom they served it.) The researcher might then analyze the association between server liability laws and the frequency of accidents caused by drunk driving (perhaps also taking into account the town's population). Because the data describe the town, towns are the units of analysis.

The important point is to know what the units of analysis are and then to evaluate whether the conclusions are appropriate in light of these units. Conclusions about processes at the individual level should be based on individual-level data; conclusions about group-level processes should be based on data collected about groups. A researcher who draws conclusions about individual-level processes from group-level data could be making what is termed an **ecological fallacy** (Exhibit 4.8). The conclusions may or may not be correct, but we must recognize that group-level data do not necessarily reflect solely individual-level processes. For example, a researcher may examine factory records and find that the higher the percentage of unskilled workers in factories, the higher the rate of employee sabotage in those factories. But the researcher would commit an ecological fallacy if he or she then

Units of analysis: The level of social life on which a measure is focused, such as individuals, groups, towns, or nations.

Ecological fallacy: An error in reasoning in which incorrect conclusions about individual-level processes are drawn from group-level data.

■ EXHIBIT 4.7   Properties of Levels of Measurement

Level of Measurement	Possible Statements About Age of Two Individuals: Sara (24) and Bill (12)	Quality of Level	Appropriate Math Operations
Nominal	Sara is an adult; Bill is an adolescent	Different from	= (≠)
Ordinal	Sara is older than Bill; Bill is younger than Sara	Greater than	> (<)
Interval/Ratio	Sara is 12 years older than Bill; Bill is 12 years younger than Sara	A year is a year is a year	+ (−)

Source: Adapted from material provided by Tajuana D. Massie, assistant professor, social sciences, South Carolina State University.

■ EXHIBIT 4.8   **Errors in Causal Conclusions**

		You make conclusions about . . .	
		Groups	**Individuals**
You collect data from . . .	Groups	More homogeneous groups tend to have stronger social bonds.	Groups with a higher average age are more conservative, so older people are more conservative. *Possible Reductionist Fallacy*
	Individuals	Students who socialize more have lower grades, so schools with more social engagement will have poorer student performance. *Possible Ecological Fallacy*	Older people tend to be more conservative.

concluded that unskilled factory workers are more likely to engage in sabotage. This conclusion is about an individual-level process (individual workers' occupation and criminal propensities), but the measures describe groups (factories). It could be that white-collar workers are the ones more likely to commit sabotage in factories with more unskilled workers, perhaps because the white-collar workers feel they won't be suspected in these settings.

Conversely, when measures about individuals are used to make inferences about group-level processes, a problem occurs that can be thought of as the mirror image of the ecological fallacy: the **reductionist fallacy**, also known as *reductionism*, or the *individualist fallacy* (Exhibit 4.8). For example, a reductionist explanation of behavior problems in grade-school classrooms would focus on the children's personalities, rather than on classroom structure, teacher behavior, or the surrounding neighborhood.

❖ Evaluating Measures

Do the operations developed to measure our variables actually do so—are they valid? If we have weighed our measurement options, carefully constructed our questions and observational procedures, and selected sensibly from the available data indicators, we should be on the right track. But we cannot have much confidence in a measure until we have empirically evaluated its validity. What good is our measure if it doesn't measure what we think it does? If our measurement procedure is invalid, we might as well go back to the starting block and try again. As a part of evaluating the validity of our measures, we must also evaluate their reliability, because reliability (consistency) is a prerequisite for measurement validity.

Measurement Validity

In Chapter 2, you learned that measurement validity refers to the extent to which measures indicate what they are intended to measure. More technically, a valid measure of a concept is one that is closely related to other apparently valid measures of the concept and to the known or supposed correlates of that concept, but that is not related to measures of unrelated concepts, irrespective of the methods used for the other different measures (Brewer & Hunter 1989:134). When a measure "misses the mark"—when it is not valid—our measurement procedure has been affected by measurement error.

The social scientist must try to reduce measurement errors and then to evaluate the extent to which the resulting measures are valid. The extent to which measurement validity has been achieved can be assessed in relation to four different standards: (1) face validity, (2) content validity, (3) criterion validity, and (4) construct validity. We'll use the concept of substance abuse to illustrate these different approaches to measurement validity.

AUDIO LINK 🌐
Measurement Validity

Reductionist fallacy (reductionism): An error in reasoning that occurs when incorrect conclusions about group-level processes are based on individual-level data; also known as an individualist fallacy.

Face validity: The type of validity that exists when an inspection of items used to measure a concept suggests that they are appropriate "on their face."

Content validity: The type of validity that exists when the full range of a concept's meaning is covered by the measure.

Face Validity

Researchers apply the term **face validity** to the confidence gained from careful review of a measure to see if it seems appropriate "on its face." More precisely, we can say that a measure is face valid if it obviously pertains to the meaning of the concept being measured more than to other concepts (Brewer & Hunter 1989:131). For example, a count of the number of drinks people had consumed in the past week would be a face-valid measure of their alcohol consumption.

Content Validity

Content validity establishes that the measure covers the full range of the concept's meaning. To determine that range of meaning, the researcher may solicit the opinions of experts and review literature that identifies the different aspects, or dimensions, of the concept.

An example of a measure that covers a wide range of meaning is the Michigan Alcoholism Screening Test (MAST). The MAST includes 24 questions representing the following subscales: recognition of alcohol problems by self and others; legal, social, and work problems; help seeking; marital and family difficulties; and liver pathology (Skinner & Sheu 1982). Many experts familiar with the direct consequences of substance abuse agree that these dimensions capture the full range of possibilities. Thus, the MAST is believed to be valid from the standpoint of content validity.

Criterion Validity

Criterion validity is established when the scores obtained on one measure can be accurately compared with those obtained with a more direct or already validated measure of the same phenomenon (the criterion). A measure of blood-alcohol concentration or a urine test could serve as the criterion for validating a self-report measure of drinking, as long as the questions we ask about drinking refer to the same time period. Chemical analysis of hair samples can reveal unacknowledged drug use (Mieczkowski 1997). Friends' or relatives' observations of a person's substance use also could serve, in some limited circumstances, as a criterion for validating self-report substance use measures.

The criterion that researchers select can be measured either at the same time as the variable to be validated or after that time. **Concurrent validity** exists when a measure yields scores that are closely related to scores on a criterion measured at the same time. A store might validate a question-based test of sales ability by administering it to sales personnel who are already employed and then comparing their test scores with their sales performance. Or a measure of walking speed based on mental counting might be validated concurrently with a stopwatch. **Predictive validity** is the ability of a measure to predict scores on a criterion measured in the future. For example, a store might administer a test of sales ability to new sales personnel and then validate the measure by comparing these test scores with the criterion—the subsequent sales performance of the new personnel.

Unfortunately, many concepts of interest to social scientists do not have another variable that can reasonably be considered a criterion. If we are measuring feelings or beliefs, such as feelings of loneliness or beliefs about conflict, what *direct* indicator could serve as a criterion—the thing itself?

Construct Validity

Measurement validity can also be established by showing that a measure is related to a variety of other measures as specified in a theory. This validation approach, known as **construct validity**, is commonly used in social research as an additional form of measurement validation or when no clear criterion exists for validation purposes. For example, Steven F. Messner, Lawrence E. Raffalovich, and Gretchen M. Sutton at the University at Albany assessed the extent to which the infant mortality rate can be used as an indicator of poverty in cross-national research. Prior research has established that measures of poverty are strong determinants of the homicide rate and criminological theory implies "that poverty is conducive to lethal violence" (Messner et al. 2010:527). Messner, Raffalovich, and Sutton examined the association between infant mortality measures and the homicide rate in an international data set and found that the infant mortality rate was associated with variation in the homicide rate, thus indicating the construct validity of the infant mortality rate as a "stand in" for poverty.

Measurement Reliability

Reliability means that a measurement procedure yields consistent scores when the phenomenon being measured is not changing (or that the measured scores change in direct correspondence to actual changes in the phenomenon). If a measure is reliable, it is affected less by random error, or chance variation, than if it is unreliable. Reliability is a prerequisite for measurement validity: We cannot really measure a phenomenon if the measure we are using gives inconsistent results. Actually, because it is usually easier to assess reliability than validity, you are more likely to see an evaluation of measurement reliability in a research report than an evaluation of measurement validity.

Problems in reliability can occur when inconsistent measurements are obtained after the same phenomenon is measured multiple times, with multiple indicators, or by multiple observers. For example, a test of your knowledge of research methods would be unreliable if every time you took it, you received a different score even though your knowledge of research methods had not changed in the interim, not even as a result of taking the test more than once. This is a problem in **test-retest reliability**.

Measurement reliability of an abstract concept can be improved by using a set of similar questions about the concept rather than just one question. The sum or average of responses to a set of

---

JOURNAL LINK
Content Analysis

RESEARCH/SOCIAL IMPACT LINK
Reliability and Validity

Criterion validity: The type of validity that is established by comparing the scores obtained on the measure being validated with those obtained with a more direct or already validated measure of the same phenomenon (the criterion).

Concurrent validity: The type of validity that exists when scores on a measure are closely related to scores on a criterion measured at the same time.

Predictive validity: The type of validity that exists when a measure predicts scores on a criterion measured in the future.

Construct validity: The type of validity that is established by showing that a measure is related to other measures as specified in a theory.

Reliability: A measurement procedure yields consistent scores when the phenomenon being measured is not changing.

Test-retest reliability: A measurement showing that measures of a phenomenon at two points in time are highly correlated, if the phenomenon has not changed, or has changed only as much as the measures have changed.

■ EXHIBIT 4.9   **Examples of Indexes: Short Form of the Center for Epidemiologic Studies (CES-D) and "Negative Outlook" Index**

At any time during the past week . . . (Circle one response on each line)	Never	Some of the Time	Most of the Time
a. Was your appetite so poor that you did not feel like eating?	1	2	3
b. Did you feel so tired and worn out that you could not enjoy anything?	1	2	3
c. Did you feel depressed?	1	2	3
d. Did you feel unhappy about the way your life is going?	1	2	3
e. Did you feel discouraged and worried about your future?	1	2	3
f. Did you feel lonely?	1	2	3
Negative outlook			
How often was each of these things true during the past week? (Circle one response on each line)	A Lot, Most, or All of the Time	Sometimes	Never or Rarely
a. You felt that you were just as good as other people.	0	1	2
b. You felt hopeful about the future.	0	1	2
c. You were happy.	0	1	2
d. You enjoyed life.	0	1	2

Source: Hawkins et al. (2007).

questions about a concept is termed an **index** (described further in Chapter 7). An index composed of questions to measure knowledge of research methods would be unreliable if respondents' answers to each question were totally independent of their answers to the others. By contrast, the index has **interitem reliability** if the component items are closely related.

Donald Hawkins, Paul Amato, and Valarie King (2007:1007) used the "CES-D" index to measure depression in their study of adolescent well-being and obtained a high level of interitem reliability. They measured "negative outlook" with a similar set of questions (Exhibit 4.9), but the interitem reliability of this set was lower. Read through the two sets of questions. Do the sets seem to cover what you think of as being depressed and having a negative outlook? If so, they seem to be *content valid* to you. Why do you think the second set of questions resulted in less consistent answers than the first set? (Why was the *interitem reliability* of the "negative outlook" index lower?)

When researchers use more than one observer to rate the same people, events, or places, **interobserver reliability** is their goal. If observers are using the same instrument to rate the same thing, their ratings should be very similar. If they are similar, we can have much more confidence that the ratings reflect the phenomenon being assessed rather than the orientations of the observers. If different instructors scored your answers differently, this would indicate a failure of interobserver reliability.

VIDEO LINK ▶
Validity vs. Reliability

Remember that a reliable measure is not necessarily a valid measure, as Exhibit 4.10 illustrates. This discrepancy is a common flaw of self-report measures of substance abuse. Most respondents answer the multiple questions in self-report indexes of substance abuse in a consistent way, so the indexes are reliable. However, a number of respondents will not admit to drinking, even though they drink a lot. Their answers to the questions are consistent, but they are consistently misleading. As a result, some indexes based on self-report are reliable but invalid. Such indexes are not useful and should be improved or discarded. Unfortunately, many measures are judged to be worthwhile on the basis of only a reliability test.

Index: The sum or average of responses to a set of questions about a concept.

Interitem reliability: An approach that calculates reliability based on the correlation among multiple items used to measure a single concept; also known as internal consistency.

Interobserver reliability: When similar measurements are obtained by different observers rating the same persons, events, or places.

The reliability and validity of measures in any study must be tested after the fact to assess the quality of the information obtained. But then, if it turns out that a measure cannot be considered reliable and valid, little can be done to save the study. Hence, it is supremely important that researchers use measures that are likely to be reliable and valid. In most cases, the best strategy is to use measures that have been used before and whose reliability and validity have been established in other contexts. But the selection of tried and true measures still does not absolve researchers from the responsibility of testing the reliability and validity of the measures in their own studies.

■ **EXHIBIT 4.10   The Difference Between Reliability and Validity: Drinking Behavior**

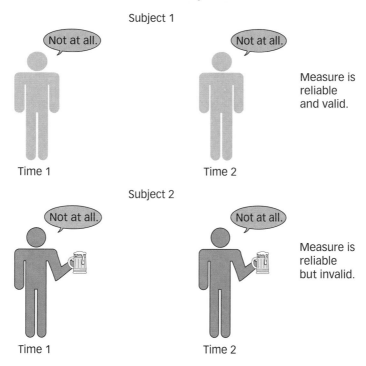

Measure: "How much do you drink?"

Subject 1

Not at all.   Not at all.

Measure is
reliable
and valid.

Time 1   Time 2

Subject 2

Not at all.   Not at all.

Measure is
reliable
but invalid.

Time 1   Time 2

❖ Conclusions

Remember always that measurement validity is a necessary foundation for social research. Gathering data without careful conceptualization or conscientious efforts to operationalize key concepts undermines the value of research. When researchers define concepts clearly and specify measurement procedures carefully, they are displaying their commitment to research quality.

Planning ahead is the key to achieving valid measurement in research projects; careful evaluation is the key to sound decisions about the validity of measures in others' research. If it appears after the fact that a measure is invalid, little can often be done to correct the situation. If statistical tests have not been used appropriately in relation to the levels of measurement of the variables in an analysis, the results may be misleading. But if a research article begins with a compelling discussion of key concepts and a convincing explanation of how they were operationalized, you know the article is off to a good start.

⋯⋯ Key Terms ⋯⋯⋯⋯⋯⋯⋯⋯⋯⋯⋯⋯⋯

····· **Highlights** ····································

- Conceptualization plays a critical role in research. In deductive research, conceptualization guides the operationalization of specific variables; in inductive research, it guides efforts to make sense of related observations.

- Concepts may refer to either constant or variable phenomena. Concepts that refer to variable phenomena may be quite similar to the actual variables used in a study, or they may be much more abstract.

- Concepts are operationalized in research by one or more indicators, or measures, which may derive from observation, self-report, available records or statistics, books and other written documents, clinical indicators, pictures, discarded materials, or some combination of these.

- Single-question measures may be closed-ended, with fixed-response choices, or open-ended, with fixed-response choices and an option to write another response.

- Indexes and scales measure a concept by combining answers to several questions, each of which measures the same concept in a slightly different way. An important question is, Does combining items in an index obscure important relationships between individual questions and other variables?

- Level of measurement indicates the type of information obtained about a variable and the type of statistics that can be used to describe its variation. The three levels measurement can be ordered by the complexity of the mathematical operations they permit: nominal (least complex), ordinal, interval/ratio (most complex). The measurement level of a variable is determined by how the variable is operationalized. Dichotomies, a special case, may be treated as measured at the nominal, ordinal, or interval/ratio level.

- We do not fully understand the variables in a study until we know the units of analysis—the level of social life—to which they refer.

- Invalid conclusions about causality may occur when relationships between variables measured at the group level are assumed to apply at the individual level (the ecological fallacy) and when relationships between variables measured at the level of individuals are assumed to apply at the group level (the reductionist fallacy). Nonetheless, many research questions point to relationships at multiple levels and so may profitably be investigated at multiple units of analysis.

- The validity of measures should always be tested. There are four basic approaches: (1) face validity, (2) content validity, (3) criterion validity (either predictive or concurrent), and (4) construct validity. Criterion validation provides the strongest evidence of measurement validity, but there often is no criterion to use in validating social measures.

- Measurement reliability is a prerequisite for measurement validity, although reliable measures are not necessarily valid. Two ways of assessing reliability are a test-retest procedure and interitem consistency.

····· **Chapter Questions** ····························

1. What does trust mean to you? Identify two examples of "trust in action" and explain how they represent *your* concept of trust. Now develop a short definition of trust (without checking a dictionary). Compare your definition with those of your classmates and what you find in a dictionary. Can you improve your definition based on some feedback?

2. What questions would you ask to measure level of trust among students? How about feelings of being "in" or "out" with regard to a group? Write five questions for an index and suggest response choices for each. How would you validate this measure using a construct validation approach? Can you think of a criterion validation procedure for your measure?

3. If you were given a questionnaire right now that asked you about your use of alcohol and illicit drugs in the past year, would you disclose the details fully? How do you think others would respond? What if the questionnaire was anonymous? What if there was a confidential ID number on the questionnaire so that the researcher could keep track of who responded? What criterion validation procedure would you suggest for assessing measurement validity?

4. Some Homeland Security practices as well as inadvertent releases of web searching records have raised new concerns about the use of unobtrusive measures of behavior and attitudes. If all identifying information is removed, do you think social scientists should be able to study the extent of prostitution in different cities by analyzing police records? How about how much alcohol different types of people use by linking de-identified credit card records to store purchases?

······ Practice Exercises ···

1. Now it's time to try your hand at operationalization with survey-based measures. Formulate a few fixed-choice questions to measure variables pertaining to the concepts you researched for the chapter questions, such as feelings of trust. Arrange to interview one or two other students with the questions you have developed. Ask one fixed-choice question at a time, record your interviewee's answer, and then probe for additional comments and clarifications. Your goal is to discover how respondents understand the meaning of the concept you used in the question and what additional issues shape their response to it.

    When you have finished the interviews, analyze your experience: Did the interviewees interpret the fixed-choice questions and response choices as you intended? Did you learn more about the concepts you were working on? Should your conceptual definition be refined? Should the questions be rewritten, or would more fixed-choice questions be necessary to capture adequately the variation among respondents?

2. Now, try index construction. You might begin with some of the questions you wrote for Practice Exercise 1. Try to write about four or five fixed-choice questions that each measure the same concept. Write each question so that it has the same response choices. Now, conduct a literature search to identify an index that another researcher used to measure your concept or a similar concept. Compare your index to the published index. Which seems preferable to you? Why?

3. The book's study site (edge.sagepub.com/schuttusw) contains lessons on units of analysis in the Interactive Exercises. Choose the "Units of Analysis" lesson from the main menu. It describes several research projects and asks you to identify the units of analysis in each.

4. One quick and easy way to check your understanding of the levels of measurement, reliability, and validity is with the interactive exercises on the study site. First, select one of the "Levels of Measurement" options from the Interactive Exercises link on the main menu, and then read the review information at the start of the lesson. You will then be presented with about 10 variables and response choices and asked to identify the level of measurement for each one. If you make a mistake, the program will give a brief explanation about the level of measurement. After you have reviewed one to four of these lessons, repeat the process with one or more of the "Valid and Reliable Measures" lessons.

5. Go to the book's study site (edge.sagepub.com/schuttusw) and review the Methods section of two of the research articles that you find there. Write a short summary of the concepts and measures used in these studies. Which article provides clearer definitions of the major concepts? Does either article discuss possible weaknesses in measurement procedures?

6. What are the "facts" about alcoholism presented by the National Council on Alcohol and Drug Dependence (NCADD) at www.ncadd.org? How is alcoholism conceptualized? Based on this conceptualization, give an example of one method that could be a valid measurement in a study of alcoholism.

    Now look at some of the other related links accessible from the NCADD website. What are some of the different conceptualizations of alcoholism that you find? How might the chosen conceptualization affect one's choice of methods of measurement?

STUDENT STUDY SITE

$SAGE edge™

The Student Study Site, available at **edge.sagepub.com/schuttusw**, includes useful study materials including eFlashcards, videos, audio resources, journal articles, and encyclopedia articles, many of which are represented by the media links throughout the text.

CHAPTER 5

Sampling and Generalizability

Learning Objectives

- ❖ Distinguish the two meanings of generalizability
- ❖ Identify the circumstances that make sampling unnecessary and the reasons they are rare
- ❖ Identify the relations among the desired sample, the obtained sample, the sampling frame, and sample quality
- ❖ Define and distinguish the major types of probability sampling method and indicate when each is preferred

- ❖ Explain when nonprobability sampling methods may be preferred
- ❖ Describe the concept of sampling error and explain how it is affected by the number of cases sampled, the heterogeneity of the population, and the fraction of the population included in the sample

A common technique in journalism is to put a "human face" on a story. For instance, a *New York Times* reporter (Hu 2014) interviewed a participant in a program called Urban Pathways for a story about the effect of severe cold weather on homeless people in New York City. "Mr. Scott" came to New York after losing his job as a restaurant cook and then finding a bus ticket in a casino. He eventually received housing from the Urban Pathways program and so what would otherwise have been a very sad story has a happy—although uncertain—ending. However, we don't know whether Mr. Scott is like most program participants, most homeless persons in New York, or most homeless persons throughout the United States—or whether he is just one person who caught the eye of this one reporter. In other words, we don't know how *generalizable* his story is. If we don't have confidence in generalizability, then the validity of this account of how the program participant became homeless is suspect: We cannot determine what the story tells us about homeless people in New York.

In this chapter, you will learn about sampling methods—the process of selecting individuals or other cases for a study. It is sampling that primarily determines the generalizability of research findings. The first section reviews the terms and logic of sampling. Specific sampling methods and their strengths and weaknesses are then discussed and a key distinction is made between probability and nonprobability sampling methods. By the chapter's end, you should understand which questions you need to ask to evaluate the generalizability of a study.

❖ Sample Planning

The purpose of sampling is to generate a set of individuals or other entities that give us a valid picture of all such individuals, or other entities. That is, a sample is a subset of the larger set of individuals or other entities in which we are interested. If researchers have done a good job of sampling, they are able to generalize what they learned from the subset to the larger set from which it was selected.

Get the edge on your studies.
edge.sagepub.com/schuttusw

- Take a quiz to find out what you've learned.
- Review key terms with eFlashcards.
- Watch videos that enhance chapter content.

The set of individuals or other entities to which findings are generalized is called the **population**. For example, a city government may want to describe the city's entire adult homeless population. If, as is usually the case, the government does not have the time or resources to survey all homeless individuals in the city, it may fund a survey of a subset of these individuals. This subset of the population of interest is a **sample**. The individual members of this sample are called **elements**, or elementary units.

Defining Sample Components and the Population

Population: The entire set of individuals or other entities to which study findings are to be generalized.

Sample: A subset of a population that is used to study the population as a whole.

Elements: The individual members of the population whose characteristics are to be measured.

Sampling frame: A list of all elements or other units containing the elements in a population.

Sampling units: Units listed at each stage of a multistage sampling design.

In many studies, we sample directly from the elements in the population of interest. For example, we may survey a sample of the entire population of students in a school, based on a list obtained from the registrar's office. This list, from which the elements of the population are selected, is termed the **sampling frame**. The students who are selected and interviewed from that list are the elements.

Sometimes, the individuals or other entities from which we collect information are not actually the elements in our study. For example, a researcher might sample schools for a survey about educational practices and then interview a sample of teachers in each sampled school to obtain the information about educational practices. Both the schools and the teachers are termed **sampling units**, because they are both sampled from (Levy & Lemeshow 1999:22). The schools are selected in the first stage of the sample, so they are *primary sampling units* (in this case, they are also the elements in the study). The teachers are *secondary sampling units* (but they are not elements because they are used to provide information about the entire school) (Exhibit 5.1).

Evaluating Generalizability

Do you recall from Chapter 2 the two different meanings of generalizability?

Can the findings from a sample of the population be generalized to the population from which the sample was selected? Did Lee Rainie, Aaron Smith, and Maeve Duggan's (2013) findings about Facebook use (see Chapter 1) apply to the United States population? This type of generalizability was defined as *sample generalizability* in Chapter 2.

Can the findings from a study of one population be generalized to another, somewhat different population? Could the Sherman and Harris (2013) findings on death rates in their long-term follow-up of inner-city residents accused of domestic violence be generalized to other populations? This type of generalizability question was defined as *cross-population generalizability* in Chapter 2.

This chapter focuses attention on the problem of sample generalizability. Sample generalizability is determined by the amount of **sampling error**—the difference between the characteristics of a sample and the characteristics of the population from which it was selected. The larger the sampling error, the less representative the sample—and thus the less generalizable the findings. To assess sample generalizability when you are planning or evaluating a study, ask yourself these questions:

- From what population were the cases selected?

- What method was used to select cases from this population?

- Do the cases that were studied represent the population from which they were selected?

■ **EXHIBIT 5.1**   **Sample Components in a Two-Stage Study**

Sample of schools

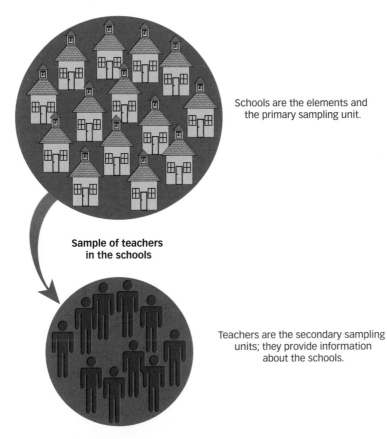

Schools are the elements and the primary sampling unit.

Sample of teachers in the schools

Teachers are the secondary sampling units; they provide information about the schools.

Source: Based on information from Levy and Lemeshow (1999).

Cross-population generalizability involves quite different considerations. Researchers are engaging in cross-population generalizability when they project their findings onto groups or populations different from those they have studied. The population to which generalizations are made in this way can be termed the **target population**—a set of elements larger than or different from the population that was sampled and to which the researcher would like to generalize any study findings. Generalizations of findings to target populations are always somewhat speculative. We must carefully consider the validity of claims that findings can be applied to other groups, geographic areas, cultures, or times.

Chapter 6, on experimental research, addresses cross-population generalizability further.

Social scientists rarely can skirt the problem of demonstrating the generalizability of their findings. If a small sample has been studied in an experiment or a field research project, the study should be replicated in different settings or, preferably, with a **representative sample** of the population to which generalizations are sought (Exhibit 5.2). The social world and the people in it are just too diverse to be considered identical in most respects. Social psychological experiments and small field studies have produced good social science, but they need to be replicated in other settings, with other subjects, to claim any generalizability. Even when we believe that we have uncovered basic social processes in a laboratory experiment or field observation, we should be very concerned with seeking confirmation in other samples and in other research.

In some circumstances, it may be feasible to skirt the issue of generalizability by conducting a **census**—studying the entire population of interest—rather than drawing a sample. This is what the federal government does every 10 years with the U.S. Census. Any study of all members of a population is a census: all employees (or students) in small organizations; all 50 states; the entire population of a particular type of organization in some area. However, in most survey situations, it is much better to survey only a limited number from the total population so that there are more resources for follow-up procedures that can overcome reluctance or indifference about participation.

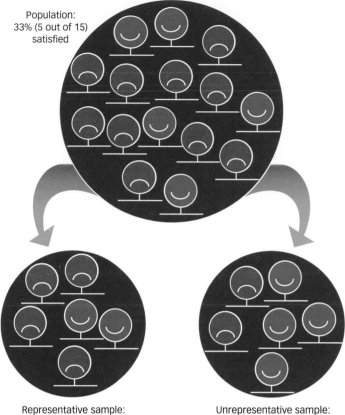

■ EXHIBIT 5.2 **Representative and Unrepresentative Samples**

Population: 33% (5 out of 15) satisfied

Representative sample: 33% (2 out of 6) satisfied

Unrepresentative sample: 67% (4 out of 6) satisfied

Sampling error: Any difference between the characteristics of a sample and the characteristics of a population; the larger the sampling error, the less representative the sample.

Target population: A set of elements larger than or different from the population sampled and to which the researcher would like to generalize study findings.

Representative sample: A sample that "looks like" the population from which it was selected in all respects potentially relevant to the study. The distribution of characteristics among the elements of a representative sample is the same as the distribution of those characteristics among the total population. In an unrepresentative sample, some characteristics are overrepresented or underrepresented.

Census: Research in which information is obtained through responses from or information about all available members of an entire population.

Probability sampling method: A sampling method that relies on a random, or chance, selection method so that the probability of selection of population elements is known.

❖ Sampling Methods

The most important distinction that needs to be made about samples is whether they are based on a probability or a nonprobability sampling method. Sampling methods that are based on knowing in advance how likely it is that any element of a population will be selected for the sample are termed **probability sampling methods**. Sampling methods that are not based on advance knowledge of the likelihood of selecting each element are termed **nonprobability sampling methods**.

Probability sampling methods rely on a random, or chance, selection procedure that is, in principle, the same as flipping a coin to decide which of two people "wins" and which one "loses." Heads and tails are equally likely to turn up in a coin toss, so both persons have an equal chance of winning. That chance, their **probability of selection**, is 1 out of 2, or .5.

Flipping a coin is a fair way to select one of two people because the selection process harbors no systematic bias. You might win or lose the coin toss, but you know that the outcome was due simply to chance, not to bias. For the same reason, a roll of a six-sided die is a fair way to choose one of six possible outcomes (the odds of selection are 1 out of 6, or .17). Dealing out a hand after shuffling a deck of cards is a fair way to allocate sets of cards in a poker game (the odds of each person's getting a particular outcome, such as a full house or a flush, are the same). Similarly, state lotteries use a

RESEARCH

In the News

CHALLENGES OF CONDUCTING A CENSUS

Conducting a census is a challenge for any government, but imagine how those challenges are multiplied as the current government in Afghanistan attempts to conduct a national census. It's not just the continued threat of violence in some areas: "Many people lack surnames, most do not know their birthday, and Afghan women generally will not speak if their husbands are out." The census director expects it to take 5 years to reach 70 percent of the population.

For Further Thought **?**

1. Based on the details provided in the text on the U.S. Census effort, to what extent do you think the U.S. government has overcome the problems facing Afghanistan?

2. For any country, what are the possible benefits of a comprehensive census of its population?

3. Would you recommend conducting a sample survey instead of a census in challenging situations like Afghanistan?

News source: Goldstein, Joseph. 2014. "For Afghans, Name and Birthdate Census Questions Are Not So Simple." *New York Times*, December 11.

random process to select winning numbers. Thus, the odds of winning a lottery, the probability of selection, are known, even though they are very much smaller (perhaps 1 out of 1 million) than the odds of winning a coin toss.

Even a good sampling frame may yield systematic bias if many sample members cannot be contacted or refuse to participate. Nonresponse is a major hazard in survey research because **nonrespondents** are likely to differ systematically from those who take the time to participate. Findings from a randomly selected sample may not be generalizable to the population from which the sample was selected if the rate of nonresponse is considerable (much above 30%).

Nonprobability sampling method: A sampling method in which the probability of selection of population elements is unknown.

Probability of selection: The likelihood that an element will be selected from the population for inclusion in the sample. In a census of all elements of a population, the probability that any particular element will be selected is 1.0. If half the elements in the population are sampled on the basis of chance (say, by tossing a coin), the probability of selection for each element is one half, or .5. As the size of the sample as a proportion of the population decreases, so does the probability of selection.

Nonrespondents: People or other entities who do not participate in a study although they are selected for the sample.

Systematic bias: Overrepresentation or underrepresentation of some population characteristics in a sample resulting from the method used to select the sample; a sample shaped by systematic sampling error is a biased sample.

Random sampling: Sampling that relies on a random, or chance, selection method so that every element of the sampling frame has a known probability of being selected.

Probability Sampling Methods

Probability sampling methods are those in which the probability of selection is known and is not zero (so there is some chance of selecting each element). These methods randomly select elements and therefore have no **systematic bias**; nothing but chance determines which elements are included in the sample (if the sampling frame is complete). This feature of probability samples makes them much more desirable than nonprobability samples when the goal is to generalize to a larger population.

Although a **random sample** has no systematic bias, it will certainly have some sampling error resulting from chance. The probability of selecting a head is .5 in a single toss of a coin and in 20, 30, or however many tosses of a coin you like. But it is perfectly possible to toss a coin twice and get a head both times. The random "sample" of the two sides of the coin is selected in an unbiased fashion, but it still is unrepresentative. Imagine selecting randomly a sample of 10 people from a population comprising 50 men and 50 women. Just by chance, can't you imagine finding that these 10 people include 7 women and only 3 men? Fortunately, we can determine mathematically the likely degree of sampling error in an estimate based on a random sample (as we'll discuss later in this chapter)—assuming that the sample's randomness has not been destroyed by a high rate of nonresponse or by poor control over the selection process.

In general, both the size of the sample and the homogeneity (sameness) of the population affect the degree of error as a result of chance; the proportion of the population that the sample represents does not. To elaborate,

- *The larger the sample, the more confidence we can have in the sample's representativeness.* If we randomly pick 5 people to represent the entire population of our city, our sample is unlikely to be very representative of the entire population in age, gender, race, attitudes, and so on. But if we randomly pick 100 people, the odds of having a representative sample are much better; with a random sample of 1,000, the odds become very good indeed.

- *The more homogeneous the population, the more confidence we can have in the representativeness of a sample of any particular size.* Let's say we plan to draw samples of 50 from each of two communities to estimate mean family income. One community is quite diverse, with family incomes varying from $12,000 to $85,000. In the other, more homogeneous community, family incomes are concentrated in a narrow range, from $41,000 to $64,000. The estimated mean family income based on the sample from the homogeneous community is more likely to be representative than is the estimate based on the sample from the more heterogeneous community. With less variation to represent, fewer cases are needed to represent the homogeneous community.

- *The fraction of the total population that a sample contains does not affect the sample's representativeness unless that fraction is large.* Other things being equal, a sample of 1,000 from a population of 1 million (with a sampling fraction of .001, or 0.1%) is much better than a sample of 100 from a population of 10,000 (although the sampling fraction for this smaller sample is .01, or 1%, which is 10 times higher). The size of the samples is what makes representativeness more likely, not the proportion of the whole that the sample represents (Sudman 1976:184).

Photo 5.1 Flipping a coin is a popular way to help select one of two options because it is entirely random. Can you think of other methods of selection that are free from bias?

©iStockphoto.com/slobo

Polls to predict presidential election outcomes illustrate both the value of random sampling and the problems that it cannot overcome. In most presidential elections, pollsters have predicted accurately the outcomes of the actual votes by using random sampling and phone interviewing to learn for which candidate the likely voters intend to vote. Exhibit 5.3 shows how close these sample-based predictions have been in the past 14 contests. The exceptions were the 1980, 1992, and 2004 elections, when third-party candidates had an unpredicted effect. Otherwise, the small discrepancies between the votes predicted through random sampling and the actual votes can be attributed to random error.

JOURNAL LINK
Probability Sampling

Nevertheless, election polls have produced some major errors in prediction. The reasons for these errors illustrate some of the ways in which unintentional systematic bias can influence sample results. In 1948, pollsters mistakenly predicted that Thomas E. Dewey would beat Harry S. Truman, based on the sampling method that George Gallup had used successfully since 1934. The problem was that pollsters stopped collecting data several weeks before the election, and in those weeks, many people changed their minds (Kenney 1987). The sample was systematically biased by underrepresenting shifts in voter sentiment just before the election. This experience convinced Gallup to use only random sampling methods (as well as to continue polling until the election).

The fast-paced 2008 presidential primary elections were also challenging for the pollsters, primarily among Democratic Party voters. In the early New Hampshire primary, polls successfully predicted Republican John McCain's winning margin of 5.5% (the polls were off by only .2%, on average). However, all the polls predicted that Barack Obama would win New Hampshire's Democratic primary by a margin of about 8 percentage points, but he lost to Hillary Clinton by 12 points (47% to 35%). In a careful review of different

■ EXHIBIT 5.3   **Presidential Election Outcomes: Predicted and Actual**

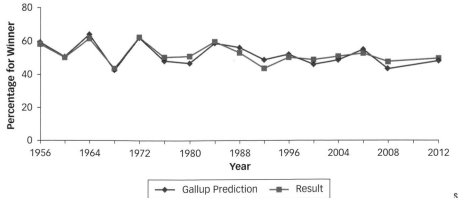

Sources: Gallup (2011); Panagopoulos (2008); Jones (2012).

explanations that have been proposed for that failure, the president of the Pew Research Center, Andrew Kohut (2008:A27), concluded that the problem was that voters who are poorer, less well educated, and white and who tend to refuse to respond to surveys tend to be less favorable to blacks than do other voters. These voters, who were unrepresented in the polls, were more likely to favor Clinton over Obama.

The four most common methods for drawing random samples are (1) simple random sampling, (2) systematic random sampling, (3) stratified random sampling, and (4) cluster sampling. These methods are described in the sections that follow.

Simple Random Sampling

Simple random sampling requires some procedure that generates numbers or otherwise identifies cases strictly on the basis of chance. As you know, flipping a coin or rolling a die can be used to identify cases strictly on the basis of chance, but these procedures are not very efficient tools for drawing a sample. A **random number table**, such as the one in Appendix C (on the study site), simplifies the process considerably. The researcher numbers all the elements in the sampling frame and then uses a systematic procedure for picking corresponding numbers from the random number table. (Practice Exercise 1 at the end of this chapter explains the process step by step.) Alternatively, a researcher may use a lottery procedure, in which each case number is written on a small card, and then the cards are mixed up and the sample is selected from the cards.

©iStockphoto.com/PeopleImages

Photo 5.2 In what ways is a sample generated by random digit dialing compromised if it does not include cell phones? How might this affect the results of a study?

When a large sample must be generated, these procedures are cumbersome. Fortunately, a computer program can easily generate a random sample of any size. The researcher must first number all the elements to be sampled (the sampling frame) and then run the computer program to generate a random selection of the numbers within the desired range. The elements represented by these numbers are the sample.

Organizations that conduct phone surveys often draw random samples using another automated procedure, called **random digit dialing**. A machine dials random numbers within the phone prefixes corresponding to the area in which the survey is to be conducted. Random digit dialing is particularly useful when a sampling frame is not available. The researcher simply replaces any inappropriate number (e.g., those that are no longer in service or that are for businesses) with the next randomly generated phone number.

As the fraction of the population that has only cell phones has increased (up to 40% in 2013), it has become essential to explicitly sample cell phone numbers as well as landline phone numbers (McGeeney & Keeter 2014). Those who use only cell phones tend to be younger; are more likely to be male, single, and black or Hispanic; and are less likely to vote compared with those who have a landline phone. As a result, failing to include cell phone numbers in a phone survey can introduce bias (Christian et al. 2010). In fact, in a 2008 presidential election survey, those who used only cell phones were less likely to be registered voters than were landline users but were considerably more favorable to Obama than landline users (Keeter 2008) (Exhibit 5.4).

The probability of selection in a true simple random sample is equal for each element. If a sample of 500 is selected from a population of 17,000 (i.e., a sampling frame of 17,000), then the probability of selection for each element is 500 to 17,000, or .03. Every element has an equal chance of being selected, just like the odds in a toss of a coin (1 to 2) or a roll of a die (1 to 6). Thus, simple random sampling is an *equal probability of selection method,* or EPSEM.

Systematic Random Sampling

Systematic random sampling is a variant of simple random sampling. The first element is selected randomly from a list or from sequential files, and then every *n*th element is selected. This is a convenient method for drawing a random sample when the population elements are arranged sequentially. It is particularly efficient when the elements are not actually printed (i.e., there is no sampling frame) but instead are represented by folders in filing cabinets.

Simple random sampling: Sampling in which every sample element is selected only on the basis of chance, through a random process.

Random number table: A table containing lists of numbers that are ordered solely on the basis of chance; it is used for drawing a random sample.

Random digit dialing: The random dialing of numbers within designated phone prefixes by a machine, which creates a random sample for phone surveys.

Systematic random sampling: Sampling in which sample elements are selected from a list or from sequential files, with every *n*th element being selected after the first element is selected randomly within the first interval.

Systematic random sampling requires the following three steps:

1. The total number of cases in the population is divided by the number of cases required for the sample. This division yields the sampling interval, the number of cases from one sampled case to another. If 50 cases are to be selected out of 1,000, the **sampling interval** is 20; every 20th case is selected.

2. A number from 1 to 20 (or whatever the sampling interval is) is selected randomly. This number identifies the first case to be sampled, counting from the first case on the list or in the files.

3. After the first case is selected, every *n*th case is selected for the sample, where *n* is the sampling interval. If the sampling interval is not a whole number, the size of the sampling interval is varied systematically to yield the proper number of cases for the sample. For example, if the

■ EXHIBIT 5.4 **Cell-Only and Landline Users in a 2008 Presidential Poll**

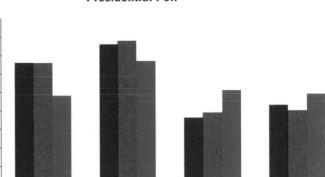

Source: Based on Keeter, Dimock, and Christian (2008).

sampling interval is 30.5, the sampling interval alternates between 30 and 31. In almost all sampling situations, systematic random sampling yields what is essentially a simple random sample. The exception is a situation in which the sequence of elements is affected by **periodicity**—that is, the sequence varies in some regular, periodic pattern. For example, the houses in a new development with the same number of houses in each block (e.g., 8) may be listed by block, starting with the house in the northwest corner of each block and

Sampling interval: The number of cases from one sampled case to another in a systematic random sample.

Periodicity: A sequence of elements (in a list to be sampled) that varies in some regular, periodic pattern.

■ EXHIBIT 5.5 **The Effect of Periodicity on Systematic Random Sampling**

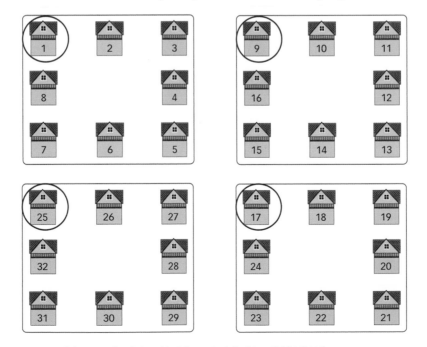

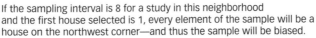

If the sampling interval is 8 for a study in this neighborhood and the first house selected is 1, every element of the sample will be a house on the northwest corner—and thus the sample will be biased.

continuing clockwise. If the sampling interval is 8, the same as the periodic pattern, all the cases selected will be in the same position (Exhibit 5.5). But in reality, periodicity and the sampling interval are rarely the same.

Stratified Random Sampling

Although all probability sampling methods use random sampling, some add steps to the sampling process to make sampling more efficient or easier. **Stratified random sampling** uses information known about the total population before sampling to make the sampling process more efficient. First, all elements in the population (i.e., in the sampling frame) are distinguished according to their value on some relevant characteristic. This characteristic might be year in school in a study of students, marital status in a study of family relations, or average property value in a study of towns. That characteristic forms the sampling strata. Next, elements are sampled randomly from within these strata. For example, race may be the basis for distinguishing individuals in some population of interest. Within each racial category, individuals are then sampled randomly. Of course, using this method requires more information before sampling than is the case with simple random sampling. It must be possible to categorize each element in one and only one stratum, and the size of each stratum in the population must be known.

> **Stratified random sampling:**
> Sampling in which sample elements are selected separately from population strata that are identified in advance by the researcher.
>
> **Proportionate stratified sampling:**
> Sampling method in which elements are selected from strata in exact proportion to their representation in the population.

This method is more efficient than drawing a simple random sample because it ensures appropriate representation of elements across strata. Imagine that you plan to draw a sample of 500 from the population of a large company to study the experiences of different ethnic groups. You know from company records that the workforce is 15% black, 10% Hispanic, 5% Asian, and 70% white. If you drew a simple random sample, you might end up with somewhat disproportionate numbers of each group. But if you created sampling strata based on race and ethnicity, you could randomly select exactly the right number of cases from each stratum: 75 blacks (15% of the sample), 50 Hispanics (10%), 25 Asians (5%), and 350 whites (70%). By using **proportionate stratified sampling**, you would eliminate any possibility of sampling error in the sample's distribution of ethnicity. Each stratum would be represented exactly in proportion to its size in the population from which the sample was drawn (Exhibit 5.6).

■ EXHIBIT 5.6 **Stratified Random Sampling**

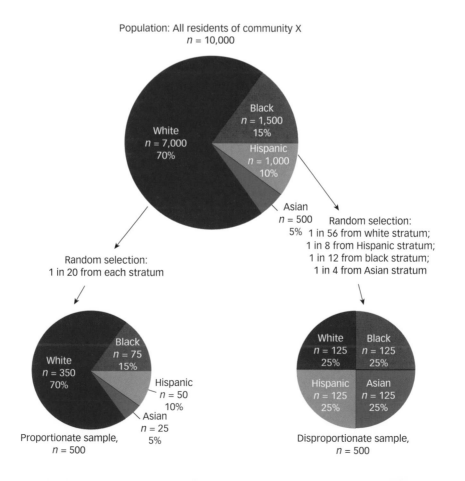

In **disproportionate stratified sampling**, the proportion of each stratum that is included in the sample is intentionally varied from what it is in the population. The usual reason for using this disproportionate approach is to ensure that smaller groups are represented by enough cases in the sample to allow separate analyses of them. For example, if research is conducted to study the factors that influence the success of Asian Americans in school in comparison to white Americans, but there is only one Asian American in the population for every twenty white Americans, a researcher may stratify the sample by race and then disproportionately sample Asian Americans.

Cluster Sampling

Cluster sampling is useful when a sampling frame of elements is not available, as often is the case for large populations spread out across a wide geographic area or among many different organizations. A **cluster** is a naturally occurring, mixed aggregate of elements of the population, with each element appearing in one, and only one, cluster. Schools could serve as clusters for sampling students, blocks could serve as clusters for sampling city residents, counties could serve as clusters for sampling the general population, and businesses could serve as clusters for sampling employees.

Drawing a cluster sample involves two (or more) stages. First, the researcher draws a random sample of clusters. A list of clusters should be much easier to obtain than a list of all the individuals in each cluster in the population. Next, the researcher draws a random sample of elements within each selected cluster. Because only a fraction of the total clusters is involved, obtaining the sampling frame of elements at this stage should be much easier.

In a cluster sample of city residents, for example, blocks could be the first-stage clusters. A research assistant could walk around each selected block and list the addresses of all occupied dwelling units. This list of addresses would be the sampling frame for that block. Or, in a cluster sample of students, a researcher could contact the schools selected in the first stage and make arrangements with the registrar to obtain lists of students at each school. Cluster samples often involve multiple stages (Exhibit 5.7), with clusters within clusters, as when a national sample of individuals might involve first sampling states, then geographic units within those states, then dwellings within those units, and finally, individuals within the dwellings. In multistage cluster sampling, the clusters at the first stage of sampling are termed the *primary sampling units* (Levy & Lemeshow 1999:228).

How many clusters should be selected, and how many individuals within each cluster should be selected? As a general rule, the sample will be more similar to the entire population if the researcher selects as many clusters as possible—even though this will mean the selection of fewer individuals within each cluster. Unfortunately, this strategy also maximizes the cost of the sample for studies using in-person interviews. The more clusters a researcher selects, the more time and money will have to be spent traveling to the different clusters to reach the individuals for interviews.

Cluster sampling is a popular method among survey researchers, but it has one general drawback: Sampling error is greater in a cluster sample than in a simple random sample because there are two steps involving random selection rather than just one. This sampling error increases as the number of clusters decreases, and it decreases as the homogeneity of cases per cluster increases. In sum, it's better to include as many clusters as possible in a sample. Also, it's more likely that a cluster sample will be representative of the population if cases are relatively similar within clusters.

Many professionally designed surveys use combinations of clusters and stratified probability sampling methods in order to achieve some of the advantages of each type.

Sampling Error

A well-designed probability sample is one that is likely to be representative of the population from which it was selected. But as you've seen, random samples still are subject to sampling error owing just to chance. To deal with that problem, social researchers consider the properties of a sampling distribution, a hypothetical distribution of a statistic across all the random samples that could be drawn from a population. Any single random sample can be thought of as just one of an infinite

Disproportionate stratified sampling: Sampling in which elements are selected from strata in different proportions from those that appear in the population.

Cluster sampling: Sampling in which elements are selected in two or more stages, with the first stage being the random selection of naturally occurring clusters and the last stage being the random selection of elements within clusters.

Cluster: A naturally occurring, mixed aggregate of elements of the population.

■ EXHIBIT 5.7　**Multistage Cluster Sampling**

Stage 1:
Randomly
select states

Stage 2:
Randomly select cities,
towns, and counties
within those states

Stage 3:
Randomly select
schools within
those cities and towns

Stage 4:
Randomly select
students within
each school

number of random samples that, in theory, could have been selected from the population. Understanding sampling distributions is the foundation for understanding how statisticians can estimate sampling error. The tool for calculating sampling error is called **inferential statistics**.

> **Inferential statistics:** A mathematical tool for estimating how likely it is that a statistical result based on data from a random sample is representative of the population from which the sample is assumed to have been selected.

> **Random sampling error (chance sampling error):** Differences between the population and the sample that are due only to chance factors (random error), not to systematic sampling error. Random sampling error may or may not result in an unrepresentative sample. The magnitude of sampling error resulting from chance factors can be estimated statistically.

> **Sample statistic:** The value of a statistic, such as a mean, computed from sample data.

> **Population parameter:** The value of a statistic, such as a mean, computed using the data for the entire population; a sample statistic is an estimate of a population parameter.

Sampling distributions for many statistics, including the mean, have a "normal" shape. A graph of a normal distribution looks like a bell, with one hump in the middle, centered on the population mean, and the number of cases tapering off on both sides of the mean. It is also called a "bell curve." Note that a normal distribution is symmetric: If you folded it in half at its center (at the population mean), the two halves would match perfectly. This shape is produced by **random sampling error**—variation owing purely to chance. The value of the statistic varies from sample to sample because of chance, so higher and lower values are equally likely. Exhibit 5.8 shows what a sampling distribution would look like if it formed a perfectly normal distribution.

The properties of a sampling distribution facilitate the process of statistical inference. In the sampling distribution, the most frequent value of the **sample statistic**—the statistic (such as the mean) computed from sample data—is identical to the **population parameter**—the statistic computed for the entire population. In other words, we can have a lot of confidence that the value at the peak of the bell curve represents the norm for the entire population. A population parameter also may be termed the *true value* for the statistic in that population. A sample statistic is an estimate of a population parameter.

In a normal distribution, a predictable proportion of cases fall within certain ranges. Inferential statistics takes advantage of this feature and allow researchers to estimate how likely it is that, given a particular sample, the true population value will be within some range of the statistic. For example, a statistician might conclude from a sample of 30 families, "We can be 95% confident that the true mean family income in the total population is between $39,037 and $89,977." The interval from $39,037 to $89,977 would then be called the *95% confidence interval for the mean*. The lower ($39,037) and upper ($89,977) bounds of this interval are termed the *confidence limits*. Exhibit 5.8 marks such confidence limits, indicating the range that encompasses 95% of the area under the normal curve; 95% of all sample means would fall within this range, as does the mean of our hypothetical sample of 30 cases.

Although all normal distributions have these same basic features, they differ from one another in the extent to which they cluster around the mean. A sampling distribution is more compact when it is based on larger samples. Stated another way, we can be more confident in estimates based on larger random samples because we know that a larger sample creates a more compact sampling distribution.

> **ENCYCLOPEDIA LINK** 📚
> Sampling Error

> **AUDIO LINK** 🌐
> Sampling Methods and Trends

> **AUDIO LINK** 🌐
> Convenience Sampling

Probability Sampling Methods Compared

Exhibit 5.9 should help you remember the key features of the different types of sampling and to determine when each is most appropriate.

Nonprobability Sampling Methods

Nonprobability sampling methods are often used in qualitative research; they also are used in quantitative studies when researchers are unable to use probability selection methods. In qualitative research, a focus on

■ EXHIBIT 5.8   **Normal Sampling Distribution: Mean Family Income**

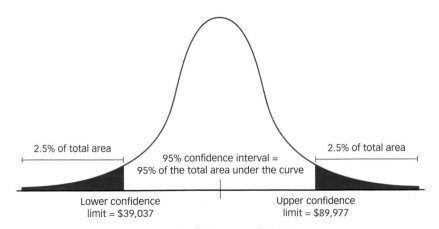

Mean Family Income = $64,507

■ EXHIBIT 5.9   **Features of Probability Sampling Methods**

Feature	Simple	Systematic	Stratified	Cluster
Selects cases without bias	Yes	Yes	Yes	Yes
Requires sampling frame	Yes	No	Yes	No
Ensures representation of key strata	No	No	Yes	No
Uses natural grouping of cases	No	No	No	Yes
Reduces sampling costs	No	No	No	Yes
Sampling error compared with simple random sample	–	Same	Lower	Higher

one setting or a small sample allows a more intensive portrait of activities and actors, but it also limits field researchers' ability to generalize and lowers the confidence that others can place in these generalizations. The use of nonprobability sampling methods in quantitative research too often reflects a lack of concern with generalizability or a lack of understanding of the importance of probability-based sampling.

There are four common nonprobability sampling methods: (1) availability sampling, (2) quota sampling, (3) purposive sampling, and (4) snowball sampling. Because these methods do not use a random selection procedure, we cannot expect a sample selected with any of these methods to yield a representative sample. They should not be used in quantitative studies if a probability-based method is feasible. Nonetheless, these nonprobability methods are useful when random sampling is not possible, when a research question calls for an intensive investigation of a small population, or when a researcher is performing a preliminary, exploratory study.

Availability sampling: Sampling in which elements are selected on the basis of convenience.

Quota sampling: A nonprobability sampling method in which elements are selected to ensure that the sample represents certain characteristics in proportion to their prevalence in the population.

Availability Sampling

Elements are selected for **availability sampling** because they're available or easy to find. Thus, this sampling method is also known as haphazard, accidental, or convenience sampling. There are many ways to select elements for an availability sample: standing on street corners and talking to whoever walks by, asking questions of employees who have time to talk when they pick up their paychecks at a personnel office, or approaching particular individuals at opportune times while observing activities in a social setting. You may find yourself interviewing available students at campus hangouts as part of a course assignment.

An availability sample may be appropriate in social research when a field researcher is exploring a new setting and trying to get some sense of the prevailing attitudes or when a survey researcher conducts a preliminary test of a new set of questions. But availability samples do not allow us to have any confidence in the generalizability of our findings.

Quota Sampling

Quota sampling is intended to overcome the most obvious flaw of availability sampling—that the sample will just consist of whoever or whatever is available, without any concern for its similarity to the population of interest. The distinguishing feature of a quota sample is that quotas are set to ensure that the sample represents certain characteristics in proportion to their prevalence in the population.

Suppose that you want to sample adult residents of a town in a study of support for a tax increase to improve the town's schools. You know from the town's annual report what the proportions of town residents are in gender, race, age, and number of children. You think that each of these characteristics might influence support for new school taxes, so you want to be sure that the sample includes men, women, whites, blacks, Hispanics, Asians, older people, younger people, big families, small families, and childless families in proportion to their numbers in the town population.

Photo 5.3   Availability sampling has convenience on its side, but the drawback is that it can limit generalizability.

CAREERS
and Research

TYLER EVANS, ACCOUNT SUPERVISOR

When Tyler Evans began his career in advertising and public relations, he did not have a particular fondness for research. "I thought my 'gut' was going to help separate my ideas from the others'." However, he found out quickly that relying on his gut would be no better than shooting at a target in the dark, blindfolded.

Like other marketers who have advanced in their careers, Tyler learned that he had to understand the "why" before he could get to the "how." Hubris—the assumption that you "just knew" what the answer was, without research—is the biggest impediment to that understanding. Talented marketers figure out quickly that to solve the complex consumer puzzle, to learn what is behind the consumer's motivation, it is imperative to understand the consumer's need states. Few realize that the process of understanding must begin with identifying fundamental consumer truths.

The person most accountable for this is the agency lead on the account, who must understand exactly who the target is, why they are the best focus for the product or service, and what strategy will best engage them. There is a saying that hangs over many computer monitors to keep that strategic focus at the forefront each day, and it reads simply: "Data beats opinions." Research must lead the strategy and, eventually, the tactics of successful marketers. This research goes beyond simple demographic information to create a knowledge base steeped in understanding consumer need states and what can be offered during their moments of need. If there is not that deep understanding at the intersection of need states and product offerings, then consumers will not make any long-term commitment to the product; many dollars will be wasted chasing unattainable targets. To be just a bit hyperbolic, the ultimate goal in working at an advertising/PR firm is to do bold work that sends shockwaves through the heart of the target audience.

Today, Tyler Evans leads an account for the advertising agency. He advises students interested in a marketing career that research is the one thing that marketers use on a daily basis to ensure a focus on what will be measurable, significant, and impactful. "Marketers should receive training in research so that they can understand consumer insights and become an impactful force in the marketing community."

This is where quotas come in (Exhibit 5.10). Let's say that 48% of the town's adult residents are men and 52% are women, and that 60% are employed, 5% are unemployed, and 35% are out of the labor force. These percentages and the percentages corresponding to the other characteristics become the quotas for the sample. If you plan to include 500 residents in your sample, 240 must be men (48% of 500), 260 must be women, 300 must be employed, and so on.

Characteristic	Population	Quota	Calculation
Sex			
Men	48%	240	(.48*500)
Women	52%	260	(.52*500)
Employment Status			
Employed	60%	300	(.60*500)
Unemployed	5%	25	(.05*500)
Out of Labor Force	35%	175	(.35*500)
Total Sample Size	500		

With the quota list in hand, you (or your research staff) can now go out into the community looking for the right number of people in each quota category. You may go door to door, bar to bar, or just stand on a street corner until you have surveyed 240 men, 260 women, and so on.

The problem is that even when we know that a quota sample is representative of the particular characteristics for which quotas have been set, we have no way of knowing if the sample is representative for any other characteristics. Realistically, researchers can set quotas for only a small fraction of the characteristics relevant to a study, so a quota sample is really not much better than an availability sample. Also, a researcher must know the characteristics of the entire population in order to set the quotas. In most cases, researchers know what the population looks like relative to no more than a few of the characteristics relevant to their concerns—and in some cases, they have no such information on the entire population.

Purposive Sampling

In **purposive sampling**, each sample element is selected for a purpose, usually because of the unique position of the sample elements. Purposive sampling may involve studying the entire population of some limited group (directors of shelters for homeless adults) or a subset of a population (mid-level managers with a reputation for efficiency). Or a purposive sample may be a *key informant survey*, which targets individuals who are particularly knowledgeable about the issues under investigation.

Of course, purposive sampling does not produce a sample that represents some larger population, but it can be exactly what is needed in a case study of an organization, a community, or some other clearly defined and relatively limited group. In an intensive organizational case study, a purposive sample of organizational leaders might be complemented with a probability sample of organizational members.

■ EXHIBIT 5.10 **Quota Sampling**

Population
50% male, 50% female
70% white, 30% black

Quota Sample
50% male, 50% female
50% white, 50% black

Representative of gender distribution in population, not representative of race distribution.

Snowball Sampling

Snowball sampling is useful for hard-to-reach or hard-to-identify populations for which there is no sampling frame, but when the members are somewhat interconnected (i.e., at least some members of the population know each other). It can be used to sample members of groups such as drug dealers, prostitutes, practicing criminals, informal organizational leaders, participants in Alcoholics Anonymous groups, gang leaders, and homeless persons. However, the initial contacts may shape the entire sample and foreclose access to some members of the population of interest. Because researchers cannot be confident that a snowball sample represents the total population of interest, generalizations must be tentative. (See Practice Exercise 2.)

❖ Generalizability in Qualitative Research

Qualitative research often focuses on populations that are hard to locate or limited in size. In consequence, nonprobability sampling methods such as availability (convenience) sampling and snowball sampling are often used. Several strategies can enhance the value of such samples (Gobo 2008:206):

- *Studying the typical.* If enough is known in advance to choose research sites on the basis of their typicality, this is preferable to simply choosing on the basis of convenience (Schofield 2002:181).

- *Studying the atypical.* A case may be selected for in-depth study because it is atypical, or deviant. Investigating social processes in a situation that differs from the norm will improve understanding of how social processes work in typical situations: "the exception that proves the rule" (Gobo 2008:204–205).

- *Performing multisite studies.* "Generally speaking, a finding emerging from the study of several very heterogeneous sites would be more . . . likely to be useful in understanding various other sites than one emerging from the study of several very similar sites" (Schofield 2002:184).

By contrast, some qualitative researchers question the value of seeking generalizability. The argument is that understanding the particulars of a situation in depth is an important object of inquiry in itself:

The interpretivist rejects generalization as a goal and never aims to draw randomly selected samples of human experience. . . . Every instance of social interaction . . . represents a slice from the life world that is the proper subject matter for interpretive inquiry. (Norman Denzin, cited in Schofield 2002:173)

Purposive sampling: A nonprobability sampling method in which elements are selected for a purpose, usually because of their unique position.

Snowball sampling: Sampling in which sample elements are selected as they are identified by successive informants or interviewees.

❖ Conclusions

Sampling is a powerful tool for social research and one that must often be used: Social researchers cannot often study all members of a population, and it is rare that all members of a population can be presumed to be identical in some way. Probability sampling methods allow a researcher to use the laws of chance, or probability, to draw samples from which population parameters can be estimated with a high degree of confidence. A sample of just 1,000 or 1,500 individuals can be used to represent the characteristics of the population of a nation comprising millions of individuals.

But representative samples are not easy to obtain. Well-designed samples require careful planning, some advance knowledge about the population to be sampled, and adherence to systematic selection procedures—all so that the selection procedures are not biased. To evaluate sample quality in a quantitative study, you must check the sampling frame used, the specific sampling method used, and the response rate obtained. Even after data are collected with a representative sample, the researcher's ability to generalize from the sample findings to the population is not completely certain: Statistics obtained with such a sample are only *likely* to represent the population with some degree of confidence. The degree of confidence that can be placed in the representativeness of a nonprobability sampling method cannot be calculated.

Qualitative research that seeks to understand a small group or setting in depth usually uses a nonprobability sampling method. The depth of insight that can be gained about people or social settings with qualitative methods can be sufficient justification for selecting cases for study that may not represent some larger population. However, the value of samples used in qualitative research can be enhanced by considering carefully the alternatives. Additional procedures for sampling in qualitative studies are introduced in Chapter 8.

····· Key Terms ·····

Availability sampling   73
Census   65
Cluster   71
Cluster sampling   71
Disproportionate stratified
    sampling   71
Elements   64
Inferential statistics   72
Nonprobability sampling method   65
Nonrespondents   66
Periodicity   69
Population   64

Population parameter   72
Probability of selection   65
Probability sampling method   65
Proportionate stratified sampling   70
Purposive sampling   75
Quota sampling   73
Random digit dialing   68
Random number table   68
Random sampling   66
Random sampling error (chance
    sampling error)   72
Representative sample   65

Sample   64
Sample statistic   72
Sampling error   64
Sampling frame   64
Sampling interval   69
Sampling units   64
Simple random sampling   68
Snowball sampling   75
Stratified random sampling   70
Systematic bias   66
Systematic random sampling   68
Target population   65

····· Highlights ·····

- Sampling theory focuses on the generalizability of descriptive findings to the population from which the sample was drawn. It also considers whether statements can be generalized from one population to another.

- Sampling is unnecessary when the elements that would be sampled are identical, but the complexity of the social world makes it difficult to argue very often that all different elements are identical. Conducting a complete census of a population also eliminates the need for sampling, but the resources required for a complete census of a large population are usually prohibitive.

- Nonresponse undermines sample quality: The obtained sample, not the desired sample, determines sample quality.

- Probability sampling methods rely on a random selection procedure to ensure no systematic bias in the selection of elements. In a probability sample, the odds of selecting elements are known, and the method of selection is carefully controlled.

- A sampling frame (a list of elements in the population) is required in most probability sampling methods. The adequacy of the sampling frame is an important determinant of sample quality.

- Simple random sampling and systematic random sampling are equivalent probability sampling methods in most situations. However, systematic random sampling is inappropriate for sampling from lists of elements that have a regular, periodic structure.

- Stratified random sampling uses prior information about a population to make sampling more efficient. Stratified sampling may be either proportionate or disproportionate. Disproportionate stratified sampling is useful when a research question focuses on a stratum or on strata that make up a small proportion of the population.

- Cluster sampling is less efficient than simple random sampling, but it is useful when a sampling frame is unavailable. It is also useful for large populations spread out across a wide area or among many organizations.

- Nonprobability sampling methods can be useful when random sampling is not possible, when a research question does not concern a larger population, and when a preliminary exploratory study is appropriate. However, the representativeness of nonprobability samples cannot be determined.

- The likely degree of error in an estimate of a population characteristic based on a probability sample decreases when the size of the sample and the homogeneity of the population from which the sample was selected increase. The proportion of the population that is sampled does not affect sampling error, except when that proportion is large. The degree of sampling error affecting a sample statistic can be estimated from the characteristics of the sample and from knowledge of the properties of sampling distributions.

Chapter Questions

1. All adult U.S. citizens are required to participate in the decennial census, but some do not. Some social scientists have argued for putting more resources into a large representative sample, so that more resources are available to secure higher rates of response from hard-to-include groups. Do you think that the U.S. Census should shift to a probability-based sampling design? Why or why not?

2. What increases sampling error in probability-based sampling designs? Stratified rather than simple random sampling? Disproportionate (rather than proportionate) stratified random sampling? Stratified rather than cluster random sampling? Why do researchers select *disproportionate* (rather than proportionate) stratified samples? Why do they select cluster rather than simple random samples?

3. What are the advantages and disadvantages of probability-based sampling designs compared with nonprobability-based designs? Could any of the research described in this chapter with a nonprobability-based design have been conducted instead with a probability-based design? What are the difficulties that might have been encountered in an attempt to use random selection? How would you discuss the degree of confidence you can place in the results obtained from research using a nonprobability-based sampling design?

4. How much pressure is too much pressure to participate in a probability-based sample survey? Is it okay for the U.S. government to mandate legally that all citizens participate in the decennial census? Should companies be able to require employees to participate in survey research about work-related issues? Should students be required to participate in surveys about teacher performance? Should parents be required to consent to the participation of their high-school-age students in a survey about substance abuse and health issues? Is it okay to give monetary incentives for participation in a survey of homeless shelter clients? Can monetary incentives be coercive? Explain your decisions.

Practice Exercises

1. Select a random sample using the table of random numbers in Appendix C (on the study site; edge.sagepub.com/schuttusw). Compute a statistic based on your sample and compare it with the corresponding figure for the entire population. Here's how to proceed:

   a. First, select a very small population for which you have a reasonably complete sampling frame. One possibility would be the list of asking prices for houses advertised in your local paper. Another would be the listing of some characteristic of states in a U.S. Census Bureau publication, such as average income or population size.

   b. The next step is to create your sampling frame, a numbered list of all the elements in the population. If you are using a complete listing of all elements, as from a U.S. Census Bureau publication, the sampling frame is the same as the list. Just number the elements (states). If your population is composed of housing ads in the local paper, your sampling frame will be those ads that contain a housing price. Identify these ads, and then number them sequentially, starting with 1.

   c. Decide on a method of picking numbers out of the random number table in Appendix C, such as taking every number in each row, row by row (or you may move down or diagonally across the columns). Use only the first (or last) digit in each number if you need to select 1 to 9 cases, or only the first (or last) two digits if you want fewer than 100 cases.

d. Pick a starting location in the random number table. It's important to pick a starting point in an unbiased way, perhaps by closing your eyes and then pointing to some part of the page.

e. Record the numbers you encounter as you move from the starting location in the direction you decided on in advance, until you have recorded as many random numbers as the number of cases you need in the sample. If you are selecting states, 10 might be a good number. Ignore numbers that are too large (or too small) for the range of numbers used to identify the elements in the population. Discard duplicate numbers.

f. Calculate the average value in your sample for some variable that was measured—for example, population size in a sample of states or housing price for the housing ads. Calculate the average by adding the values of all the elements in the sample and dividing by the number of elements in the sample.

g. Go back to the sampling frame and calculate this same average for all elements in the list. How close is the sample average to the population average?

2. Draw a snowball sample of people who are involved in bungee jumping or some other uncommon sport that does not involve teams. Ask friends and relatives to locate a first contact, and then call or visit this person and ask for names of others. Stop when you have identified a sample of 10. Review the problems you encountered, and consider how you would proceed if you had to draw a larger sample.

3. Identify one article at the book's study site (edge.sagepub.com/schuttusw) that used a survey research design. Describe the sampling procedure. What type was it? Why did the author(s) use this particular type of sample?

STUDENT STUDY SITE

⑤SAGE edge™

The Student Study Site, available at **edge.sagepub.com/schuttusw**, includes useful study materials including eFlashcards, videos, audio resources, journal articles, and encyclopedia articles, many of which are represented by the media links throughout the text.

Causation and Experimental Design

Learning Objectives

❖ List the three criteria for establishing a causal relationship and the two cautions that can improve understanding of a causal connection

❖ Explain the meaning of the expression "correlation does not prove causation"

❖ List the essential components of a true experimental design

❖ Distinguish the concepts of random assignment (randomization) and random sampling

❖ Explain the advantages and disadvantages of using quasi-experimental and experimental designs

❖ Define five threats to validity in research

❖ Discuss the most distinctive ethical challenges in experimental research

I dentifying causes—figuring out why things happen—is the goal of most social research. Unfortunately, valid explanations of the causes of social phenomena do not come easily. Why has the rate of homicides declined in the United States since the early 1990s, even during the 2008–2010 recession (Exhibit 6.1)? Arizona State University criminologist Scott Decker points to the low levels of crime committed by illegal immigrants to explain the falling crime rate in his state (Archibold 2010), while criminal justice advocates in Texas point to the state's investment in community treatment and diversion programs (Grissom 2011). Police officials in New York City emphasize the effect of CompStat, a computer program that highlights the location of crimes (Dewan 2004a:A25; Dewan 2004b:A1; Kaplan 2002:A3), but others think New York City has benefited from a decline in crack cocaine use (Dewan 2004b:C16). And why did the rate of homicides rise again in several cities in 2015? Should we worry about the increasing number of drug arrests nationally (Bureau of Justice Statistics 2011) and a rise in abuse of prescription drugs (Goodnough 2010)? What type of research design can help us answer questions like these?

What does it mean to say that one phenomenon causes another? What features should a research design include in order to test causal hypotheses? This chapter begins with answers to these questions and then focuses on experimental designs, which are the strongest research designs for identifying causes. The chapter then identifies features of experimental designs that underlie their ability to test causal hypotheses, some concerns that remain when experimental designs are used, and reasons for using "quasi-experimental" designs in some circumstances. The chapter concludes with a discussion of ethical issues of concern in social research using experimental designs.

Causal explanation: An explanation that identifies common influences on a number of cases or events.

❖ Causal Explanations and Experimental Design

A **causal explanation** is one involving the belief that an independent variable (X) has produced a change in a dependent variable (Y), when all other things are equal (*ceteris paribus*). Researchers who claim a **causal effect** have concluded that the value of cases on the dependent variable differs from what their value would have been in the absence of variation in the independent variable. For instance, researchers might evaluate the claim that the likelihood of committing violent crimes is higher for individuals exposed to media violence than it would be if these same individuals had not been exposed to media violence.

We can test causal hypotheses with research methods that allow us to examine the impact on the dependent variable of variation in the independent variable alone, holding other things constant—that is, *ceteris paribus*. Even though it may appear in Photo 6.1 that the ball broke the window, there may have been a different cause. We need to devise a test.

True experiments are the strongest research design for testing causal effects. They must have at least three features:

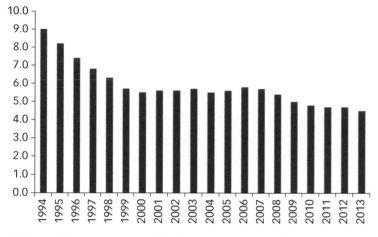

■ EXHIBIT 6.1 **Rate of Murder and Nonnegligent Homicide in the United States, 1994–2013**

Source: Federal Bureau of Investigation. 2013. "Table 1: Crime in the United States." *Uniform Crime Reports.*

- Two groups (in the simplest case, an experimental and a control group)

- Variation in the independent variable (the "treatment" or "stimulus") before assessment of change in the dependent variable

- **Random assignment** to the two (or more) comparison groups

Ceteris paribus: Latin phrase meaning "other things being equal."

Causal effect: When variation in one phenomenon, an independent variable, leads to or results, on average, in variation in another phenomenon, the dependent variable.

CAREERS
and Research

JENNIFER A. HERBERT, CRIME INTELLIGENCE ANALYST

Jennifer Herbert graduated with a double major in political science and justice studies from James Madison University in 2007. She had aspirations of becoming a police officer and eventually a detective. She was hired as a police officer after graduation, but she realized while at the police academy that she wanted to pursue the crime analysis career path in law enforcement. She became a crime analyst with a county police department. While working full time as an analyst, Herbert pursued an M.A. degree in intelligence at the American Military University. She then accepted a promotion to crime intelligence analyst with a county police division. After working as a crime analyst for six years, she cannot imagine doing anything else.

Every day is different working as a crime intelligence analyst. Some days, Herbert analyzes phone records and maps a suspect's whereabouts during the time of a crime. Other days, she maps the latest residential burglary trends and predicts where the next burglary will occur. She also completes research projects that examine quality-of-life issues for the community, including estimating crimes per 1,000 residents by neighborhood. Herbert's role as a crime analyst is equally important in preventing crime and in apprehension of offenders by patrol officers. She thinks the most rewarding part of her job is helping people who have been victimized by apprehending offenders and improving the quality of life for county residents. Herbert has some good advice for students interested in careers involving analysis:

If crime analysis interests you, ask your local police department if you can do an internship (paid or unpaid) to gain experience. Be sure to network with other crime analysts and let them know you are interested in pursuing a career in crime analysis. Courses in all forms of data analysis and geographic information systems (GIS) are almost essential to a career in crime analysis.

©iStockphoto.com/Charles Mann

Photo 6.1 Determining cause and effect is one of the many goals of an experiment. Did the ball break the window?

The combination of these features permits us to have much greater confidence in the validity of causal conclusions (internal validity) than is possible in other research designs. Two other features further enhance our confidence in the validity of an experiment's findings:

- Identification of the causal mechanism

- Control over the context of an experiment

A causal **mechanism** is some process that creates the connection between variation in an independent variable and the variation in the dependent variable that the independent variable is hypothesized to cause (Cook & Campbell 1979:35; Marini & Singer 1988). Many social scientists (and scientists in other fields) argue that no causal explanation is adequate until a causal mechanism is identified (Costner 1989; Hedström & Swedberg 1998). In statistical analysis, variables that involve a mechanism are termed **mediators**.

Identification of the **context** in which a causal relationship occurs can help us understand that relationship. In statistical analysis, variables that identify contexts for the effects of other variables are termed **moderators.**

The police response to domestic violence experiments introduced you to experimental design in Chapter 2. Recall from that chapter that Sherman and Berk (1984) found in the first of these experiments that, in Minneapolis, mandatory arrest reduced subsequent offenses. The Milwaukee Police Department hosted one of the replications of that experiment between 1987 and 1988 (Sherman et al. 1992). During that period, 1,200 eligible cases—about half of all domestic violence cases during this period—were treated randomly based on a computer-generated "lottery" procedure (suspects were not eligible for the study if there was an outstanding warrant or evidence of serious injury). Police officers arrested one third of the suspects and required them to post bail, they arrested another third but then released them on their personal recognizance, and they read a verbal warning to another third instead of making an arrest. The researchers then measured subsequent calls about domestic violence involving the same suspects for 22 months after the precipitating incident. After 23 years, Sherman and Harris (2013) checked death records to see if there was a long-term effect of the arrest experience on death rates among the suspects.

Let's review the features that make the Milwaukee study an experiment:

True experiment: Experiment in which subjects are assigned randomly to an experimental group that receives a treatment or other manipulation of the independent variable and a comparison group that does not receive the treatment or receives some other manipulation; outcomes are measured in a posttest.

Random assignment: A procedure by which each experimental subject is placed in a group randomly.

Mechanism: A discernible process that creates a causal connection between two variables.

Context: A set of interrelated circumstances that alters a relationship between other variables or social processes.

Mediator: A variable involved in a causal mechanism (intervening variable).

Moderator: A variable that identifies a context for the effect of other variables.

- There was a treatment group (actually two treatment groups, with different types of arrest experience) and a comparison group that did not receive the treatment of interest.

- The variation in the independent variable (the treatment or stimulus) occurred before the repeat offense rate—the dependent variable (or the *outcome*)—was measured.

- Cases were assigned randomly to the three groups.

In addition to having these three criteria of a true experimental design, this research provided information about the two other important issues in experimental design:

- In 1997, Larry Paternoster and others reported an investigation of records of police interaction with suspects in an attempt to identify the mechanism by which the experience of arrest might influence suspects.

- Sherman et al. (1992) sought to identify the context in which the experimental treatment had an effect by comparing the effect of arrest for those who were unemployed to its effect for those who were employed at the time of arrest. The comparison of results between the police response to domestic violence experiments in six different cities also allowed consideration of the effect of context on the hypothesized effect (Sherman 1992).

The initial results of the Milwaukee domestic violence experiment did not support the hypothesis based on specific deterrence theory that mandatory arrest would reduce recidivism. Instead, there were indications that the likelihood of repeat incidents increased among those who were arrested, as predicted by labeling theory. The long-term follow-up also supported the impression of an unintended effect: Suspects who had been arrested were more likely to have died due to homicide over the next 23 years (Exhibit 6.2). Sherman and Harris (2013) speculate about the possible reasons for this unintended effect of arrest, but because they do not have systematic data on what happened to the suspects as a result of being arrested, we cannot be sure about the underlying causal mechanism that produced this effect.

The next sections provide more information about how the design of true experiments achieves each of the three criteria for testing a causal effect, using as an example Alexander Czopp, Margo Monteith, and Aimee Mark's (2006) study of reducing racial bias among students through interpersonal confrontation.

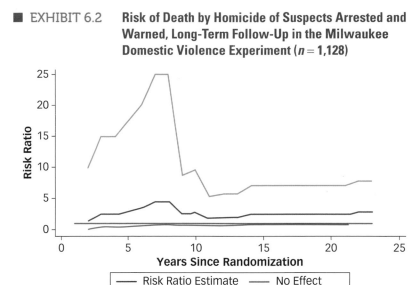

■ EXHIBIT 6.2   **Risk of Death by Homicide of Suspects Arrested and Warned, Long-Term Follow-Up in the Milwaukee Domestic Violence Experiment ($n = 1,128$)**

Source: Sherman et al. (1992); Sherman and Harris (2013).

Association

The first criterion for a causal effect is that there is an association between the independent and dependent variable. This is determined in a true experiment by comparing scores on the dependent variable between a treatment group and a comparison group. Czopp and his colleagues (2006) used several comparison groups in an experiment about interpersonal confrontation. For this experiment, Czopp et al. recruited 111 white students from introductory psychology classes and assigned them randomly to one of the four groups. At the time of the experiment, individual students came to a laboratory, sat before a computer, and were told that they would be working with a student in another room through a computer to complete a task. Unknown to the student recruits, the other student was actually the experimenter. Also without their knowledge, the student recruits were assigned randomly to one of the four conditions in the experiment.

The students first answered some "getting to know you" questions from the "other student." The "other student" did mention that he was white. After this brief Q&A, the student subjects were shown images of various people, of different races, and asked to write a comment about them to the "other student." The "other student" did the same thing, according to a standard script, and had an opportunity to give some feedback about these comments. Here is the type of feedback that students in the Racial Confrontation condition soon received (the particular words varied according to what the student subject had actually written):

> I thought some of your answers seemed a little offensive. The Black guy wandering the streets could be a lost tourist and the Black woman could work for the government. People shouldn't use stereotypes, you know? (Czopp et al. 2006:795)

Students in the Nonracial Confrontation condition received a response like, "I thought some of your answers seemed a little goofy." Students in the No-Confrontation Control condition were told only, "I thought you typed fast. Good job."

The study results indicated that the interpersonal confrontations were effective in curbing racial bias (stereotypic responding), whether the confronter was white or black. In other words, there was an **association** between interpersonal response and expression of racial bias. An empirical (observed) association between the independent and dependent variables is the first criterion for identifying a causal effect.

In the simplest type of experiment, the group that receives a "treatment" or "stimulus"—involving a manipulation of the value of the independent variable—is termed the *experimental group*, while another group—that does not receive the treatment—is termed the *control group*.

VIDEO LINK
Control Groups and Social Experiments

Association: A criterion for establishing a causal relationship between two variables; variation in one variable is related to variation in another variable.

Time order: A criterion for establishing a causal relation between two variables; the variation in the presumed cause (the independent variable) must occur before the variation in the presumed effect (the dependent variable).

Time Order

The second criterion for a true experiment is that researchers must ensure that the cause came before the supposed effect; that is, that variation in the independent variable occurred before variation in the dependent variable (the outcome). This is the criterion of **time order**.

ENCYCLOPEDIA LINK
Spurious Relationship

All true experiments have a **posttest**—that is, measurement of the outcome in both groups after the experimental group has received the treatment. Many true experiments also have **pretests** that measure the dependent variable before the experimental intervention. A pretest is exactly the same as a posttest, just administered at a different time. A randomized experimental design with a pretest and a posttest is termed a **randomized comparative change design** or a *pretest–posttest control group design*.

A true experiment does not *require* a pretest, because the experimental and comparison groups' initial scores on the dependent variable and all other variables should be the same at the start of the experiment due to random assignment. Any difference in outcome (in the posttest) between the experimental and comparison groups is therefore likely to result from the intervention. This is fortunate, because the dependent variable in some experiments cannot be measured in a pretest. In the Sherman and Berk (1984) research, likelihood of repeat offending could not be measured before suspects had had a first offense. Czopp et al. (2006:797) couldn't measure racial bias in attitudes of student subjects toward the "other student" who had confronted them until after the interaction in which the confrontation occurred, although they could measure general "attitude toward blacks" in a pretest and a posttest. Exhibit 6.3 diagrams the Czopp study. If there is no pretest, a true experimental design is termed a *posttest-only control group design*, or the **randomized comparative posttest design**.

Posttest: In experimental research, the measurement of an outcome (dependent) variable after an experimental intervention or after a presumed independent variable has changed for some other reason.

Pretest: In experimental research, the measurement of an outcome (dependent) variable before an experimental intervention or change in a presumed independent variable for some other reason. The pretest is exactly the same "test" as the posttest, but it is administered at a different time.

Randomized comparative change design: The classic true experimental design in which subjects are assigned randomly to two groups; both groups receive a pretest, then one group receives the experimental intervention, and then both groups receive a posttest. Also known as a *pretest–posttest control group design.*

Nonspuriousness

The third criterion for establishing the existence of a causal effect of an independent variable on a dependent variable is **nonspuriousness**; this criterion is established in an experimental design through **randomization**—or random assignment. A relationship between two variables is not spurious when it is not caused by variation in a third variable. Have you heard the adage "correlation does not prove causation"? It reminds us that an association between two variables might be

■ **EXHIBIT 6.3**   **Diagram of Czopp Confrontation Experiment**

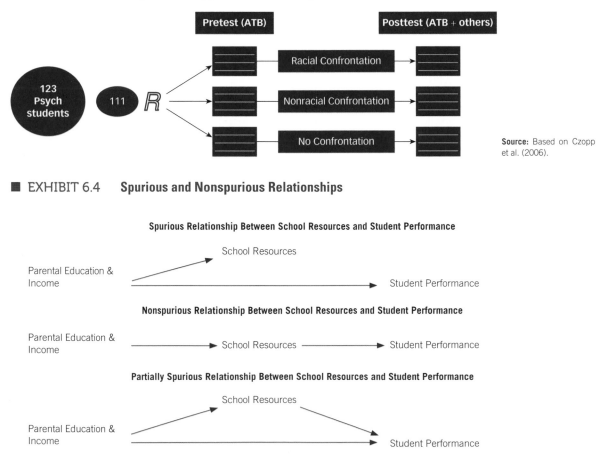

Source: Based on Czopp et al. (2006).

■ **EXHIBIT 6.4**   **Spurious and Nonspurious Relationships**

caused by something other than an effect of the presumed independent variable on the dependent variable—that is, it might be a **spurious relationship** (Exhibit 6.4). If we measure children's shoe sizes and their academic knowledge, for example, we will find a positive association. However, the association results from the fact that older children have larger feet as well as more academic knowledge. Age (the **extraneous variable**) causes variation in the other two variables.

If you think this point is obvious, consider a social science example. Do schools with more resources produce better student outcomes? Before you answer the question, consider the fact that parents with more education and higher income tend to live in neighborhoods that spend more on their schools. These parents also are more likely to have books in the home and to provide other advantages for their children. So do the children in schools with more resources do better because of the schools or because they are more likely to have parents who provided them with other advantages? Can you see the need for research to figure this out?

Randomization is what makes the comparison group in a true experiment such as Czopp et al.'s such a powerful tool for identifying the effects of the treatment. A randomized comparison group can provide a good estimate of the outcome that would have occurred if the subjects who were exposed to the treatment had not been exposed but otherwise had had the same experiences (Mohr 1992:3; Rossi & Freeman 1989:229). A researcher cannot determine for sure what the unique effects of a treatment are if the comparison group differs from the experimental group in any way other than not receiving the treatment.

Assigning subjects randomly to the experimental and comparison groups ensures that systematic bias does not affect the assignment of subjects to groups. Of course, random assignment cannot guarantee that the groups are perfectly identical at the start of the experiment. Randomization removes bias from the assignment process, but only by relying on chance, which itself can result in some intergroup differences (Bloom 2008:116). Fortunately, researchers can use statistical methods to determine the odds of ending up with groups that differ very much on the basis of chance, and these odds are low even for groups of moderate size.

Note that the random assignment of subjects to experimental and comparison groups is not the same as random sampling of individuals from some larger population (Exhibit 6.5). In fact, random assignment (randomization) does not help at all to ensure that the research subjects are representative of some larger population; instead, representativeness is the goal of random sampling. What random assignment does—create two (or more) equivalent groups—is useful for maximizing the likelihood of internal validity, not generalizability (Bloom 2008:116).

Randomized comparative posttest design: A true experimental design in which subjects are assigned randomly to two groups —one group receives the experimental intervention and both groups receive a posttest; there is no pretest. Also known as a *posttest-only control group design*.

Nonspuriousness: A criterion for establishing a causal relation between two variables; when a relationship between two variables is not caused by variation in a third variable.

Randomization: The random assignment of cases, as by the toss of a coin.

Spurious relationship: A relationship between two variables that is caused by variation in a third variable.

Extraneous variable: A variable that influences both the independent and the dependent variables, creating a spurious association between them that disappears when the extraneous variable is controlled.

RESEARCH

In the News

LONG-TERM IMPACT: HOW CAN RESEARCH MAKE THE CONNECTION?

Researchers are analyzing census data and data from the National Federation of State High School Associations on high school sports participation to test the long-term effects of Title IX—which required equal treatment for men and women in educational activities—on women's health and overall educational success. By controlling factors such as school size, income, and social differences, Betsey Stevenson was able to conclude that Title IX had a positive effect on female achievement. Robert Kaestner found that female athletes have a 7% lower risk of obesity years after participation in high school sports.

For Further Thought **?**

1. What are some advantages of using census data to test hypotheses like this one?

2. Name one variable that is unlikely to be measured in the census but that you feel would be useful in an analysis of the long-term effects of Title IX.

3. How could a randomized experiment help to improve confidence in the conclusion about Title IX's impact?

News source: Parker-Pope, Tara. 2010. "As Girls Become Women, Sports Pay Dividends." *New York Times,* February 16:D5.

Limitations of True Experimental Designs

The distinguishing features of true experiments—experimental and comparison groups, pretests (which are not always used) and posttests, and randomization—can be implemented most easily in laboratory settings with participants such as students who are available for the experiments. For this reason, true experimental designs are used most often in social psychological experiments that focus on research questions about reactions to conditions that can easily be created in laboratories on college campuses. However, this focus on college students in laboratory settings raises the question of whether findings can be generalized to other populations and settings. This problem of generalizability is the biggest limitation of true experimental designs.

True experimental designs also do not guarantee that the researcher has been able to maintain control over the conditions to which subjects are exposed after they are assigned to the experimental and comparison groups. If these conditions begin to differ, the variation between the experimental and comparison groups will not be what was intended. Such unintended variation is often not much of a problem in laboratory experiments, where the researcher has almost complete control over the conditions (and can ensure that these conditions are nearly identical for both groups). But control over conditions can become a big concern for **field experiments**, experimental studies that are conducted in the field, in real-world settings. The field experiment that Sherman and Berk (1984) designed to study the police response to domestic violence (see Chapter 2) is an example of a well-designed field experiment, but the researchers found evidence that some police officers did not adhere consistently to the random assignment procedure. As a result of this concern, subsequent replications of the experiment in other cities reduced the discretion of individual police officers and used a more centralized procedure for assigning cases to the treatment and comparison conditions.

Field experiment: A study using an experimental design that is conducted in a real-world setting.

■ EXHIBIT 6.5 **Random Sampling Versus Random Assignment**

Random sampling (a tool for maximizing generalizability):
Individuals are randomly selected from a population to participate in a study.

Random assignment, or randomization (a tool for maximizing internal validity):
Individuals who are to participate in a study are randomly divided into an experimental group and a comparison group.

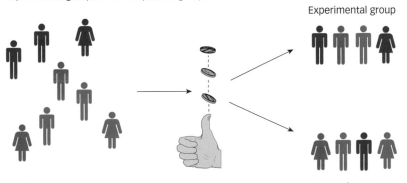

Population   Sample

Study participants   Experimental group   Comparison group

❖ Quasi-Experiments

Often, testing a hypothesis with a true experimental design is not feasible with the desired participants and in the desired setting. Such a test may be too costly or take too long to carry out, it may not be ethical to randomly assign subjects to the different conditions, or it may be too late to do so. In these situations, researchers may instead use *quasi-experimental* designs that retain several features of experimental designs but do not randomly assign participants to different conditions.

A **quasi-experimental design** is one in which the comparison group is predetermined to be comparable with the treatment group in critical ways, such as being eligible for the same services or being in the same school cohort (Rossi & Freeman 1989:313). These research designs are quasi-experimental because subjects are not randomly assigned to the comparison and experimental groups. As a result, we cannot be as confident in the comparability of the groups as in true experimental designs. Nonetheless, to term a research design quasi-experimental, we have to be sure that the comparison groups meet specific criteria that help lessen the possibility of preexisting differences between groups.

Once research moves outside of laboratories on college campuses and samples of available students, it becomes much harder to control what people do and what type of experiences they will have. When random assignment is not possible, an alternative approach to testing the effect of some treatment or other experience can be to find a comparison group that matches the treatment group in many ways but differs in exposure to the treatment—known as a **nonequivalent control group design**. However, it is important in a nonequivalent control group design that individuals have not been able to choose whether to join the group that had one experience or the other. Nonequivalent control group designs represent the most common type of quasi-experimental design.

An interesting study by doctoral student Stephen Hoffman (2014) at Harvard's Graduate School of Education provides a good example of a nonequivalent control group design. Since the mid-1990s, many high schools have adopted zero-tolerance discipline policies that mandate the automatic suspension or expulsion of students for offenses such as alcohol and drug violations, physical assault and fighting, and criminal damage to property (Hoffman 2014:72). Hoffman sought to investigate the impact of these policies on racial disparities in school discipline. For this purpose, he examined a mid-sized urban school district that had abruptly expanded the number of offenses subject to mandatory suspension and possible expulsion in September 2007.

Hoffman's research design was a quasi-experimental nonequivalent control group design. He compared discipline rates by race before and after the expansion of zero-tolerance policies in 15 schools in this district and contrasted these rates to those in 28 comparable schools that had not changed their policies. Students (and their parents) were not able to choose whether to attend a school using zero-tolerance policies, so they could not select to change to (or out of) the schools with the new policies. Hoffman found that the percentage of black secondary students recommended for expulsion more than doubled after the policy change, while the corresponding percentages for white and Hispanic secondary students increased by only a small amount (Exhibit 6.6).

However, it is important to recognize that simply comparing outcome measures in two groups that offer different programs is not in itself a quasi-experiment. If individuals can choose which group to join, partly on the basis of what programs they offer, then the groups will differ in preference for the treatment as well as in having had the treatment. When such selection bias is possible, the design is nonexperimental rather than quasi-experimental. This design is termed an **ex post facto control group design**. More generally, the validity of this design depends on the adequacy of matching of the comparison group with the treatment group (Cook & Wong 2008:151).

The common feature of **before-and-after designs** is the absence of a comparison group. Because all cases are exposed to the experimental treatment, the basis for comparison is provided by comparing the pretreatment with the posttreatment measures. These designs are thus useful for studies of interventions that are experienced by virtually every case in some population, including total-coverage programs such as Social Security or studies of the effect of a new management strategy in a single organization. The simplest type of before-and-after design has just one pretest and one posttest, but **repeated-measures panel designs** are stronger because the inclusion of several pretest and posttest observations allows study of the process by which an intervention or treatment has an impact over time.

Photo 6.2 Once an experiment is moved out of the lab and into the field, it's more difficult to control the conditions. What are some environmental factors that could influence an experiment?

©iStockphoto.com/SensorSpot

▶ **VIDEO LINK**
Correlation vs. Causality

Quasi-experimental design: A research design in which there is a comparison group that is very similar to the experimental group in critical ways, but subjects are not randomly assigned to the comparison and experimental groups.

Nonequivalent control group design: A quasi-experimental research design in which experimental and comparison groups are designated before the treatment occurs but are not created by random assignment.

Ex post facto control group design: A nonexperimental design in which comparison groups are selected after the treatment, program, or other variation in the independent variable has occurred, but when the participants were able to choose the group in which they participated. Often confused with a quasi-experimental design.

Before-and-after design: A quasi-experimental design consisting of a before-after comparison involving the same variables but no comparison group.

Repeated-measures panel design: A quasi-experimental design consisting of several pretest and posttest observations of the same group.

■ EXHIBIT 6.6 **Effect of New Zero-Tolerance Discipline Policies on Black, White, and Hispanic Students**

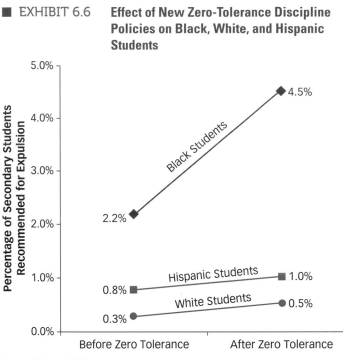

Source: Hoffman (2014).

■ EXHIBIT 6.7 **Divorce Rates in Oklahoma Before and After the 1995 Oklahoma City Bombing**

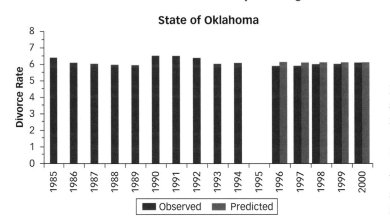

Source: Nakonezny, Paul A., Rebecca Reddick, and Joseph Lee Rodgers. 2004. "Did Divorces Decline After the Oklahoma City Bombing?" *Journal of Marriage and Family*, 66:90–100. Copyright © 2004, John Wiley & Sons. Reprinted with permission.

ENCYCLOPEDIA LINK 📖
Internal Validity

Time series design: A quasi-experimental design consisting of many observations of the same group before and after an intervention.

Threat to internal validity: A feature of a research design that creates the potential for an influence on the dependent variable (outcome scores) other than the experimental treatment or stimulus.

In a **time series design**, the trend in the dependent variable until the date of the intervention or event whose effect is being studied is compared with the trend in the dependent variable after the intervention. A substantial disparity between the preintervention trend and the postintervention trend is evidence that the intervention or event had an impact (Rossi & Freeman 1989:260–261, 358–363).

Time series designs are particularly useful for studies of the impact of unique events of new laws or new social programs that affect everyone and that are readily assessed by some ongoing measurement. For example, Paul A. Nakonezny, Rebecca Reddick, and Joseph Lee Rodgers (2004) used a time series design to identify the impact of the Oklahoma City terrorist bombing in April 1995 on the divorce rate in Oklahoma. They hypothesized that people would be more likely to feel a need for support in the aftermath of such a terrifying event and thus be less likely to divorce. Nakonezny et al. (2004) first calculated the average rate of change in divorce rates in Oklahoma's 77 counties in the 10 years before the bombing and then projected these rates forward to the 5 years after the bombing. As they hypothesized, they found that the actual divorce rate in the first years after the bombing was lower than the prebombing trend would have predicted, but this effect diminished to nothing by the year 2000 (Exhibit 6.7).

❖ Validity in Experimental Designs

Issues of both causal (internal) validity and generalizability must be considered when evaluating experimental designs.

Causal (Internal) Validity

You now know that randomization is used to create a comparison group that is identical to the experimental group at the start of the experiment—with a certain margin of error that occurs with a process of random assignment. For this reason, a true experiment—a design with random assignment—is prone to fewer sources of internal invalidity than is a quasi-experiment or a non-experiment.

The most common **threat to internal validity** in a comparison of outcomes between two or more groups is selection bias. **Selection bias** occurs when participants can select the group they enter based on the treatment they expect to receive. True experimental design is used largely to eliminate this source of bias. In a true experiment, randomization equates the groups' characteristics and so selection bias is not possible—although the groups may differ initially due to chance. When subjects are not assigned randomly to treatment and comparison groups, the threat of selection bias can be great.

Having a comparison group even without randomization allows much greater confidence that it was the treatment in the experimental group that caused the observed change, but there are more bases for concern. What is referred to as a **history effect** can occur when external events during the experiment (things that happen outside the experiment such as a community disaster or public shooting) change subjects' outcome scores. An effect of *testing* can occur when taking the pretest itself influences posttest scores. An effect of *maturation* can occur during a lengthy treatment period if participants age, gain experience, or grow in knowledge as part of a natural maturational process. However, because they affect the control group as well as the experimental group, these additional threats to internal invalidity are not a concern with a true randomized experimental design.

The particulars of the experimental conditions must also be assessed in order to assess the likelihood that other problems during the experiment itself led to changes in the outcome scores of the participants that could have been confused with the effect of treatment. A problem of **differential attrition** occurs when the groups become different after the experiment begins because more participants drop out of one of the groups than out of the other(s) for various reasons. When the comparison group in an experiment is in some way affected by, or affects, the treatment group, there is a problem with **contamination**. This problem basically arises from the failure to control adequately the conditions of the experiment. If the experiment is conducted in

Photo 6.3 How might an event, such as the shooting death of Michael Brown by a police officer in Ferguson, Missouri, have represented a source of causal invalidity to an ongoing research study regarding public opinion of the police?

a laboratory, if members of the experimental group and the comparison group have no contact while the study is in progress, and if the treatment is relatively brief, contamination is not likely to be a problem.

Change among experimental subjects may also result from the positive expectations of the experimental staff who are delivering the treatment rather than from the treatment itself. **Expectancies of experimental staff** may alter the experimental results if staff—even well-trained staff—convey their enthusiasm for an experimental program to the subjects in subtle ways. This is a special concern in evaluation research, when program staff and researchers may be biased in favor of the program for which they work and eager to believe that their work is helping clients. Such positive staff expectations thus create a self-fulfilling prophecy.

In experiments on the effects of treatments such as medical drugs, **double-blind procedures** can be used so that staff delivering the treatments do not know which subjects are getting the treatment and which are receiving a **placebo**—something that looks like the treatment but has no effect. In some circumstances, though, members of the treatment group may change relative to the dependent variable because their participation in the study makes them feel special. This is termed a **Hawthorne effect**, after a famous productivity experiment at the Hawthorne electric plant outside Chicago. As the story has been told, the workers worked harder no matter what physical or economic conditions the researchers changed to influence productivity; the motivation for the harder work simply seemed to be that the workers felt special because of being in the experiment (Whyte 1955:34).

Generalizability

The need for generalizable findings can be thought of as the Achilles heel of true experimental design. The design components that are essential for a true experiment and that minimize the threats to causal validity make it more difficult to achieve sample generalizability (being able to apply the findings to some clearly defined larger population) and cross-population generalizability (generalizing across subgroups and to other populations and settings). Nonetheless, no one conducts experiments just to find out how freshman psychology students react to confrontation (or some other experimental "treatment") at their university. Because experimental researchers are seeking to learn about general processes, we have to worry about the generalizability of their results.

Sample Generalizability

Subjects who can be recruited for a laboratory experiment, randomly assigned to a group, and kept under carefully controlled conditions for the study's duration are unlikely to be a representative sample of any large population of interest to social scientists. Can they be expected to react to the experimental treatment in the same way as members of the larger population? The generalizability

---

Selection bias: A source of internal (causal) invalidity that occurs when characteristics of experimental and comparison group subjects differ in any way that influences the outcome.

History effect: A source of causal invalidity that occurs when events external to the study influence posttest scores; also called an *effect of external events*.

Differential attrition (mortality): A problem that occurs in experiments when comparison groups become different because subjects are more likely to drop out of one of the groups for various reasons.

Contamination: A source of causal invalidity that occurs when either the experimental or the comparison group is aware of the other group and is influenced in the posttest as a result.

Expectancies of experimental staff: A source of treatment misidentification in experiments and quasi-experiments that occurs when change among experimental subjects results from the positive expectancies of the staff who are delivering the treatment rather than from the treatment itself; also called a *self-fulfilling prophecy*.

Double-blind procedure: An experimental method in which neither the subjects nor the staff delivering experimental treatments know which subjects are getting the treatment and which are receiving a placebo.

Placebo: A fake "treatment" given to a comparison group to make sure their experience is no different from that of the experimental group except for the actual treatment.

of the treatment and of the setting for the experiment also must be considered (Cook & Campbell 1979:73–74). The more artificial the experimental arrangements, the greater the problem will be (Campbell & Stanley 1966:20–21).

In some field experiments, participants can even be selected randomly from the population of interest, and, thus, the researchers can achieve results generalizable to that population. For example, some studies of the effects of income supports on the work behavior of poor persons have randomly sampled persons within particular states before randomly assigning them to experimental and comparison groups. When random selection is not feasible, the researchers may be able to increase generalizability by selecting several different experimental sites that offer marked contrasts on key variables (Cook & Campbell 1979:76–77).

Factorial Surveys

Factorial surveys (or survey experiments) embed the features of true experiments into a survey design to maximize generalizability. In the most common type of factorial survey, respondents are asked for their likely responses to one or more vignettes about hypothetical situations. The content of these vignettes is varied randomly among survey respondents to create "treatment groups" that differ in particular variables reflected in the vignettes.

Greet Van Hoye and Filip Lievens (2003) used a factorial survey design to test the effect of job applicants' sexual orientation on ratings of their hirability by professionals who make personnel decisions. Van Hoye and Lievens first identified 252 selection professionals—people involved daily in personnel selection and recruitment—from consulting firms and company human resource departments. The researchers mailed to each of these professionals a packet with four items: (1) a letter inviting their participation in the study, (2) a job posting that described a company and a particular job opening in that company, (3) a candidate profile that described someone ostensibly seeking that job, and (4) a response form on which the selection professionals could rate the candidate's hirability.

Hawthorne effect: A type of contamination in research designs that occurs when members of the treatment group change relative to the dependent variable because their participation in the study makes them feel special.

Factorial survey (or survey experiments): A survey in which randomly selected subsets of respondents are asked different questions, or are asked to respond to different vignettes, to determine the causal effect of the variables represented by these differences.

The experimental component of the survey was created by varying the candidate profiles. Van Hoye and Lievens created nine different candidate profiles. Each profile used very similar language to describe a candidate's gender (they were all male), age, nationality, family situation, education, professional experience, and personality. However, the family situations were varied to distinguish candidates as heterosexual, homosexual, or "possibly homosexual"—single and older than 30. Other characteristics were varied to distinguish candidates who were "poor," "moderate," and "excellent" matches to the job opening.

The combination of three different descriptions of family situation and three different levels of candidate quality resulted in nine different candidate profiles. Each selection professional was randomly assigned to receive one of these nine candidate profiles. As a result, there was no relationship between who a particular selection professional was and the type of candidate profile he or she received.

The results of the study appear in Exhibit 6.8. The average hirability ratings did not differ between candidates who were gay, heterosexual, or single, but hirability increased in direct relation to candidate quality. Van Hoye and Lievens (2003:26) concluded that selection professionals based their evaluations of written candidate profiles on candidate quality, not on their sexual orientation—at least in Flanders, Belgium.

Because Van Hoye and Lievens surveyed real selection professionals at their actual workplaces, we can feel more comfortable with the generalizability of their results than if they had just recruited college students for an experiment in a laboratory. However, there is still an important limitation to the generalizability of factorial surveys such as this: A factorial survey research design indicates only what respondents say they would do in situations that have been described to them. If the selection professionals had to make a recommendation for hiring to an actual employer, we cannot be sure that they would act in the same way. So factorial surveys do not completely resolve the problems caused by the difficulty of conducting true experiments with representative samples. Nonetheless, by combining some of the advantages of experimental and survey designs, factorial surveys can provide stronger tests of causal hypotheses than can other surveys and more generalizable findings than can experiments.

JOURNAL LINK
Validity of Cross-
Cultural Social Studies

■ EXHIBIT 6.8 **Average Hirability Ratings in Relation to Candidate Quality and Sexual Orientation**

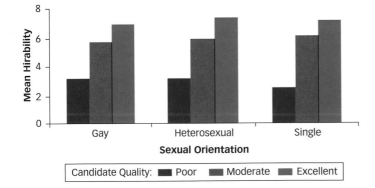

Candidate Quality: ■ Poor ■ Moderate ■ Excellent

Source: Van Hoye, Greet, and Filip Lievens. 2003. "The Effects of Sexual Orientation on Hirability Ratings: An Experimental Study." *Journal of Business and Psychology* 18:15–30. Copyright © 2003, Human Science Press, Inc. Reprinted with permission from Springer.

Factorial surveys and some other types of experiments can now also be conducted through the web, greatly expanding the potential pool of participants although also limiting it to those engaged in the Internet and interested in participating in online experiments. Some web experiments are offered on sites that recruit participants to an ongoing panel in which they then sign up for experiments that involve some type of interaction in which conditions are randomly varied. Amazon maintains a Mechanical Turk site on which individuals can participate in a survey experiment or other type of survey and receive monetary compensation (such as $1.25 for a 30-minute experiment). Ron Kohavi and colleagues (Kohavi et al. 2007; Kohavi et al. 2009) provide background information on web experiments and links to relevant sites. A factorial experiment on the web is a relatively easy way to test out questions and causal propositions that can be presented in a web format.

Photo 6.4 There is often a gap between how people report they would behave and how they actually behave in the real world. For example, if asked earlier, this person might have responded that he would order a salad for lunch, because that seemed like the socially desirable response, but when it came time to order, he selected the cheeseburger.

External Validity

Researchers are often interested in determining whether treatment effects identified in an experiment hold true for subgroups of subjects and across different populations, times, or settings. Of course, determining that a relationship between the treatment and the outcome variable holds true for certain subgroups does not establish that the relationship also holds true for these subgroups in the larger population, but it suggests that the relationship might be externally valid.

We have already seen examples of how the existence of treatment effects in particular subgroups of experimental subjects can help us predict the cross-population generalizability of the findings. For example, Sherman and Berk's (1984) research (see Chapter 2) found that arrest did not deter subsequent domestic violence for unemployed individuals; arrest also failed to deter subsequent violence in communities with high levels of unemployment. Richard H. Price, Michelle Van Ryn, and Amiram D. Vinokur (1992) found that intensive job search assistance reduced depression among individuals who were at high risk for depression because of other psychosocial characteristics; however, the intervention did not influence the rate of depression among individuals at low risk for depression. This is an important interaction effect that limits the generalizability of the treatment, even if Price et al.'s sample was representative of the population of unemployed persons.

Interaction of Testing and Treatment

A variant on the problem of external validity occurs when the experimental treatment has an effect only when particular conditions created by the experiment occur. One such problem occurs when the treatment has an effect only if subjects have had the pretest. The pretest sensitizes the subjects to some issue, so that when they are exposed to the treatment, they react in a way that differs from how they would have reacted had they not taken the pretest. In other words, testing and treatment interact to produce the outcome. For example, answering questions in a pretest about racial prejudice may sensitize subjects so that when exposed to the experimental treatment—seeing a film about prejudice—their attitudes are different from what they would have been otherwise. In this situation, the treatment truly had an effect, but it would not have had an effect had it been provided without the sensitizing pretest.

The possibility that a treatment has an effect only if it is preceded by a pretest can be evaluated with the **Solomon four-group design** (Exhibit 6.9). The Solomon four-group design is a true experimental design that combines a randomized comparative change design (the pretest–posttest control group design) with the randomized comparative posttest design (posttest-only control group design). This design allows comparison of the effect of the independent variable on groups that had a pretest (O_1) with its effect on groups that have not had a pretest. Whenever there is reason to think that taking the pretest may itself influence how participants react to the treatment, the Solomon four-group design should be considered. If the pretest had such an effect, the difference in outcome scores between the experimental and comparison groups will be different for subjects who took the pretest (the pretest–posttest design) compared with those who did not (the posttest-only design).

As you can see, no single procedure establishes the external validity of experimental results. Ultimately, we must base our evaluation of external validity on the success of replications taking place at different times and places and using different forms of the treatment.

There is always an implicit trade-off in experimental design between maximizing causal validity and generalizability. The more the assignment to treatments is randomized and all experimental conditions are controlled, the less likely it is that the research subjects and setting will be representative

> **Solomon four-group design:** A type of experimental design that combines a randomized pretest–posttest control group design with a randomized posttest-only design, resulting in two experimental groups and two comparison groups.

■ EXHIBIT 6.9   **Solomon Four-Group Design: Testing the Interaction of Pretesting and Treatment**

Experimental Group	R	O_1	X	O_2
Comparison Group	R	O_1		O_2
Experimental Group	R		X	O_2
Comparison Group	R			O_2

Key:

R = Random assignment

O = Observation (pretest or posttest)

X = Experimental treatment

of the larger population. College students are easy to recruit and assign to artificial but controlled manipulations, but both practical and ethical concerns preclude this approach with many groups and with respect to many treatments. Even so, although we need to be skeptical about the generalizability of the results of a single experimental test of a hypothesis, the body of findings accumulated from many experimental tests with different people in different settings can provide a solid basis for generalization (Campbell & Russo 1999:143).

❖ Ethical Issues in Experimental Research

Social science experiments can raise difficult ethical issues. Nonetheless, experimental research continues because of the need for good evidence about cause-effect relationships to inform social theory as well as social policy. The particular strength of randomized experiments for answering causal questions means that they can potentially prevent confusion in social theory and avoid wasting time and resources on ineffective social programs (Mark & Gamble 2009:203).

Two ethical issues are of special importance in experimental research designs. Deception is an essential part of many experimental designs, despite the ethical standard of subjects' informed consent. As a result, contentious debate continues about the interpretation of this standard. In addition, experimental evaluations of social programs pose ethical dilemmas because they require researchers to withhold possibly beneficial treatment from some subjects just on the basis of chance (Boruch 1997).

Deception

Deception is used in social experiments to create more "realistic" treatments, often within the confines of a laboratory. You learned in Chapter 3 about Milgram's (1964) use of deception in his classic study of obedience to authority. Volunteers were recruited for what they were told was a study of the learning process, not a study of "obedience to authority." The experimenter told the volunteers that they were administering electric shocks to a "student" in the next room, when there were actually neither students nor shocks. Most subjects seemed to believe the deception.

JOURNAL LINK
Ethics in Fieldwork

Whether or not you believe that you could be deceived in this way, you are not likely to be invited to participate in an experiment such as Milgram's. Current federal regulations preclude deception in research that might trigger such upsetting feelings.

David Willer and Henry A. Walker (2007) pay particular attention to debriefing after deception in their book about experimental research. They argue that every experiment involving deception should be followed immediately for each participant with dehoaxing, in which the deception is explained, and then by desensitization, in which participants' questions are answered to their satisfaction and those participants who still feel aggrieved are directed to a university authority to file a complaint or to a counselor for help with their feelings. This is sound advice.

RESEARCHER INTERVIEW LINK
Experimental Design

Selective Distribution of Benefits

Field experiments conducted to evaluate social programs also can involve issues of informed consent (Hunt 1985:275–276). One ethical issue that is somewhat unique to field experiments is the **selective distribution of benefits**: How much are subjects harmed by the way treatments are distributed in the experiment? For example, Sherman and Berk's (1984) experiment, and its successors, required police to make arrests in domestic violence cases largely on the basis of a random process. When arrests were not made, did the subjects' abused spouses suffer? Price et al. (1992) randomly assigned unemployed individuals who had volunteered for job search help to an intensive program. Were the unemployed volunteers assigned to the comparison group at a big disadvantage?

Selective distribution of benefits: An ethical issue about how much researchers can influence the benefits that subjects receive as part of the treatment being studied in a field experiment.

Random distribution of benefits is justified when the researchers do not know whether some treatment is beneficial or not—and, of course, it is the goal of the experiment to find out (Mark & Gamble 2009:205). Chance is as reasonable a basis for distributing the treatment as any other. Also, if insufficient resources are available to fully fund a benefit for every eligible person, distribution of the benefit on the basis of chance to equally needy persons is ethically defensible (Boruch 1997:66–67).

❖ Conclusions

True experiments play two critical roles in social research. First, they are the best research design for testing causal hypotheses. Even when conditions preclude use of a true experimental design, many research designs can be improved by adding some experimental components. Second, true experiments also provide a comparison point for evaluating the ability of other research designs to achieve causally valid results.

Despite obvious strengths, true experiments are used infrequently to study many research problems that interest social scientists. There are three basic reasons: (1) The experiments required to test many important hypotheses require far more resources than are often available; (2) many research problems of interest to social scientists are not amenable to experimental designs, for reasons ranging from ethical considerations to the limited possibilities for randomly assigning people to different conditions in the real world; and (3) the requirements of experimental design usually preclude large-scale studies and so limit generalizability to a degree that is unacceptable to many social scientists. Quasi-experiments can be an excellent design alternative.

Even laboratory experiments are inadvisable when they do not test the real hypothesis of interest, but test instead a limited version amenable to laboratory manipulation. The intersecting complexity of societies, social relationships, and social beings—of people and the groups to which they belong—is so great that it often defies reduction to the simplicity of a laboratory or restriction to the requirements of experimental designs. Yet the virtues of experimental designs mean that they should always be considered when explanatory research is planned.

Key Terms

REVIEW
key terms with
eFlashcards.
⑤ SAGE edge™

Association   83
Before-and-after design   87
Causal effect   81
Ceteris paribus   81
Contamination   89
Context   82
Differential attrition (mortality)   89
Double-blind procedure   89
Ex post facto control group design   87
Expectancies of experimental staff   89
Extraneous variable   85
Factorial survey (or survey experiments)   90
Field experiment   86

Hawthorne effect   89
History effect   88
Mechanism   82
Mediator   82
Moderator   82
Nonequivalent control group design   87
Nonspuriousness   84
Placebo   89
Posttest   84
Pretest   84
Quasi-experimental design   87
Random assignment   81
Randomization   84

Randomized comparative change design   84
Randomized comparative posttest design   84
Repeated-measures panel design   87
Selection bias   88
Selective distribution of benefits   92
Solomon four-group design   91
Spurious relationship   85
Threat to internal validity   88
Time order   83
Time series design   88
True experiment   81

Highlights

- Three criteria are generally viewed as necessary for identifying a causal relationship: (1) association between the variables, (2) proper time order, and (3) nonspuriousness of the association. In addition, the basis for concluding that a causal relationship exists is strengthened by the identification of a causal mechanism and the context for the relationship.

- Association between two variables is in itself insufficient evidence of a causal relationship. This point is commonly made with the expression "correlation does not prove causation."

- Experiments use random assignment to make comparison groups as similar as possible at the outset of an experiment to reduce the risk of spurious effects resulting from extraneous variables.

- Ethical and practical constraints often preclude the use of experimental designs.

- The independent variable in an experiment is represented by a treatment or other intervention. Some subjects receive one type of treatment; others may receive a different treatment or no treatment. In true experiments, subjects are assigned randomly to comparison groups.

- Experimental research designs have three essential components: (1) use of at least two groups of subjects for comparison, (2) measurement of the change that occurs as a result of the experimental treatment, and (3) use of random assignment. In addition, experiments may include identification of a causal mechanism and control over experimental conditions.

- Random assignment of subjects to experimental and comparison groups eliminates systematic bias in group assignment. The odds of a difference between the experimental and comparison groups because of chance can be calculated.

- Both random assignment and random sampling rely on a chance selection procedure, but their purposes differ. Random assignment involves placing predesignated subjects into two or more groups on the basis of chance; random sampling involves selecting subjects out of a larger population on the basis of chance.

- Quasi-experiments include features that maximize the comparability of the control and experimental groups and make it unlikely that self-selection determines group membership.

- Causal conclusions derived from experiments can be invalid due to threats to internal validity including selection bias, effects of external events, and cross-group contamination. In true experiments, randomization, use of a comparison group, and pretests and posttests should eliminate most of these sources of internal invalidity. However, when conditions are not carefully controlled during an experiment, differential attrition, contamination, and expectancies of experimental staff can create differences between groups and threaten the validity of causal conclusions.

- Quasi-experiments may provide more generalizable results than do true experiments, but they are more prone to some problems of internal invalidity because of their lack of random assignment (although some quasi-experimental designs allow the researcher to rule out almost as many potential sources of internal invalidity as does a true experiment). The generalizability of experimental results declines if the study conditions are artificial and the experimental subjects are unique. Field experiments are likely to produce more generalizable results than experiments conducted in the laboratory.

- The external validity of causal conclusions is determined by the extent to which they apply to different types of individuals and settings. When causal conclusions do not apply to all the subgroups in a study, they are not generalizable to corresponding subgroups in the population—and so they are not externally valid with respect to those subgroups. Causal conclusions can also be considered externally invalid when they occur only under the experimental conditions.

- Subject deception is common in laboratory experiments and poses unique ethical issues. Researchers must weigh the potential harm to subjects and debrief subjects who have been deceived. In field experiments, a common ethical problem is selective distribution of benefits. Random assignment may be the fairest way of allocating treatment when treatment openings are insufficient for all eligible individuals and when the efficacy of the treatment is unknown.

Chapter Questions

1. What research questions are suitable for research with an experimental design? Propose hypotheses about influences on student performance, on neighborhood violence, on worker satisfaction, and on international migration. Propose an experimental design to test each hypothesis. What characteristics of a research question make it unsuited to an experimental study? Now propose a quasi-experimental design to test each hypothesis. What does this experience suggest to you about the potential value of quasi-experimental designs?

2. Randomization is a key feature of experimental designs that are often used to investigate the efficacy of new treatments for serious and often incurable, terminal diseases. What ethical issues do these techniques raise in studies of experimental treatments for such diseases? Would you make an ethical argument that there are situations when it is *more* ethical to use random assignment than usual procedures for deciding whether patients receive a new treatment?

TEST your understanding of chapter content. Take the practice quiz. $SAGE edge

Practice Exercises

1. Go to the Crime Stoppers USA (CSUSA) website at www.crimestoppersusa.com. Check out "Profile" and then "FAQ." How is CSUSA "fighting crime"? What does CSUSA's approach assume about the cause of crime? Do you think CSUSA's approach to fighting crime is based on valid conclusions about causality? Explain.

2. Try out the process of randomization. Go to the website www.randomizer.org and click on "Randomize Now" at the bottom of the page. Type numbers into the randomizer for an experiment with 2 groups and 20 individuals per group. Repeat the process for an experiment with 4 groups and 10 individuals per

group. Plot the numbers corresponding to each individual in each group. Does the distribution of numbers within each group truly seem to be random?

3. Try out a Web experiment! Go to a site that will connect you to current Web experiments, such as http://www.exp-platform .com/Pages/hippo_long.aspx, and enroll in one. How much does the experience seem like what you might experience in an on-campus experiment? What do you think about the potential generalizability of results from such Web experiments?

STUDENT STUDY SITE

$SAGE edge™

The Student Study Site, available at **edge.sagepub.com/schuttusw**, includes useful study materials including eFlashcards, videos, audio resources, journal articles, and encyclopedia articles, many of which are represented by the media links throughout the text.

Survey Research

Learning Objectives

- Identify the reasons for the popularity of survey research
- Discuss the advantages and disadvantages of including "don't know" and neutral responses among response choices and of using open-ended questions
- List the different methods for improving survey questions
- Outline a cover letter for a survey that contains each of the required elements
- List the strengths and weaknesses of each type of survey design, giving particular attention to response rates
- Explain the rationale for a mixed-mode survey
- Discuss the key ethical issues in survey research

Survey research involves the collection of information from a sample of individuals through their responses to questions. Because it can be used to collect data from a broad spectrum of individuals and social settings, **survey research** has become a multibillion-dollar industry that shapes what we read in the newspapers, see on television, and find in government reports (Tourangeau 2004:776).

This chapter reviews the major features of surveys, guidelines for writing survey questions, alternatives in survey design, and related ethical issues. The methods presented here help to reduce error in responding to survey questions and increase the likelihood of completing surveys. The section on alternative survey designs provides current data about the implications of different designs for response rates and population coverage.

Survey research: Research in which information is obtained from a sample of individuals through their responses to questions about themselves or others.

Omnibus survey: A survey that covers a range of topics of interest to different social scientists.

❖ Survey Research in the Social Sciences

Survey research owes its popularity to three advantages: versatility, efficiency, and generalizability. First, survey methods are *versatile*. Politicians campaigning for election use surveys, as do businesses marketing a product, governments assessing community needs, agencies monitoring program effectiveness, and social scientists investigating almost any research question you can think of. Surveys also are popular because they are *efficient*: Data can be collected from many people at relatively low cost and, depending on the survey design, relatively quickly. In addition, survey research is well suited to maximizing *generalizability* of findings, since survey methods lend themselves to sampling from large populations.

An **omnibus survey** shows just how versatile, efficient, and generalizable a survey can be. An omnibus survey covers a range of topics of interest to different social scientists, in contrast to the typical survey that is directed at a specific research question. Many omnibus surveys are funded by the government and are conducted regularly to provide data about such vital social issues as population mobility, income levels, and the unemployment rate, while others are sponsored by professional survey organizations to provide data for analysis in academic research and reporting in popular media. One of the most successful omnibus surveys, the General Social Survey, is administered by the National Opinion Research Center at the University of Chicago biennially to a probability sample of at least 3,000 Americans (4,820 in 2012), with a wide range of questions and topic areas chosen by a board of overseers.

❖ Errors in Survey Research

It might be said that surveys are *too* easy to conduct. Organizations and individuals often decide that a survey will help solve some important problem because it seems so easy to write up some questions and distribute them. But without careful attention to sampling, measurement, and overall survey design, the effort is likely to be a flop. Such flops are too common for comfort, so the responsible survey researcher must take the time to design surveys properly and to convince sponsoring organizations that this time is worth the effort (Turner & Martin 1984:68).

For a survey to succeed, it must minimize four types of error (Groves 1989:vi, 10–12): (1) poor measurement, (2) nonresponse, (3) inadequate coverage of the population, and (4) sampling error.

Poor Measurement

Measurement error was a key concern in Chapter 4, but there is much more to be learned about how to minimize these errors of observation in the survey process. The theory of satisficing can help us understand the problem. It takes effort to answer survey questions carefully: Respondents have to figure out what each question means, then recall relevant information, and finally decide which answer is most appropriate. Survey respondents satisfice when they reduce the effort required to answer a question by interpreting questions superficially and giving what they think will be an acceptable answer (Krosnick 1999:547–548). Presenting clear and interesting questions in a well-organized questionnaire will help reduce measurement error by encouraging respondents to answer questions carefully and to take seriously the request to participate in the survey. Tailoring questions to the specific population surveyed is also important. In particular, persons with less education are more likely to satisfice in response to more challenging questions (Holbrook, Green, & Krosnick 2003; Narayan & Krosnick 1996).

©iStockphoto.com/hocus-focus

Photo 7.1 What would it take to get you to respond to a request to participate in a survey?

Nonresponse

Nonresponse is a major and growing problem in survey research in the United States and Western Europe. We can understand the problem in terms of benefits and costs of participation: The perceived benefits of survey participation have declined with decreasing levels of civic engagement and with longer work hours (Groves, Singer, & Corning 2000; Krosnick 1999:539–540), but relative costs have increased with the widespread use of telemarketing—a turnoff to answering the phone—and the ease of screening out calls from unknown parties with answering machines and caller ID. In addition, since some cell phone plans require users to pay for usage time, the ratio of costs to benefits worsens for surveys attempting to reach persons using cell phones (Nagourney 2002).

Inadequate Coverage of the Population

A poor sampling frame can invalidate the results of an otherwise well-designed survey. The importance of a good sampling frame was considered in Chapter 5; this chapter reviews special coverage problems related to each of the particular survey methods.

Sampling Error

The process of random sampling can result in differences between the characteristics of the sample members and the population simply on the basis of chance. You learned about this problem in Chapter 5 and so this chapter does not discuss it further.

❖ Writing Survey Questions

Questions are the centerpiece of survey research. Because the way questions are worded can have a great effect on the way they are answered, selecting good questions is the single most important concern for survey researchers. All hope for achieving measurement validity is lost unless the questions in a survey are clear and convey the intended meaning to respondents.

Adherence to a few basic principles will go a long way toward ensuring clear and meaningful questions. Each of these principles summarizes a great deal of research, although none of them should be viewed as an inflexible mandate (Alwin & Krosnick 1991). Every survey has its own unique requirements and constraints; sometimes violating one principle is necessary to achieve others.

Avoid Confusing Phrasing

There are several ways to avoid confusing phrasing. In most cases, a simple direct approach to asking a question minimizes confusion. Use shorter rather than longer words and sentences; for example, "brave" rather than "courageous," "job concerns" rather than "work-related employment issues" (Dillman 2000:52). Breaking up complex issues into simple parts also reduces confusion. Try to keep the total number of words to 20 or fewer and the number of commas to 3 or fewer (Peterson 2000:50). However, questions shouldn't be abbreviated in a way that results in confusion: To ask, "In what city or town do you live?" is to focus attention clearly on a specific geographic unit, a specific time, and a specific person (you); the simple format,

Residential location: _____,

does not do this.

Sometimes, when sensitive issues or past behaviors are the topic, longer questions can provide cues that make the respondent feel comfortable or aid memory (Peterson 2000:51).

A sure way to muddy the meaning of a question is to use **double negatives**: "Do you *disagree* that there should *not* be a tax increase?" Respondents have a hard time figuring out which response matches their sentiments. So-called **double-barreled questions** are also guaranteed to produce uninterpretable results because they actually ask two questions but allow only one answer. For example, during the Watergate scandal, Gallup poll results indicated that when the question was "Do you think President Nixon should be impeached and compelled to leave the presidency, or not?" only about a third of Americans supported impeaching President Richard M. Nixon. But when the Gallup organization changed the question to ask respondents if they "think there is enough evidence of possible wrongdoing in the case of President Nixon to bring him to trial before the Senate, or not," over half answered yes. Apparently, the first, double-barreled version of the question confused support for impeaching Nixon—putting him on trial before the Senate—with concluding that he was guilty before he had had a chance to defend himself (Kagay & Elder 1992:E5).

It is also important to ask a question only of the respondents who may have the desired information. Respondents will be annoyed if asked questions that do not apply to them (Schaeffer & Presser 2003:74). Use **filter questions** to create **skip patterns** and indicate that pattern clearly with an arrow or other mark in the questionnaire. For example, in Exhibit 7.1, respondents who answer *no* to the

> **Double negative:** A question or statement that contains two negatives, which can muddy the meaning of the question.
>
> **Double-barreled question:** A single survey question that actually asks two questions but allows only one answer.
>
> **Filter question:** A survey question used to identify a subset of respondents who then are asked other questions.
>
> **Skip pattern:** The unique combination of questions created in a survey by filter questions and contingent questions.

■ EXHIBIT 7.1   **Filter Questions and Skip Patterns**

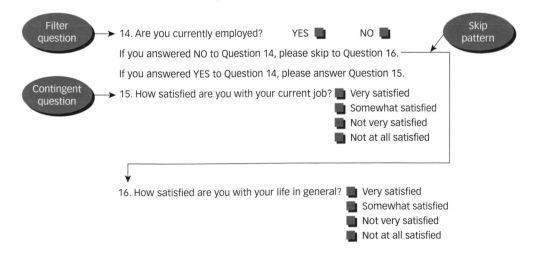

filter question about current employment (14) are told to skip to question 16, but those who answer *yes* are asked the **contingent question** (15) about their job satisfaction before they go on to question 16.

Minimize the Risk of Bias

Specific words in survey questions should not trigger biases, unless that is the researcher's conscious intent. Biased or loaded words and phrases tend to produce misleading answers. For example, a 1974 survey near the end of the Vietnam War found that only 18% of respondents supported sending U.S. troops "if a situation like Vietnam were to develop in another part of the world." But when the question was reworded to mention sending troops to "stop a communist takeover"—"communist takeover" being a loaded phrase—favorable responses rose to 33% (Schuman & Presser 1981:285).

Responses can also be biased when response alternatives do not reflect the full range of possible sentiment on an issue. If the response alternatives for a question fall on a continuum from positive to negative, the number of positive and negative categories should be balanced so that one end of the continuum doesn't seem more attractive than the other (Dillman 2000:57–58). If you ask respondents, "How satisfied are you with the intramural sports program here?" and include "completely satisfied" as the most positive possible response, then "completely dissatisfied" should be included as the most negative possible response. This is called a *bipolar* scale.

Maximize the Utility of Response Categories

Response choices should be considered carefully because they help respondents to understand what the question is about and what types of responses are viewed as relevant (Clark & Schober 1994). Single questions with fixed response choices must provide one and only one possible response for everyone who is asked the question—that is, the response choices must be exhaustive and mutually exclusive. Ranges of ages, incomes, years of schooling, and so forth should not overlap and should provide a response option for all respondents.

Sometimes, problems with response choices can be corrected by adding questions. For example, if you ask, "How many years of schooling have you completed?" someone who dropped out of high school but completed the requirements for a General Equivalency Diploma (GED) might not be sure how to respond. By asking a second question, "What is the highest degree you have received?" you can provide the correct alternative for those with a GED as well as for those who graduated from high school.

One common approach for measures of attitude intensity is to present a statement and then ask respondents to indicate their degree of agreement or disagreement. A **Likert item** phrases an attitude in terms of one end of a continuum, so that the responses ranging from "strongly agree" to "strongly disagree" cover the full range of possible agreement. A range of five response choices seems to result in the highest-quality agree/disagree responses (Revilla, Saris, & Krosnick 2013).

Other words used to distinguish points on an ordinal scale of attitude intensity are shown in the response choices in Exhibit 7.2. One important decision is whether to use unipolar distinctions, such as "not at all" to "extremely," or bipolar distinctions, such as "very comfortable" to "very uncomfortable." The advantages of using **bipolar response options** are discussed in the next section. Responses are more reliable when these categories are labeled (**labeled unipolar response options**) rather than identified only by numbers (**unlabeled unipolar response options**) (Krosnick 1999:544; Schaeffer & Presser 2003:78). A special consideration for ratings is whether to include a neutral middle response option.

Avoid Making Either Disagreement or Agreement Disagreeable

People often tend to "agree" with a statement just to avoid seeming disagreeable. This is termed *agreement bias*, **social desirability bias**, or an *acquiescence effect*. Numerous studies of agreement bias suggest that about 10% of respondents will "agree" just to be agreeable, without regard to what they really think (Krosnick 1999:553).

As a general rule, you should present both sides of attitude scales in the question itself (Dillman 2000:61–62): "In general, do you believe that *individuals* or *social conditions* are more to blame for crime and lawlessness in the United States?" The response choices themselves should be phrased to make each one seem as socially approved, as "agreeable," as the others (Schaeffer & Presser 2003:80–81).

When an illegal or socially disapproved behavior or attitude is the focus, you have to be concerned that some respondents will be reluctant to agree that they have ever done or thought such a thing. In this situation, the goal is to write a question and response choices that make agreement seem more acceptable. For example, Dillman (2000:75) suggests that you ask, "Have you ever taken anything from a store without paying for it?" rather than "Have

---

Contingent question: A question that is asked of only a subset of survey respondents.

Likert item: A statement followed by response choices ranging from "strongly agree" to "strongly disagree."

Bipolar response options: Response choices to a survey question that include a middle category and parallel responses with positive and negative valence (can be labeled or unlabeled).

Labeled unipolar response options: Response choices for a survey question that use words to identify categories ranging from low to high (or vice versa).

Unlabeled unipolar response options: Response choices for a survey question that use numbers to identify categories ranging from low to high (or vice versa).

Social desirability bias: The tendency to "agree" with a statement just to avoid seeming disagreeable.

■ EXHIBIT 7.2   **Labeled Unipolar, Unlabeled Unipolar, and Bipolar Response Options**

Original

>Q72a< How free do you feel to disagree with the person who
supervises your work? Are you . . .

<1> Not at all free,

<2> Somewhat free,

<3> Largely but not completely free, or

<4> Completely free to disagree?

<7> NO CODED RESPONSE APPLICABLE

<8> DON'T KNOW

<9> REFUSED

Labeled unipolar version

How comfortable do you feel disagreeing with the person who supervises your work? (Please circle one number to indicate your
response.)

1. Extremely comfortable

2. Very comfortable

3. Quite comfortable

4. Somewhat comfortable

5. Not at all comfortable

Labeled bipolar version

Do you feel comfortable or uncomfortable disagreeing with the person who supervises your work? (Please circle one number to indicate
your response.)

1. Very comfortable

2. Mostly comfortable

3. Slightly comfortable

4. Feel neither comfortable nor uncomfortable

5. Slightly uncomfortable

6. Mostly uncomfortable

7. Very uncomfortable

Unlabeled unipolar version

Please circle a number from 1 to 10 to indicate how comfortable you feel disagreeing with the person who supervises your work. 1
means "not at all comfortable" and 10 means "extremely comfortable."

How comfortable do you feel disagreeing with the person who supervises your work?

Not at all									Extremely
1	2	3	4	5	6	7	8	9	10

Source: Based on Mirowsky and Ross (2001:9).

you ever shoplifted something from a store?" Asking respondents about a variety of behaviors or attitudes that range from
socially acceptable to socially unacceptable will also soften the impact on them of agreeing with those statements that are
socially unacceptable.

Minimize Fence-Sitting and Floating

Fence-sitters, people who see themselves as being neutral, may skew the results if you force them
to choose between opposites. In most cases, about 10% to 20% of such respondents—those who do
not have strong feelings on an issue—will choose an explicit middle, neutral alternative (Schuman &
Presser 1981:161–178). Having an explicit neutral response option identifies fence-sitters and tends to
increase measurement reliability (Schaeffer & Presser 2003:78).

Fence-sitters: Survey respondents who
see themselves as being neutral on an issue
and choose a middle (neutral) response that
is offered.

■ EXHIBIT 7.3   **The Effect of Floaters on Public Opinion Polls**

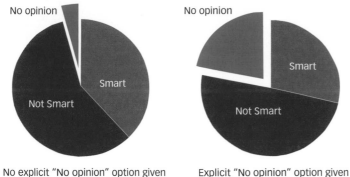

Response to "Are government leaders smart"?

No explicit "No opinion" option given   Explicit "No opinion" option given

Source: Based on Schuman and Presser (1981: 121).

Even more people can be termed **floaters**: respondents who choose a substantive answer when they really don't know or have no opinion. A third of the public will provide an opinion on a proposed law that they know nothing about if they are asked for their opinion in a closed-ended survey question that does not include "don't know" as an explicit response choice. However, 90% of these persons will select the "don't know" response if they are explicitly given that option. On average, offering an explicit response option increases the "don't know" or "no opinion" responses by about one fifth (Exhibit 7.3) (Schuman & Presser 1981:113–160).

Unfortunately, the inclusion of an explicit "don't know" response choice leads some people who do have a preference to take the easy way out—to choose "don't know." This is particularly true in surveys of less-educated populations (Schuman & Presser 1981:113–146). As a result, survey experts recommend use of **forced-choice questions** without a "don't know" or "no opinion" option (Krosnick 1999:558; Schaeffer & Presser 2003:80).

Combine Questions in Indexes

Writing single questions that yield usable answers is always a challenge. Simple though they may seem, single questions are prone to error because of **idiosyncratic variation**, which occurs when individuals' responses vary because of their reactions to particular words or ideas in the question.

In some cases, the effect of idiosyncratic variation can be dramatic. For example, when people were asked in a survey whether they would "forbid" public speeches against democracy, 54% agreed. When the question was whether they would "not allow" public speeches against democracy, 75% agreed (Turner & Martin 1984:chap. 5). Respondents are less likely to respond affirmatively to the question, "Did you see a broken headlight?" than they are to the question, "Did you see *the* broken headlight?" (Turner & Martin 1984:chap. 9).

The best option is often to develop multiple questions about a concept and then to average the responses to those questions in a composite measure termed an *index* or *scale,* as mentioned in Chapter 4. The index can be considered a more complete measure of the concept than can any one of the component questions.

Creating an index is not just a matter of writing a few questions that seem to focus on a concept. Questions that seem to you to measure a common concept might seem to respondents to concern several different issues. The only way to know that a given set of questions does, in fact, form an index is to administer the questions to people like those you plan to study. If a common concept is being measured, people's responses to the different questions should display some consistency. In other words, responses to the different questions should be correlated. You learned in Chapter 4 that this is the measurement criterion of interitem reliability.

Because of the popularity of survey research, indexes already have been developed to measure many concepts, and some of these indexes have proved to be reliable in a range of studies. Use of a preexisting index both simplifies the work involved in designing a study and facilitates comparison of findings to those obtained in other studies.

The questions in Exhibit 7.4 are from a set of questions that make up an index to measure perceived risk of drug use in the 2013 Massachusetts Youth Health Survey designed by the University of Massachusetts Boston's Center for Survey Research and funded by the Massachusetts departments of Public Health and Elementary and Secondary Education. Note that each question concerns perceived risk of using a particular drug. People may have idiosyncratic reasons for feeling a particular drug is risky without feeling that way about illicit drug use in general; for example, a youth who is prescribed Ritalin may feel there is no risk in taking it, even though the question specifies that it is about risk when it has not been prescribed. But by combining the answers to questions about several drugs, the index score reduces the impact of this idiosyncratic variation. An index score is usually calculated as the arithmetic average or sum of responses to the component questions, so that every question that goes into the index counts equally.

Floaters: Survey respondents who provide an opinion on a topic in response to a closed-ended question that does not include a "don't know" option, but who will choose "don't know" if it is available.

Forced-choice questions: Closed-ended survey questions that do not include "don't know" as an explicit response choice.

Idiosyncratic variation: Variation in responses to questions that is caused by individuals' reactions to particular words or ideas in the question instead of by variation in relation to the concept that the question is intended to measure.

❖ Designing Questionnaires

Survey questions are answered as part of a **questionnaire** (or **interview schedule**, as it's often called in interview-based studies), not in isolation from other questions. The context created by the

■ EXHIBIT 7.4   **Example of an Index: Selected Questions From the Perceived Drug Risk Index**

64.   How much do you think people risk harming themselves if they <u>occasionally</u> use:

	No Risk	Slight Risk	Moderate Risk	Great Risk
a. Marijuana	☐	☐	☐	☐
b. Narcotics (such as Methadone, Opium, Morphine, Codeine, Oxycontin, Percodan, Demerol, Percocet, Ultram and Vicodin from prescriptions that aren't your own)	☐	☐	☐	☐
c. Ritalin or Adderall (from prescriptions that aren't your own)	☐	☐	☐	☐
d. Tranquilizers (such as Valium, Xanax, Klonopin, Ativan and Librium from prescriptions that aren't your own)	☐	☐	☐	☐
e. Inhalants (sniffing glue, breathing the contents of aerosol spray cans, or inhaling any paints or sprays to get high)	☐	☐	☐	☐
f. Heroin	☐	☐	☐	☐

Source: Center for Survey Research. 2013. *Massachusetts Youth Health Survey.* Boston, MA: Center for Survey Research, University of Massachusetts Boston. Reproduced by permission.

questionnaire has a major impact on how individual questions are interpreted and whether they are even answered. As a result, survey researchers must give very careful attention to the design of the questionnaire as well as to the individual questions that it includes.

The key principles that should guide the design of any questionnaire are described in the sections that follow.

Build on Existing Instruments

If another researcher already has designed a set of questions to measure a key concept, and evidence from previous surveys indicates that this measure is reliable and valid, then, by all means, use that instrument. Resources such as Delbert Miller and Neil J. Salkind's (2002) *Handbook of Research Design and Social Measurement*, 6th ed. (SAGE Publications, of course!), can give you many ideas about existing instruments; your literature review at the start of a research project should be an even better source.

Refine and Test Questions

Adhering to the preceding question-writing guidelines will go a long way toward producing a useful questionnaire. However, simply asking what appear to you to be clear questions does not ensure that people have a consistent understanding of what you are asking. You need some external feedback—the more of it the better. One important form of feedback results from simply discussing the questionnaire content with others. Persons who should be consulted include expert researchers, key figures in the locale or organization to be surveyed (e.g., elected representatives, company presidents, and community leaders), and some individuals from the population to be sampled.

Another increasingly popular form of feedback comes from guided discussions among potential respondents, called *focus groups*, to check for consistent understanding of terms and to identify the range of events or experiences about which people will be asked to report. By listening to and observing the focus group discussions, researchers can validate their assumptions about what level of vocabulary is appropriate and what people are going to be reporting (Fowler 1995). (See Chapter 8 for more about this technique.)

Professional survey researchers also use a technique for improving questions called the **cognitive interview** (Dillman 2000:66–67; Fowler 1995). The researcher asks a test question, then probes with follow-up questions about how the respondent understood one or more words in the question, how confusing it was, and so forth (Schaeffer & Presser 2003:82). This method can identify many problems with proposed questions (Presser et al. 2004:109–130).

In a traditional **survey pretest**, interviewers administer the questionnaire to a small set of respondents (perhaps 15–25) who are similar to those who will be sampled in the planned survey. After the interviews are completed, the interviewers discuss the experience with the researcher and, through this discussion, try to identify questions that caused problems.

▶ ◀ **RESEARCHER INTERVIEW LINK**
Writing Survey Questions

Questionnaire: The survey instrument containing the questions in a self-administered survey.

Interview schedule: The survey instrument containing the questions asked by the interviewer in an in-person or phone survey.

Cognitive interview: A technique for evaluating questions in which researchers ask people test questions and then probe with follow-up questions to learn how they understood the question and what their answers mean.

Survey pretest: A method of evaluating survey questions and procedures by testing them on a small sample of individuals like those to be included in the actual survey and then reviewing responses to the questions and reactions to the survey procedures.

Add Interpretive Questions

A survey researcher can also include **interpretive questions** in the survey itself to help the researcher understand what the respondent meant by his or her responses to particular questions. An example from a study of people with motor vehicle driving violations illustrates the importance of interpretive questions:

When asked whether their emotional state affected their driving at all, respondents would reply that their emotions had very little effect on their habits. Then, when asked to describe the circumstances surrounding their last traffic violation, respondents typically replied, "I was mad at my girlfriend," or "I had a quarrel with my wife," or "We had a family quarrel," or "I was angry with my boss." (Labaw 1980:71)

Maintain Consistent Focus

A survey (with the exception of an omnibus survey) should be guided by a clear conception of the research problem under investigation. Until the research objective is formulated clearly, survey design cannot begin. Throughout the process of questionnaire design, this objective should be the primary basis for making decisions about what to include and exclude and what to emphasize or treat in a cursory fashion. Moreover, the questionnaire should be viewed as an integrated whole, with a logical division of topics in sections, and each section and every question serving a clear purpose related to the study's objective.

Interpretive questions: Questions included in a questionnaire or interview schedule to help explain answers to other important questions.

Order the Questions

The order in which questions are presented will influence how respondents react to the questionnaire as a whole and how they may answer some questions (Schwarz 2010:47). The first question deserves special attention because it signals to the respondent what the survey is about, whether it will be interesting, and how easy it will be to complete. For these reasons, the first question should connect to the primary purpose of the survey, be interesting and easy, and apply to everyone in the sample (Dillman 2000:92–94). Mirowsky and Ross (1999) began a phone survey about health and related issues with a question about the respondent's overall health:

CAREERS
and Research

GRANT A. BACON, RESEARCH ASSOCIATE

Grant Bacon graduated with degrees in history education and political science from the University of Delaware in 1998. He initially aspired to give back to the community, especially by helping young people as a teacher. Although he started out teaching, he found his calling by working more directly with at-risk youth as a court liaison and eventually program coordinator for a juvenile drug court/drug diversion program. It was during this time working with these drug court programs that Bacon first came into contact with a university-based center for drug and health studies, which was beginning an evaluation of one such program. In 2001, he accepted an offer to become a research associate with the center, where he has continued to work on many different research projects. Two of his most recent projects include research that investigated factors affecting the reentry experiences for inmates returning to the community and another evaluating a parole program.

Bacon is happy to be working in the field on both qualitative and quantitative research. He loves working with people who share a vision of using research findings to help people in a number of ways, and to give back to the world in a meaningful manner. Every day is different. Some days, Bacon and other associates are on the road visiting criminal justice or health-related facilities or are trying to locate specific individual respondents or study participants. Other days, he may be gathering data, doing intensive interviewing, or administering surveys. He thinks the most rewarding part of his job is helping people who have been part of the criminal justice system and giving them a voice.

Bacon's advice to students interested in research is the following:

If doing research interests you, ask your teachers how you can gain experience through internships or volunteering. Be sure to network with as many people from as many human services organizations as possible. Being familiar with systems like geographic information systems (GIS) and data analysis is becoming important as well. If you did not receive this training during your undergraduate studies, many community colleges offer introductory and advanced classes in GIS, Microsoft Excel, Access, and SPSS. Take them!

RESEARCH

In the News

MOVIE "FACTS" . . . OR FANTASY?

Movies based on true stories often gain a wide audience. *Selma. American Sniper. The Theory of Everything. The Imitation Game.* But how accurate are they?

Research by psychologists has led to the conclusion that viewers tend to reshape their understanding of historical events based on films, even when they know the films are not accurate. The key problem is that viewers do not remember the source for their memories.

For Further Thought

1. What are the implications of this problem for survey researchers? For qualitative researchers who conduct intensive interviews?

2. Do mixed methods provide a way to lessen the distortions this problem introduces into our understanding of the social world?

News source: Zacks, Jeffrey. 2015. "Why Movie 'Facts' Prevail." *New York Times,* March 8. Retrieved from www.nytimes.com/2015/02/15/opinion/sunday/why-movie-facts-prevail.html?_r=0

First, I'd like to ask you about your health. In general, would you say your health is . . .

1. <1> Very good,
2. <2> Good,
3. <3> Satisfactory,
4. <4> Poor, or
5. <5> Very poor?

The individual questions should be sorted into broad thematic categories, which then become separate sections in the questionnaire. Throughout the design process, the grouping of questions in sections and the ordering of questions within sections should be adjusted to maximize the questionnaire's overall coherence. One or more filter or screening questions may also appear early in the survey to identify respondents for whom the questionnaire is not intended or perhaps to determine which sections of a multipart questionnaire a respondent is to skip (Peterson 2000:106–107).

Question order can lead to **context effects** when one or more questions influence how subsequent questions are interpreted (Schober 1999:88–89). For example, when a sample of the general public was asked, "Do you think it should be possible for a pregnant woman to obtain a legal abortion if she is married and does not want any more children?" Fifty-eight percent said yes. However, when this question was preceded by a less permissive question that asked whether the respondent would allow abortion of a defective fetus, only 40% said yes. Asking the question about a defective fetus altered respondents' frame of reference, perhaps by making abortion simply to avoid having more children seem frivolous by comparison (Turner & Martin 1984:135). Context effects have also been identified in the measurement of general happiness, in what is termed a **part-whole question effect** (Peterson 2000:113). Married people tend to report that they are happier "in general" if the general happiness question is preceded by a question about their happiness with their marriage (Schuman & Presser 1981:23–77).

Some questions may be presented in a *matrix* format. **Matrix questions** are a series of questions that concern a common theme and that have the same response choices. The questions are written so that a common initial phrase applies to each one (see question 36 in Exhibit 7.5). This format shortens the questionnaire by reducing the number of words that must be used for each question. It also emphasizes the common theme among the questions and so invites answering each question in relation to other questions in the matrix. It is very important to provide an explicit instruction to "Check one response on each line" in a matrix question, because some respondents will think that they have completed the entire matrix after they have responded to just a few of the specific questions.

Make the Questionnaire Attractive

An attractive questionnaire is more likely to be completed and less likely to confuse either the respondent or, in an interview, the interviewer. An attractive questionnaire also should increase the likelihood that different respondents interpret the same questions in the same way.

Context effects: Effects that occur when one or more survey questions influence how subsequent questions are interpreted.

Part-whole question effects: Effects that occur when responses to a general or summary survey question about a topic are influenced by responses to an earlier, more specific question about that topic.

Matrix questions: A series of questions that concern a common theme and that have the same response choices.

Printing a multipage questionnaire in booklet form usually results in the most attractive and simple-to-use questionnaire (Dillman 2000:80–86). An attractive questionnaire does not look cramped; plenty of white space—more between questions than within question components—makes the questionnaire appear easy to complete. Response choices are distinguished clearly and consistently, perhaps by formatting them with light print (while questions are formatted with dark print) and keeping them in the middle of the pages. Response choices are listed vertically rather than horizontally across the page. The proper path through the questionnaire for each respondent is identified with arrows or other graphics and judicious use of spacing and other aspects of layout as well as with clear instructions (Dillman & Christian 2005:43–48).

■ EXHIBIT 7.5   **A Page From the Youth Health Survey**

34. Did you do any of the following in the past 12 months?

	YES	No
a. Bully or push someone around	☐	☐
b. Use texting, e-mail, or social networking sites to make fun of, threaten, or insult another kid, or try to hurt another kid's reputation	☐	☐
c. Threaten to hurt, physically hurt, or try to hurt a date or someone you were going out with	☐	☐

QUESTIONS ABOUT YOUR FAMILY AND PEERS

35. How would your parent(s) react if they found out you regularly drank alcohol. Would they be:

☐ Extremely Upset
☐ Fairly Upset
☐ A Little Upset
☐ Not Upset at All

36. Do you think most people your age do the following?

	YES	No
a. Drink alcohol	☐	☐
b. Smoke cigarettes	☐	☐
c. Smoke marijuana	☐	☐
d. Use other illegal drugs	☐	☐
e. Bully, threaten, or push around other kids	☐	☐

QUESTIONS ABOUT ALCOHOL

The next 7 questions ask about drinking alcohol. This includes drinking beer, wine, wine coolers, hard lemonade, hard cider, and liquor such as rum, gin, vodka, or whiskey. For these questions, drinking alcohol does not include drinking a few sips of wine for religious purposes.

37. During your life, on how many days have you had at least one drink of alcohol?

☐ 0 days
☐ 1 or 2 days
☐ 3 to 9 days
☐ 10 to 19 days
☐ 20 to 39 days
☐ 40 to 99 days
☐ 100 or more days

38. How old were you when you had your first drink of alcohol other than a few sips?

☐ I have never had a drink of alcohol other than a few sips →
   If you have NEVER had alcohol, go to Question 42
☐ 8 years old or younger
☐ 9 or 10 years old
☐ 11 or 12 years old
☐ 13 or 14 years old
☐ 15 or 16 years old
☐ 17 years old or older

39. During the past 30 days, on how many days did you have at least one drink of alcohol?

☐ 0 days
☐ 1 or 2 days
☐ 3 to 5 days
☐ 6 to 9 days
☐ 10 to 19 days
☐ 20 to 29 days
☐ All 30 days

40. During the past 30 days, on how many days did you have 5 or more drinks of alcohol in a row, that is, within a couple of hours?

☐ 0 days
☐ 1 day
☐ 2 days
☐ 3 to 5 days
☐ 6 to 9 days
☐ 10 to 19 days
☐ 20 or more days

Source: Center for Survey Research. 2013. *Massachusetts Youth Health Survey.* Boston, MA: Center for Survey Research, University of Massachusetts Boston. Reproduced by permission.

Exhibit 7.5 is a page from the Youth Health Survey (Center for Survey Research 2013) that illustrates the questionnaire features reviewed here: It has an attractive, open layout, with clear instructions, logical sections, vertical arrangement, and a distinctive format for response choices.

Consider Translation

Should the survey be translated into one or more languages? In the 21st century, no survey plan in the United States or many other countries can be considered complete until this issue has been considered. In the United States in 2011, 13% of the population was foreign born (Motel & Patten, 2013:Table 1) and more than half of the foreign-born adults said that they did not speak English very well (Pew Hispanic Center 2013:Table 21).

❖ Organizing Surveys

There are five basic social science survey designs: (1) mailed, self-administered (2) group-administered, (3) phone, (4) in-person, and (5) web. Survey researchers can also combine elements of two or more of these basic designs in mixed-mode surveys.

Differences by Survey Type

Different designs are most appropriate for different purposes and populations and their relative merits have been affected in different ways by the development of modern information technology. Exhibit 7.6 summarizes the typical features of the five basic survey designs.

Manner of Administration

The five survey designs differ in the manner in which the questionnaire is administered (Exhibit 7.6). Mailed, group, and web surveys are completed by the respondents themselves. During phone and in-person interviews, the researcher or a staff person asks the questions and records the respondent's answers. However, new mixed-mode surveys break down these distinctions. For example, in audio computer-assisted self-interviewing (or audio-CASI), the interviewer gives the respondent a laptop and a headset (Tourangeau 2004:790–791). The respondent reads the questions on the computer screen, hears the questions in the headset, and responds by choosing answers on the computer screen.

Questionnaire Structure

Survey designs also differ in the extent to which the researcher structures the content and order of questions in advance. Most mailed, group, phone, and web surveys are highly structured, fixing in advance the content and order of questions and response choices. Some of these types of surveys, particularly mailed surveys, may include some open-ended questions (respondents write in their answers rather than checking off one of several response choices). In-person interviews are often highly structured, but they may include many questions without fixed response choices. Moreover, some interviews may proceed from an interview guide rather than a fixed set of questions. In these relatively unstructured interviews, the interviewer covers the same topics with respondents but varies questions according to the respondent's answers to previous questions. Extra questions are added as needed to clarify or explore answers to the most important questions (Tourangeau 2004:789).

Setting

Most surveys are conducted in settings where only one respondent completes the survey at a time; most mail and web surveys and phone interviews are intended for completion by only one respondent. The same is usually true of in-person interviews, although

■ EXHIBIT 7.6   **Typical Features of the Five Survey Designs**

Design	Manner of Administration	Setting	Questionnaire Structure	Cost
Mailed survey	Self	Individual	Mostly structured	Low to moderate
Group survey	Self	Group	Mostly structured	Very low
Phone survey	Professional	Individual	Structured	Moderate
In-person interview	Professional	Individual	Structured or unstructured	High
Web survey	Self	Individual	Mostly structured	Low

sometimes researchers interview several family members at once. A variant of the standard survey is a questionnaire distributed simultaneously to a group of respondents, such as students in a classroom, who complete the survey while the researcher (or assistant) waits.

Cost

As mentioned earlier, in-person interviews are the most expensive type of survey. Phone interviews are much less expensive, although costs are rising because of the need to make more calls to reach potential respondents. Surveying by mail is cheaper yet. Web surveys can be the least expensive method because there are no interviewer costs, no mailing costs, and, for many designs, almost no costs for data entry. However, extra staff time and programming expertise are required to prepare web surveys (Tourangeau, Conrad, & Couper 2012).

Mailed, Self-Administered Surveys

A **mailed survey** is conducted by mailing a questionnaire to respondents, who then administer the survey themselves. The central concern in a mailed survey is maximizing the response rate. Even an attractive questionnaire full of clear questions will probably be returned by no more than 30% of a sample unless extra steps are taken to increase the rate of response. Fortunately, the conscientious use of a systematic survey design method can be expected to lead to an acceptable 70% or higher rate of response to most mailed surveys (Dillman 2000).

Sending follow-up mailings to nonrespondents is the single most important requirement for obtaining an adequate response rate to a mailed survey. The follow-up mailings explicitly encourage initial nonrespondents to return a completed questionnaire; implicitly, they convey the importance of the effort. Dillman (2000:155–158, 177–188) has demonstrated the effectiveness of a standard procedure for the mailing process:

- A few days before the questionnaire is to be mailed, send a brief letter to respondents that notifies them of the importance of the survey they are to receive.

- Send the questionnaire with a well-designed, personalized cover letter (see the following description); a self-addressed, stamped return envelope; and, if possible, a token monetary reward (Dillman 2000:174–175).

- Send a reminder postcard, thanking respondents and reminding nonrespondents, to all sample members 2 weeks after the initial mailing. The postcard should be friendly in tone and must include a phone number for those people who may not have received the questionnaire.

- Send a replacement questionnaire with a new cover letter only to nonrespondents, 2 to 4 weeks after the initial questionnaire mailing. This cover letter should be a bit shorter and more insistent than the original cover letter. It should note that the recipient has not yet responded, and it should stress the survey's importance. Of course, a self-addressed, stamped return envelope must be included.

- The final step is taken 6 to 8 weeks after the initial survey mailing. This step uses a different mode of delivery (either priority or special delivery) or a different survey design—usually an attempt to administer the questionnaire over the phone. These special procedures emphasize the importance of the survey and encourage people to respond.

The **cover letter** for a mailed questionnaire is critical to the success of a mailed survey. This statement to respondents sets the tone for the questionnaire. A carefully prepared cover letter should increase the response rate and result in more honest and complete answers to the survey questions; a poorly prepared cover letter can have the reverse effects.

The cover letter or introductory statement must be

- *Credible:* The letter should establish that the research is being conducted by a researcher or organization that the respondent is likely to accept as a credible, unbiased authority. Government sponsors, well-known universities, and recognized research organizations tend to elicit high rates of response. Publishing firms, students (sorry!), and private associations elicit the lowest response rates.

- *Personalized:* The cover letter should include a personalized salutation (using the respondent's name, e.g., not just "Dear Student"), close with the researcher's signature (blue ballpoint pen is best because that makes it clear that the researcher has signed personally), and refer to the respondent in the second person ("Your participation . . .").

Mailed survey: A survey involving a mailed questionnaire to be completed by the respondent.

Cover letter: The letter sent with a mailed questionnaire that explains the survey's purpose and auspices and encourages the respondent to participate.

- *Interesting:* The statement should interest the respondent in the contents of the questionnaire. Try to put yourself in the respondent's shoes before composing the statement, and then test your appeal with a variety of potential respondents.

- *Responsible:* Reassure the respondent that the information you obtain will be treated confidentially, and include a phone number to call if the respondent has any questions or would like a summary of the final report. Point out that the respondent's participation is completely voluntary (Dillman 1978:165–172).

Exhibit 7.7 is an example of a cover letter for a questionnaire.

Even in the era of the Internet, mailed questionnaires can still be a good survey option and may be simpler to organize than a mixed-mode survey needed to overcome problems with phone survey response (see below). Among new mothers previously surveyed by phone in a health survey in Britain, for example, 87% returned a mailed questionnaire, compared to 71% who completed a computer-assisted telephone interview (described later in this chapter) (Rocheleau et al. 2012).

Group-Administered Surveys

A **group-administered survey** is completed by individual respondents assembled in a group. The response rate is not usually a major concern in surveys that are distributed and collected in a group setting because most group members will participate. With the exception of students, employees, members of the armed forces, and some institutionalized populations, most populations cannot be surveyed in this way.

A standard introductory statement should be read to the group that expresses appreciation for their participation, describes the steps of the survey, and emphasizes (in classroom surveys) that the survey is not the same as a test. A cover letter like the one used in mailed surveys also should be distributed with the questionnaires. To emphasize confidentiality, respondents should be given an envelope in which to seal their questionnaires after they are completed. The introductory statement for the Youth Health Survey administered in Massachusetts high schools and middle schools appears in Exhibit 7.8.

Phone Surveys

In a **phone survey**, interviewers question respondents over the phone and then record respondents' answers. Procedures can be standardized more effectively, quality control maintained, and processing speed maximized when phone interviewers use **computer-assisted telephone interviews (CATI)**.

Computerized **interactive voice response (IVR)** survey technology allows even greater control over interviewer-respondent interaction. In an IVR survey, respondents receive automated calls and answer questions by pressing numbers on their touch-tone phones or

> **SAGE JOURNAL ARTICLE**
> Phone Surveys _

> **Group-administered survey:** A survey completed by individual respondents who are assembled in a group.

> **Phone survey:** A survey in which interviewers question respondents over the phone and then record their answers.

> **Computer-assisted telephone interview (CATI):** A phone interview in which a questionnaire is programmed into a computer, along with relevant skip patterns, and only valid entries are allowed; incorporates the tasks of interviewing, data entry, and checking data for invalid responses.

■ EXHIBIT 7.7 **Sample Questionnaire Cover Letter**

University of Massachusetts Boston
Department of Sociology

Jane Doe
AIDS Coordinator
Shattuck Shelter

Dear Jane:

AIDS is an increasing concern for homeless people and for homeless shelters. The enclosed survey is about the AIDS problem and related issues confronting shelters. It is sponsored by the Life Lines AIDS Prevention Project for the Homeless—a program of the Massachusetts Department of Public Health.

As an AIDS coordinator/shelter director, you have learned about homeless persons' problems and about implementing programs in response to those problems. The Life Lines Project needs to learn from your experience. Your answers to the questions in the enclosed survey will improve substantially the base of information for improving AIDS prevention programs.

Questions in the survey focus on AIDS prevention activities and on related aspects of shelter operations. It should take about 30 minutes to answer all the questions.

Every shelter AIDS coordinator (or shelter director) in Massachusetts is being asked to complete the survey. And every response is vital to the success of the survey: The survey report must represent the full range of experiences.

You may be assured of complete confidentiality. No one outside of the university will have access to the questionnaire you return. (The ID number on the survey will permit us to check with nonrespondents to see if they need a replacement survey or other information.) All information presented in the report to Life Lines will be in aggregate form, with the exception of a list of the number, gender, and family status of each shelter's guests.

Please mail the survey back to us by Monday, June 4, and feel free to call if you have any questions.

Thank you for your assistance.

Yours sincerely,

Russell K. Schutt

Russell K. Schutt, PhD
Project Director

Stephanie Howard

Stephanie Howard
Project Assistant

■ EXHIBIT 7.8 **Introductory Statement in Youth Health Survey**

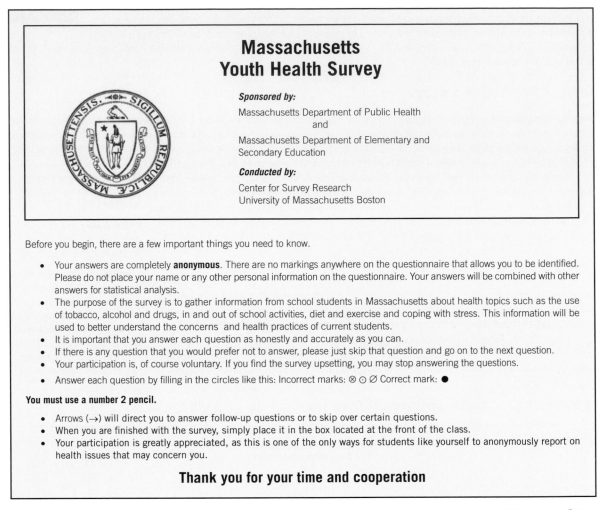

Massachusetts
Youth Health Survey

Sponsored by:

Massachusetts Department of Public Health
and
Massachusetts Department of Elementary and
Secondary Education

Conducted by:

Center for Survey Research
University of Massachusetts Boston

Before you begin, there are a few important things you need to know.

- Your answers are completely **anonymous**. There are no markings anywhere on the questionnaire that allows you to be identified. Please do not place your name or any other personal information on the questionnaire. Your answers will be combined with other answers for statistical analysis.
- The purpose of the survey is to gather information from school students in Massachusetts about health topics such as the use of tobacco, alcohol and drugs, in and out of school activities, diet and exercise and coping with stress. This information will be used to better understand the concerns and health practices of current students.
- It is important that you answer each question as honestly and accurately as you can.
- If there is any question that you would prefer not to answer, please just skip that question and go on to the next question.
- Your participation is, of course voluntary. If you find the survey upsetting, you may stop answering the questions.
- Answer each question by filling in the circles like this: Incorrect marks: ⊗ ⊙ ⊘ Correct mark: ●

You must use a number 2 pencil.

- Arrows (→) will direct you to answer follow-up questions or to skip over certain questions.
- When you are finished with the survey, simply place it in the box located at the front of the class.
- Your participation is greatly appreciated, as this is one of the only ways for students like yourself to anonymously report on health issues that may concern you.

Thank you for your time and cooperation

Source: Center for Survey Research. 2013. Massachusetts Youth Health Survey. Boston, MA: Center for Survey Research, University of Massachusetts Boston. Reproduced by permission.

by speaking numbers that are interpreted by computerized voice recognition software. These surveys can also record verbal responses to open-ended questions for later transcription. IVR surveys have been used successfully with short questionnaires and when respondents are highly motivated to participate (Dillman 2000:402–411).

Reaching Sample Units

Procedures and problems differ if the survey involves only landline phones or mobile phones, or both. Most surveys to landline phones use random digit dialing at some point in the sampling process (Lavrakas 1987). A machine calls random phone numbers within the designated exchanges, whether or not the numbers are published. When the machine reaches an inappropriate household (such as a business in a survey directed to the general population), the phone number is simply replaced with another. Most survey research organizations use special methods to identify sets of phone numbers that are likely to include working numbers and so make the random digit dialing more efficient (Tourangeau 2004:778–780). In surveys of landline phones, interviewers must ask a series of questions after the phone is answered to ensure that they are speaking to the appropriate member of the household; this is generally not done when calling cell phones.

Cell phones must be included in phone surveys to obtain adequate coverage of most populations. Nine in ten American adults owned a cell phone in early 2014, and 43% lived in households with a cell phone but no landline phone (Pew Research Center 2014). The Pew Research Center, one of the largest survey organizations, now makes two thirds of its calls in typical national phone surveys to cell phone numbers, and the University of Michigan's Survey of Consumers is calling only cell phones (Keeter 2015). Current federal law in the United States prohibits random digit dialing of cell phone numbers, so the use of more dialing by interviewers is increasing the cost of phone interviews, but

RESEARCH/SOCIAL IMPACT LINK
Sample Units

Interactive voice response (IVR):
A survey in which respondents receive automated calls and answer questions by pressing numbers on their touch-tone phones or speaking numbers that are interpreted by computerized voice recognition software.

■ EXHIBIT 7.9   **Percentage of Adults Living in Wireless-Only Households by Age and Poverty**

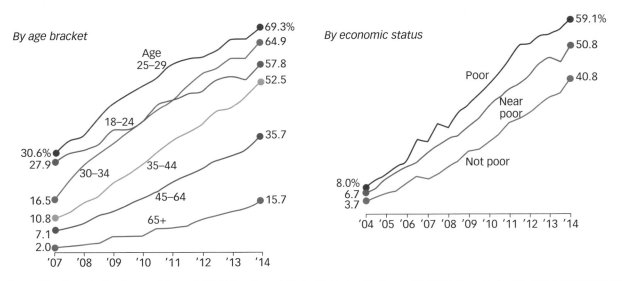

Source: "Pew Research will call more cellphones in 2015," Pew Research Center, Washington, DC (January, 2015) http://www.pewresearch.org/fact-tank/2015/01/07/pew-research-will-call-more-cellphones-in-2015/.

leaving out cell-phone-only households can result in severe survey biases. Cell-phone-only households are much more likely to be poor than those that also have landlines, and their members tend to be younger. By contrast, only 16% of adults 65 or older live in a cell-phone-only household (Exhibit 7.9) (Desilver 2013; Keeter 2015). Cell phone usage is even more prevalent in some other countries, both developed and developing (Mahfoud et al. 2014:41).

Maximizing Response to Phone Surveys

Because people often are not home, multiple callbacks will be needed in landline phone surveys for many sample members. Those with more money and education are more likely to be away from home; such persons are more likely to vote Republican, so the results of political polls can be seriously biased if few callback attempts are made (Kohut 1988). In addition, because of the large fraction of the U.S. population that is foreign born (13% in 2012), surveys must be translated into multiple foreign languages if the results are to be generalized to the entire population (Grieco et al. 2012:2; Tourangeau 2004:783).

Since the late 1970s, the average response rate in phone surveys has plummeted from a historic high of about 75% (Tourangeau 2004:781–783) (see Exhibit 7.10). The Pew Research Center reports a decline in the response rate based on all those sampled, from 36% in 1997 to only 9% in 2012. The number of callbacks needed to reach respondents by phone has increased greatly, with increasing numbers of single-person households, dual-earner families, and out-of-home activities. High-effort phone surveys can improve the response somewhat, but even with extended callbacks, monetary incentives for respondents, letters to nonrespondents, and the use of the most skilled interviewers, the response rate improves only from about 1 in 10 to 1 in 5 (Kohut et al. 2012).

> **In-person survey:** A survey in which an interviewer questions respondents face-to-face and records their answers.

In-Person Surveys

What is unique to the **in-person survey**, compared with the other survey designs, is the face-to-face social interaction between interviewer and respondent. If money is no object, in-person interviewing is often the best survey design because people are more likely to agree to be interviewed and are less likely to end prematurely.

But researchers must be alert to some special hazards resulting from the presence of an interviewer. Respondents should experience the interview process as a personalized interaction with an interviewer who is very interested in the respondent's experiences and opinions. At the same time, however, every respondent should have the same interview experience—asked the same questions in the same way by the

Photo 7.2   How might the presence of an interviewer affect the results of an in-person survey?

■ EXHIBIT 7.10 **Response Rates to High-Effort and Standard-Effort Phone Surveys, 1997–2012**

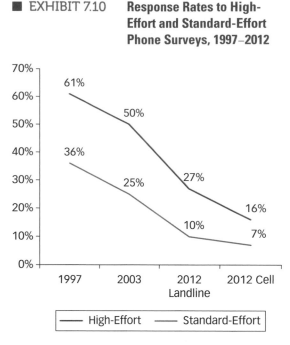

Source: Kohut et al. (2012:8).

....

Computer-assisted personal interview (CAPI): A personal interview in which a laptop computer is used to display interview questions and to process responses that the interviewer types in, as well as to check that these responses fall within allowed ranges.

Web survey: A survey accessed and responded to on the World Wide Web.

same type of person, who reacts similarly to the answers (de Leeuw 2008:318). Careful training and supervision are essential because small differences in intonation or emphasis on particular words can alter how respondents interpret questions (Groves 1989:404–406; Peterson 2000:24).

As with phone interviewing, computers can be used to increase control of the in-person interview. In a **computer-assisted personal interview (CAPI)** project, interviewers carry a laptop computer that is programmed to display the interview questions and to process the responses that the interviewer types in, as well as to check that these responses fall within allowed ranges (Tourangeau 2004:790–791). Interviewers seem to like CAPI, and the data obtained are comparable in quality to data obtained in a noncomputerized interview (Shepherd et al. 1996).

Exhibit 7.11 displays the breakdown of nonrespondents to the 1990 General Social Survey (GSS). Of the total original sample of 2,165, only 86% (1,857) were determined to be valid selections of dwelling units with potentially eligible respondents. Among these potentially eligible respondents, the response rate was 74%. The GSS is a well-designed survey using carefully trained and supervised interviewers, so this response rate indicates the difficulty of securing respondents from a sample of the general population even when everything is done "by the book."

Web Surveys

Web surveys have become an increasingly useful survey method for two reasons: growth in the fraction of the population using the Internet—84% in 2015—and technological advances that make web survey design relatively easy. Many specific populations have very high rates of Internet use, so a web survey can be a good option for groups such as professionals, residents of middle-class communities, members of organizations, and, of course, college students. Because of the Internet's global reach, web surveys also make it possible to conduct large, international surveys. However, coverage remains a problem with some segments of the population (Tourangeau et al. 2012): About 15% of U.S. households were not connected to the Internet in 2015 (Couper & Miller 2008:832; File 2013; Perrin & Duggan 2015).

The extent to which the population of interest is connected to the web is the most important consideration when deciding whether to conduct a survey through the web. Exhibit 7.12 illustrates that rates of Internet usage are considerably lower among those with a high school education or less (Perrin & Duggan 2015). How might the use of the Internet shown in Exhibit 7.12 skew the results of a web survey? There are also differences in Internet use in the United States by income, race and ethnicity, and city type (rural lower than urban), but not by gender.

■ EXHIBIT 7.11 **Reasons for Nonresponse in Personal Interviews (1990 General Social Survey)**

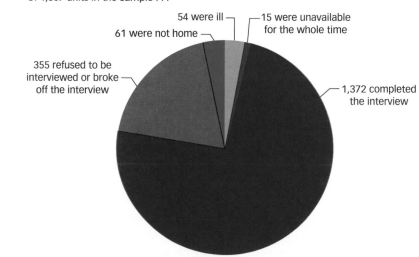

Source: Data from Davis and Smith (1992:54).

Internationally, Internet usage varies dramatically by region, with a low in 2014 of 27.5% in Africa and a high of 87% in North America (Exhibit 7.13).

There are several different approaches to engaging people in web surveys, each with unique advantages and disadvantages and somewhat different effects on the coverage problem. Many web surveys begin with an e-mail message to potential respondents that contains a direct "hot-link" to the survey website (Gaiser & Schreiner 2009:70). It is important that such e-mail invitations include a catchy phrase in the subject line as well as attractive and clear text in the message itself (Sue & Ritter 2012:110–114). This approach is particularly useful when a defined population with known e-mail addresses is to be surveyed. The researcher can then send e-mail invitations to a representative sample without difficulty. To ensure that the appropriate people respond to a web survey, researchers may require that respondents enter a personal identification number (PIN) to gain access to the web survey (Dillman 2000:378; Sue & Ritter 2012:103–104).

Web surveys that use volunteer samples may instead be linked to a website that is used by the intended population, and everyone who visits that site is invited to complete the survey. Although this approach can generate a large number of respondents (50,000 persons completed Survey 2000), the resulting sample will necessarily reflect the type of people who visit that website (middle-class, young North Americans, in Survey 2000) and thus be a biased representation of the larger population (Couper 2000:486–487; Dillman 2000:355).

■ EXHIBIT 7.12　**Use of the Internet by Education Level, 2000–2015**

While Less-Educated Adults Are Catching Up, Their Internet Adoption Rates Are Still Below Those of College Graduates

Among all American adults, the % who use the Internet, by education level

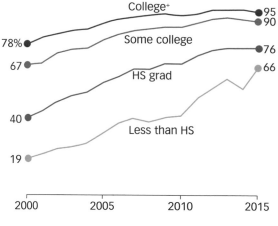

Source: Perrin and Duggan (2015).

Web surveys have some unique advantages for increasing measurement validity (Selm & Jankowski 2006; Tourangeau et al. 2012). Pictures, sounds, and animation can be used as a focus of particular questions, and graphic and typographic variation can be used to enhance visual survey appeal. Definitions of terms can also "pop up" when respondents scroll over them (Dillman 2007:458–459). Questionnaires completed on the web can elicit more honest reports about socially undesirable behavior or experiences, including illicit behavior and victimization in the general population and failing course grades among college students, when compared with results with phone interviews (Kreuter, Presser, & Tourangeau 2008; Parks, Pardi, & Bradizza 2006). A study by Pew Research Center found that white Americans were more likely to agree with the response choice that blacks face "a lot of discrimination" when they were asked by a phone interviewer than when they responded in a web survey, while black Americans were less likely to agree that they face "a lot of discrimination" when interviewed on the phone than when they answered the question in a web version of the same survey (Exhibit 7.14).

Coverage bias is the single biggest problem with web surveys of the general population and of segments of the population without a high level of Internet access, and none of the different web survey methods fully overcome this problem. Although providing computers and Internet access to all who agree to participate in a web survey panel reduces coverage bias, many potential respondents do

■ EXHIBIT 7.13　**Worldwide Internet Penetration Rates by Region, 2014**

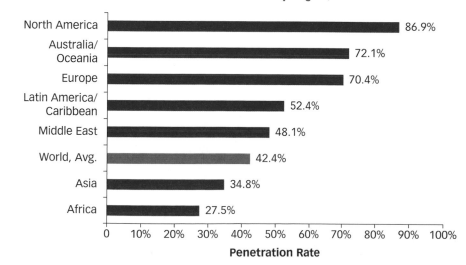

Source: Internet World Stats, www.internetworldstats.com/stats.htm. Copyright © 2015, Miniwatts Marketing Group. Reprinted with permission.

■ EXHIBIT 7.14 **Racial Divide on Discrimination Against Blacks in Society, by Survey Mode, 2014**

% who say blacks face "a lot of discrimination"

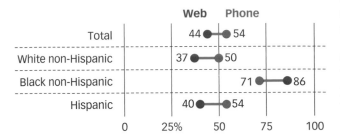

Source: "From Telephone to the Web: The Challenge of Mode of Interview Effects in Public Opinion Polls," Pew Research Center, Washington, DC (May, 2015) http://www.pewresearch.org/2015/05/13/from-telephone-to-the-web-the-challenge-of-mode-of-interview-effects-in-public-opinion-polls/.

not agree to participate in such surveys: The rate of agreement to participate was 57% in one Knowledge Networks survey and just 41.5% in a survey of students at the University of Michigan (Couper 2000:485–489). In addition, this approach increases the cost of the survey considerably, so it is typically used as part of creating the panel of respondents who agree to be contacted for multiple surveys over time. The start-up costs can then be spread across many surveys (Couper & Miller 2008:832–833).

Only about one third of Internet users contacted in phone surveys agree to provide an e-mail address for a web survey and then only one third of those actually complete the survey (Couper 2000:488). Web surveys that take more than 15 minutes are too long for most respondents (de Leeuw 2008:322). Surveys by phone continue to elicit higher rates of response (Kreuter et al. 2008). Some researchers have found that when people are sent a mailed survey that also provides a link to a web survey alternative, they overwhelmingly choose the paper survey (Couper 2000:488).

Surveys are also now being conducted on smartphones and via text messages, as well as through social media such as Facebook (Bhutta 2012; Sue & Ritter 2012:119–122). Research continues into the ways that the design of web surveys can influence rates of initial response, the likelihood of completing the survey, and the validity of the responses (see Exhibit 7.15) (Couper, Traugott, & Lamias 2001; Kreuter et al. 2008; Porter & Whitcomb 2003; Tourangeau et al. 2012). With about two thirds of Americans owning a smartphone and about half saying it is something they "couldn't live without," designing surveys for delivery on smartphones is an increasingly attractive survey option, although ownership rates differ by education and other social characteristics (Pew Research Center 2015:2,7).

Mixed-Mode Surveys

Survey researchers increasingly are combining different survey designs to improve the overall participation rate and to take advantage of the unique strengths of different methods. **Mixed-mode surveys** allow the strengths of one survey design to compensate for the weaknesses of another, and they can maximize the likelihood of securing data from different types of respondents (Dillman 2007:451–453;

■ EXHIBIT 7.15 **Mobile Web Survey Screen**

Mobile web browser screen shots

Please note all the places where you used your smart phone IN THE PAST HOUR.

[Check all that apply]

☑ At work

☑ At a community place like a coffee shop or park

☑ Riding in a car or on public transit

☑ Exercising

☑ At home

☑ Walking from place to place

☑ Waiting in line or for something else to happen

◉ None of the above

◻ Saving screenshot...

[Check all that apply]

☑ At work

☑ At a community place like a coffee shop or park

☑ Riding in a car or on public transit

☑ Exercising

☑ At home

☑ Walking from place to place

☑ Waiting in line or for something else to happen

◉ None of the above

[Back]   [Next]

Source: "App vs. Web for Surveys of Smartphone Users," Pew Research Center, Washington, DC (April, 2015) http://www.pewresearch.org/files/2015/03/2015-04-01_smartphones-METHODS_final-3-27-2015.pdf.

Selm & Jankowski 2006). For example, a survey may be sent electronically to sample members who have e-mail addresses and mailed to those who don't. Phone reminders may be used to encourage responses to web or paper surveys, or a letter of introduction may be sent in advance of calls in a phone survey (Guterbock 2008). Alternatively, nonrespondents in a mailed survey may be interviewed in person or over the phone. In one comparative study, the response rate to a phone survey rose from 43% to 80% when it was followed by a mailed questionnaire (Dillman 2007:456). Mixing modes in this way can reduce total costs by starting with the cheapest method and then adding more effort as needed, and some research indicates that measurement reliability is not lessened by mixing modes (Cernat 2015).

Photo 7.3 Web surveys don't reach everyone, but they can still reach a broad audience.

Comparing Survey Designs

Which survey design should be used when? Group-administered surveys are similar, in most respects, to mailed surveys, except that they require the unusual circumstance of having access to the sample in a group setting. We therefore don't need to consider this survey design by itself; what applies to mailed surveys applies to group-administered survey designs, with the exception of sampling issues. The features of mixed-mode surveys depend on the survey types that are being combined. Thus, we can focus our comparison on the four survey designs that involve the use of a questionnaire with individuals sampled from a larger population: (1) mailed surveys, (2) phone surveys, (3) in-person surveys, and (4) web surveys. Exhibit 7.16 summarizes their strong and weak points.

The most important consideration in comparing the advantages and disadvantages of the four methods is the likely response rate they will generate. Declining rates of response to phone surveys have reduced the appeal of this method below that of mailed surveys. In-person surveys are preferable in the possible length and complexity of the questionnaire itself, as well as with respect to the researcher's ability to monitor conditions while the questionnaire is completed. Mailed and web surveys often are preferable for asking sensitive questions, although this problem can be lessened in an interview by giving respondents a separate sheet to fill out or a laptop on which to enter their answers. Some survey organizations have also switched to having in-person interviews completed entirely by the respondents on a laptop as they listen to prerecorded questions.

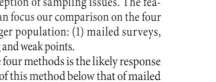

▶ **VIDEO LINK**
Accuracy of Surveys

📖 **ENCYCLOPEDIA LINK**
Anonymity

▶ **VIDEO LINK**
Using Survey Data

The advantages and disadvantages of web surveys must be weighed in light of the population that is to be surveyed and the capabilities at the time the survey is to be conducted. At this time, too many people lack Internet connections for survey researchers to use the Internet to survey the general population.

The "best" survey design for any particular study will be determined by the study's unique features and goals rather than by any absolute standard for the best survey design.

❖ Ethical Issues in Survey Research

Survey research usually poses fewer ethical dilemmas than do experimental or field research designs. Potential respondents to a survey can easily decline to participate, and a cover letter or introductory statement that identifies the sponsors of, and motivations for, the survey gives them the information required to make this decision. Current federal regulations to protect human subjects allow survey research to be exempted from formal review unless respondents can be identified and disclosure of their responses could place them at risk.

Confidentiality is most often the primary focus of ethical concern in survey research. Many surveys include some essential questions that might, in some way, prove damaging to the subjects if their answers were disclosed. To prevent any possibility of harm to subjects because of the disclosure of such information, the researcher must preserve subject confidentiality. Nobody but research personnel should have access to information that could be used to link respondents to their responses, and even that access should be limited to what is necessary for specific research purposes.

Not many surveys can provide true **anonymity**, so that no identifying information is ever recorded to link respondents with their responses. The main problem with anonymous surveys is that they preclude follow-up attempts to encourage participation by initial nonrespondents, and they prevent panel designs, which measure change through repeated surveys of the same individuals.

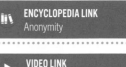

Mixed-mode survey: A survey conducted by more than one method, allowing the strengths of one survey design to compensate for the weaknesses of another and maximizing the likelihood of securing data from different types of respondents; for example, nonrespondents in a mailed survey may be interviewed in person or over the phone.

Confidentiality: Provided by research in which identifying information that could be used to link respondents to their responses is available only to designated research personnel for specific research needs.

Anonymity: Provided by research in which no identifying information is recorded that could be used to link respondents to their responses.

■ EXHIBIT 7.16 **Advantages and Disadvantages of the Four Survey Designs**

Characteristics of Design	Mail Survey	Phone Survey	In-Person Survey	Web Survey
Representative sample				
Opportunity for inclusion is known				
For completely listed populations	High	High	High	Medium
For incompletely listed populations	Medium	Medium	High	Low
Selection within sampling units is controlled (e.g., specific family members must respond)	Medium	High	High	Low
Respondents are likely to be located				
If samples are heterogeneous	Medium	Medium	High	Low
If samples are homogeneous and specialized	High	High	High	High
Questionnaire construction and question design				
Allowable length of questionnaire	Medium	Medium	High	Medium
Ability to include				
Complex questions	Medium	Low	High	High
Open questions	Low	High	High	Medium
Screening questions	Low	High	High	High
Tedious, boring questions	Low	High	High	Low
Ability to control question sequence	Low	High	High	High
Ability to ensure questionnaire completion	Medium	High	High	Low
Distortion of answers				
Odds of avoiding social desirability bias	High	Medium	Low	High
Odds of avoiding interviewer distortion	High	Medium	Low	High
Odds of avoiding contamination by others	Medium	High	Medium	Medium
Administrative goals				
Odds of meeting personnel requirements	High	High	Low	Medium
Odds of implementing quickly	Low	High	Low	High
Odds of keeping costs low	High	Medium	Low	High

Source: Adapted from Dillman (1978 and 2007). *Mail and Telephone Surveys: The Total Design Method.* Reprinted by permission of John Wiley & Sons, Inc.

In-person surveys rarely can be anonymous because an interviewer must, in almost all cases, know the name and address of the interviewee. However, phone surveys that are meant only to sample opinion at one point in time, as in political polls, can safely be completely anonymous. When no future follow-up is desired, group-administered surveys also can be anonymous. To provide anonymity in a mail survey, the researcher should omit identifying codes from the questionnaire but could include a self-addressed, stamped postcard so that the respondent can notify the researcher that the questionnaire has been returned without creating any linkage to the questionnaire itself (Mangione 1995:69).

❖ Conclusions

Survey research is an exceptionally efficient and productive method for investigating a wide array of social research questions. One or more of the six survey designs reviewed in this chapter (including mixed mode) can be applied to almost any research question. But the relative ease of conducting at least some types of survey research leads many people to imagine that no particular training or systematic procedures are required. Nothing could be further from the truth. As a result of this widespread misconception, however, you will encounter a great many nearly worthless survey results. You must be prepared to examine carefully the procedures used in any survey before accepting its findings as credible. And if you decide to conduct a survey, you must be prepared to invest the time and effort that proper procedures require.

Key Terms

Anonymity   115
Bipolar response options   100
Cognitive interview   103
Computer-assisted personal interview (CAPI)   112
Computer-assisted telephone interview (CATI)   109
Confidentiality   115
Context effects   105
Contingent question   100
Cover letter   108
Double-barreled question   99
Double negative   99

Fence-sitters   101
Filter question   99
Floaters   102
Forced-choice questions   102
Group-administered survey   109
Idiosyncratic variation   102
In-person survey   111
Interactive voice response (IVR)   109
Interpretive questions   104
Interview schedule   102
Labeled unipolar response options   100
Likert item   100
Mailed survey   108

Matrix questions   105
Mixed-mode survey   114
Omnibus survey   97
Part-whole question effects   105
Phone survey   109
Questionnaire   102
Skip pattern   99
Social desirability bias   100
Survey pretest   103
Survey research   97
Unlabeled unipolar response options   100
Web survey   112

Highlights

- Surveys are the most popular form of social research because of their versatility, efficiency, and generalizability. Data from many surveys, such as the GSS, are available for social scientists to use in teaching and research.

- Omnibus surveys cover a range of topics of interest and generate data useful to multiple sponsors.

- Survey designs must minimize the risk of poor measurement, nonresponse, inadequate coverage of the population, and sampling error.

- Questions must be worded carefully to avoid confusing respondents, encouraging a less-than-honest response, or triggering biases. Inclusion of "don't know" choices and neutral responses may help, but the presence of such options also affects the distribution of answers. Open-ended questions can be used to determine the meaning that respondents attach to their answers. Answers to any survey questions may be affected by the questions that precede them in a questionnaire or interview schedule.

- Sets of questions that comprise an index can reduce idiosyncratic variation in measurement of a concept.

- Interpretive questions should be used in questionnaires to help clarify the meaning of responses to critical questions.

- A survey questionnaire or interview schedule should be designed as an integrated whole, with each question and section serving some clear purpose and complementing the others.

- The cover letter for a mailed questionnaire should be credible, personalized, interesting, and responsible.

- Response rates in mailed surveys are typically well below 70% unless multiple mailings are made to nonrespondents and the questionnaire and cover letter are attractive, interesting, and carefully planned. Response rates for group-administered surveys are usually much higher.

- Phone interviews using random digit dialing allow fast turnaround and efficient sampling. Multiple callbacks are often required, and the rate of nonresponse to phone interviews is rising. Response rates to phone surveys have declined dramatically due to cell phones and caller ID.

- In-person interviews have several advantages over other types of surveys: They allow longer and more complex interview schedules, monitoring of the conditions when the questions are answered, probing for respondents' understanding of the questions, and high response rates. However, the interviewer must balance the need to establish rapport with the respondent with the importance of maintaining control over the delivery of the interview questions.

- Electronic surveys may be e-mailed or posted on the web. Interactive voice response (IVR) systems using the phone are another option. At this time, use of the Internet is not sufficiently widespread to allow web surveys of the general population, but these approaches can be fast and efficient for populations with high rates of computer use.

- Mixed-mode surveys allow the strengths of one survey design to compensate for the weaknesses of another. However, questions and procedures must be designed carefully to reduce the possibility that responses to the same question will vary as a result of the mode of delivery.

- In deciding which survey design to use, researchers must consider the unique features and goals of the study. In general, in-person interviews are the strongest, but most expensive, survey design.

- Most survey research poses few ethical problems because respondents are able to decline to participate—an option that should be stated clearly in the cover letter or introductory statement. Special care must be taken when questionnaires are administered in group settings (to "captive audiences") and when sensitive personal questions are to be asked; subject confidentiality should always be preserved.

⋯⋯ **Chapter Questions** ⋯⋯⋯⋯⋯⋯⋯⋯⋯⋯⋯⋯⋯⋯

1. Response rates to phone surveys are declining, even as phone usage increases. Part of the problem is that lists of cell phone numbers are not available and wireless service providers may not allow outside access to their networks. Cell phone users may also have to pay for incoming calls. Do you think regulations should be passed to increase the ability of survey researchers to include cell phones in their random digit dialing surveys? How would you feel about receiving survey calls on your cell phone? What problems might result from "improving" phone survey capabilities in this way?

2. In-person interviews have for many years been the "gold standard" in survey research because the presence of an interviewer increases the response rate, allows better rapport with the interviewee, facilitates clarification of questions and instructions, and provides feedback about the interviewee's situation. However, researchers who design in-person interviewing projects are now making increasing use of technology to ensure consistent questioning of respondents and to provide greater privacy for respondents answering questions. But having a respondent answer questions on a laptop while the interviewer waits is a very different social process from asking the questions verbally. Which approach would you favor in survey research? What trade-offs might there be in quality of information collected, rapport building, and interviewee satisfaction?

3. Group-administered surveys are easier to conduct than other types of surveys, but they always raise an ethical dilemma. If a teacher allows a social research survey to be distributed in his or her class, or if an employer allows employees to complete a survey on company time, is the survey truly voluntary? Is it sufficient to read a statement to the group members stating that their participation is entirely up to them? How would you react to a survey in your class? What general guidelines should be followed in such situations?

4. Patricia Tjaden and Nancy Thoennes (2000) sampled adults with random digit dialing to study violent victimization from a nationally representative sample of adults. What ethical dilemmas do you see in reporting victimizations that are identified in a survey? What about when the survey respondents are under the age of 18? What about children under the age of 12?

⋯⋯ **Practice Exercises** ⋯⋯⋯⋯⋯⋯⋯⋯⋯⋯⋯⋯⋯⋯⋯⋯

1. Who does survey research, and how do they do it? These questions can be answered through careful inspection of ongoing surveys and the organizations that administer them at www .ciser.cornell.edu/info/polls.shtml. Spend some time reading about the different survey research organizations, and write a brief summary of the types of research they conduct, the projects in which they are involved, and the resources they offer on their websites. What are the distinctive features of different survey research organizations?

2. Go to the Research Triangle Institute site at www.rti.org. Click on "Survey Research & Services" and then "Innovations." Read about their methods for computer-assisted interviewing and their cognitive laboratory methods for refining questions. What does this information add to the chapter's treatment of these topics?

3. Go to the UK Data Service at http://discover.ukdataservice .ac.uk/variables. In the search box, enter topics of interest such as "health" or "inequality." Review five questions for two topic areas and critique them in terms of the principles for question writing that you have learned. Do you find any question features that might be attributed to the use of British English?

STUDENT STUDY SITE

⊛SAGE edge™

CHAPTER 8

Qualitative Methods

Hurricane Katrina roared ashore in Louisiana on August 29, 2005, at 7:10 a.m. Eastern Standard Time (National Oceanic & Atmospheric Administration [NOAA] 2005). The combined force of winds of up to 125 miles per hour and heavy rain soon breached several levees designed to protect New Orleans from surrounding lakes; by August 31, 80% of New Orleans was under as much as 20 feet of floodwater (Photo 8.1). With more than 1,000 deaths, 1 million displaced, and total costs in excess of $100 billion, Katrina was one of the most devastating natural disasters in U.S. history.

How can we understand the resulting disruptions in individual lives and social patterns? What happened to the New Orleans social world (Rodríguez, Trainor, & Quarantelli 2006)? Sociologist Kai Erikson sent me the following verbal "picture" of New Orleans as he began research a few days after Katrina:

> The carnage stretches out almost endlessly: more than a hundred thousand [crumpled] homes, at least fifty thousand [flattened] automobiles, the whole mass being covered by a crust of grey mud, dried as hard as fired clay by the sun. It was the silence of it, the emptiness of it; that is the story.

In the words of one 30-year-old resident,

> I have stopped planning ahead. All I thought I had has been taken away. I lost my job, my home. When I was evacuated, I didn't know where I would go. You had to live one day at a time. (Davis & Land 2007:76)

It is through observing and participating in natural settings, listening to the words of others and engaging with them, that qualitative researchers contribute to understanding the social world. This chapter reviews the major methods of qualitative research, including participant observation, intensive interviewing, and focus groups, and illustrates them with research on disasters and a range of other social phenomena. The chapter gives particular attention to new qualitative methods for studying the social world online and to ethical issues that are of particular concern in qualitative research.

Qualitative researchers must observe keenly, take notes systematically, question respondents strategically, and prepare to spend more time and invest more of their whole selves than often occurs with experiments or surveys. Moreover, if we are to have any confidence in a qualitative study's conclusions, each element of its design must be reviewed as carefully as we would review the elements of an experiment or survey. The result of careful use of these methods can be insights into the features of the social world and social processes that defy quantification and are ill suited to investigation with experiments or surveys.

Photo 8.1   New Orleans after Hurricane Katrina.

❖ Fundamentals of Qualitative Methods

The term *qualitative methods* refers to a variety of research techniques that share some basic features (Denzin & Lincoln 1994; Maxwell 2005; Wolcott 1995):

- *Collection primarily of qualitative rather than quantitative data.* Any research design may collect both qualitative and quantitative data, but qualitative methods emphasize observations about natural behavior and artifacts that capture social life as participants experience it, rather than in categories the researcher predetermines.

- *Exploratory research questions, with a commitment to inductive reasoning.* Qualitative researchers typically begin their projects seeking not to test preformulated hypotheses but to discover what people think, how they act, and why, in some social setting.

- *A focus on previously unstudied processes and unanticipated phenomena.* Qualitative methods have their greatest appeal when we need to explore new issues, investigate hard-to-study groups, or determine the meaning people give to their lives and actions. In these circumstances, it won't be clear which hypothesis to test in an experimental design or exactly which questions to include in a survey.

- *An orientation to social context, to the interconnections between social phenomena rather than to their discrete features.* The context of concern may be a program or an organization, a community, or a broader social context.

- *A focus on human subjectivity, on the meanings that participants attach to events and that people give to their lives.* "Through life stories, people 'account for their lives.' . . . The themes people create are the means by which they interpret and evaluate their life experiences and attempt to integrate these experiences to form a self-concept" (Kaufman 1986:24–25).

- *Adaptive research design, in which the design develops as the research progresses.* The activities of collecting and analyzing data, developing and modifying theory, elaborating or refocusing the research questions, and identifying and eliminating validity threats are usually all going on more or less simultaneously, each influencing all of the others (Maxwell 2005).

- *Sensitivity to the subjective role of the researcher (reflexivity).* Qualitative researchers recognize that their perspective on social phenomena will reflect in part their own background and current situation. Who the researcher is and "where he or she is coming from" can affect what the research "finds."

You can understand better how these different features make qualitative methods so distinct by learning the basics of specific qualitative methods and some of the insights those methods have produced. This section illustrates the way in which qualitative research can produce insights about whole settings and cultures by presenting the basics of case study research and ethnographic research, and the new online "netnography" version of ethnography. The rest of the chapter presents the primary qualitative methods: participant observation, intensive interviewing (and online interviewing), and focus groups.

SAGE JOURNAL ARTICLE
Neighborhood Politics

VIDEO LINK
Qualitative Studies

RESEARCH/SOCIAL IMPACT LINK
Qualitative Methods

Adaptive research design: A research design that develops as the research progresses.

Reflexivity: Sensitivity of and adaptation by the researcher to his or her influence in the research setting.

The Case Study

Qualitative research projects often have the goal of developing an understanding of an entire slice of the social world, not just discrete parts of it. A **case study** may focus on an organization, a community, a social group, a family, or even an individual; as far as the qualitative researcher is concerned, it must be understood in its entirety. The idea is that the social world really functions as an integrated whole; social researchers therefore need to develop "deep understanding of particular instances of phenomena" (Mabry 2008:214).

Much case study research seeks to develop a **thick description** of the setting studied—a description that provides a sense of what it is like to experience that setting from the standpoint of the natural actors in that setting (Geertz 1973). For instance, Annette Lareau (2002) provides a thick description of a middle-class black child's interaction with his mother in her qualitative study of social class and childrearing in black and white families. The description helps us to understand the childrearing approach she terms "concerted cultivation":

> Sometimes Alexander complains that "my mother signs me up for everything!" Generally, however, he likes his activities. He says they make him feel "special," and without them life would be "boring." His sense of time is thoroughly entwined with his activities: He feels disoriented when his schedule is not full. This unease is clear in the following field-note excerpt. The family is driving home from a Back-to-School night. The next morning, Ms. Williams will leave for a work-related day trip and will not return until late at night. Alexander is grumpy because he has nothing planned for the next day. He wants to have a friend over, but his mother rebuffs him. Whining, he wonders what he will do. His mother, speaking tersely, says:

> You have piano and guitar. You'll have some free time. [Pause] I think you'll survive for one night. [Alexander does not respond but seems mad. It is quiet for the rest of the trip home.] (p. 754)

Just this one segment from Lareau's thick description of Alexander's relationship with his mother provides a compelling picture of the family's childrearing approach. Lareau subsequently contrasts this style with the "accomplishment of natural growth" style that she found more often in working-class families. Although Lareau's multiphase study was not itself a case study—it ultimately involved interviews and observations of 88 white and African American children and their families—her artful and detailed presentations of case studies representing distinct social patterns demonstrate the value of the case study approach. As Lareau (2002:749) explains, "Quantitative studies of children's activities offer valuable empirical evidence but only limited ideas about how to conceptualize the mechanisms through which social advantage is transmitted." Her qualitative approach provides such ideas to help assess "the role of social structural location in shaping daily life."

Case study: A setting or group that the analyst treats as an integrated social unit that must be studied holistically and in its particularity.

Thick description: A rich description that conveys a sense of what it is like from the standpoint of the natural actors in that setting.

Ethnography: The study of a culture or cultures that some group of people share, using participant observation over an extended period.

Ethnography

Ethnography is the study of a culture or cultures that a group of people share (Van Maanen 1995). As a method, it is usually meant to refer to the process by which a single investigator immerses himself or herself in a group for a long time (often one or more years), gradually establishing trust and experiencing the social world as do the participants (Madden 2010). Ethnographic research can be called *naturalistic,* because it seeks to describe and understand the natural social world as it is, in all its richness and detail. This goal is best achieved when an ethnographer is fluent in the local language and spends enough time in the setting to know how people live, what they say about themselves and what they actually do, and what they value (Armstrong 2008).

Code of the Street, Elijah Anderson's (1999) award-winning study of Philadelphia's inner city, captures the flavor of this approach:

> My primary aim in this work is to render ethnographically the social and cultural dynamics of the interpersonal violence that is currently undermining the quality of life of too many urban neighborhoods. . . . How do the people of the setting perceive their situation? What assumptions do they bring to their decision making? (pp. 10–11)

A thick description of life in the inner city emerges as Anderson's work develops. We feel the community's pain in Anderson's (1999) description of "the aftermath of death":

©iStockphoto.com/KIVILCIM PINAR

Photo 8.2 Ethnographies offer great opportunities for researchers to explore cultures outside their own. What culture or subculture might you be interested in studying?

When a young life is cut down, almost everyone goes into mourning. The first thing that happens is that a crowd gathers about the site of the shooting or the incident. The police then arrive, drawing more of a crowd. Since such a death often occurs close to the victim's house, his mother or his close relatives and friends may be on the scene of the killing. When they arrive, the women and girls often wail and moan, crying out their grief for all to hear, while the young men simply look on, in studied silence. . . . Soon the ambulance arrives. (p. 138)

Anderson (1999) uses this description as a foundation on which he develops key concepts, such as "code of the street":

The "code of the street" is not the goal or product of any individual's action but is the fabric of everyday life, a vivid and pressing milieu within which all local residents must shape their personal routines, income strategies, and orientations to schooling, as well as their mating, parenting, and neighbor relations. (p. 326)

Netnography

Communities can refer not only to people in a common physical location, but also to relationships that develop online. Online communities may be formed by persons with similar interests or backgrounds, perhaps to create new social relationships that location or schedules did not permit, or to supplement relationships that emerge in the course of work or school or other ongoing social activities. Like communities of people who interact face-to-face, online communities can develop a culture and become sources of identification and attachment (Kozinets 2010). And as with physical communities, researchers can study online communities through immersion in the group for an extended period. **Netnography**, also termed *cyberethnography* and *virtual ethnography* (James & Busher 2009:34–35), is the use of ethnographic methods to study online communities.

Unlike in-person ethnographies, netnographies can focus on communities whose members are physically distant and dispersed. The selected community should be relevant to the research question, involve frequent communication among actively engaged members, and have a number of participants who, as a result, generate a rich body of textual data (Kozinets 2010). A netnographer must keep both observational and reflective field notes but, unlike a traditional ethnographer, can return to review the original data—the posted text—long after it was produced. As reflected in comments by social media researcher danah boyd (2015), the traditional ethnographic process of immersion in a community can also occur online:

Online, I participate in and gather data from MySpace, Facebook, YouTube, Twitter, Xanga, LiveJournal, Formspring, and a host of smaller social media services. I follow teen-oriented "Trending Topics" and download countless profiles to analyze. I have watched teen girls "catfight" on uStream and tracked discussions of proms, SAT tests, and political mobilization over immigration issues. I have read teens' messages to Beyoncé and watched their obsession with Justin Bieber and Lady Gaga grow.

Netnography: The use of ethnographic methods to study online communities; also termed *cyberethnography* and *virtual ethnography.*

CAREERS and Research

DZENAN BERBEROVIC, DIRECTOR OF DEVELOPMENT

Dzenan Berberovic was the first in his immediate family to attend college. While at the University of South Dakota, he earned a bachelor's degree in media and journalism with minors in communication studies and sociology.

During Berberovic's third year at the university, he was exposed to a research course. The use of research in marketing was eye-opening. It allowed him to see the important role of research in nearly every profession.

Berberovic's love for helping others, combined with his interest in both sociology and research, led him to pursue a career in the nonprofit sector. He now serves as the director of development for the University of South Dakota Foundation. Every day, he uses data and research completed on trends in the nonprofit and giving fields.

Dzenan's advice for students studying research methods is compelling: "Research is all around us. It will continue to grow, especially through the use of data analytics. Most professions will utilize a form of research, thus it is important to take advantage of the opportunities you are given as an undergraduate student. Even in careers like nonprofit—in my case—you may initially not think of research as a component of it. However, it plays a large role in moving organizations in the right direction."

VIDEO LINK
Ethnography

RESEARCHER INTERVIEW LINK
Ethnographic Research

SAGE JOURNAL ARTICLE
Ethnography

VIDEO LINK ▶
Netnography

Can a researcher gain a sufficient understanding of the social world if data about people and their interactions in that world are obtained only online? Does the "net" part have to be supplemented with some in-person "eth"nography? danah boyd (2015) offers a compelling explanation for her preference for collecting data about people both online and offline:

I have found that I cannot get a deep understanding of people's mediated practices without engaging with them face-to-face in at least one of the physical environments that they inhabit. Given that most of my work concerns a population whose interactions span multiple modes and media, . . . I . . . traipse across the United States because . . . I have found that it is the only way that I can get a decent picture of teens' lives. When I meet teens face-to-face, they offer depth and context to what I see online. More importantly, they show me where my first impressions were inaccurate or wrong. Thus, I purposefully collect data both online and offline.

Interviews by Alice Marwick and danah boyd (2011:4) with teens about the online gendered interactions they call "drama" rather than "cyberbullying" result in a good example of the deeper understanding of online behavior that can result from offline research:

Although drama does not need to take place on social media sites, it often does.
    danah: How does it [drama] come out on Facebook?
    Alicia, 17, North Carolina: Well, there's a girl from West Beverly that got in an argument with a girl from South Beverly and they were at a party. So then when I looked on Facebook the next day there were all of these comments on [there] like "I love you, I don't think you're a—whatever the girl called her." So it's all really immature and they'll put statuses up like "oh my gosh I'm so over this." So that's how drama gets on Facebook.

. . . Not only can friends respond with supportive comments, but they can also click the "Like" button, which appears on each message to show their affiliation in an interpersonal interaction. This is just one way in which Facebook is employed in teen dramas.

On the other hand, members of an online community may only be accessible to a researcher through online interaction, so social research based on only online data will certainly continue. Be sure to consider what you might be missing about social context or individual situations when you read netnographic research that relies exclusively on online data.

RESEARCH

In the News

FACELESSNESS AND SOCIAL RESEARCH

Is "the world of faces" dissonant from "the world without faces"? This question is posed in a *New York Times* article on the social problem created by our ability to communicate directly with others through social media without actually seeing or hearing them. For example, a part-time delivery driver in England was recently sentenced to 18 weeks in prison for tweeting violent messages to a member of Parliament.

Although the focus of the *Times* article is on the moral problem of unethical behavior that can emerge through Internet connections, the "inability to recognize shared humanity with another" when we are unable to see faces also creates a problem for social research. One of the great appeals of qualitative methods such as participant observation and intensive interviewing has been the ability to learn about people while experiencing their facial expressions, emotions, and tone of voice.

For Further Thought ?

1. Have you seen instances of a shocking lack of social inhibition in communications sent over e-mail or social media?

2. How much do we lose when we try to understand social behavior through analyzing e-mails, "tweets," or Facebook posts?

News source: Marchie, Stephen. 2015. "The Epidemic of Facelessness." *New York Times,* February 14.

❖ Primary Qualitative Methods

The specifics of qualitative methods can best be understood by reviewing the three distinctive qualitative research techniques: **participant observation, intensive (in-depth) interviewing**, and **focus groups**. Participant observation and intensive interviewing are often used in the same project, whereas focus groups combine some elements of these two approaches into a unique data-collection strategy. These techniques are most often used as the primary method in a social research project, but they can also be used to enrich experimental and survey research.

Participant Observation

Participant observation is the classic **field research** method—a means for seeing the social world as the research subjects see it, in its totality, and for understanding subjects' interpretations of that world (Wolcott 1995). By observing people and interacting with them during their normal activities, **field researchers** seek to avoid the artificiality of experimental design and the unnatural structured questioning of survey research (Koegel 1987). This method encourages consideration of the context in which social interaction occurs, of the complex and interconnected nature of social relations, and of the sequencing of events (Bogdewic 1999).

Choosing a Role

The term *participant observation* actually refers to several different specific roles that a qualitative researcher can adopt (Exhibit 8.1). The first concern of every participant observer is to decide what balance to strike between observing and participating and whether to reveal one's role as a researcher. These decisions must take into account the specifics of the social situation being studied, the researcher's own background and personality, the larger sociopolitical context, and ethical concerns. The balance of participating and observing that is most appropriate may change during a project, sometimes many times.

Covert Observation: In social settings involving many people, in which observing while standing or sitting does not attract attention, covert observation is possible and is unlikely to have much effect on social processes. As a **covert observer**, a researcher observes others without participating in social interaction and does not self-identify as a researcher. However, the way in which actions of a covert observer may have affected the actions of others in that setting should also be considered.

Overt Observation: In many settings, a qualitative researcher will function as a **complete observer**, who does not participate in group activities and is publicly defined as a researcher. The overt, or complete, observer announces his or her role as a research observer. Because it is not "natural" in most social situations for someone to be recording his or her observations for research and publication purposes, individuals may alter their behavior in ways that create a problem of **reactive effects**. However, in most situations, overt observers find that their presence seems to be ignored by participants after a while and to have no discernible impact on social processes.

These two relatively passive roles contrast with the role of a researcher who participates actively in the setting.

Participant Observation (Overt Participation): Most field researchers adopt a role that involves some active participation in the setting. If the researcher publicly acknowledges being

■ EXHIBIT 8.1 **The Participant Observation Continuum**

To study an activist group, you could take the role of a covert observer.

You could take the role of an overt observer:

You could take the role of a participant and observer:

You could take the role of a covert participant:

....

Participant observation: A qualitative method for gathering data that involves developing a sustained relationship with people while they go about their normal activities.

Intensive (in-depth) interviewing: A qualitative method that involves open-ended, relatively unstructured questioning in which the interviewer seeks in-depth information about the interviewee's feelings, experiences, and perceptions.

a researcher but nonetheless participates in group activities, unlike a complete observer, he or she is an *overt participant,* or a true **participant observer**.

Usually, participant observers inform some group members of their research interests and then participate in group activities to develop rapport with members and to gain a direct sense of group members' experiences. This involves a balancing act between maintaining research goals while still discarding the symbolic "white lab coat" of a researcher and engaging with people in their everyday lives (Wolcott 1995:100).

VIDEO LINK ▶
Participant Observation

Complete (Covert) Participation: A qualitative researcher is a **complete participant** (also known as a *covert participant*) when he or she acts just like other group members and does not disclose his or her research role.

Some field researchers have adopted this role, keeping their research secret and trying their best to act similar to other participants in a social setting or group, in order to gain entry to otherwise inaccessible settings and to lessen the potential for reactive effect. Laud Humphreys (1970) took the role of a covert participant when he served as a "watch queen" so that he could learn about the men engaging in homosexual acts in a public restroom. Randall Alfred (1976) joined a group of Satanists to investigate the group members and their interaction. Erving Goffman (1961) worked as a state hospital assistant while studying the treatment of psychiatric patients.

Although the role of a covert participant lessens some of the reactive effects encountered by the complete observer, covert participants confront other problems:

- *Covert participants cannot take notes openly or use any obvious recording devices.* They must write up notes based solely on their memory and must do so at times when it is natural for them to be away from the group members.

- *Covert participants cannot ask questions that will arouse suspicion.* Thus, they often have trouble clarifying the meaning of other participants' attitudes or actions.

- *The role of a covert participant is difficult to play successfully.* Regular participants have entered the situation from different social backgrounds and with goals different from that of the researcher, so researchers' spontaneous reactions to every event are unlikely to be consistent with those of the regular participants (Mitchell 1993). Researchers may experience enormous psychological strain, particularly in situations where they are expected to choose sides in intragroup conflict or to participate in criminal or other acts.

Entering the Field

Entering the field, the setting under investigation, is a critical stage in a participant observation project because it can shape many subsequent experiences. Finding a participant who can make introductions—a **gatekeeper** who could grant access—is often critical and may be very time-consuming (Rossman & Rallis 1998). On the other hand, access may proceed easily from a researcher's social contacts. Jane Ward (2000) gained access to Heath House, the AIDS care facility she studied, through contacts made during her past work as a volunteer at a local AIDS organization and connections she had gained at another care facility while visiting a sick friend.

Field researchers must be very sensitive to the impression they make and to the ties they establish when entering the field. This stage lays the groundwork for collecting data from people who have different perspectives and for developing relationships that the researcher can use to surmount the problems in data collection that inevitably arise in the field. The researcher should be ready with a rationale for his or her participation and some sense of the potential benefits to participants (Rossman & Rallis 1998).

Developing and Maintaining Relationships

Researchers must be careful to manage their relationships in the research setting so that they can continue to observe and interview diverse members of the social setting throughout the long period typical of participant observation (Maxwell 2005). In his landmark qualitative study, *Street Corner Society*, William Foote Whyte developed and maintained a relationship with a street-corner man named Doc, who in turn provided access to others in the neighborhood. Doc became a **key informant** in the research setting—a knowledgeable insider who knew the group's culture and was willing to share access and insights with the researcher (Gilchrist & Williams 1999).

Jane Ward (2000) developed relations with several residents of the AIDS care house she studied and four became her primary informants:

Focus groups: A qualitative method that involves unstructured group interviews in which the focus group leader actively encourages discussion among participants about the topics of interest.

Field research: Research in which natural social processes are studied as they happen and left relatively undisturbed.

Field researcher: A researcher who uses qualitative methods to conduct research in the field.

Covert observer: A role in participant observation in which the researcher does not participate in group activities and is not publicly defined as a researcher.

Complete (or overt) observer: A role in participant observation in which the researcher does not participate in group activities and is publicly defined as a researcher.

Reactive effects: The changes in individual or group behavior that result from being observed or otherwise studied.

Participant observer (overt participant): A researcher who gathers data through participating and observing in a setting where he or she develops a sustained relationship with people while they go about their normal activities. The term *participant observer* is also used more broadly to refer to a continuum of possible roles, from *complete observer* to *complete participant*.

Complete (or covert) participant: A role in field research in which the researcher does not reveal his or her identity as a researcher to those who are observed while participating.

Gatekeeper: A person in a field setting who can grant researchers access to the setting.

Key informant: An insider who is willing and able to provide a field researcher with superior access and information, including answers to questions that arise in the course of the research.

Being a participant observer and a volunteer at Heath House necessitated developing intimate relationships with the residents, an experience that was both part of a natural progression in the research and a strategy for gaining greater access to the very private life of the house. I became emotionally invested in the lives of the residents, and . . . considered the extent to which it was important, or possible, to create and maintain a professional boundary between myself and my research participants. . . . My approach . . . was to become immersed in the lives of my primary informants while simultaneously being explicit with them about the progress of my work. As I came to know the residents well, . . . four of the seven residents became primary informants, spending considerable time away from the house (most often in bars or restaurants) sharing their thoughts about its atmosphere and operation, as well as their strategies for coping with illness and group living. (p. 254)

Sampling People and Events

Most qualitative researchers limit their focus to just one or a few sites or programs, but this does not mean that sampling is unimportant. The researcher must be reasonably confident about gaining access and that the site can provide relevant information. The sample must be appropriate and adequate for the study, even if it is not representative. The qualitative researcher may select a *critical case* that is unusually rich in information pertaining to the research question, a *typical case* precisely because it is judged to be typical, or a *deviant case* that provides a useful contrast (Kuzel 1999). Within a project, plans may be made to sample different settings, people, events, and artifacts. Selecting more than one case or setting with some type of intentional sampling strategy almost always strengthens causal conclusions and makes the findings more generalizable (King, Keohane, & Verba 1994).

An intentional sampling strategy was essential in Annette Lareau's investigation of the intersecting influences of social class and race on childrearing practices. In the last phase of her investigation, she arranged to be a participant observer in the homes of 12 families that spanned the continuum she focused on in terms of social class and race. Two families from each of 6 different race-class combinations were chosen to provide insight into the daily lives of the larger group of 88 she had interviewed in an earlier phase of the research (Exhibit 8.2).

Theoretical sampling is a systematic approach to sampling that may emerge in the course of participant observation studies (Glaser & Strauss 1967). When field researchers discover in an investigation that particular processes seem to be important, inferring that certain comparisons should be made or that similar instances should be checked, the researchers then choose new settings or individuals that permit these comparisons or checks (Ragin 1994) (Exhibit 8.3).

> **Theoretical sampling:** A sampling method recommended for field researchers by Glaser and Strauss (1967). A theoretical sample is drawn in a sequential fashion, with settings or individuals selected for study as earlier observations or interviews indicate that these settings or individuals are influential.

Taking Notes

Notes are the primary means of recording participant observation data (Emerson, Fretz, & Shaw 1995). It is almost always a mistake to try to take comprehensive notes while engaged in the

■ EXHIBIT 8.2   **Sampling Plan for Participant Observation Study of Class and Race Differences in Childrearing**

Social Class	White	Black	Total
Middle class[a]	18 (Garrett Tallinger) (Melanie Handlon)	18 (Alexander Williams) (Stacey Marshall)	36
Working class[b]	14 (Billy Yanelli) (Wendy Driver)	12 (Tyrec Taylor) (Jessica Irwin)[c]	26
Poor[d]	12 (Karl Greeley) (Katie Brindle)	14 {Harold McAllister) (Tara Carroll)	26
Total sample	44	44	88

Note: The names in each cell of the table indicate the children selectcd to take place in the family-observation phase of the study.

[a]Middle-class children are those who live in households in which at least one parent is employed in a position that either entails substantial managerial authority or that draws upon highly complex, educationally certified skills (i.e., college-level).

[b]Working class children are those who live in households in which neither parent is employed in a middle-class position and at least one parent is employed in a position with little or no managerial authority and that does not draw on highly complex, educationally certified skills. This category includes lower-level white-collar workers.

[c]An inter-racial girl who has a black father and a white mother.

[d]Poor children are those who live in households in which parents receive public assistance and do not participate in the labor force on a regular, continuous basis.

Source: Lareau (2002:75).

■ EXHIBIT 8.3   **Theoretical Sampling**

Original cases interviewed in a study of cocaine users:

Realization: Some cocaine users are businesspeople.
Add businesspeople to sample:

Realization: Sample is low on women.
Add women to sample:

Realization: Some female cocaine users are mothers of young children.
Add mothers to sample:

field—the process of writing extensively is just too disruptive. The usual procedure is to jot down brief notes, called **jottings**, about highlights of the observation period, whether on paper or with a smartphone, a tablet, or another electronic device. The researcher then writes the actual **field notes** later that day or the next, outside of the "field." A daily log should also be used to record each day's activities (Bogdewic 1999).

Careful note taking yields a big payoff. On page after page, field notes will suggest new concepts, causal connections, and theoretical propositions. Social processes and settings can be described in rich detail, with ample illustrations. Exhibit 8.4, for example, contains field notes recorded by Norma Ware, an anthropologist studying living arrangements for homeless mentally ill persons in the Boston housing study for which I was a coinvestigator (Schutt 2011). The notes contain observations of the setting, the questions the anthropologist asked, the answers she received, and her analytic thoughts about one of the residents. The mood of the house at this time is evident in just this one page of field notes, with joking, casual conversation, and close friendships. "Dick" remarks on problems with household financial management, and, at the same time, we learn a bit about his own activities and personality (a regular worker who appears to like systematic plans). The field notes also provide the foundation for a more complete picture of one resident, describing "Jim's" relationships with others, his personal history, his interests and personality, and his orientation to the future. We see analytic concepts emerge in the notes, such as the concept of pulling himself together and of some house members working as a team.

Notes may be supplemented by still pictures, videotapes, and printed material circulated or posted in the research setting. Such visual material can bring an entirely different qualitative dimension into the analysis and call attention to some features of the social situation and actors within it that were missed in the notes (Grady 1996).

ENCYCLOPEDIA LINK
Field Notes

Managing the Personal Dimensions

Jottings: Brief notes written in the field about highlights of an observation period.

Field notes: Notes that describe what has been observed, heard, or otherwise experienced in a participant observation study. These notes usually are written after the observational session.

There is no formula for successfully managing the personal dimension of a field research project. It is much more an art than a science and flows more from the researcher's own personality and natural approach to other people than from formal training. Sharing similarities such as age, race, or gender with those who are studied may help create mutual feelings of comfort, but such social similarities may mask more important differences in perspective resulting from education, social class, and having the role of researcher (Doucet & Mauthner 2008). Don't place too much confidence in participant observers' reports unless they provide information about their role in the setting and how they

■ EXHIBIT 8.4   **Field Notes From an Evolving Consumer Household (ECH)**

I arrive around 4:30 p.m. and walk into a conversation between Jim and somebody else as to what color jeans he should buy. There is quite a lot of joking going on between Jim and Susan. I go out to the kitchen and find Dick about to take his dinner out to the picnic table to eat (his idea?) so I go ask if I can join him. He says yes. In the course of the conversation, I find out that he works 3 days a week in the "prevoc" program at the local day program, Food Services branch, for which he gets $10 per week. Does he think the living situation will work out? Yes. All they need is a plan for things like when somebody buys something and then everybody else uses it. Like he bought a gallon of milk and it was gone in two days, because everyone was using it for their coffee. I ask if he's gone back to the shelter to visit and he says, "No. I was glad to get out of there." He came to [the ECH] from [a shelter] through homeless outreach [a Department of Mental Health program]. Had been at [the shelter] since January. Affirms that [the ECH] is a better place to live than the shelter. Why? Because you have your own room and privacy and stuff. How have people been getting along with each other? He says, "Fine."

   I return to the living room and sit down on the couch with Jim and Susan. Susan teases Jim and he jokes back. Susan is eating a T.V. dinner with M & M's for dessert. There is joking about working off the calories from the M & M's by doing sit-ups, which she proceeds to demonstrate. This leads to a conversation about exercise during which Jim declares his intention to get back into exercise by doing sports, like basketball.

   Jim seems to have his mind on pulling himself together, which he characterizes as "getting my old self back." When I ask him what he's been doing since I saw him last, he says, "Working on my appearance." And in fact, he has had a haircut, a shave, and washed his clothes. When I ask him what his old self was like, he says, "You mean before I lost everything?" I learn that he used to work two jobs, had "a family" and was into "religion." This seems to have been when he was quite young, around eighteen. He tells me he was on the street for 7–8 years, from 1978 [to] 1985, drinking the whole time. I ask him whether he thinks living at [the ECH] will help him to get his "old self back" and he says that it will "help motivate me." I observe that he seems pretty motivated already. He says yes, "but this will motivate me more."

   Jim has a warm personality, likes to joke and laugh. He also speaks up—in meetings he is among the first to say what he thinks and he talks among the most. His "team" relationship with Bill is also important to him—"me and Bill, we work together."

Source: Field notes from an ECH made available by Norma Ware, unpublished ethnographic notes, 1991.

dealt with personal problems. A good example is Jane Ward's (2003) description of her role while studying a grassroots organization (Christopher Street West, or CSW) that organized an annual gay pride festival:

> As a lesbian inclined to be involved in community organizing, and as a regular attendee of pride festivals, my service on CSW's board of directors was, in many ways, not incongruous with my social and political identity. . . . I . . . was understood by other board members to be volunteering in, and later studying, an organization representing my own community. . . . Yet at the same time, I also held an "outsider" status as a woman on an all-male board. . . . Later, as my research interests shifted to an examination of class conflict in pride festivals, it was my identity as a middle class doctoral student volunteering alongside working class gay men that became more important. . . . [T]his shift in my analysis—from looking at gender to looking at class—allowed me to consider the ways in which I was . . . being both "insider" and "outsider," . . . assisted in my ability to avoid both the pitfalls of total immersion or "going native," and conversely, the pitfalls of professional distance. (pp. 72–73)

Intensive Interviewing

Intensive or depth interviewing is a qualitative method of finding out about people's experiences, thoughts, and feelings. Although intensive interviewing can be an important element in a participant observation study, it is often used by itself (Wolcott 1995). Unlike the more structured interviewing that may be used in survey research (discussed in Chapter 7), intensive or depth interviewing relies on open-ended questions. Rather than asking standard questions in a fixed order, intensive interviewers may allow the specific content and order of questions to vary from one interviewee to another. Rather than presenting fixed responses that presume awareness of the range of answers that respondents might give, intensive interviewers expect respondents to answer questions in their own words.

   So, similar to participant observation studies, intensive interviewing engages researchers more actively with subjects than occurs in standard survey research. The researchers must listen to lengthy explanations and ask follow-up questions, resulting in much longer interviews than most standardized interviews. Intensive interviewers actively try to probe understandings and engage interviewees in a dialogue about what they mean by their comments. Some call it "a conversation with a purpose" (Rossman & Rallis 1998:126).

   The intensive interview follows a preplanned outline of topics. It may begin with a few simple questions that gather background information while building rapport. These are often followed by a few general **grand tour questions** that are meant to elicit lengthy narratives (Miller & Crabtree 1999). As an example, Gloria González-López (2004) included the following question in her intensive interviews with Mexican fathers about attitudes toward their daughters' sexuality: "Would you like your daughter(s) to have sex before they get married? Why?"

SAGE JOURNAL ARTICLE
Qualitative Interviews

AUDIO LINK
Interviewing

Grand tour question: A broad question at the start of an interview that seeks to engage the respondent in the topic of interest.

■ **EXHIBIT 8.5** **The Saturation Point in Intensive Interviewing**

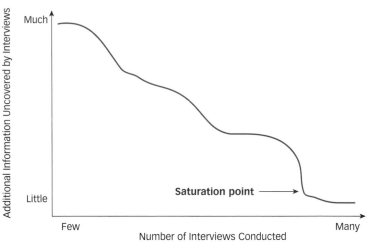

Qualitative interviewers must adapt nimbly throughout the interview, paying attention to non-verbal cues, expressions with symbolic value, and the ebb and flow of the interviewee's feelings and interests. According to Herbert J. Rubin and Irene S. Rubin (1995), "You have to be free to follow your data where they lead" (p. 64).

Random selection is rarely used to select respondents for intensive interviews, but the selection method still must be considered carefully. Researchers should try to select interviewees who are knowledgeable about the subject of the interview, who are open to talking, and who represent the range of perspectives (Rubin & Rubin 1995). Selection of new interviewees should continue, if possible, at least until the **saturation point** is reached, the point when new interviews seem to yield little additional information (Exhibit 8.5). As new issues are uncovered, additional interviewees may be selected to represent different opinions about these issues.

Establishing and Maintaining a Partnership

Because intensive interviewing does not engage researchers as participants in subjects' daily affairs, the problems of entering the field are much reduced. However, it is important to establish rapport with subjects by considering in advance how they will react to the interview arrangements and by developing an approach that does not violate their standards for social behavior. danah boyd's (2015) description of her approach to interviewing teens is instructive:

> My interviews are most effective when teens see me as someone who shares their values so I try hard to minimize signals that might be off-putting. . . . When I meet a teen, I try to find common ground as quickly as possible and verbally signal allegiance. When I interview teens, they fill out a simple questionnaire about their media habits, interests, demographics, and tastes before our conversation; I scan this to find connections. I also typically open up the interview by asking them about what they are most passionate about or interested in and hope that I will be able to ask intelligent questions about whatever topic emerges. I also use references to current events or pop culture as opening topics. . . . Creating an environment in which teens feel comfortable opening up about their lives is the hardest part of interviewing teens.

RESEARCHER INTERVIEW LINK
Interviewing

An appropriate pace is also important, so that interviewees can reflect, elaborate, and generally not feel rushed (Gordon 1992). Interviewees should be treated with respect, as knowledgeable partners whose time is valued, and a commitment to confidentiality should be stated and honored (Rubin & Rubin 1995). When an interview covers emotional or otherwise stressful topics, the interviewer should give the interviewee an opportunity to unwind at the interview's end (Rubin & Rubin 1995).

Asking Questions and Recording Answers

Intensive interviewers must plan their main questions around an outline of the interview topic. The questions should generally be short and to the point. More details can then be elicited through nondirective probes (e.g., "Can you tell me more about that?" or "uh-huh," echoing the respondent's comment, or just maintaining a moment of silence). Follow-up questions can then be tailored to answers to the main questions. Text from an interview by González-López (2004:1125), in her study of Mexican fathers' attitudes about their daughters losing their virginity, illustrates this type of probing:

> It would hurt me, because as a father, I want the best for my daughters.

> *I probed to learn more about his concerns. He responded,*

Saturation point: The point at which subject selection is ended in intensive interviewing, when new interviews seem to yield little additional information.

> I am so afraid, yes, because I don't know, because of all the things that you find out there, things that happen, that happen these days.

Tape recorders commonly are used to reduce the distraction of taking notes and improve accuracy of records. Most researchers who have tape-recorded interviews (including me) feel that they do not inhibit most interviewees and, in fact, are routinely ignored.

Interviewing Online

Our social world now includes many connections initiated and maintained through e-mail and other forms of web-based communication, so it is only natural that interviewing has also moved online. Online interviewing can facilitate interviews with others who are separated by physical distance; it also is a means to conduct research with those who are known only through such online connections as a discussion group, an e-mail distribution list, or social media (James & Busher 2009; Salmons 2012).

Online interviews can be either *synchronous*—in which the interviewer and interviewee exchange messages as in online chatting or with text messages—or *asynchronous*—in which the interviewee can respond to the interviewer's questions whenever it is convenient, usually through e-mail, but perhaps through a blog, a wiki, or an online forum (Salmons 2012). Both styles of online interviewing have advantages and disadvantages (James & Busher 2009). Synchronous interviewing provides an experience more similar to an in-person interview, thus giving more of a sense of obtaining spontaneous reactions, but it requires careful attention to arrangements and is prone to interruptions. Asynchronous interviewing allows interviewees to provide more thoughtful and developed answers, but it may be difficult to maintain interest and engagement if the exchanges continue over many days. Adding video to the exchange can increase engagement, whether through real-time videoconferencing or by sending video clips or podcasts (Salmons 2012).

Allison Deegan (2012) initially tried synchronous interviewing in her study of teenage girls who had participated in the WriteGirl mentoring program in Los Angeles. She had learned that most program alumnae used Facebook and so contacted them on Facebook and began to set up "chat" sessions. However, her first interviews turned out to be too slow and seemed jerky; Deegan learned that the problem was that some respondents did multiple other tasks while they were in the chat sessions. So Deegan began arranging asynchronous interviews so that respondents could return their answers to the interview questions by e-mail when it was convenient for them.

Whether a synchronous or asynchronous approach is used, online interviewing can facilitate the research process by creating a written record of the entire interaction without the need for typed transcripts. The relative anonymity of online communications can also encourage interviewees to be more open and honest about their feelings than they would be if interviewed in person (James & Busher 2009). However, online interviewing lacks some of the most appealing elements of qualitative methods: The revealing subtleties of facial expression, intonation, and body language are lost unless video is also added, and the intimate rapport that a good intensive interviewer can develop in a face-to-face interview cannot be achieved.

If people are creating personas online to connect with others, that too becomes an important part of the social world to investigate—even if these online personas differ from the people who create them. Second Life is a three-dimensional virtual world in which real people are represented by avatars they create or purchase. Such virtual environments are part of the social world that millions of users experience and so are starting to become objects of investigation by qualitative researchers. In such virtual worlds, avatars interact with others in communities of various types and can buy and sell clothes, equipment, buildings, and do almost anything that people do in the real world.

Ann Randall (2012) wondered whether Second Life members would experience beneficial effects from being interviewed in Second Life through their avatars, in the same way that "real people" report benefits from participating in qualitative interviews. To explore this issue, Randall e-mailed an invitation to Second Life members who were included on lists for educators and educational researchers. Randall's avatar then arranged to interview the avatars of those who agreed to be interviewed by returning a consent form with their avatar's name (retaining the anonymity of the interview). She then arranged for interviews with an availability sample of nine experienced Second Life members. Three chose to be interviewed in their own Second Life home while the other six came to virtual locations that Randall created for the purpose, such as a beach house with reclining chairs.

Randall (2012) emphasized the importance of exploring the specific virtual world(s) in which interviews would be conducted and of maintaining respectful communications based on the knowledge that each avatar represents a person with feelings that may not be expressed openly but that could be affected by the reactions of others.

Focus Groups

Focus groups are groups of unrelated individuals that are formed by a researcher and then led in group discussion of a topic for 1 to 2 hours (Krueger & Casey 2009). The researcher asks specific questions and guides the discussion to ensure that group members address these questions, but

Photo 8.3 Advances in technology have opened new avenues for interview-based research. What additional opportunities and challenges do these options bring to research studies?

©iStockphoto.com/pixdeluxe

the resulting information is qualitative and relatively unstructured. There are usually several focus groups in a focus group project. In each one, 5 to 10 individuals are recruited who have the time to participate, have some knowledge pertinent to the focus group topic, and share key characteristics with the target population.

A focus group discussion mimics the natural process of forming and expressing opinions, with open-ended questions posed by the researcher (or group leader). The researcher, or group moderator, uses an interview guide, but the dynamics of group discussion often require changes in the order and manner in which different topics are addressed (Brown 1999). When differences in attitudes between different types of people are a concern, separate focus groups may be conducted that include these different types, and then the analyst can compare comments between them (Krueger & Casey 2009). Participants usually do not know one another. Homogeneous groups may be more convivial and willing to share feelings, but heterogeneous groups may stimulate more ideas (Brown 1999).

Keith Elder and his colleagues at the University of South Carolina and elsewhere (2007:S125) used focus groups to study the decisions by African Americans not to evacuate New Orleans before Hurricane Katrina. Elder et al. conducted six focus groups with 53 evacuees who were living in hotels in Columbia, South Carolina, between October 3 and October 14, 2005. African American women conducted the focus groups after American Red Cross relief coordinators announced them at a weekly "town hall" meeting.

One of the themes identified in the focus groups was the confusion resulting from inconsistent messages about the storm's likely severity. "Participants reported confusion about what to do because of inappropriate timing of mandatory evacuation orders and confusing recommendations from different authorities" (Elder et al. 2007:S126):

> The mayor did not say it was a mandatory evacuation at first. One or two days before the hurricane hit, he said it was mandatory. It was too late then.

> They didn't give us no warning. . . . When they said leave, it was already too late.

> After [the] levees broke the mayor said mandatory evacuation, before then he was not saying mandatory evacuation.

> Governor said on TV, you didn't want to go, you didn't have to go, cause it was no threat to us, she said.

AUDIO LINK 🔊
Focus Groups

RESEARCH/SOCIAL IMPACT LINK 🌐
Qualitative Studies

Like other qualitative methods, focus group methods emphasize discovering unanticipated findings and exploring hidden meanings. They can be an indispensable aid for developing hypotheses and survey questions, for investigating the meaning of survey results, and for quickly assessing the range of opinions about an issue. The group discussion reveals the language participants used to discuss topics and think about their experiences (Smithson 2008). Because it is not possible to conduct focus groups with large, representative samples, it is always important to consider how recruitment procedures have shaped the generalizability of focus group findings.

❖ Ethical Issues in Qualitative Research

When qualitative researchers engage actively in the social world—in other words, when they are doing their job—they encounter unique ethical challenges. When a participant observer becomes an accepted part of a community or other group, natural social relations and sentiments will develop over time despite initial disclosure of the researcher's role. Just as in everyday social interaction, a qualitative researcher's engagement with others "in the field" can go in a direction that was not anticipated in the formal research plan (Bosk & De Vries 2004). As an example, Martin Levinson (2010:196–197) recounts his effort to gain the consent of a potential interviewee in his ethnographic study of Romani gypsies in the United Kingdom:

Me [Levinson]: So, would you mind answering a few questions?
No response.
. . .

Me: What I'm hoping is that this research will be of some use in . . .

Smithy: I'm not f—king interested in what you say your work's about. I told you to f—k off.

Me: Look, I tell you what. I won't even ask you any questions. Just talk to me for five minutes—about whatever you like, then I'll f—k off.

It seemed to me that his expression softened. . . . Perhaps, too, I had passed some test of maleness.

Smithy: Buy me a drink, and I'll talk to you.

The specific ethical issues in a particular project vary with the type of qualitative methods used and the specific circumstances in which a project is conducted. The following six issues should be considered: (1) voluntary participation, (2) subject well-being, (3) identity disclosure, (4) confidentiality, (5) appropriate boundaries, and (6) researcher safety.

Voluntary Participation

The first step in ensuring that subjects are participating in a study voluntarily is to provide clear information about the research and the opportunity to decline to participate (King & Horrocks 2010). However, even when such information is provided, the ongoing interaction between the researcher and the participant can blur the meaning of voluntary participation:

> A skilled researcher can establish rapport and convince subjects to reveal almost anything, including things the researcher may not want to be responsible for knowing. (Sieber & Tolich 2013:164)

Few researchers or institutional review boards are willing to condone covert participation because it offers no way to ensure that participation by the subjects is voluntary. However, interpreting the standard of voluntary participation can be difficult even when the researcher's role is more open.

Some researchers recommend adherence to a **process consent** standard. Researchers using process consent check with participants at each stage of the project about their willingness to continue in the project (Sieber & Tolich 2013).

Information about the research that is provided to research participants must also be tailored to their capacities, interests, and needs if they are able to give truly informed consent (Hammersley & Traianou 2012). Jim Birckhead commented that he "never felt that" the fundamentalist Christian serpent-handlers he studied in the southern United States "fully comprehended what I was actually doing in their midst" (as quoted in Hammersley & Traianou 2012:97).

Subject Well-Being

Every field researcher should consider carefully before beginning a project how to avoid harm to subjects. Researchers can avoid harm, in part, by maintaining the confidentiality of research subjects. Such concerns were raised after publication of a book by sociologist Sudhir Venkatesh (2008) about a gang in a Chicago housing project. Venkatesh had gained the trust of housing residents after being given access to them by a local gang leader and the project's manager and so was able to ask residents about their sources of unreported income, such as through babysitting, prostitution, and car repair. Venkatesh then reviewed with the gang leader what he had learned, leading the gang leader to extort more money from residents who had sources of income about which he had been unaware and leading Venkatesh to be shunned by the residents who had shared their income secrets with him (Sieber & Tolich 2013).

The well-being of the group or community studied as a whole should also be considered in relation to publication or other forms of reporting findings. Carolyn Ellis (1995) returned to a Chesapeake fishing community in the hope of conducting a follow-up to her ethnographic study; she was surprised to learn that residents had read excerpts from her book about the community (provided by another researcher!) and some were very upset with how they had been portrayed (pp. 79–80).

> "I thought we was friends, you and me, just talkin.' I didn't think you would put it in no book."

> "'But I told people down here I was writing a book,' I reply feebly."

> "But I still thought we was just talkin.' And you said we're dirty and don't know how to dress." . . . "It's my life, not anybody else's business. Weren't yours neither."

These problems are less likely in intensive interviewing and focus groups, but researchers using these methods should try to identify negative feelings both after interviews and after reports are released and then help distressed subjects cope with their feelings through debriefing or referrals for professional help. Online interviewing can create additional challenges for interviews in which respondents become inappropriately personal over time (King & Horrocks 2010).

Identity Disclosure

Most people would argue that the standard of informed consent cannot be met in any meaningful way if researchers do not fully disclose their identity. But how much disclosure about the study is necessary, and how hard should researchers try to make sure that their research purposes are understood? In field research on Codependents Anonymous, Leslie Irvine (1998) found that the emphasis on anonymity and expectations for group discussion made it difficult to disclose her identity.

Internet-based research can violate the principles of voluntary participation and identity disclosure when researchers participate in discussions and record and analyze text but do not identify themselves as researchers (Jesnadum 2000). By contrast, members of online communities can disguise their identities, as men may masquerade as women and children as adults, or vice versa. Netnographers can lessen the risks caused by these uncertainties by making their own identities known, stating clearly their expectations for participation, and providing an explicit informed consent letter that is available as discussion participants come and go (Denzin & Lincoln 2008).

Process consent: An interpretation of the ethical standard of voluntary consent that allows participants to change their decision about participating at any point by requiring that the researcher check with participants at each stage of the project about their willingness to continue in the project.

Confidentiality

Field researchers typically use fictitious names for the characters in their reports, but doing so does not always guarantee confidentiality to their research subjects. Individuals in the setting studied may be able to identify those whose actions are described and thus may become privy to some knowledge about their colleagues or neighbors that had formerly been kept from them. Therefore, researchers should make every effort to expunge possible identifying material from published information and to alter unimportant aspects of a description when necessary to prevent identity disclosure. Focus groups create a particular challenge because the researcher cannot guarantee that participants will not disclose information that others would like to be treated as confidential. Social media researcher danah boyd (2015) explains that she replaces names with pseudonyms, and she uses more elaborate procedures to maintain confidentiality:

> I also purposefully obscure data that I collect as part of my online observations and content analysis. I work to scrub identifying information from all digital material. When I use screen shots of profiles in talks or in papers, they are typically heavily modified (using Photoshop) to erase identifying information. I either blur photos or use substitute photos from friends, my childhood, or young adults who have content available through Creative Commons. When I quote text from profiles, I often alter the quotes to maintain the meaning but to make the quote itself unsearchable.

Appropriate Boundaries

Maintaining appropriate boundaries between the researcher and research participants is a uniquely important issue in qualitative research projects that creates challenges for identity disclosure, subject well-being, and voluntary participation. The long-term relationships that can develop in participant observation studies can make it seem natural for researchers to offer tangible help to research participants, such as taking a child to school or lending funds. These involvements can in turn make it difficult to avoid becoming an advocate for the research participants, rather than a sympathetic observer. Mitch Duneier (1999) explains that he resolved this issue in his study of impoverished sidewalk book vendors in New York City by doing "everything I could to be helpful" when personal problems were discussed, "but I never gave advice, opinions, or help beyond what was asked for" (p. 355).

©iStockphoto.com/eyecrave

Photo 8.4 Safety of the researchers and participants should always be considered. What safety considerations need to be made when conducting research in disaster areas, such as this town that was devastated by a tornado?

Researcher Safety

Research "in the field" about disasters or simply unfamiliar neighborhoods or nations should not begin until any potential risks to researcher safety have been evaluated. As Virginia Dickson-Swift, Erica James, Sandra Kippen, and Pranee Liamputtong (2008) note, risks in qualitative research can be emotional as well as physical:

> Look after yourself—have someone who you can debrief with, in fact have two people who you can debrief with. . . . Think there is always a risk in this research. You have got to remember that sometimes we go into spaces in people's lives that others have not been and that has the potential to be risky, both physically if the environment is not a safe one, or emotionally if the research affects you in some way. (pp. 137–138)

Few qualitative research projects will be barred by consideration of the ethical issues discussed here, but almost all projects require careful attention to them. The more important concern for researchers is to identify the ethically troublesome aspects of their proposed research and resolve them before the project begins and to act on new ethical issues as they come up during the project.

❖ Conclusions

Qualitative research allows the careful investigator to obtain a richer and more intimate view of the social world than is possible with more structured methods. It is not hard to understand why so many qualitative studies have become classics in the social science literature. The emphases in qualitative research on inductive reasoning and incremental understanding help stimulate and inform other research approaches. Exploratory research to chart the dimensions of previously unstudied social settings and intensive investigations of the subjective meanings that motivate individual action are particularly well served by the techniques of participant observation, intensive interviewing, and focus groups.

Key Terms

Adaptive research design   121
Case study   122
Complete (or covert) participant   126
Complete (or overt) observer   125
Covert observer   125
Ethnography   122
Field notes   128
Field research   125
Field researcher   125

Focus groups   125
Gatekeeper   126
Grand tour question   129
Intensive (in-depth) interviewing   125
Jottings   128
Key informant   126
Netnography   123
Participant observation   125

Participant observer
(overt participant)   126
Process consent   133
Reactive effects   125
Reflexivity   121
Saturation point   130
Theoretical sampling   127
Thick description   122

Highlights

- Qualitative methods are most useful in exploring new issues, investigating hard-to-study groups, and determining the meaning people give to their lives and actions. In addition, most social research projects can be improved, in some respects, by taking advantage of qualitative techniques.

- Qualitative researchers tend to develop ideas inductively, try to understand the social context and sequential nature of attitudes and actions, and explore the subjective meanings that participants attach to events. These researchers rely primarily on participant observation, intensive interviewing, and focus groups.

- Case studies use thick description and other qualitative techniques to provide a holistic picture of a setting or group.

- Ethnographers attempt to understand the culture of a group.

- Participant observers may adopt one of several roles for a particular research project. Each role represents a different balance between observing and participating. Many field researchers prefer a moderate role, participating as well as observing in a group but acknowledging publicly the researcher role. Such a role avoids the ethical issues that covert participation poses while still allowing the insights into the social world derived from participating directly in it. The role that the participant observer chooses should be based on an evaluation of the problems that are likely to arise from reactive effects and the ethical dilemmas of covert participation.

- Field researchers must develop strategies for entering the field, developing and maintaining relations in the field, sampling, and recording and analyzing data. Selection of sites or other units to study may reflect an emphasis on typical cases, deviant cases, or critical cases that can provide more information than others.

- Netnographers use ethnographic techniques to study online communities.

- Recording and analyzing notes is a crucial step in field research. Jottings are used as brief reminders about events in the field, and daily logs are useful to chronicle the researcher's activities. Detailed field notes should be recorded and analyzed daily. Analysis of the notes can guide refinement of methods used in the field and of the concepts, indicators, and models developed to explain what has been observed.

- Theoretical sampling methods can improve generalizability of qualitative research findings.

- Intensive interviews involve open-ended questions and follow-up probes, with specific question content and order varying from one interview to another. Intensive interviews can supplement participant observation data.

- Focus groups combine elements of participant observation and intensive interviewing. They can increase the validity of attitude measurement by revealing what people say when they present their opinions in a group context instead of in the artificial one-on-one interview setting.

- Six ethical issues that should be given particular attention in field research concern (1) voluntary participation, (2) subject well-being, (3) identity disclosure, (4) confidentiality, (5) appropriate boundaries, and (6) researcher safety. Process consent procedures may be appropriate in ongoing field research projects. Qualitative research conducted online, with discussion groups or e-mail traffic, raises special concerns about voluntary participation and identity disclosure.

- Adding qualitative elements to structured survey projects and experimental designs can enrich understanding of social processes.

⋯⋯ **Chapter Questions** ⋯⋯⋯⋯⋯⋯⋯⋯⋯⋯⋯

1. Review the experiments and surveys described in previous chapters. Pick one, and propose a field research design that would focus on the same research question but with participant observation techniques in a local setting. Propose the role that you would play in the setting, along the participant observation continuum, and explain why you would favor this role. Describe the stages of your field research study, including your plans for entering the field, developing and maintaining relationships, sampling, and recording and analyzing data. Then, discuss what you would expect your study to add to the findings resulting from the study described in the book.

2. Intensive interviews are the core of many qualitative research designs. How do they differ from the structured survey procedures that you studied in Chapter 7? What are their advantages and disadvantages over standardized interviewing? How does intensive interviewing differ from the qualitative method of participant observation? What are the advantages and disadvantages of these two methods?

3. Research on disasters poses a number of methodological challenges. In what ways are qualitative methods suited to disaster research? What particular qualitative methods would you have emphasized if you had been able to design research in New Orleans in the immediate aftermath of Hurricane Katrina? What unique challenges would you have confronted because of the nature of the disaster?

⋯⋯ **Practice Exercises** ⋯⋯⋯⋯⋯⋯⋯⋯⋯⋯⋯⋯

1. Conduct a brief observational study in a public location on campus where students congregate. A cafeteria, a building lobby, or a lounge would be ideal. You can sit and observe, taking occasional notes unobtrusively, without violating any expectations of privacy. Observe for 30 minutes. Write up field notes, being sure to include a description of the setting and a commentary on your own behavior and your reactions to what you observed.

2. Develop an interview guide that focuses on a research question addressed in one of the studies in this book. Using this guide, conduct an intensive interview with one person who is involved with the topic in some way. Take only brief notes during the interview, and then write up as complete a record of the interview as you can immediately afterward. Turn in an evaluation of your performance as an interviewer and note taker, together with your notes.

3. Devise a plan for using a focus group to explore and explain student perspectives on some current event. How would you recruit students for the group? What types of students would you try to include? How would you introduce the topic and the method to the group? What questions would you ask? What problems would you anticipate, such as discord between focus group members or digressions from the chosen topic? How would you respond to these problems?

4. Review postings to an online discussion group. How could you study this group using netnography? What challenges would you encounter?

STUDENT STUDY SITE

⑤SAGE edge™

The Student Study Site, available at **edge.sagepub.com/schuttusw**, includes useful study materials including eFlashcards, videos, audio resources, journal articles, and encyclopedia articles, many of which are represented by the media links throughout the text.

Unobtrusive Methods

A re you an extraordinary person? Are you a born leader? These questions are part of the Narcissistic Personality Inventory developed by Robert Raskin and Calvin Hall (1979) and adapted for survey research by psychologist Robert Emmons (1984). Management researchers Arijit Chatterjee and Donald C. Hambrick (2007) didn't think chief executive officers (CEOs) would give honest answers to these questions, so they turned to **unobtrusive methods** to study narcissism among computer industry CEOs. There are several types of unobtrusive methods and many reasons for using them.

This chapter introduces five different unobtrusive methods: **unobtrusive measures** of behavior, secondary data analysis of previously collected data, "Big Data" records of social life, historical and comparative analysis, and content analysis. The chapter highlights special opportunities and challenges involved in the use of unobtrusive methods as well as ethical issues of particular concern. You may be surprised to learn that there are many indirect sources of data for social research.

❖ Unobtrusive Measures of Behavior

Chatterjee and Hambrick (2007) identified five different unobtrusive measures of CEO narcissism and combined them into a narcissism index: (1) the prominence of the CEO's photograph in the company's annual report; (2) the CEO's prominence in the company's press releases; (3) the CEO's use of first-person singular pronouns in interviews; (4) the CEO's cash compensation divided by that of the second-highest-paid executive in the firm; and (5) the CEO's noncash compensation divided by that of the second-highest-paid executive in the firm. Chatterjee and Hambrick (2007) use French CEO Jean-Marie Messier as an example of the type of CEO who would score high on these indicators. Messier sometimes referred to himself in e-mails as "J6M," "Jean-Marie Messier

Myself, Master of the World" (in French). Over time, more narcissistic CEOs generated more big wins and big losses in their companies (performance extremeness), with no net advantage over companies led by less narcissistic CEOs (Chatterjee and Hambrick 2007). Exhibit 9.1 graphs the association between CEO narcissism and performance extremeness in terms of return on assets (ROA).

In their classic book on unobtrusive measures, Eugene Webb and his colleagues (2000) also discussed the use of physical trace evidence as an unobtrusive measure of behavior. To measure the prevalence of drinking in college dorms or fraternity houses, we might count the number of empty bottles of alcoholic beverages in the surrounding dumpsters. Student interest in the college courses they are taking might be measured by counting the number of times that books left on reserve are checked out or by the number of class handouts left in trash barrels outside a lecture hall. Webb et al. (2000:37) suggested measuring the interest in museum exhibits by the frequency with which tiles in front of the exhibits needed to be replaced. Social variables can also be measured by observing clothing, hair length, or reactions to such stimuli as dropped letters or jaywalkers.

Such unobtrusive measures can improve measurement validity by avoiding the bias of self-reports about socially desirable or undesirable behavior. They also allow researchers to measure behavior that has already occurred and that may not be directly observable for such reasons as time and money or ethical constraints. However, because such measures often cannot be linked to particular individuals, they are most useful for measuring the behavior of people in the aggregate.

❖ Secondary Data Analysis

Secondary data analysis is the method of using preexisting data in a different way or to answer a different research question than intended by those who collected the data. The most common sources of **secondary data**—previously collected data that are used in a new analysis—are social science surveys and data collected by government agencies, often with survey research

■ **EXHIBIT 9.1**   **CEO Narcissism and Extremeness in Company Performance**

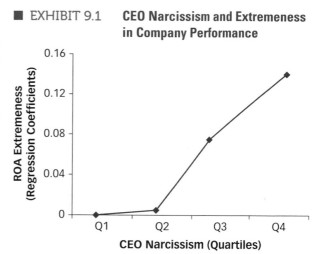

Source: Page 376, figure 2b from Chatterjee, Arijit, and Donald C. Hambrick. 2007. "It's All About Me: Narcissistic Chief Executive Officers and Their Effects on Company Strategy and Performance." *Administrative Science Quarterly* 52:351–386.

Unobtrusive methods: Research methods in which data are collected without the knowledge or participation of the individuals or groups that generated the data.

Unobtrusive measure: A measurement based on physical traces or other data that are collected without the knowledge or participation of the individuals or groups that generated the data.

Secondary data analysis: The method of using preexisting data in a different way or to answer a different research question than intended by those who collected the data.

Secondary data: Previously collected data that are used in a new analysis.

RESEARCH

In the News

TRASH: THE FOCUS OF ANTHROPOLOGICAL RESEARCH IN NEW YORK

New York University anthropologist Robin Nagle has found "a gold mine for garbage pickers." New York's Department of Sanitation collects almost 3.5 million tons of trash each year. The contents range from discarded photos of a divorced spouse and bottles from those with a drinking problem to diapers from new babies and clothing discarded as no longer in fashion. Professor Nagle realized that she could improve understanding of our modern "throw-away culture" by systematically studying this trash. She became the "anthropologist-in-residence" for the sanitation department; has worked as a regular, salaried sanitation worker; has helped to publicize the value of "the most important workers that we have in this city"; and has published books on her findings.

For Further Thought ?

1. What can social researchers understand about the social world by investigating this most unobtrusive of indicators?

2. What problems do you suppose Professor Nagle has to overcome in this research approach?

News source: Dobnik, Verena. 2015. "Trash Offers Peek Into New Yorkers' Lives." *New York Times,* August 31:A5.

SAGE JOURNAL ARTICLE
Geography and Social Networks

RESEARCHER INTERVIEW LINK
Secondary Data Analysis

methods. It is also possible to reanalyze data that have been collected in experimental studies or with qualitative methods. Secondary data are readily available through various websites and provide the foundation for a great many social science articles and books.

Irish researchers Richard Layte (Economic and Social Research Institute) and Christopher Whelan (University College Dublin) used secondary analysis of data from the European Community Household Panel Survey to improve understanding of poverty in Europe. The data they obtained from Eurostat, the Statistical Office of the European Communities (Eurostat 2003) represented the years from 1994 to 1998, thus allowing Layte and Whelan (2003) to investigate whether poverty tends to persist more in some countries than in others. They found a tendency for individuals and households to be "trapped" in poverty, but to an extent that varied with the social welfare supports available in a country.

Secondary Data Sources

University researchers can obtain many data sets for secondary analyses with no more effort than a few clicks on a website; a number of important data sets can be analyzed directly on the web by users who lack their own statistical software (see my example of doing this in Chapter 11). A major source of social science data sets is the **Inter-university Consortium for Political and Social Research (ICPSR)** website at the University of Michigan (http://www.icpsr.umich.edu/icpsrweb/landing.jsp). More than 8,000 data sets from the United States and more than 130 other countries are available through ICPSR. The University of California at Berkeley's Survey Documentation and Analysis (SDA) archive provides several data sets from national omnibus surveys, as well as from the U.S. Census, surveys on racial attitudes and prejudice, and several labor and health surveys (https://sda.berkeley.edu/archive.htm). The National Archive of Criminal Justice Data (https://www.icpsr.umich.edu/icpsrweb/NACJD/) is an excellent source of data in the area of criminal justice, although, like many other data collections, including key data from the U.S. Census, it is also available through the ICPSR. Much of the statistical data collected by U.S. federal government agencies can be accessed through the consolidated FedStats website, www.fedstats.gov.

ICPSR also catalogs reports and publications containing analyses that have used ICPSR data sets since 1962—67,215 citations were in this archive on September 6, 2015. This superb resource provides an excellent starting point for the literature search that should precede a secondary data analysis. In most cases, you can learn from detailed study reports a great deal about the study methodology, including the rate of response in a sample survey and the reliability of any indexes constructed. Published articles provide examples of how others have described the study methodology as well as research questions that have already been studied with the data set and issues that remain to be resolved. You can search this literature at the ICPSR site simply by entering the same search terms that you used to find data sets or by entering the specific study number of the data set on which you have focused (Photo 9.1). Don't start a secondary analysis without reviewing such reports and publications.

ICPSR (Inter-university Consortium for Political and Social Research): Academic consortium that archives data sets online from major surveys and other social research and makes them available for analysis by others.

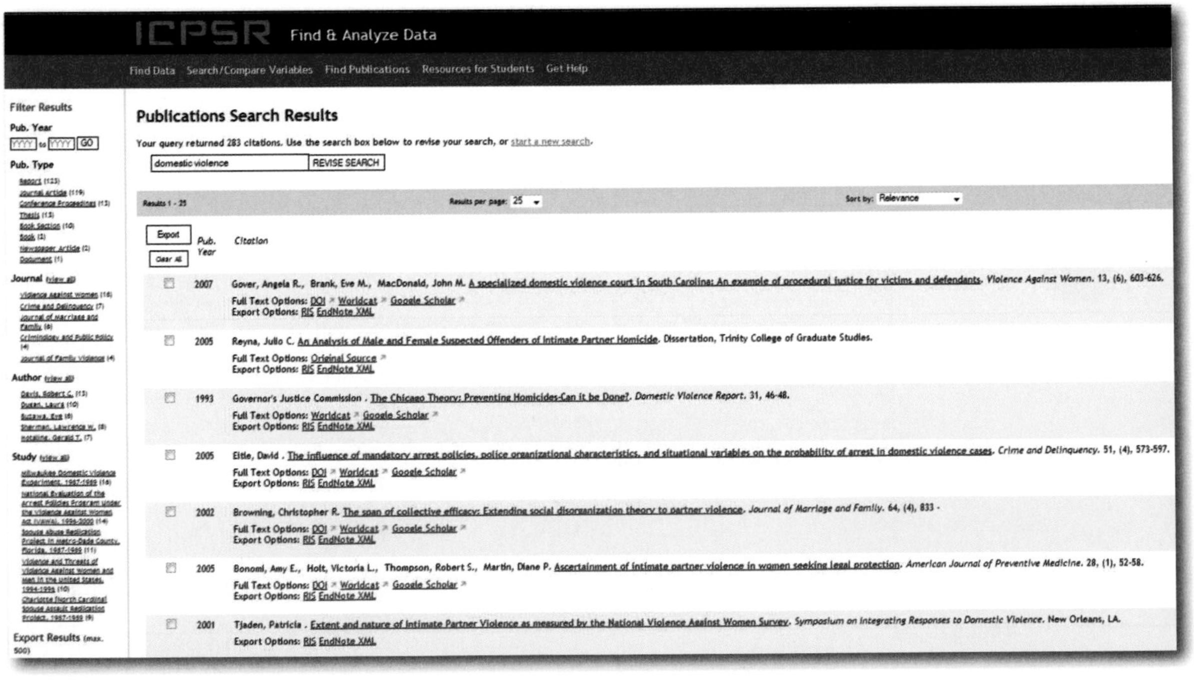

Photo 9.1 ICPSR bibliography search.

Source: Reprinted with permission from the Inter-university Consortium for Political and Social Research.

CAREERS
and Research

LEE RAINIE, PEW RESEARCH CENTER

You already know of Lee Rainie's research from findings presented in Chapter 1 from the Pew Research Center Internet Project. Rainie received his B.A. from Harvard University and has an M.A. in political science from Long Island University.

He was for many years managing editor at *U.S. News & World Report,* but since 1999 he has directed the Pew Internet Project, a nonprofit, nonpartisan "fact tank" that studies the social impact of the Internet. Since December 1999, the Washington, D.C., research center has explored how people's Internet use affects their families, communities, health care, education, civic and political life, and workplaces.

The U.S. government has conducted a census of the population every 10 years since 1790; since 1940, this census has also included a census of housing. This decennial Census of Population and Housing is a rich source of social science data (Lavin 1994). Participation in the census is required by law, and confidentiality of the information obtained is mandated by law for 72 years after collection. Census data are reported for geographic units, including states, metropolitan areas, counties, census tracts (small, relatively permanent areas within counties), and even blocks (Exhibit 9.2). The Census Bureau's monthly *CPS* provides basic data on labor force activity that is then used in U.S. Bureau of Labor Statistics reports. The Census Bureau also collects data on agriculture, manufacturers, construction and other business, foreign countries, and foreign trade. Census data are used to apportion seats in the U.S. House of Representatives and to determine federal and state legislative district boundaries, as well as to inform other decisions by government agencies.

The U.S. Census website (www.census.gov) provides much information about the nearly 100 surveys and censuses that the Census Bureau directs each year, including direct access to many statistics for particular geographic units. An interactive data retrieval system, American FactFinder, is the primary means for distributing results from the 2010 Census: You can review its organization and download data at http://factfinder2.census.gov/main.html. The catalog of the ICPSR (www.icpsr.umich.edu/icpsrweb/ICPSR/) also lists many census reports. An even more accessible way to use U.S. Census data is through the website maintained by the Social Science Data Analysis Network, at www.ssdan.net/. Check out the DataCounts! options.

Far fewer qualitative data sets are available for secondary analysis, but the number is growing. European countries, particularly England, have been at the forefront of efforts to promote archiving of qualitative data. The United Kingdom's Economic and Social Research Council established the Qualitative Data Archiving Resource Center at the University of Essex in 1994 (Heaton 2008:507). Now part of the Economic and Social Data Service, UK Data Service QualiBank (http://ukdataservice.ac.uk/get-data/explore-online/qualibank/qualibank) provides access to data from 888 qualitative research projects. After registering at the UK Data Service site, you can browse or search interview transcripts and other materials from many qualitative

▶ **VIDEO LINK**
Secondary Data Resources

RESEARCH/SOCIAL IMPACT LINK
Sharing Research

■ EXHIBIT 9.2   **Census Small-Area Geography**

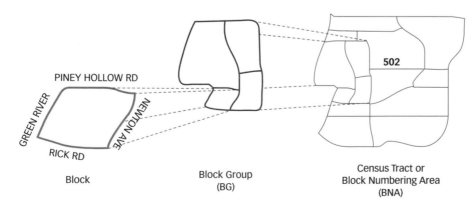

PINEY HOLLOW RD
GREEN RIVER
NEWTON AVE
RICK RD
502

Block

Block Group
(BG)

Census Tract or
Block Numbering Area
(BNA)

Source: U.S. Bureau of the Census (1994:8).

studies, but access to many studies is restricted to users in the United Kingdom or according to other criteria. In the United States, the ICPSR collection includes an expanding number of studies containing qualitative data (380 data sets as of September 2015).

The Library of Congress (http://www.loc.gov/) offers many resources, including an extensive collection of life stories from veterans (http://lcweb2.loc.gov/diglib/vhp/html/search/search.html) and others. The University of Southern Maine's Center for the Study of Lives (http://usm.maine.edu/lifestorycenter/) collects interview transcripts that record the life stories of people of diverse ages and backgrounds. Their collection includes transcripts representing more than 35 different ethnic groups, experiences of historical events ranging from the Great Depression to the Vietnam War, and reports on health problems such as HIV/AIDS. Access requires registration.

Challenges for Secondary Data Analyses

The use of secondary data analysis methods has several advantages for social researchers (Rew et al. 2000:226):

- It allows analyses of social processes in otherwise inaccessible settings.

- It saves time and money.

- It allows the researcher to avoid data collection problems.

- It facilitates comparison with other samples.

- It may allow inclusion of many more variables and a more diverse sample than otherwise would be feasible.

- It may allow data from multiple studies to be combined.

However, the secondary data analyst also faces some unique challenges. It may not be possible for a secondary data analyst to focus on the specific research question of original interest or to use the most appropriate sampling or measurement approach for studying that research question. Secondary data analysis inevitably involves a trade-off between the ease with which the research process can be initiated and the specific hypotheses that can be tested and methods that can be used (Riedel 2000).

Data quality is always a concern with secondary data, even when the data are collected by an official government agency. Government actions result, at least in part, from political processes that may not have as their first priority the design or maintenance of high-quality data for social scientific analysis. For example, political opposition to the British Census's approach to recording ethnic origin led to changes in the 1991 census that rendered its results inconsistent with prior years and that demonstrated the "tenuous relationship between enumeration [Census] categories and possible social realities" (Fenton 1996:155).

The need for concern is much greater in research across national boundaries because different data collection systems and definitions of key variables may have been used (Glover 1996). Census counts can be distorted by incorrect answers to census questions as well as by inadequate coverage of the entire population (Rives & Serow 1988). National differences in the division of labor between genders within households can confuse the picture when comparing household earnings between nations without accounting for these differences (Jarvis 1997).

Confidence in any secondary analysis will increase if satisfactory answers can be given to the following questions (adapted from Riedel 2000:55–69; Stewart & Kamins 1993:17–31):

1. *What were the agency's or researcher's goals in collecting the data?* The goals of the researcher, research, or research sponsor influence every step in the process of designing a research project, analyzing the resulting data, and reporting the results. Some of these goals will be stated quite explicitly, but others may only be implicit—reflected in the decisions made but not acknowledged in the research report or other publications. When the research question or other goals in the secondary analysis diverge from those of the original investigator, you should consider how this divergence affects the use of the resulting data for a different purpose.

   For example, Pamela Paxton (2002) studied the role of secondary organizations in democratic politics in a sample of 101 countries but found that she could measure the prevalence of only international nongovernmental associations (INGOs) because comparable figures on purely national associations were not available. She cautioned, "INGOs represent only a specialized subset of all the associations present in a country" (Paxton 2002:261). We need to consider this limitation when interpreting the results of her secondary analysis.

2. *What data were collected, when were they collected, and what were they intended to measure?* A report based on a secondary data analysis should provide a clear description of the data collection system and its purpose. Consider reviewing the guidelines that agency personnel were supposed to follow in processing cases (Riedel 2000). Both historical and comparative analyses can be affected by differences in measurement over time. For example, the percentage of the U.S. population not counted in the U.S. Census appears to have declined since 1880 from about 7% to 1%, but undercounting continues to be more common

among poorer urban dwellers and recent immigrants (King & Magnuson 1995; see also Chapter 5). The relatively successful 2000 U.S. Census reduced undercounting (Forero 2000b) but still suffered from accusations of shoddy data collection procedures in some areas (Forero 2000a).

3. *What specific methods were used for data collection?* Copies of the forms used for data collection should be available, specific measures should have been inspected, and the ways in which these data were processed by the agency/agencies should have been reviewed.

4. *What is known about the success of the data collection effort? How are missing data indicated? What kind of documentation is available? How consistent are the data with data available from other sources?* The U.S. Census Bureau provides extensive documentation about data quality, including missing data, and it documents the efforts it makes to improve data quality. The 2010 Census Program for Evaluations and Experiments was designed to improve the decennial census in 2020, as well as other Census Bureau censuses and surveys. This is an ongoing effort, since 1950, with tests of questionnaire design and other issues. You can read more about it at http://www.census.gov/2010census/about/cpex.php.

Photo 9.2 Thanks to the Internet and social media, massive amounts of data produced by human activity are now available online. What might be some of the opportunities and challenges presented to researchers looking to use these data?

Answering these questions helps ensure that the researcher is familiar with the data he or she will analyze and can help identify any problems with it.

❖ Big Data

Big Data refers to data involving an entirely different order of magnitude than what we are used to thinking about as large data sets. Each year, if you're an "average" person, you produce about eight trillion terabytes of data—the equivalent of answering eight trillion yes-or-no questions! (Aiden & Michel 2013:11).

Here are some examples of what now qualifies as Big Data (Mayer-Schönberger & Cukier 2013:8–9): Facebook users upload more than 10 million photos every hour and leave a comment or click on a "like" button almost 3 billion times per day; YouTube users upload more than an hour of video every second; and Twitter users sent more than 500 million tweets per day in 2015 (https://about.twitter.com/company).

Here's a quick demonstration: Would you like to know how popular your discipline is? One way to answer that question is to see how frequently the name of the discipline has appeared in all the books ever written in the world. It may surprise you to learn that it is possible right now to answer that question, though with two key limitations: We can examine *only* those books written in English and in several other languages and, as of 2013, we were limited to "only" one quarter of all books ever published—30 million books (Aiden & Michel 2013:16).

To check this out, go to the Google **Ngrams** site (https://books.google.com/ngrams), type in "sociology, political science, anthropology, criminology, psychology, economics," and check the "case-insensitive" box (and change the ending year to 2015). Exhibit 9.3 shows the resulting screen (if you don't obtain a graph, try using a different browser). Note that the height of a graph line represents the percentage that the term represents of all words in books published in each year, so a rising line means greater relative interest in the word, not more books being published. You can see that psychology emerges in the mid-19th century, while sociology, economics, anthropology, and political science appear in the latter part of that century, and criminology arrives in the early 20th century. Interest in sociology soared as the 1960s progressed, but then dropped off sharply in the 1980s. What else can you see in the graph? It's hard to stop checking other ideas by adding in other terms, searching in other languages, or shifting to another topic entirely.

Big Data: Massive data sets reflecting human activity that are accessible in computer-readable form, available to social scientists, and manageable with today's computers.

Ngrams: Frequency graphs produced by Google's database of all words printed in more than one quarter of the world's books over time (with coverage still expanding).

Make no mistake about it. The potential for Big Data is not just of academic interest—Big Data work is already changing lives. For example, Jeremy Ginsberg and some colleagues (2009) at Google realized they could improve the response to the spread of flu around the world by taking advantage of the fact that about 90 million U.S. adults search online for information about specific illnesses each year. Ginsberg et al. started a collaboration with the U.S. Centers for Disease Control and Prevention (CDC), which collects data from about 2,700 health centers about patients' flu symptoms each year (Butler 2013). By comparing these official CDC data with information from the Google searches, Ginsberg and his colleagues were able to develop a Big Data–based procedure for predicting the onset of the flu. You can see the latest trends yourself at https://www.google.com/publicdata/explore?ds=z3bsqef7ki44ac_.

VIDEO LINK ▶
Big Data

AUDIO LINK ⊕
Big Data

But there's also a cautionary tale in Google's experience with predicting flu trends. In the 2013 flu season, Google Flu Trends predicted a much higher peak level of flu than actually occurred. The problem seems to have been that widespread media coverage and the declaration of a public health emergency in New York City led many more people than usual to search for flu-related information, even though they were not experiencing symptoms themselves. Google has been refining its procedures to account for this problem, and other researchers have shifted their attention to analysis of flu-related tweets or to data from networks of thousands of volunteers who report symptoms experienced by family members to a central database (Butler 2013). So having incredible amounts of data does not allow us to forget about the potential for problems in measurement or sampling.

The sources of Big Data are increasing rapidly. One billion people use Facebook, thereby creating digital records that can, with appropriate arrangements, be analyzed to better understand social behavior (Aiden & Michel 2013). Big Data are also generated by global positioning system (GPS) users, social media, smartphones, wristband health monitors, student postings, and even student activity in online education programs (Mayer-Schönberger & Cukier 2013). The U.S. Geological Survey is using tweets to collect data regarding earthquakes (Earle et al. 2015). Public utilities, government agencies, and private companies can learn about their customers by analyzing patterns revealed in their records. Big Data is creating possibilities for investigation of the social world that could not have been envisioned even 20 years ago.

In a striking example, Robert Bond, James Fowler, and others at Facebook and the University of California, San Diego, conducted a randomized experiment with Facebook on the day of the 2010 congressional elections (Bond et al. 2012). Here is their description of the research design:

> Users [of Facebook] were randomly assigned to a "social message" group, an "informational message" group, or a control group. The social message group ($n = 60,055,176$) was shown a statement at the top of their "News Feed." This message encouraged the user to vote, provided a link to find local polling places, showed a clickable button reading "I Voted," showed a counter indicating how many other Facebook users had previously reported voting, and displayed up to six small randomly selected "profile pictures" of the user's Facebook friends who had already clicked the I Voted button. . . . The informational message group ($n = 611,044$) was shown the message, poll information, counter, and button, but they were not shown any faces of friends. The control group ($n = 613,096$) did not receive any message at the top of their News Feed. (p. 295)

As indicated in Exhibit 9.4, individuals in the group that received the personalized message about their friends having voted were more likely to vote—and the effect was higher the more closely connected they were to those friends. Bond et al. (2012:297) estimate that receiving this message led 60,000 more people to vote in 2010, while the effect of friends having seen the message could have increased turnout by 280,000 votes!

But researchers must understand the medium they are collecting data from in order to benefit from it. danah boyd (2011) at Microsoft Research has identified a racial difference in the use of MySpace and Facebook for social networking among teens, so

■ **EXHIBIT 9.3   Ngram of Social Sciences**

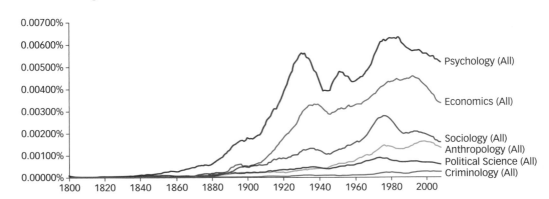

■ EXHIBIT 9.4   **Facebook Experiment on Voter Turnout**

a   Informational message

Social message

b

Examples of (a) the informational message and social message Facebook treatments and (b) their direct effect on voting behavior.

Sources: Adapted from Bond et al. (2012:296); row of photos: © istockpoto.com/franckreporter.

limitation of a study to one of these social media sites would skew findings. In fact, boyd has shed some light on the impact of race and class on adolescent social patterns by comparing trends in usage of both sites.

❖ Historical and Comparative Research Methods

Although the United States and several European nations have maintained democratic systems of governance for more than 100 years, democratic rule has more often been brief and unstable, when it has occurred at all. What explains the presence of democratic practices in one country and their absence in another? Are democratic politics a realistic option for every nation? What about Libya? Egypt? Iraq? Are there some prerequisites in historical experience, cultural values, or economic resources (Markoff 2005)?

The central insight behind historical and comparative research is that we can improve our understanding of social processes when we make comparisons to other times and places. However, because this broader focus involves collecting data from records about the past or from other nations, the methods used in historical and comparative investigations present unique challenges to social researchers.

Historical Social Science Methods

Much historical (and comparative) research is qualitative. This style of historical social research tends to have several features that are similar to those used in other qualitative methodologies. First, like other qualitative methods, qualitative historical research is inductive: It develops an explanation for what happened from the details discovered about the past. In addition, qualitative historical research is **case-oriented**; it focuses on the nation or other unit as a whole, rather than only on different parts of the whole in isolation from each other (Ragin 2000). This could be considered the most distinctive feature of qualitative research on historical processes. The research question is "What was Britain like at the time?" rather than "What did Queen Elizabeth do?" Related to this case orientation, qualitative historical research is **holistic** as well as **conjunctural**—concerned with the context in which events occurred and the

SAGE JOURNAL ARTICLE
Quantitative Research of the Democratization Process

ENCYCLOPEDIA LINK
Comparative Research

Case-oriented research: Research that focuses attention on the nation or other unit as a whole.

interrelations between different events and processes: "how different conditions or parts fit together" (Ragin 1987:25–26). Charles Ragin (2000) uses the example of case-oriented research on the changing relationship between income and single parenthood in the United States after World War II:

In the end, the study is also about the United States in the second half of the twentieth century, not just the many individuals and families included in the analysis. More than likely, the explanation of the changing relation between income and single parenthood would focus on interrelated aspects of the United States over this period. For example, to explain the weakening link between low income and single parenthood the researcher might cite the changing status of women, the decline in the social significance of conventional family forms, the increase in divorce, the decrease in men's job security, and other changes occurring in the United States over this period. (pp. 67–68)

Qualitative historical research is also **temporal** because it looks at the related series of events that unfold over time. It is therefore also likely to be *historically specific*—limited to the specific time(s) and place(s) studied. Qualitative historical research uses **narrative explanations** in which the research tells a story involving specific actors and events (Abbott 1994).

The focus on the past presents special methodological challenges:

- Documents and other evidence may have been lost or damaged.

- Available evidence may represent a sample biased toward more newsworthy figures.

- Written records will be biased toward those who were more prone to writing.

- Feelings of individuals involved in past events may be hard, if not impossible, to reconstruct.

Before you judge historical social research as credible, you should look for convincing evidence that each of these challenges has been addressed.

Holistic research: Research concerned with the context in which events occurred and the interrelations between different events and processes.

Conjunctural research: Research that considers the complex combinations in which causal influences operate.

Temporal research: Research that accounts for the related series of events that unfold over time.

Narrative explanation: A causal explanation that involves developing a narrative of events and processes that indicate a chain of causes and effects.

Historical research can also use quantitative techniques. The units of analysis in quantitative analyses of historical processes are nations or larger entities, and researchers use a longitudinal design to identify changes over time. For example, David John Frank, Ann Hironaka, and Evan Schofer (2000) treated the entire world as their "case" for their deductive test of alternative explanations for the growth of national activities to protect the natural environment during the 20th century. Were environmental protection activities a response to environmental degradation and economic affluence within nations, as many had theorized? Or, instead, were they the result of a "top-down" process in which a new view of national responsibilities was spread by international organizations? Frank et al.'s measures of environmental protectionism included the number of national parks among all countries in the world and memberships in international environmental organizations; one of their indicators of global changes was the cumulative number of international agreements (see Exhibit 9.5 for a list of some of their data sources).

Exhibit 9.6a charts the growth of environmental activities identified around the world. Compare the pattern in this exhibit with the pattern of growth in the number of international environmental agreements and national environmental laws shown in Exhibit 9.6b, and you can see that environmental protectionism at the national level was rising at the same time that it was becoming more the norm in international relations. In more detailed analyses, Frank and colleagues (2000) attempt to

■ EXHIBIT 9.5   **Variables for Historical Analysis of Environmental Protectionism**

Dependent Variables	Definition	Data Source(s)	Period of Analysis
National parks and protected areas	Annual cumulative numbers of parks per nation-state	IUCN (1990)	1900–1990
Country chapters of international environmental nongovernmental associations	Annual numbers of chapters per nation-state	Fried (1905–1911); League of Nations (1921, 1938); UIA (1948–1990)	1900–1988
Nation-state memberships in intergovernmental environmental organizations	Annual numbers of memberships per nation-state	Fried (1905–1911); League of Nations (1921, 1938); UIA (1948–1990)	1900–1984
Environmental impact assessment laws	Year of founding	Wood (1995)	1966–1992
National environmental ministries	Year of founding	Europa Year Book (1970–1995)	1970–1995

Source: Frank et al. (2000).

■ EXHIBIT 9.6   **International Environmental Activity**

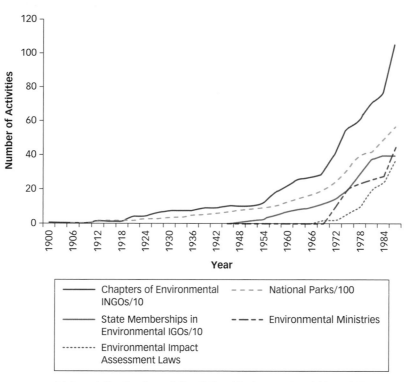

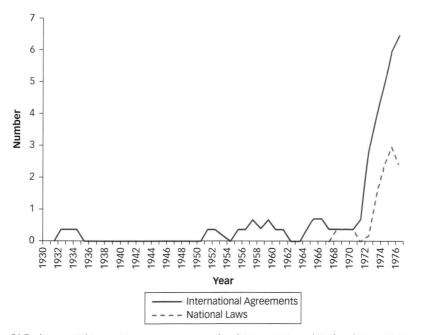

(a) Cumulative Numbers of Five National Environment Activities, 1900 to 1988

Note: INGOs are international nongovernment organizations; IGOs are
intergovernmental organizations.

(b) Environmental Impact Assessment: International Agreements and National Laws, 1930 to 1977

Source: Frank et al. (2000:98, 102).

show that the growth in environmental protectionism was not explained by increasing environmental problems or economic affluence within nations. As in most research that relies on historical or comparative data, however, some variables that would indicate alternative influences (such as the strength of national environmental protest movements) could not be measured (Buttel 2000). Therefore, further research is needed.

One common measurement problem in historical research projects is the lack of data from some historical periods (Rueschemeyer, Stephens, & Stephens 1992; Walters, James, & McCammon 1997). For example, the widely used U.S. Uniform Crime Reporting System did not begin until 1930 (Rosen 1995). Sometimes, alternative sources of documents or estimates for missing quantitative data can fill in gaps (Zaret 1996), but even when measures can be created for key concepts, multiple measures of the same concepts are likely to be out of the question. As a result, tests of reliability and validity may not be feasible. Whatever the situation, researchers must assess the problem honestly and openly (Bollen, Entwisle, & Alderson 1993; Paxton 2002).

Those measures that are available are not always adequate. What is included in the historical archives may be an unrepresentative selection of materials that still remain from the past. At various times, some documents could have been discarded, lost, or transferred elsewhere for a variety of reasons. Original documents may be transcriptions of spoken words or handwritten pages and could have been modified slightly in the process; they could also be outright distortions (Erikson 1966; Zaret 1996). It is important to develop a systematic plan for identifying and evaluating relevant documents.

Comparative Social Science Methods

Variable-oriented research: Research that focuses attention on variables representing particular aspects of the cases studied and then examines the relations between these variables across sets of cases.

Comparisons between countries during one time period can help social scientists identify the limitations of explanations based on single-nation research. Such comparisons can suggest the relative importance of universal factors in explaining social phenomena compared with unique factors rooted in specific times and places (de Vaus 2008). These comparative studies may focus on a period in either the past or the present. Historical and comparative research that is quantitative may obtain data from national statistics or other sources of published data; if it is contemporary, such research may rely on cross-national surveys. Like other types of quantitative research, quantitative historical and comparative research can be termed **variable-oriented research**, with a focus on variables representing particular aspects of the units studied (Demos 1998).

For example, Clem Brooks and Jeff Manza (2006) deduce from three theories about welfare states—national values, power resources, and path dependency theory—the hypothesis that voters' social policy preferences will influence welfare state expenditures. Using country-level survey data collected by the International Social Survey Program (ISSP) in 15 democracies in five different years and expenditure data from the Organisation for Economic Co-operation and Development (OECD), Brooks and Manza were able to identify a consistent relationship between popular preferences for social welfare spending and the actual national expenditures (Exhibit 9.7).

Cross-national research confronts unique challenges (de Vaus 2008). The meaning of concepts and the definitions of variables may differ between nations or regions (Erikson 1966). For example, the concept of being a *good son or daughter* refers to a much broader range of behaviors in China than in most Western countries (Ho 1996). Rates of physical disability cannot be compared between nations because standard definitions are lacking (Martin & Kinsella 1995). Individuals in different cultures may respond differently to the same questions (Martin & Kinsella 1995). The value of statistics for particular geographic units such as counties in the United States may vary over time simply because

■ **EXHIBIT 9.7**   **Interrelationship of Policy Preferences and Welfare State Output**

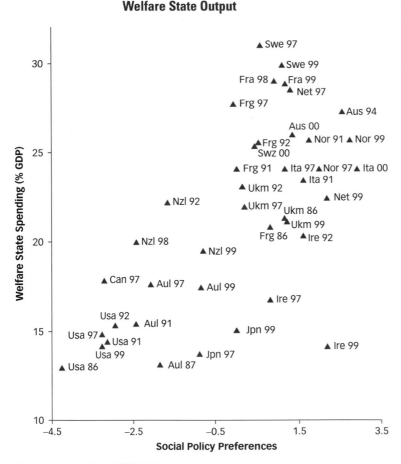

Source: Brooks and Manza (2006:484).

Note: Scattergram shows data for policy preferences and welfare state spending in 15 OECD democracies. Data are from the ISSP/OECD (International Social Survey Program/Organisation for Economic Co-operation and Development).

of changes in the boundaries of these units (Walters et al. 1997). Such possibilities should be considered, and any available opportunity should be taken to test for their effects.

Comparative Historical Methods

The combination of historical analysis with comparisons between nations or other units often leads to the most interesting results. Comparisons may be either quantitative or qualitative.

There are several stages for a systematic, qualitative, comparative historical study (Ragin 1987; Rueschemeyer et al. 1992):

1. Specify a theoretical framework and identify key concepts or events that should be examined to explain a phenomenon.

2. Select cases (such as nations) that vary in terms of the key concepts or events.

3. Identify similarities and differences between the cases in these key concepts or events and the outcome to be explained.

4. Propose a causal explanation for the historical outcome and check it against the features of each case. The criterion for success in this method is to explain the outcome for each case, without allowing deviations from the proposed causal pattern.

Kathleen Fallon, Liam Swiss, and Jocelyn Viterna (2012) designed a historical comparative research project to investigate what has been called a "democracy paradox": An increase in democratic freedoms in nations has often led to a decline in representation of women in powerful political positions. Fallon, Swiss, and Viterna designed a quantitative study of the "democratization process" in 118 developing countries over a 34-year period. The dependent variable in the analysis was the percentage of seats held by women in the national legislature or its equivalent. The researchers distinguished countries transitioning from civil strife, authoritarian regimes, and communist regimes and they accounted for the use of quotas for women as well as the extent of democratic practices and the differences in national culture.

The results indicate that women's legislative representation drops after democratizing changes begin, but then increases with additional elections. However, the strength of this pattern varies with the type of pre-democratic regime and the use of quotas. Exhibit 9.8 displays the process of change in countries that shifted from communist to democratic governance. The nature of the *process* of democratic change is critical to understanding its outcome for women.

Cautions for Historical and Comparative Analysis

Historical and comparative methods allow for rich descriptions of social and political processes in different nations or regions as well as for causal inferences that reflect a systematic, defensible weighing of the evidence. Data of increasingly good quality are available on a rapidly expanding number of nations, creating many opportunities for comparative research. We cannot expect one study comparing the histories of a few nations to control adequately for every plausible alternative causal influence, but repeated investigations can refine our understanding and lead to increasingly accurate causal conclusions (King et al. 1994).

However, when geographic units such as nations are sampled for comparative purposes, it is assumed that each nation can be treated as a separate case for identifying possible chains of causes and effects. In an interdependent world, this assumption may be misplaced—nations may develop as they do because of how other nations are developing (and the same can be said of cities and other units). As a result, comparing the particular histories of different nations may overlook the influence of global culture, international organizations, or economic dependency—just the type of influence identified in Frank et al.'s study of environmental protectionism (Skocpol 1984; compare

■ EXHIBIT 9.8 **Levels of Women's Representation for Select Countries Transitioning from Communism, 1975–2009**

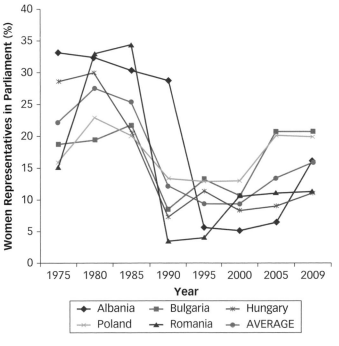

Source: Fallon, Swiss, & Viterna (2012:396).

©iStockphoto.com/JianGang Wang

Photo 9.3 Researchers must be cautious when comparing different cultures. What are some of the many factors that can complicate comparative and historical research?

Chase-Dunn & Hall 1993). The possibility of such complex interrelations should always be considered when evaluating the plausibility of a causal argument based on a comparison between two apparently independent cases (Jervis 1996).

❖ Content Analysis

Content analysis, "the systematic, objective, quantitative analysis of message characteristics," is a method particularly well suited to the study of popular culture and many other issues concerning human communication (Neuendorf 2002:1). Content analysis usually begins with text, speech broadcasts, or visual images. The content analyst develops procedures for coding various aspects of the textual, aural (spoken), or visual material and then analyzes this coded content.

The various steps in a content analysis are represented in the flowchart in Exhibit 9.9. Note that the steps are comparable to the procedures in quantitative survey research. Use this flowchart as a checklist when you design or critique a content analysis project.

Kimberly Neuendorf's (2002) analysis of medical prime-time network television programming introduces the potential of content analysis. As Exhibit 9.10 shows, medical programming has been dominated by noncomedy shows, but there have been two significant periods of comedy medical shows—during the 1970s and early 1980s and then again in the early 1990s. It took a qualitative analysis of medical show content to reveal that the 1960s shows represented a very distinct "physician-as-God" era, which shifted to a more human view of the medical profession in the 1970s and 1980s. This era has been followed, in turn, by a mixed period that has had no dominant theme.

Identify a Population of Documents or Other Textual Sources

The population of sources should be selected so that it is appropriate to the research question of interest. Perhaps the population will be all newspapers published in the United States, college student newspapers, nomination speeches at political party conventions, or "state of the nation" speeches by national leaders. Books or films are also common sources for content analysis projects. Often, a comprehensive archive can provide the primary data for the analysis (Neuendorf 2002). For a fee, the LexisNexis service makes a large archive of newspapers available for analysis. For her analysis of prime-time programming since 1951, Neuendorf (2002) used a published catalog of all TV shows.

Determine the Units of Analysis

The units of analysis could be items such as newspaper articles, whole newspapers, speeches, or political conventions, or they could be more microscopic units such as words, interactions, time periods, or other bits of a communication (Neuendorf 2002). The content analyst has to decide what units are most appropriate to the research question and how the communication content can be broken into those units. If the units are individual issues of a newspaper, in a study of changes in news emphases, this step may be relatively easy. The units of analysis for Neuendorf (2002:2) were "the individual medically oriented TV program." However, if the units are most appropriately the instances of interaction between characters in a novel or a movie, in a study of conflict patterns between different types of characters, it will require a careful process of testing to determine how to define operationally the specific units of interaction (Weber 1990).

Content analysis: A research method for systematically analyzing and making inferences from recorded human communication, including books, articles, poems, constitutions, speeches, and songs.

Select a Sample of Units From the Population

The simplest strategy to select a sample might be a simple random sample of documents. However, a stratified sample might be needed to ensure adequate representation of community newspapers in large and in small cities, or of weekday and Sunday papers, or of political speeches during election years and in off years (Weber 1990). Neuendorf (2002) included the entire population of medically oriented TV programs between 1951 and 1998. Nonrandom sampling methods have also been used in content analyses when the entire population of interest could not be determined (Neuendorf 2002).

SAGE JOURNAL ARTICLE
Sampling the Population

Design Coding Procedures for the Variables to Be Measured

Quantitative researchers use content analysis to measure aspects of media such as the frequency of use of particular words or ideas or the consistency with which authors convey a particular message in their stories. An investigation of the drinking climate on campuses

■ EXHIBIT 9.9   **Flowchart for the Typical Process of Content Analysis Research**

1. *Theory and rationale:* What content will be examined, and *why*? Are there certain *theories* or perspectives that indicate that this particular message content is important to study? Library work is needed here to conduct a good literature review. Will you be using an integrative model, linking content analysis with other data to show relationships with source or receiver characteristics? Do you have *research questions? Hypotheses?*

2. *Conceptualizations:* What *variables* will be used in the study, and how do you define them *conceptually* (i.e., with dictionary-type definitions)? Remember, you are the boss! There are many ways to define a given construct, and there is no one right way. You may want to screen some examples of the content you're going to analyze, to make sure you've covered everything you want.

3. *Operationalizations (measures):* Your measures should match your conceptualizations. . . . What *unit of data collection* will you use? You may have more than one unit (e.g., a by-utterance coding scheme and a by-speaker coding scheme). Are the variables measured well (i.e., at a high *level of measurement,* with categories that are *exhaustive and mutually exclusive)?* An *a priori* coding scheme describing all measures must be created. Both face validity and content validity may also be assessed at this point.

Human Coding   Computer Coding

4a. *Coding schemes:* You need to create the following materials:

   a. *Codebook* (with all variable measures *fully* explained)
   b. *Coding form*

4b. *Coding schemes:* With computer text content analysis, you still need a codebook of sorts—a full explanation of your *dictionaries* and method of applying them. You may use standard dictionaries (e.g., those in Hart's program, *Diction*) or originally created dictionaries. When creating custom dictionaries, be sure to first generate a frequencies list from your text sample and examine for key words and phrases.

Human Coding   Computer Coding

(Continued)

■ EXHIBIT 9.9 **(Continued)**

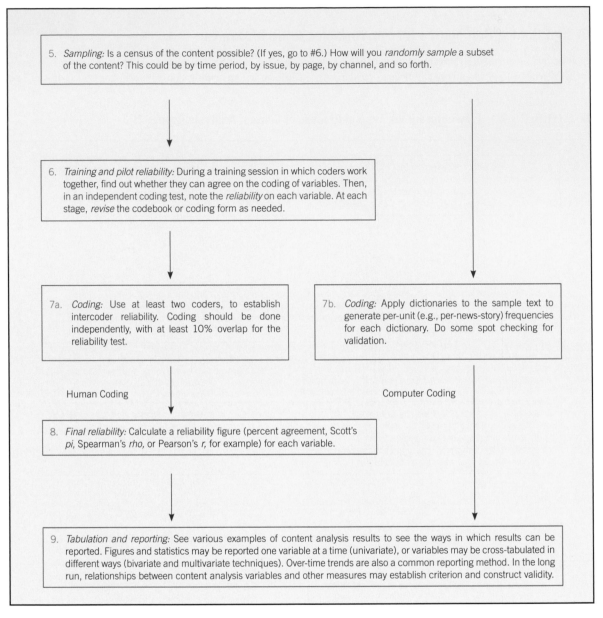

5. *Sampling:* Is a census of the content possible? (If yes, go to #6.) How will you *randomly sample* a subset of the content? This could be by time period, by issue, by page, by channel, and so forth.

6. *Training and pilot reliability:* During a training session in which coders work together, find out whether they can agree on the coding of variables. Then, in an independent coding test, note the *reliability* on each variable. At each stage, *revise* the codebook or coding form as needed.

7a. *Coding:* Use at least two coders, to establish intercoder reliability. Coding should be done independently, with at least 10% overlap for the reliability test.

7b. *Coding:* Apply dictionaries to the sample text to generate per-unit (e.g., per-news-story) frequencies for each dictionary. Do some spot checking for validation.

Human Coding

Computer Coding

8. *Final reliability:* Calculate a reliability figure (percent agreement, Scott's *pi,* Spearman's *rho,* or Pearson's *r,* for example) for each variable.

9. *Tabulation and reporting:* See various examples of content analysis results to see the ways in which results can be reported. Figures and statistics may be reported one variable at a time (univariate), or variables may be cross-tabulated in different ways (bivariate and multivariate techniques). Over-time trends are also a common reporting method. In the long run, relationships between content analysis variables and other measures may establish criterion and construct validity.

Source: Neuendorf (2002:50–51).

might include a count of the amount of space devoted to ads for alcoholic beverages in a sample of issues of the student newspaper. Photographs record individual characteristics and social events, so they can also become an important tool for investigating the social world. As cameras embedded in cell phones and the use of websites and social media encourage taking and sharing photos, social scientists are increasingly coding photos to indicate peoples' orientations in other times and places (Tinkler 2013).

The researcher must first decide what variables to measure, using the unit of text to be coded such as words, sentences, themes, or paragraphs. Then, the categories into which the text units are to be coded must be defined. These categories may be broad, such as *supports democracy,* or narrow, such as *supports universal suffrage.* Reading or otherwise reviewing some of the documents or other units to be coded is an essential step in thinking about variables that should be coded and in developing coding procedures. Development of clear instructions and careful training of coders are essential.

Developing reliable and valid coding procedures deserves special attention in a content analysis, for it is not an easy task. The meaning of words and phrases is often ambiguous. Homographs create special problems (words such as *mine* that have different meanings in different contexts), as do many phrases that have special meanings (such as *point of no return*)

(Weber 1990). As a result, coding procedures cannot simply categorize and count words; text segments in which the words are embedded must also be inspected before codes are finalized. Because different coders may perceive different meanings in the same text segments, explicit coding rules are required to ensure coding consistency. Special dictionaries can be developed to keep track of how the categories of interest are defined in the study (Weber 1990).

Neuendorf's (2002) analysis of medical programming measured two variables that did not need explicit coding rules: length of show in minutes and the year(s) the program was aired. She also coded shows as comedies or noncomedies, as well as medical or not, but she did not report the coding rules for these distinctions (Exhibit 9.10).

> **SAGE JOURNAL ARTICLE**
> Organizing Data

■ EXHIBIT 9.10　**Medical Prime-Time Network Television Programming, 1951–1998**

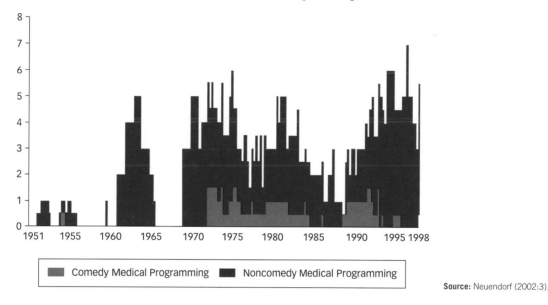

Source: Neuendorf (2002:3).

Develop Appropriate Statistical Analyses

The content analyst creates variables for analysis by counting occurrences of particular words, themes, or phrases and then tests relations between the resulting variables. In many cases, computer-aided qualitative analysis programs, like those you will learn about in Chapter 12, can help to develop coding procedures and then carry out the content coding. The simple chart that Neuendorf (2002) used to analyze the frequency of medical programming appears in Exhibit 9.10.

Gerth and Siegert (2012) use both charts and percentage distributions to test hypotheses they posed about media attention to different political perspectives in election campaigns. Exhibit 9.11 shows how the use of different perspectives (or "frames") varied over the weeks of the campaign, with an emphasis on the "rule of law" being the most common way of framing the issue of naturalization.

The criteria for judging quantitative content analyses of text are the same standards of validity applied to data collected with other quantitative methods. We must review the sampling approach, the reliability and validity of the measures, and the controls used to strengthen any causal conclusions.

■ EXHIBIT 9.11　**Frames per Campaign Week**

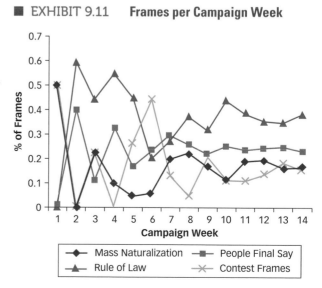

Source: Gerth and Siegert (2012:290).

❖ Ethical Issues in Unobtrusive Methods

Secondary Data Analysis and Big Data

Analysis of data collected by others does not create the same potential for immediate harm as does the collection of primary data, but neither ethical nor related political considerations can be ignored. First, because in most cases the secondary researchers did not collect the data, a key ethical obligation is to cite the original investigators, as well as the data source, such as the ICPSR. When secondary data are obtained from an archive, procedures used to preserve subject confidentiality should be reviewed and noted. All information that could identify individuals should have been removed from the records to be analyzed so that no link is possible to the identities of living subjects or the living descendants of subjects (Huston & Naylor 1996).

AUDIO LINK 🌐
Data Farm and Big Data

VIDEO LINK ▶
Research Results and
Publication

Some university institutional review boards require that researchers submit for approval any plans to use data on human subjects in a secondary analysis, even if the data are deidentified and from a responsible source (Code of Federal Regulations, 45 CFR 46.101, paragraph b, category 4).

Ethical concerns can be much greater in research across national boundaries. Social and political pressures may influence the success of a census in different ways in different countries. Some Mexicans were concerned that the results of Mexico's 2000 Census would be "used against them" by the government, and nearly 200,000 communities were inaccessible for follow-up except by a day's mule travel (Burke 2000). In rural China, many families who had flouted the government's official one-child policy sought to hide their "extra" children from census workers (Rosenthal 2000).

Big Data creates some new concerns about research ethics. When enormous amounts of data are available for analysis, the usual procedures for making data anonymous may no longer ensure that it stays that way. In 2006, AOL released for research purposes 20 million search queries from 657,000 users, after all personal information had been erased and only a unique numeric identifier remained to link searches. However, staff at the *New York Times* conducted analyses of sets of search queries and were able quickly to identify a specific individual user by name and location, based on their searches. The collection of Big Data also makes possible surveillance and prediction of behavior on a large scale. Crime control efforts and screening for terrorists now often involve developing predictions from patterns identified in Big Data. Strict rules and close monitoring are needed to prevent potential invasions of privacy and unwarranted suspicions (Mayer-Schönberger & Cukier 2013).

Mika Raento, Antti Oulasvirta, and Nathan Eagle (2009) highlight ethical concerns related to using data from smartphones. Because of the quantity of data available, neither the researcher nor the user may know entirely what is included in the database. In addition, users habituated to using their smartphones may forget about their having consented to data collection—a problem that Raento and his colleagues lessen by "beeping" research participants' smartphones when calls are being recorded. Additional risks emerge when those who have not consented to the research interact with the smartphone users or when a smartphone being used in research is lost.

Historical and Comparative Research and Content Analysis

Analysis of historical documents, documents from other countries, or content in media does not create the same potential for harm to human subjects that can be a concern when collecting primary data. It is still important to be honest and responsible in working out arrangements for data access when data must be obtained from designated officials or data archivists, but many data are easy to find in libraries or on the web. Researchers in the United States who conclude that they are being denied access to public records of the federal government may be able to obtain the data by filing a Freedom of Information Act (FOIA) request. The FOIA stipulates that all persons have a right to access all federal agency records unless the records are specifically exempted (Riedel 2000). Researchers who review historical or government documents must also try to avoid embarrassing or otherwise harming named individuals or their descendants by disclosing sensitive information.

Ethical concerns are multiplied when surveys are conducted or other data are collected in other countries. If the outside researcher lacks much knowledge of local norms, values, and routine activities, the potential for inadvertently harming subjects is substantial. For this reason, cross-cultural researchers should spend time learning about each of the countries in which they plan to collect primary data and strike up collaborations with researchers in those countries (Hantrais & Mangen 1996). Local advisory groups may also be formed in each country so that a broader range of opinion is solicited when key decisions must be made. Such collaboration can also be invaluable when designing instruments, collecting data, and interpreting results.

Cross-cultural researchers who use data from other societies have a particular obligation to try to understand the culture and norms of those societies before they begin secondary data analyses. It is a mistake to assume that questions asked in other languages or cultural contexts will have the same meaning as when asked in the researcher's own language and culture, so a careful, culturally sensitive process of review by knowledgeable experts must precede measurement decisions in these projects. Ethical standards themselves may vary between nations and cultures, so cross-cultural researchers should consider collaborating with others in the places to be compared, and they should take the time to learn about cultural practices, gender norms, and ethical standards (Ayhan 2001; Stake & Rizvi 2009).

❖ Conclusions

Unobtrusive data, secondary data, and Big Data multiply the methods social researchers can use to understand the social world, whereas historical and comparative methods and content analysis connect to areas of the social world that other methods overlook. Use of these methods may each be combined with others, resulting in an unparalleled range of options. Each of these techniques can help researchers gain new insights into complex social processes such as democratization and stimulate inductive reasoning and deductive tests about related processes.

Each of these methods draws attention to new possibilities but also significant challenges. Increasing our understanding of the social world with any of these unobtrusive methods requires careful attention to their specific strengths and weaknesses as well as to unique issues in ethical practice that emerge during their use.

Key Terms

Big Data   143
Case-oriented research   145
Conjunctural research   145
Content analysis   150
Holistic research   145

ICPSR (Inter-university Consortium for
    Political and Social Research)   140
Narrative explanation   146
Ngrams   143
Secondary data   139

Secondary data analysis   139
Temporal research   146
Unobtrusive measure   138
Unobtrusive methods   138
Variable-oriented research   148

Highlights

- Secondary data analysts should have a good understanding of the research methods used to collect the data they analyze. Data quality is always a concern, particularly with historical data.

- Secondary data for historical and comparative research are available from many sources. The ICPSR provides the most comprehensive data archive.

- Collection of massive sets of Big Data permits analysis of large-scale social patterns and trends.

- The central insight behind historical and comparative methods is that we can improve our understanding of social processes when we make comparisons with other times and places.

- Qualitative historical process research uses a narrative approach to causal explanation, in which historical events are treated as part of a developing story. Narrative explanations are temporal, holistic, and conjunctural.

- Methodological challenges for comparative and historical research include missing data, variation in the meaning of words and phrases and in the boundaries of geographic units across historical periods and between cultures, bias or inaccuracy of historical documents, a limited number of cases, and interdependence of cases selected.

- Content analysis is a tool for systematic quantitative analysis of documents and other textual data. It requires careful testing and control of coding procedures to achieve reliable measures.

Chapter Questions

1. What historical events have had a major influence on social patterns in the nation? The possible answers are too numerous to list, ranging from any of the wars to major internal political conflicts, economic booms and busts, scientific discoveries, and legal changes. Pick one such event in your own nation for this exercise. Find one historical book on this event and list the sources of evidence used. What additional evidence would you suggest for a social science investigation of the event?

2. Consider the media that you pay attention to in your social world. How could you design a content analysis of the messages conveyed by these media? What research questions could you help to answer by adding a comparison to another region or country to this content analysis?

3. What are the strengths and weaknesses of secondary data analysis? Do you think it's best to encourage researchers to try to address their research questions with secondary data if at all possible?

4. What are the similarities and differences between secondary data analysis and Big Data analysis? Do you feel one of these approaches is more likely to yield valid conclusions? Explain your answer.

Practice Exercises

1. Using your library's government documents collection or the U.S. Census site on the web, select one report by the U.S. Census Bureau about the population of the United States or some segment of it. Outline the report and list all the tables included in it. Summarize the report in two paragraphs. Suggest a historical or comparative study for which this report would be useful.

2. Review the Interactive Exercises on the study site (edge.sagepub .com/schuttusw) for a lesson that will help you master the terms used in historical and comparative research.

3. Explore the ICPSR website. Start by browsing their list of subject headings and then write a short summary of the data sets available about one subject. You can start at www.icpsr.umich.edu/icpsrweb/ICPSR.

STUDENT STUDY SITE

$SAGE edge™

The Student Study Site, available at **edge.sagepub.com/schuttusw**, includes useful study materials including eFlashcards, videos, audio resources, journal articles, and encyclopedia articles, many of which are represented by the media links throughout the text.

CHAPTER 10

Evaluation and Mixed-Methods Research

D rug Abuse Resistance Education (D.A.R.E.) is offered in elementary schools, middle schools, and high schools across the United States and in 49 other countries (D.A.R.E. 2014). Since its inception as an innovative effort of the Los Angeles Police Department in 1983, D.A.R.E. has grown to include 15,000 police officers and as many as 75% of U.S. school districts (Berman & Fox 2009). For parents worried about drug abuse among youth and for many concerned citizens, the program has immediate appeal. It brings a special police officer into the schools once a week to talk to students about the hazards of drug abuse and to establish a direct link between local law enforcement and young people. Although there are many substance abuse prevention programs, none has achieved the popularity or developed the infrastructure of D.A.R.E.

But does it work? Do students who participate in D.A.R.E. education become more resistant to the use of illicit drugs? Are they less likely to use illicit drugs while they are enrolled in the program or, more important, in the years after they have finished the program? Do students benefit in other ways from participation in D.A.R.E.? Are there beneficial effects for schools and communities? Although the idea of providing students with information about the harmful effects of substance abuse has intuitive appeal, the history of evaluation research about D.A.R.E. drives home an important point: To know whether a social program works, and to understand how it works, we have to evaluate it systematically and fairly, whether we personally think the program sounds like a good idea or not.

The U.S. Department of Justice paid for an evaluation of D.A.R.E. by Susan Ennett, Christopher Ringwalt, and Robert Flewelling at the Research Triangle Institute in North Carolina, and Nancy Tobler at the State University of New York in Albany. Ennett and her colleagues (1994) located eight quantitative studies of the effects of D.A.R.E. that had used an experimental or quasi-experimental design with a focus on a particular state or locality. Across these studies, D.A.R.E. had no effect on drug or alcohol use at the time students completed D.A.R.E., although it led to a small reduction in tobacco use (and see Ringwalt et al. 1994; West & O'Neal 2004). D.A.R.E. participants did improve their knowledge about substance use, as well as their social skills related to resisting substance abuse, attitudes toward the police, attitudes about drug use, and self-esteem, but these positive attitudinal effects were less than those identified in evaluations of other types of substance abuse prevention programs. A 6-year randomized field experiment of D.A.R.E.'s effectiveness in a sample of Illinois schools also found no long-term beneficial effects (Rosenbaum & Hanson 1998). As a result, some school districts stopped using D.A.R.E. (Rosenbaum 2007).

Yet this was not the end of the story. Federal officials convened a meeting of researchers and D.A.R.E. administrators to consider program changes and more research. As a result, the Robert Wood Johnson Foundation funded substance abuse researcher Zili Sloboda at the University of Akron to develop a new educational approach and a rigorous evaluation of its long-term impact (Berman & Fox 2009). Surprisingly, Sloboda and her colleagues (2009) found that this new program, Take Charge of Your Life, actually led to increased use of alcohol and cigarettes and no change in marijuana use. So D.A.R.E. administrators rejected that approach, adopted a different model ("keepin' it REAL"), and retooled once again (Toppo 2002; West & O'Neal 2004):

> Gone is the old-style approach to prevention in which an officer stands behind a podium and lectures students in straight rows. New D.A.R.E. officers are trained as "coaches" to support kids who are using research-based refusal strategies in high-stakes peer-pressure environments. (D.A.R.E. 2008)

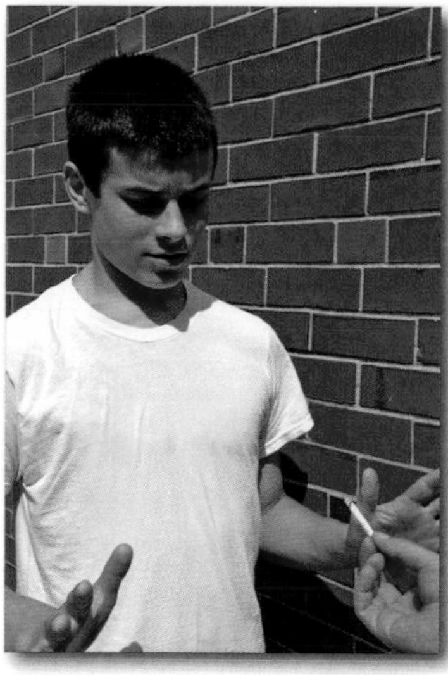

Of course, the "new D.A.R.E." is now being evaluated, too. Sorry to say, one early quasi-experimental evaluation in 17 urban schools, funded by D.A.R.E. America, found no effect of the program on students' substance use (Vincus et al. 2010). Some researchers have concluded that the program should simply be ended, while others have concluded that some communities have had good reasons for continuing to offer the program (Berman & Fox 2009; Birkeland, Murphy-Graham, & Weiss 2005).

This may seem like a depressing way to begin a chapter on evaluation research. If, like me, you have a child who enjoyed D.A.R.E., or were yourself a D.A.R.E. student, you may know how appealing the program can be and how important its message is. But that should help to drive home the key point: Government agencies and other bodies that fund social programs must invest the necessary resources to evaluate their effectiveness, no matter how appealing they seem on their surface. Resources are too scarce to spend millions of dollars on a national program that does not achieve its intended goals. As we review more of the story of evaluation research on D.A.R.E. and other programs in this chapter, you will also learn that program evaluations can give us much more insight into the complexity of the social world. Evaluation findings can convince us that our preconceptions about human motivations or program processes need to be revised; they can identify differences in how different people react to the same program and how the same program may have different effects in different social contexts; and they can alert us to the importance of some program outcomes—both harmful and beneficial—that we may have overlooked. Moreover, the efforts of federal officials to encourage reexamination of and change in the D.A.R.E. program demonstrate that program evaluations can have real impacts on public policy.

This chapter examines different types of evaluation research and the decisions that researchers must make when they plan to evaluate the impact of social programs. It also covers how and why quantitative and qualitative methods are often used as mixed methods in evaluation research and other types of research. By the end of the chapter, you will understand why agencies so often require evaluation research to test the effectiveness of government programs.

Photo 10.1 One of the key goals of evaluation research is to measure the effectiveness of social programs, like D.A.R.E. What kind of policy implications might this type of research have?

SAGE JOURNAL ARTICLE
Life-Course and Adolescents

❖ Evaluation Research Basics

Evaluation research is not a method of data collection, like survey research or experiments, nor is it a unique component of research designs, like sampling or measurement. Instead, evaluation research is social research that is conducted for a distinct purpose: to investigate social programs (e.g., substance abuse treatment programs, welfare programs, criminal justice programs, or employment and training programs). For each project, an evaluation researcher must select a research design and a method of data collection that are useful for answering the particular research questions posed and appropriate for the particular program investigated.

Exhibit 10.1 illustrates the process of evaluation research as a simple systems model. First, clients, customers, students, or some other persons or units—cases—enter the program as **inputs**. (Notice that this model treats programs like machines, with people functioning as raw materials to be processed.) Students may begin a new school program, welfare recipients may enroll in a new job training program, or crime victims may be sent to a victim advocate. The resources and staff a program requires are also program inputs.

Next, some service or treatment is provided to the cases. This may be attendance in a class, assistance with a health problem, residence in new housing, or receipt of special cash benefits.

Inputs: The resources, raw materials, clients, and staff that go into a program.

■ EXHIBIT 10.1   A Model of Evaluation

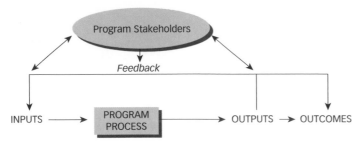

Source: Adapted from Martin and Kettner (1996).

The **program process** may be simple or complicated, short or long, but it is designed to have some impact on the cases.

The direct product of the program's service delivery process is its **output**. Program outputs may include clients served, case managers trained, food parcels delivered, or arrests made. The program outputs may be desirable in themselves, but they primarily indicate that the program is operating.

Program **outcomes** indicate the impact of the program on the cases that have been processed. Outcomes can range from improved test scores or higher rates of job retention to fewer criminal offenses and lower rates of poverty. Any social program is likely to have multiple outcomes—some intended and some unintended, some positive and others that are viewed as negative.

Variation in both outputs and outcomes, in turn, influences the inputs to the program through a **feedback** process. If not enough clients are being served, recruitment of new clients may increase. If too many negative side effects result from a trial medication, the trials may be limited or terminated. If a program does not appear to lead to improved outcomes, clients may go elsewhere.

Evaluation research is simply a systematic approach to feedback: It strengthens the feedback loop through credible analyses of program operations and outcomes. Evaluation research also broadens this loop to include connections to parties outside the program itself. A funding agency or political authority may mandate the research, outside experts may be brought in to conduct the research, and the evaluation research findings may be released to the public, or at least the funders, in a formal report.

The evaluation process as a whole, and feedback in particular, can be understood only in relation to the interests and perspectives of program stakeholders. **Stakeholders** are those individuals and groups who have some basis of concern with the program. They might be clients, staff, managers, funders, or the public. The board of a program or agency, the parents or spouses of clients, the foundations that award program grants, the auditors who monitor program spending, the members of Congress—each is a potential stakeholder, and each has an interest in the outcome of any program evaluation. Some may fund the evaluation; some may provide research data; and some may review, or even approve, the research report (Martin & Kettner 1996). Who the program stakeholders are and what role they play in the program evaluation will have tremendous consequences for the research.

❖ Questions for Evaluation Research

Evaluation projects can focus on several questions related to the operation of social programs and the impact they have:

- Is the program needed?
- How does the program operate?
- What is the program's impact?
- How efficient is the program?

The specific methods used in an evaluation research project depend partly on which of these foci the project has.

Program process: The complete treatment or service delivered by the program.

Outputs: The services delivered or new products produced by the program process.

Outcomes: The impact of the program process on the cases processed.

Feedback: Information about service delivery system outputs, outcomes, or operations that can guide program input.

Stakeholders: Individuals and groups who have some basis of concern with the program.

Needs Assessment

Is a new program needed or an old one still required? Is there a need at all? A **needs assessment** attempts to answer these questions with systematic, credible evidence. Need may be assessed by social indicators, such as the poverty rate or the level of home ownership; by interviews of local experts, such as school board members or team captains; by surveys of populations in need; or by focus groups composed of community residents (Rossi & Freeman 1989).

Needs assessment is not as easy as it sounds (Posavac & Carey 1997). Whose definitions or perceptions should be used to shape our description of the level of need? How will we deal with ignorance of need? How can we understand the level of need without understanding the social context from which that level of need emerges? (Short answer to that one: We can't!) What, after all, does *need* mean in the abstract? We won't really understand what the level of need is until we develop plans for implementing a program in response to the identified needs.

A wonderful little tale, popular with evaluation researchers, reveals the importance of thinking creatively about what people need:

> The manager of a 20-story office building had received many complaints about the slowness of the elevators. He hired an engineering consultant to propose a solution. The consultant measured traffic flow and elevator features and proposed replacing the old with new ones, which could shave 20 seconds off the average waiting time. The only problem: It cost $100,000. A second consultant proposed adding 2 additional elevators, for a total wait time reduction of 35 seconds and a cost of $150,000. Neither alternative was affordable. A third consultant was brought in. He looked around for a few days and announced that the problem was not really the waiting times, but boredom. For a cost of less than $1,000, the manager had large mirrors installed next to the elevators so people could primp and observe themselves while waiting for an elevator. The result: no more complaints. Problem solved. (Witkin & Altschuld 1995:38)

Photo 10.2 Congress is often a program stakeholder because many social programs are funded by the government. Why is it important to consider stakeholders when conducting evaluation research?

Process Evaluation

What actually happens in a social program? The New Jersey Income Maintenance Experiment was designed to test the effect of some welfare recipients receiving higher payments than others (Kershaw & Fair 1976). Did that occur? In the Minneapolis experiment on the police response to domestic violence (Sherman & Berk 1984), police officers were to either arrest or warn individuals accused of assaulting their spouses on the basis of a random selection protocol, unless they concluded that they must override the experimental assignment to minimize the risk of repeat harm. Did the police officers follow this protocol? How often did they override it because of concerns about risk? Questions like these about program implementation must be answered before it is possible to determine whether the program's key elements had the desired effect. Answers to such program implementation questions are obtained through **process evaluation**—research to investigate the process of service delivery.

Process evaluation is even more important when more complex programs are evaluated. Many social programs comprise multiple elements and are delivered over an extended period, often by different providers in different areas. Because of this complexity, it is quite possible that the program as delivered is not the same for all program recipients or consistent with the formal program design.

The process evaluation of D.A.R.E. (they called it an *implementation assessment*) was an ambitious research project in itself, with site visits, informal interviews, discussions, and surveys of D.A.R.E. program coordinators and advisers (Ringwalt et al. 1994). These data indicated that D.A.R.E. was operating as designed and was running relatively smoothly. As shown in Exhibit 10.2, drug prevention coordinators in D.A.R.E. school districts rated the program components as much more satisfactory than did coordinators in school districts with other types of alcohol and drug prevention programs.

The term **formative evaluation** may be used instead of process evaluation when the evaluation findings are used to help shape and refine the program (Rossi & Freeman 1989). Formative evaluation procedures that are incorporated into the initial development of the service program can specify the treatment process and lead to changes in recruitment procedures, program delivery, or measurement tools (Patton 2002).

Qualitative methods are often a key component of process evaluation studies because they can be used to understand internal program dynamics—even those that were not anticipated (Patton 2002; Posavac & Carey 1997). Qualitative researchers may develop detailed descriptions of how program participants engage with each other, how the program experience varies for different people, and how the program changes and evolves over time.

Impact Analysis

The core questions of evaluation research are "Did the program work?" and "Did it have the intended result?" This part of the research is variously called *impact analysis*, **impact evaluation**, or **summative evaluation**. Formally speaking, impact analysis compares what happened after a program with what would have happened had there been no program.

RESEARCHER INTERVIEW LINK
Evaluation Research

SAGE JOURNAL ARTICLE
Evaluations

AUDIO LINK
Different Results

Needs assessment: A type of evaluation research that attempts to determine the needs of some population that might be met with a social program.

Process evaluation: Evaluation research that investigates the process of service delivery.

Formative evaluation: Process evaluation that is used to shape and refine program operations.

Impact evaluation (or analysis): Analysis of the extent to which a treatment or other service has an effect; also known as **summative evaluation.**

■ EXHIBIT 10.2 **Components of D.A.R.E. and Other Alcohol and Drug Prevention Programs Rated as Very Satisfactory (%)**

Components	D.A.R.E. Program (N = 222)	Other AOD* Programs (N = 406)
Curriculum	67.5%	34.2%
Teaching	69.7%	29.8%
Administrative Requirements	55.7%	23.1%
Receptivity of Students	76.5%	34.6%
Effects on Students	63.2%	22.8%

*Alcohol and Other Drugs

Source: Ringwalt et al. (1994:58).

■ EXHIBIT 10.3 **Impact of D.A.R.E. on Attitudes Toward Police Among African American Youth**

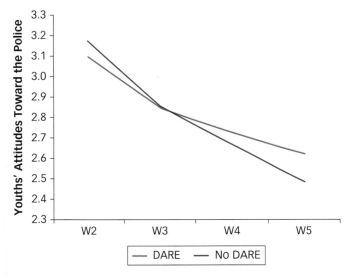

Source: Based on Schuck (2013).

Think of the program—a new strategy for combating domestic violence, an income supplement, whatever—as manipulating an independent variable and the result it seeks as a change in a dependent variable. The D.A.R.E. program (independent variable), for instance, tries to reduce drug use (dependent variable). When the program is present, we expect less drug use. In a more elaborate study, we might have multiple values of the independent variable; for instance, we might look at *no program, D.A.R.E. program,* and *other drug/alcohol education* conditions and compare the results of each.

Amie Schuck (2013) at the University of Illinois at Chicago focused on the impact of program participation on students' attitudes toward the police in her evaluation of D.A.R.E. She was able to use for this evaluation data already collected in a large randomized experiment that had tested the impact of D.A.R.E. in 12 pairs of urban and suburban schools in Illinois. Students' attitudes toward police had been measured with their answers to five questions asked in seven waves of data collection over a 7-year period.

Schuck found that student attitudes toward the police became considerably more negative from the 5th and 6th grades, when the study began, to the 11th and 12th grades, when the study concluded, although by this point the decline was reduced (Exhibit 10.3). These changes in attitudes are similar to what has been found in other studies of youth attitudes toward the police. However, participation in the D.A.R.E. program delayed the decline in attitudes toward the police and then was associated with improved attitudes toward the police. This association was particularly strong for African American youth. Schuck highlights several implications of her study for criminal justice policy.

As in other areas of research, an experimental design is the preferred method for maximizing internal validity—that is, for making sure your causal claims about program impact are justified. Cases are assigned randomly to one or more experimental treatment groups and to a control group so that there is no systematic difference between the groups at the outset (see Chapter 6). Impact analyses that do not use an experimental design can still provide useful information and may be all that is affordable, conceptually feasible, or ethically permissible in many circumstances.

Efficiency Analysis

Whatever the program's benefits, are they sufficient to offset the program's costs? Are the taxpayers getting their money's worth? What resources are required by the program? These efficiency questions can be the primary reason why funders require evaluation of the programs they fund.

A **cost-benefit analysis** must identify the specific program costs and the procedures for estimating the economic value of specific program benefits. This type of analysis also requires that the analyst identify whose perspective will be used to determine what can be considered a benefit rather than a cost. Program clients will have a different perspective on these issues than will taxpayers or program staff. Exhibit 10.4 lists the factors that can be considered as costs or benefits in an

Cost-benefit analysis: A type of evaluation research that compares program costs with the economic value of program benefits.

employment and training program, from the standpoint of program participants, the rest of society, and society as a whole (the combination of program participants and the rest of society) (Orr 1999). Note that some anticipated impacts of the program, on welfare benefits and wage subsidies, are considered a cost to one group and a benefit to another group, whereas some are not relevant to one of the groups.

■ EXHIBIT 10.4   **Conceptual Framework for Cost-Benefit Analysis of an Employment and Training Program**

Costs/Benefits	Perspective of Program Participants	Perspective of Rest of Society	Perspective of Entire Society*
Costs			
Operational costs of the program	0	–	–
Forgone leisure and home production	–	0	–
Benefits			
Earnings gains	+	0	+
Reduced costs of nonexperimental services	0	+	+
Transfers			
Reduced welfare benefits	–	+	0
Wage subsidies	+	–	0
Net benefits	±	±	±

*Entire society = program participants + rest of society.

– = program costs; + = program benefits; ± = program costs and benefits; 0 = no program costs or benefits.

Source: Orr (1999:224, Table 6.5).

In addition to measuring services and their associated costs, a cost-benefit analysis must be able to make some type of estimation of how clients benefited from the program. Typically, this will involve a comparison of some indicators of client status before and after clients received program services or between clients who received program services and a comparable group that did not.

A recent study of therapeutic communities (TCs) provides a clear illustration. A TC is a method for treating substance abuse in which abusers participate in an intensive, structured living experience with other addicts who are attempting to stay sober. Because the treatment involves residential support as well as other types of services, it can be quite costly. Are those costs worth it?

Stanley Sacks and colleagues (2002) conducted a cost-benefit analysis of a modified TC. In the study, 342 homeless, mentally ill chemical abusers were randomly assigned to either a TC or a "treatment-as-usual" comparison group. Employment status, criminal activity, and utilization of health care services were each measured for the 3 months before entering treatment and the 3 months after treatment. Earnings from employment in each period were adjusted for costs incurred by criminal activity and utilization of health care services.

Photo 10.3   A cost-benefit analysis is one way to evaluate the efficiency of a program. What impact might this have on the program that's being evaluated? Was it worth it?

The average cost of TC treatment for a client was $20,361. In comparison, the economic benefit (based on earnings) to the average TC client was $305,273, which declined to $273,698 after comparing postprogram with preprogram earnings, and it was still $253,337 even after adjustment for costs. The resulting benefit-cost ratio was 13:1, although this ratio declined to only 5.2:1 after further adjustments (for cases with extreme values). Nonetheless, the TC program studied seems to have had a substantial benefit relative to its costs.

❖ Mixed Methods

Evaluation research projects often combine qualitative and quantitative methods to provide a more comprehensive picture of program operation or impact. In other words, they used **mixed methods**. Qualitative methods may

▶ **VIDEO LINK**
Evaluation Research

📖 **ENCYCLOPEDIA LINK**
Mixed-Methods Research

be used before or after quantitative methods; that is, the sequencing of the two approaches can differ. In addition, one method may be given priority in a project, or qualitative and quantitative methods may be given equal priority. Distinguishing the sequencing and priority of the qualitative and quantitative methods used in any mixed-methods project results in a number of different types. Before discussing these types, it will help to learn some basic conventions for naming them:

- The primary method used in a mixed-methods project is written in all caps (QUAN or QUAL).

- The secondary method is written in lowercase letters (quan or qual).

- If both methods are given equal priority, they are both written in all caps.

- If one method is used before the other, the sequence is indicated with an arrow (QUAL→ quan, or qual→ QUAN, or QUAN→QUAL, etc.).

- If two methods are used concurrently, but one has priority, the secondary method is said to be "embedded" in the primary method. This is indicated as follows: QUAL(quan) or QUAN(qual).

- If two methods are used concurrently, but they have equal priority, the relation between the two methods is indicated with a +: QUAL+QUAN.

This section discusses research projects using integrated, embedded, and staged methods. There are many more possibilities, since each of these types of mixed methods can be combined in the same research project.

Integrated Designs

In an **integrated mixed-methods design**, qualitative and quantitative methods are used concurrently and both are given equal importance. Findings produced from these methods are then integrated and compared during the analysis of project data. This is the QUAL+QUAN design. Susan McCarter (2009) extended prior research on juvenile justice processing with an integrated mixed-methods investigation of case processing and participant orientations in Virginia. Her hope was to use the results of the two methods to triangulate the study's findings, that is, to show that different methods lead to similar conclusions and therefore become more credible.

The large quantitative data set McCarter (2009) used in her research was secondary data collected on 2,233 African American and Caucasian males in Virginia's juvenile justice system:

> The quantitative data set ($n = 2,920$) is a disproportionate, stratified, random sample of juvenile cases from all 35 Virginia Court Service Units (CSU) where each CSU was treated as a separate stratum. These data were collected by the Joint Legislative Audit and Review Commission (JLARC) in an examination of court processing and outcomes of delinquents and status offenders in Virginia.
>
> JLARC collected data on the juveniles' previous felonies; previous misdemeanors; previous violations of probation/parole; previous status offenses; recent criminal charges, intake action on those charges, pre-disposition(s) of those charges, court disposition(s) of those charges; and demographics such as sex, race, data of birth, CSU, and geotype (urban, suburban, rural). For a subset of these cases, data included information from the youth's social history, which required judicial request. (p. 535)

Qualitative data were obtained from 24 in-depth interviews with juvenile judges, the commonwealth's attorneys, defense attorneys, police officers, juveniles, and their families (McCarter 2009):

> The juvenile justice personnel were from six Court Service Units across the state, including two urban, two suburban, two rural, two from Region I, two from Region II, and two from Region III. . . . Participants from each CSU were chosen to provide maximum diversity in perspectives and experiences, and thus varied by race, sex, and age; and the justice personnel also varied in length of employment, educational discipline and educational attainment. (p. 536)

The in-depth interviews included both open- and closed-ended questions. The open-ended responses are coded into categories that distinguished how participants perceived the role of race in the juvenile justice system (McCarter 2009). A direct connection with the quantitative findings was made in the interviews themselves:

> Respondents were read the quantitative findings from this study and then asked whether or not their experiences and/or perceptions of the juvenile justice system were congruent with the findings. They were also asked how commonly they believed instances of racial or ethnic bias occurred in Virginia. (McCarter 2009:540)

RESEARCHER INTERVIEW LINK
Mixed Methods

Mixed methods: Research that combines qualitative and quantitative methods in an investigation of the same or related research question(s).

Integrated mixed-methods design: Qualitative and quantitative methods are used concurrently, and both are given equal importance.

Comments made in response to this qualitative question supported the quantitative finding that race mattered in the juvenile justice system:

> Juvenile justice professionals as well as youth and their families cited racial bias by individual decision-makers and by the overall system, and noted that this bias was most likely to occur by the police during the Alleged Act or Informal Handling stages. However, although race was considered a factor, when compared to other factors, professionals did not think race played a dominant role in affecting a youth's treatment within the juvenile justice system. . . . Eighteen of the juvenile justice professionals stated that they felt a disparity [between processing of African American and white juveniles] existed, four did not feel that a disparity existed, and two indicated that they did not know. (McCarter 2009:540)

Photo 10.4 Mixed-methods designs allow research to look at complex issues such as family and adulthood using different methods.

In this way, the qualitative and quantitative findings were integrated and the study's key conclusion about race-based treatment was strengthened because it was based on triangulated identification (McCarter 2009)—supporting earlier conclusions of quantitative research by Dannefer and Schutt (1982).

Embedded Designs

Maria Testa, Jennifer A. Livingston, and Carol VanZile-Tamsen (2011) supplemented their quantitative study of violence against women with a qualitative component because violence against women is "a complex, multifaceted phenomenon, occurring within a social context that is influenced by gender norms, interpersonal relationships, and sexual scripts" and "understanding of these experiences of violence is dependent on the subjective meaning for the woman and cannot easily be reduced to a checklist" (p. 237). This was an **embedded**, QUAN(qual), design.

VIDEO LINK
Embedded Research

Victims' responses to structured questions indicated an association between alcohol and rape, but when victims elaborated on their experiences in qualitative interviews, their comments led to a new way of understanding this quantitative association. Although this association has often been interpreted as suggesting "impaired judgment" about consent by intoxicated victims, the women interviewed by Testa et al. (2011) revealed that they had had so much to drink that they were unconscious or at least unable to speak at the time of the rape. Testa and her colleagues concluded that the prevalence of this type of "incapacitated rape" required a new approach to the problem of violence against women (p. 242). They determined that insights yielded by the qualitative data analysis fully justified the time-consuming process of reading and rereading interviews, coding text, and discussing and reinterpreting the codes (p. 245).

Staged Designs

Migration in search of employment creates family strains and lifestyle changes in countries around the world. Nowhere is this as true as in contemporary China, where millions of young people have migrated from rural villages to industrial cities. Juan Zhong and Jeffrey Arnett (2014) sought to understand the impact of such migration on Chinese women workers' views of themselves as adults. The researchers chose for this purpose a **staged** QUAN→qual design, in which a quantitative survey of 119 women workers, ages 18 to 29, from a factory in Guangdong, China, preceded and was the basis for qualitative interviews with 15 of them.

The structured questionnaire included questions about feelings of adulthood and the importance attached to various markers as indicating whether a person was an adult. Only 44% responded that they felt like they had reached adulthood, whereas most of the rest indicated that they felt adult in some ways but not in others. The five markers rated most often as important were (1) Learn to care for parents, (2) If a man, become capable of supporting a family financially, (3) Settle into a long-term career, (4) If a woman, become capable of caring for children, and (5) If a man, become capable of keeping family physically safe.

Analysis of the survey data indicated that being married and having children were associated with feeling like an adult, irrespective of age. The three markers of adulthood identified as most important in the quantitative survey were "Learn to care for parents," "Settle into a long-term career," and "Become capable of caring for children."

Embedded mixed-methods design: Qualitative and quantitative methods are used concurrently in the research but one is given priority.

Staged mixed-methods design: Qualitative and quantitative methods are used in sequence in the research and one is given priority.

The qualitative component began with interviews with 15 of the women workers who had responded to the questionnaire. Zhong read the transcripts and coded the themes identified about conceptions of adulthood. Arnett replicated this process and the two compared their results and resolved discrepancies. Ultimately, they settled on four major domains that captured the expressed views about adulthood: family obligations and capacities, relational maturity, role transitions, and individualism. In the following sections of their article, each domain of markers for adulthood was elaborated with illustrations from the interviews.

As in the quantitative survey, the theme of family obligations and capacities was often emphasized as associated with feelings of adulthood. A quote from a married 23-year-old woman who had a 1-year-old son provided more insight into the basis for this association:

> I am married now, I should have a sense of responsibility toward family; I am also a mother, I should take care of my child. My parents-in-law are taking care of him, and we must send a few thousand yuan to them every year. Right now, he is only 1 year old. When it's time for him to go to school, I will go back home and take care of him myself. After all, my parents-in-law, who are not well educated, only care about if he is full [well-fed] or warm. They don't know how to teach him, so it's better for me to take care of him. (Zhong & Arnett 2014:260)

Strengths and Limitations of Mixed Methods

Combining qualitative and quantitative methods within one research project can strengthen the project's design by enhancing measurement validity, generalizability, causal validity, or authenticity. At the same time, combining methods creates challenges that may be difficult to overcome and ultimately limit the extent to which these goals are enhanced.

Measurement validity is enhanced when questions to be used in a structured quantitative survey are first refined through qualitative cognitive interviewing or focus groups. After quantitative measures are used, qualitative measures can be added to clarify the meaning of numerical scores. You learned about this advantage of combining methods in Chapter 7, on survey research. Alternatively, quantitative measures can provide a more reliable indicator of the extent of variation between respondents that has already been described based on naturalistic observations or qualitative interviews.

SAGE JOURNAL ARTICLE
Mixed Methods

Measurement validity is also enhanced when measures using different methods result in a similar picture. If people are observed to do what they say they do, then the validity of a self-report measure is strengthened by measurement triangulation. McCarter's (2009) qualitative interviews on juvenile justice decisions corroborated the impression that emerged from quantitative data of racial bias in decisions.

RESEARCH

In the News

CAN WE SAVE (MORE) BABIES?

Some 800 cities and towns have adopted a home visiting program for young mothers in an ambitious effort to reduce infant mortality in the United States. Although home visiting programs have been used for more than a century, their popularity increased dramatically due to results of an ambitious program of evaluation research.

In randomized clinical trials designed by child development expert David Olds in the 1970s, nurses visited homes of impoverished mothers in several cities. As a result, death rates dropped, child abuse and neglect plummeted, maternal employment and children's subsequent GPAs improved, and arrest rates for the children when they were older dropped.

For Further Thought ?

1. Do you find these results compelling? What else would you like to know about the research in order to assess its quality?

2. What could qualitative methods add to our understanding of the effect of home visiting?

3. Do you think that it can be ethical to allocate people to a social program on a random basis in order to test the value of the program? Why or why not?

News source: Morales, Andrea. 2015. "Visiting Nurses, Helping Mothers on the Margins." *New York Times,* March 8.

The most common way that causal, or internal, validity is strengthened with a mixed-methods design is when qualitative interviews or observations are used to explore the mechanism involved in a causal effect. A mixed-methods design can also improve external validity when a quantitative study is repeated in different contexts. Qualitative comparisons between these different contexts can then help make sense of the similarities and differences between outcomes across these contexts and thus help identify the conditions for the effects.

The generalizability of qualitative findings can also be improved when a representative sample developed with a quantitative design is used to identify cases to study more intensively with qualitative methods. This was the approach used by Zhong and Arnett (2014) when they selected Chinese women for qualitative interviews from among those who had participated in their structured survey.

Mixed methods also create extra challenges for researchers because different types of expertise are required for effective use of quantitative and qualitative methods. Recruiting multiple researchers for a project who then work as a team from conception to execution of the project may be the best way to overcome this limitation. The researchers also have to acknowledge in planning the study timetable that the time required for collection, coding, and analysis of qualitative data can challenge a quantitative researcher's expectation of more rapid progress.

❖ Ethics in Evaluation

Evaluation research can make a difference in people's lives while the research is being conducted as well as after the results are reported. Job opportunities, welfare requirements, housing options, treatment for substance abuse, and training programs are each potentially important benefits, and an evaluation research project can change both the type and the availability of such benefits. This direct impact on research participants, and potentially their families, heightens the attention that evaluation researchers have to give to human subject concerns (Wolf, Turner, & Toms 2009). Although the particular criteria that are at issue and the decisions that are judged most ethical vary with the type of evaluation research conducted and the specifics of a particular project, there are always serious ethical as well as political concerns for the evaluation researcher (Boruch 1997; Dentler 2002).

When program impact is the focus, human subject considerations multiply. What about assigning persons randomly to receive some social program or benefit? One justification that evaluation researchers give for this approach has to do with the scarcity of these resources. If not everyone in the population who is eligible for a program can receive it, because of resource limitations, what could be a fairer way to distribute the program benefits than through a lottery? Random assignment also seems like a reasonable way to allocate potential program benefits when a new program is being tested with only some members of the target recipient population. However, when an ongoing entitlement program is being evaluated and experimental subjects would typically be eligible for program participation, it may not be ethical simply to bar some potential participants from the programs. Instead, evaluation researchers may test alternative treatments or provide some alternative benefit while the treatment is being denied.

CAREERS
and Research

AMANDA AYKANIAN, RESEARCH ASSOCIATE

Amanda Aykanian majored in psychology at Framingham State University and found that she enjoyed the routine and organization of research. After graduating, Aykanian didn't want to go to graduate school right away; instead she wanted to explore her interests and get a sense of what she could do with research. She found a position as a research assistant with a research and consulting firm. Her initial tasks ranged from taking notes, writing agendas, and assembling project materials to entering research data, cleaning data, and proofing reports. As she contributed more to project reports, she began to think about data from a more theoretical standpoint. She also completed a master's in applied sociology and then entered a Ph.D. program while continuing to work for the same organization.

Aykanian has helped to lead program evaluation research, design surveys and write survey questions, conduct phone and qualitative interviews, and lead focus groups. Her program evaluation research almost always uses a mixed-methods approach, so Aykanian has learned a lot about how qualitative and quantitative methods can complement each other. She has received a lot of on-the-job training in data analysis and has learned how to think about and write proposals in response to federal funding opportunities.

There are many other ethical challenges in evaluation research:

- How can confidentiality be preserved when the data are owned by a government agency or are subject to discovery in a legal proceeding?

- Who decides what level of burden an evaluation project may tolerably impose on participants?

- Is it legitimate for research decisions to be shaped by political considerations?

- Must evaluation findings be shared with stakeholders rather than only with policy makers?

- Is the effectiveness of the proposed program improvements really uncertain?

- Will a randomized experiment yield more defensible evidence than the alternatives?

- Will the results actually be used?

The problem of maintaining subject confidentiality is particularly thorny because researchers, in general, are not legally protected from the requirements that they provide evidence requested in legal proceedings, particularly through the process known as "discovery." However, several federal statutes have been passed specifically to protect research data about vulnerable populations from legal disclosure requirements. For example, the Crime Control and Safe Streets Act (28 CFR Part 11) includes the following stipulation:

> Copies of [research] information [about persons receiving services under the act or the subjects of inquiries into criminal behavior] shall be immune from legal process and shall not, without the consent of the persons furnishing such information, be admitted as evidence or used for any purpose in any action, suit, or other judicial or administrative proceedings. (Boruch 1997:60)

Ethical concerns must also be given special attention when evaluation research projects involve members of vulnerable populations as subjects. To conduct research on children, parental consent usually is required before the child can be approached directly about the research. Adding this requirement to an evaluation research project can dramatically reduce participation because many parents simply do not bother to respond to mailed consent forms. Since nonconsent is likely to be higher among those who are more at risk of substance abuse, the likelihood of identifying program impact can be diminished (Tigges 2003). Sloboda and colleagues' (2009) evaluation of the Take Charge of Your Life program used an "active consent" procedure for gaining parental consent and student assent: Parents and students had to sign forms before the student could participate; the result was that only 58% of the 34,000 eligible seventh-grade students were enrolled in the study. Other research indicates that use of a "passive consent" procedure—through which students can participate as long as their parents do not return a form indicating their lack of consent—can result in much higher rates of participation.

Researchers who combine methods must be aware of the ethical concerns involved in using each of the separate methods, but some ethical challenges are heightened in mixed-methods projects. One special challenge is defining the researcher's role in relation to the research participants. Every researcher creates an understanding about his or her role with research participants (Mertens 2012). Researchers using quantitative methods often define themselves as outside experts who design a research project and collect research data using objective procedures that are best carried out without participant involvement. By contrast, qualitative researchers often define themselves as engaging in research in some type of collaboration with the community or group they are studying, with much input from their research participants into the research design and the collection and analysis of research data.

AUDIO LINK
Varying Methods

A researcher using mixed methods needs some degree of autonomy when designing quantitative research plans but will not be able to collect intensive qualitative data if participants do not accord her or him some degree of trust as an insider. The challenge is compounded by the potential for different reactions of potential participants to the different roles. Authorities who control access to program clients or employees or to community members may be willing to agree to a structured survey but not to a long-term engagement with researchers as participant observers, so that a mixed-methods project that spans programs, communities, or other settings may involve a biased sampling for the qualitative component. Natalia Luxardo, Graciela Colombo, and Gabriela Iglesias (2011) confronted this challenge in their study of Brazilian family violence services and as a result focused their qualitative research on one service that supported the value of giving voice to their service recipients.

Weighing both roles and the best combination of them is critical at the outset of a mixed-methods project. Luxardo and her colleagues (2011) adopted a flexible qualitative interviewing approach to allow participants to avoid topics they did not want to discuss:

> We tried to consider what was important for that adolescent during the interview and, many times, we had to reframe the content of the encounters according to the expectations they had. So, if they were not willing to share during an interview but still had complaints, doubts, or comments to share, we tried to focus on those instead of subtly directing the talk to the arena of the research interests. (p. 996)

❖ Conclusions

Hopes for evaluation research are high: Society could benefit from the development of programs that work well, that accomplish their policy goals, and that serve the people who genuinely need them. At least those are the hopes. It is costly to society and potentially harmful to participants to maintain ineffective programs. In the long run, at least, it may be more ethical to conduct an evaluation study than to let the status quo remain in place.

In many respects, evaluation research is an idea whose time has come. We may never achieve Donald Campbell's (Campbell & Russo 1999) vision of an "experimenting society," in which research is consistently used to evaluate new programs and to suggest constructive changes, but we are close enough to continue trying.

When an evaluation research project is designed to answer multiple research questions and investigate a complex social setting, a mixed-methods design is often beneficial. No matter what your methodological preference is at this point, increased understanding of these issues in mixed methods will improve your own research practice and your ability to critique the research of others.

Key Terms

Cost-benefit analysis   162
Embedded mixed-methods design   165
Feedback   160
Formative evaluation   161
Impact evaluation (or analysis)   161
Inputs   159

Integrated mixed-methods design   164
Mixed methods   163
Needs assessment   160
Outcomes   160
Outputs   160
Process evaluation   161

Program process   160
Staged mixed-methods design   165
Stakeholders   160
Summative evaluation   161

Highlights

- Evaluation research is social research that is conducted for a distinct purpose: to investigate social programs.

- The evaluation process can be modeled as a feedback system, with inputs entering the program, which generates outputs and then outcomes, which feed back to program stakeholders and affect program inputs.

- Four types of program evaluation are (1) needs assessment, (2) process evaluation (including formative evaluation), (3) impact evaluation (also termed as *summative evaluation*), and (4) efficiency (cost-benefit) analysis.

- Evaluation research is done for a client, and its results may directly affect the services, treatments, or punishments that program users receive. Evaluation researchers differ in the extent to which they attempt to orient their evaluations to program stakeholders.

- Evaluation research raises complex ethical issues because it may involve withholding desired social benefits.

- Researchers use mixed methods because a single method may not represent adequately the complexity of the social world that they are trying to understand.

- Mixed methods combine qualitative and quantitative methods in a systematic way in an investigation of the same or related research questions.

- In an integrated mixed-methods design, qualitative and quantitative methods are used concurrently, and both are given equal priority.

- In an embedded mixed-methods design, qualitative and quantitative methods are used concurrently, but one has priority.

- In a staged mixed-methods design, one method is used in a sequence before the other, but one is given priority.

- Measures are said to be triangulated when different types of measures of the same phenomenon give consistent results.

Chapter Questions

1. What would be the advantages and disadvantages of using qualitative methods to evaluate the D.A.R.E. program, as described in the section on Impact Analysis? What were the advantages and disadvantages of the quantitative methods used by Amie Schuck? Which approach would you prefer and why?

2. Imagine that you are evaluating a group home for persons with serious mental illness and learn that a house resident has been talking about cutting himself. What do you see as the ethical response for a researcher in this situation? Would you immediately inform house staff about the resident's plan? What if the resident asked you not to tell anyone? In what circumstances would you feel it is ethical to take action to prevent the likelihood of a subject's harming himself or herself or others?

3. Which of the types of mixed methods reviewed do you feel is likely to be most useful for investigating the social world? Would you favor more single-method or more mixed-methods studies? Explain your reasoning.

4. Should separate consent forms and processes be used for the qualitative and quantitative components of a mixed-methods project? What would be the advantages and drawbacks of this approach?

5. Consider how ready you feel to design a mixed-methods research project. Do you think mixed-methods researchers should generally try to collaborate with another researcher who specializes in the methodology they are not so familiar with? Or should researchers seek to become experts in multiple methods so that they can combine them in research projects that they direct themselves?

······· Practice Exercises ························

1. Identify the key stakeholders in a local social or educational program. Interview several stakeholders to determine what their goals for the program are and what tools they use to assess goal achievement. Compare and contrast the views of each stakeholder and try to account for any differences you find.

2. Visit the book's study site (edge.sagepub.com/schuttusw) and identify an article that reports an evaluation research study. What type of evaluation research does this study represent? What alternatives did the author(s) select when designing the research? After reading the entire article, do you agree with the author's (or authors') choices? Why or why not?

3. Describe the resources available for evaluation researchers at one of the following three websites: the Evaluation Center at Western Michigan University (www.wmich.edu/evalctr), the

National Network of Libraries of Medicine (https://nnlm.gov/mcr/evaluation/tools.html), and the Independent Evaluation Group of the World Bank Group (http://ieg.worldbankgroup.org).

4. Read the National Institute of Health's online report on *Best Practices of Mixed Methods Research in the Health Sciences*. What additional desirable features of mixed-methods research are identified? https://www2.jabsom.hawaii.edu/native/docs/tsudocs/Best_Practices_for_Mixed_Methods_Research_Aug2011.pdf

5. Read one of the SAGE mixed-methods research articles highlighted in this chapter (available on the study site at edge.sagepub.com/schuttusw). What would have been lost if this study had been a single-method study?

STUDENT STUDY SITE

ⓢSAGE edge™

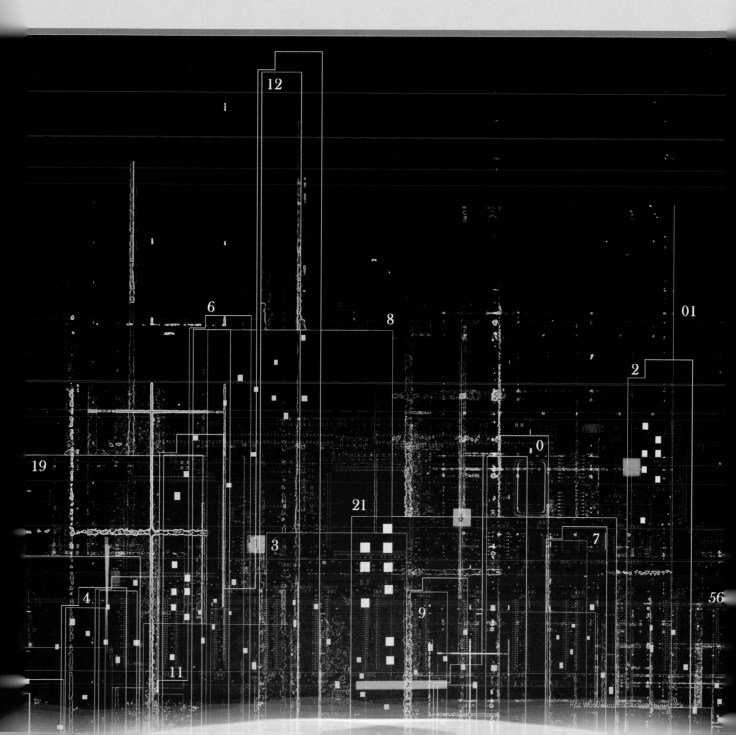

CHAPTER 11

Quantitative Data Analysis

There's been a lot of discussion about the way morals and attitudes about sex are changing in the United States. If a man and a woman have sex relations before marriage, do you think that it is always wrong, almost always wrong, wrong only sometimes, or not wrong at all?

You learned in Chapter 7 that fixed-choice questions like this one are often used in surveys. This particular question has often appeared in the biennial General Social Survey of a nationally representative sample of the U.S. population. Do you wonder what fraction of respondents chose "always wrong" or "not wrong at all" in answer to this question? Do you think attitudes have changed over time? The focus in this chapter is on how quantitative data collected in surveys or with other methods can be described and analyzed in order to answer such questions. You will learn how several common statistics are used and interpreted in social research. Think of it as a review of fundamental social statistics, if you have already studied them, or as an introductory overview, if you have not.

❖ Introducing Statistics

Some statistics are useful primarily to describe the results of measuring single variables and using multi-item scales. These statistics include frequency distributions, graphs, and measures of central tendency and of variation. Other statistics describe the association between variables. All of these statistics are termed **descriptive statistics** because they are used to describe the distribution of and relationship between variables.

You learned in Chapter 5 that *inferential statistics* are used to estimate the degree of confidence that can be placed in generalizations from a sample to the population from which the sample was selected. This chapter explains how inferential statistics are also used in hypothesis tests involving sample data.

❖ Displaying Univariate Distributions

For some statistical reports, the analysis may go no further than a display of variation in each variable of interest. Frequency distributions and graphs are the most common approaches for displaying the distribution of single variables. Graphs have the advantage of providing a picture that is easier to comprehend, although frequency distributions are preferable when exact numbers of cases having particular values must be reported and when many distributions must be displayed in a compact form.

Frequency Distributions

How did adults in the United States respond to the question about premarital sex in the 2012 survey? Of the 1,301 persons in the GSS sample who answered the question, 277—21.9% of the total—said premarital sex is "always wrong" and another 5% said it is "almost always wrong," but

Photo 11.1   Statistics is an important tool that helps researchers make sense of important data, such as individuals' attitudes toward premarital sex. What areas would you like to explore using statistics?

RESEARCHER INTERVIEW LINK
GSS

a majority—57.5%—said it is "not wrong at all." The complete frequency distribution of responses, with percentages, appears in Exhibit 11.1.

A **frequency distribution** displays the number of cases and/or the **percentage** (the relative frequency) of cases corresponding to each of a variable's values or group of values. The components of the frequency distribution should be labeled clearly, with a title, a stub (labels for the values of the variable), a caption (identifying whether the distribution includes frequencies, percentages, or both), and the total number of cases or 100%, as well as a footnote indicating the source. If, as is usually the case, only percentages are presented, the total number of cases in the distribution (the **base number N**) should be indicated in parentheses under the 100%.

You can learn more about frequency distributions by generating one yourself. To do this, you can use General Social Survey data available from the National Opinion Research Center at http://www3.norc.org/GSS+Website/. Replicate the steps in my analysis below by clicking on the link to "Data Analysis Using SDA" and then on the first link under "General Social Survey": General Social Survey (GSS) Cumulative Datafile 1972-2014 - release 2 (SDA 4.0). This takes you to the SDA site at the University of California, Berkeley. SDA allows you to analyze data from the GSS and other surveys online.

If you are following along online, you'll now see a screen like the one in Exhibit 11.2. On the left, click on "PERSONAL CONCERNS," then on "Human Nature," and then on "WORLD1." Now click on the "Copy to: Row" tab above and on the left. You will see that the WORLD1 variable name is moved into the Row position for analysis. Also

■ **EXHIBIT 11.1**   **Frequency Distribution of Attitudes About Sex Before Marriage**

Value	Number	Percentage
Always wrong	277	21.9%
Almost always wrong	65	5.1
Sometimes wrong	196	15.5
Not wrong at all	729	57.5
Total	1,267	100.0%

Source: Smith, Tom W., and Jaesok Son. 2013. *General Social Survey 2012 Final Report: Trends in Public Attitudes About Sexual Morality.* (Chicago: National Opinion Research Center, University of Chicago, p. 10). (Numbers from report adjusted to remove "don't know" responses from base *N*.)

choose "CHART OPTIONS/Type of Chart: Bar Chart" and check "Show percents." Make sure Bar Chart Options/Orientation is set to Vertical. Now click "Run the Table."

You will now see a new window with a frequency distribution for WORLD1 (Exhibit 11.3), followed by a bar chart for the same variable. The frequency produced by SDA includes both the percentage and the number of cases in each cell. In this analysis, responses are included from every year in which the question was asked (1985 to 2002). If you generate a table like this for a report, you should reformat it so that it looks like the distribution in Exhibit 11.1. How would you describe the distribution of beliefs about the world? It appears that few people believe the world is evil (just 5.7% completely endorse this view), with the largest concentration of cases in the middle category (28.5%) and the next-most-positive category (24.5%). What else can you say based on the distribution? (We'll review the bar chart in a bit.)

A frequency distribution is difficult to examine if it has many categories, so it is often a good idea to group together some categories prior to presentation. Consider grouping categories in a frequency distribution in either of two circumstances:

Descriptive statistics: Statistics used to describe the distribution of and relationship between variables.

Frequency distribution: Numerical display showing the number of cases, and usually the percentage of cases (the relative frequencies), corresponding to each value or group of values of a variable.

■ **EXHIBIT 11.2**   **Screenshot of GSS Analysis Screen at UC Berkeley SDA Site**

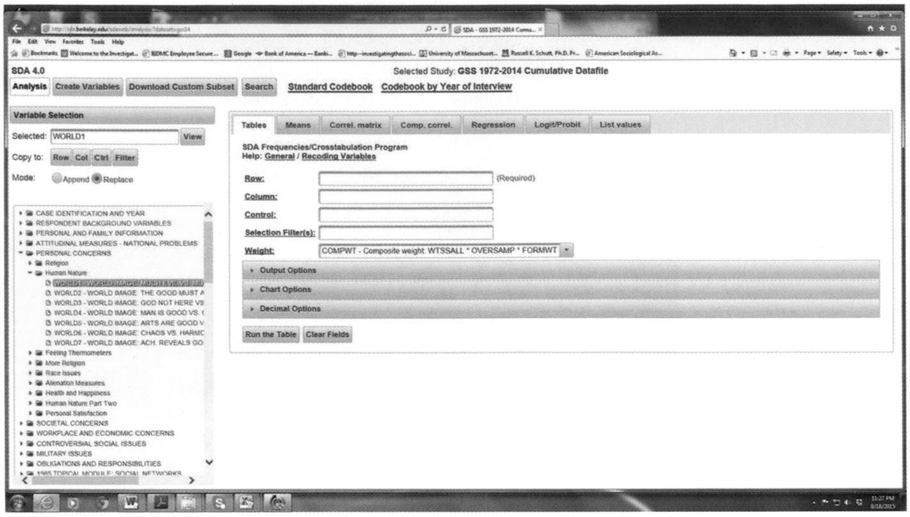

Source: Smith, Tom W., and Jaesok Son. 2013. *General Social Survey 2012 Final Report: Trends in Public Attitudes about Sexual Morality.* (Chicago: National Opinion Research Center, University of Chicago, p. 10). (Numbers from report adjusted to remove "don't know" responses from base N.)

■ **EXHIBIT 11.3**   **Frequency Distribution of Beliefs That World Is Evil or Good**

WORLD1	1: WORLD IS EVIL	5.7 936.3*
	2	3.5 576.1
	3	8.1 1,330.8
	4	28.5 4,685.1
	5	24.5 4,039.0
	6	15.0 2,468.2
	7: WORLD IS GOOD	14.8 2,430.0
	COL TOTAL	*100.0* *16,465.5*

*Number of cases includes fractional values due to GSS weighting procedures.

Source: General Social Survey, SDA Site, UC Berkeley. Retrieved from http://sda .berkeley.edu/sdaweb/analysis/?dataset=gss14

Percentage: Relative frequency, computed by dividing the frequency of cases in a particular category by the total number of cases and then multiplying by 100.

Base number (*N*): The total number of cases in a distribution.

Histogram: A graphic for quantitative variables, in which the variable's distribution is displayed with adjacent bars.

- There are more than 15 to 20 values to begin with, a number too large to be displayed in an easily readable table.
- The distribution of the variable will be clearer or more meaningful if some of the values are combined.

Categories must be used that do not distort the distribution. Adhering to the following guidelines for combining values in a frequency distribution will prevent many problems:

- Categories should be logically defensible and preserve the distribution's shape.
- Categories should be mutually exclusive and exhaustive, so that every case should be classifiable in one and only one category.

The most logically defensible categories may vary in size. A good example would be grouping years of education as less than 8 (did not finish grade school), 811 (finished grade school), 12 (graduated high school), 1315 (some college), 16 (graduated college), and 17 or more (some postgraduate education). Such a grouping captures the most meaningful distinctions in the educational distribution and preserves the information that would be important for many analyses (Exhibit 11.4).

Graphs

There are many types of graphs, but the most common and most useful are histograms, bar charts, and frequency polygons. Each has two axes, the vertical axis (the *y*-axis) and the horizontal axis (the *x*-axis), and labels to identify the variables and the values, with tick marks showing where each indicated value falls along the axis. **Histograms,** in which the bars are adjacent, are used to display the distribution of quantitative variables that vary along a continuum that has no necessary gaps. The histogram in Exhibit 11.5 was created with the frequency distribution in Exhibit 11.3. It is easy to quickly grasp the shape of the distribution with this graphic display (although the SDA site calls it a "bar chart").

Exhibit 11.6 is a histogram of the highest year of school completed from the 2012 GSS data. It has many more values than the variable displayed in Exhibit 11.5. The distribution has a clump of cases at 12 years—about one third of the total. The percentage of cases tapers off to the low end much more quickly, with a long tail, compared with the shape of the distribution toward the high end.

A **bar chart** contains solid bars separated by spaces. It is a good tool for displaying the distribution of variables measured at the nominal level because there is, in effect, a gap between each of the categories. The bar chart of marital status in Exhibit 11.7 indicates that almost half of adult Americans were married at the time of the survey. Smaller percentages were divorced, separated, or widowed, and more than one quarter had never married.

In a **frequency polygon,** a continuous line connects the points representing the number or percentage of cases with each value. The frequency polygon is an alternative to the histogram when the distribution of a quantitative variable must be displayed; this alternative is particularly useful when the variable has a wide range of values. It is easy to see in the frequency polygon of years of education in Exhibit 11.8 that the most common value is 12 years, high school completion, and that this value also seems to be at the center of the distribution. There is moderate variability in the distribution, with many cases having more than 12 years of education and almost one third having completed at least 4 years of college (16 years). The distribution is highly skewed in the negative direction, with few respondents reporting fewer than 10 years of education.

If graphs are misused, they can distort, rather than display, the shape of a distribution. Compare, for example, the two graphs in Exhibit 11.9. The first graph shows that high school seniors reported relatively stable rates of lifetime use of cocaine between 1980 and 1985. The second graph, using exactly the same numbers, appeared in a 1986 *Newsweek* article on the "coke plague" (Orcutt & Turner 1993). Looking at this graph, you would think that the rate of cocaine usage among high school seniors had increased dramatically during this period. But, in fact, the difference between the two graphs is due simply to changes in how the graphs are drawn. In the "plague graph," the percentage scale on the vertical axis begins at 15 rather than at 0, making what was about a 1-percentage point increase look very big indeed. In addition, omission from the plague graph of the more rapid increase in reported usage between 1975 and 1980 makes it look as if the tiny increase in 1985 were a new, and thus more newsworthy, crisis.

Photo 11.2 Grouping data into logical categories helps researchers present their findings more clearly. How could this also distort data in some situations?

■ **EXHIBIT 11.4** **Years of Education Completed**

Years of Education	Percentage
Less than 8	3.2%
8–11	12.9
12	27.4
13–15	26.5
16	15.6
17 or more	14.4
	100.0% (1972)

Source: General Social Survey (National Opinion Research Center 2013).

Bar chart: A graphic for qualitative variables, in which the variable's distribution is displayed with solid bars separated by spaces.

■ EXHIBIT 11.5 **Histogram of Beliefs That World Is Evil or Good**

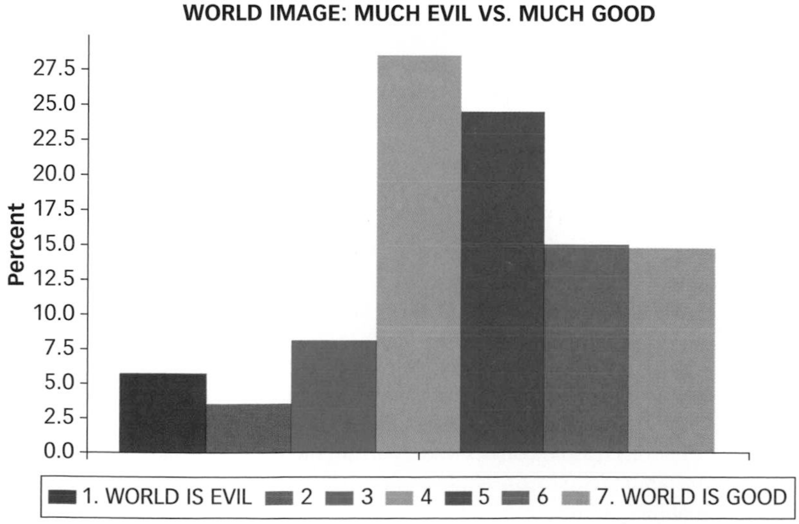

WORLD IMAGE: MUCH EVIL VS. MUCH GOOD

■ 1. WORLD IS EVIL ■ 2 ■ 3 ■ 4 ■ 5 ■ 6 ■ 7. WORLD IS GOOD

■ EXHIBIT 11.6   **Histogram of Years of School Completed**

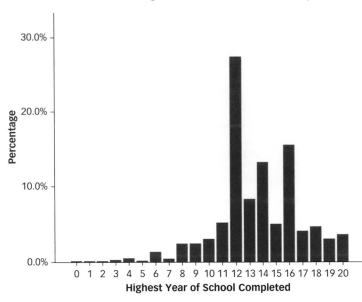

Source: General Social Survey (National Opinion Research Center 2013).

■ EXHIBIT 11.7   **Bar Chart of Marital Status**

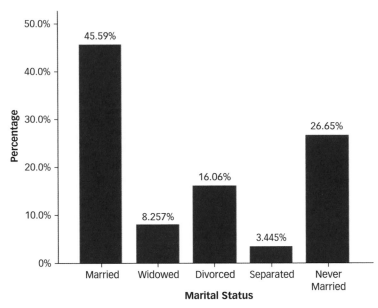

Source: General Social Survey (National Opinion Research Center 2013).

....

Frequency polygon: A graphic for quantitative variables, in which a continuous line connects data points representing the variable's distribution.

Central tendency: The most common value (for variables measured at the nominal level) or the value around which cases tend to center (for a quantitative variable).

Be on the lookout for several specific problems that can distort the impression of a distribution in a graph (Tufte 1983; Wallgren et al. 1996):

- The difference between bars can be exaggerated by cutting off the bottom of the vertical axis and displaying less than the full height of the bars (this is the type of problem in Exhibit 11.9). Instead, the graph of a quantitative variable should begin at 0 on both axes. It may be reasonable, at times, to violate this guideline, as when an age distribution is presented for a sample of adults, but in this case be sure to mark the break clearly on the axis.

- Bars of unequal width, including pictures instead of bars, can make particular values look as if they carry more weight than their frequency warrants. Bars should be of equal width.

- Either shortening or lengthening the vertical axis will obscure or accentuate the differences in the number of cases between values. The two axes usually should be of approximately equal length.

- Chart "junk" that can confuse the reader and obscure the distribution's shape should be avoided. Junk can be a lot of verbiage or umpteen marks, lines, lots of cross-hatching, etc.

❖ Summarizing Univariate Distributions

Summary statistics are often useful for representing key features of the distribution of a variable. Three features of shape are important: **central tendency**, **variability**, and **skewness** (lack of symmetry).

Summary statistics can facilitate comparison between distributions. For example, if the goal is to report variation in income by state in a form that is easy for most audiences to understand, it would usually be better to present average incomes than a detailed display containing 50 frequency distributions. A display of average incomes would also be preferable to multiple frequency distributions if the only purpose were to provide a general idea of differences in incomes between states.

Of course, representing a distribution in one number loses information about other aspects of the distribution's shape and so creates the possibility of obscuring important information. If you need to focus on differences in income inequality between states, for example, measures of central tendency would miss the point entirely. You would either have to present the 50 frequency distributions or use some special statistics that represent the extent to which the state income distributions are unequal. For this reason, analysts who report summary measures of central tendency usually also report a summary measure of variability and sometimes several measures of central tendency, variability, or both.

■ EXHIBIT 11.8   **Frequency Polygon of Years of Education**

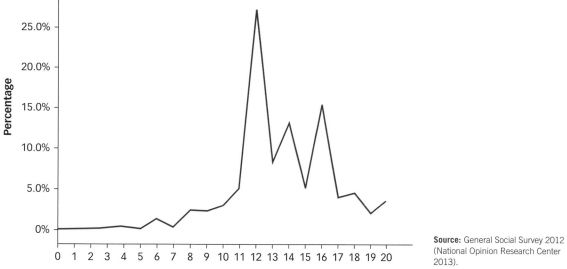

Source: General Social Survey 2012 (National Opinion Research Center 2013).

Measures of Central Tendency

Central tendency is usually summarized with one of three statistics: the mode, the median, or the mean. For any particular application, one of these statistics may be preferable, but each has a role to play in data analysis. To choose an appropriate measure of central tendency, the analyst must consider a variable's level of measurement, the skewness of a quantitative variable's distribution, and the purpose for which the statistic is used. In addition, the analyst's personal experiences and preferences inevitably will play a role.

Mode

The **mode** is the most frequent value in a distribution. It is also termed the probability average because, being the most frequent value, it is the most probable. For example, if you were to pick a case at random from the distribution of attitudes toward premarital sex (refer back to Exhibit 11.1), the probability of the case having checked "not wrong at all" would be .575 out of 1, or 57.5%—the most probable value in the distribution.

The mode is used much less often than the other two measures of central tendency because it can so easily give a misleading impression of a distribution's central tendency. One problem with the mode occurs when a distribution is **bimodal**, in contrast to being **unimodal**. A bimodal (or trimodal, etc.) distribution has two or more nonadjacent categories with an equal number of cases and with more cases than any of the other categories. There is no single mode. Imagine that a particular distribution has two categories, each having just about the same number of cases but that are far

■ EXHIBIT 11.9   **Two Graphs of Cocaine Usage**

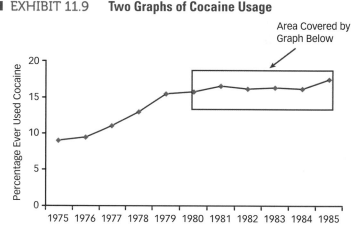

A. University of Michigan Institute for Social Research
   Time Series for Lifetime Prevalence of Cocaine Use

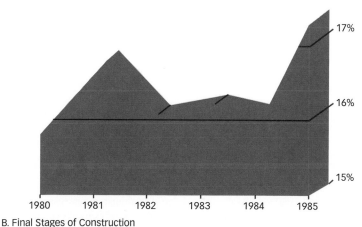

B. Final Stages of Construction

Source: Adapted from Orcutt and Turner (1993). Copyright 1993 by the Society for the Study of Social Problems. Reprinted by permission.

RESEARCH

In the News

GOOGLING AS SOCIAL DATA

The horrific tragedy of the April 2013 marathon bombing in Boston sent many people to the web. In the four days after the bombing, total searches for news rose 50% to 160%, but total searches for religion dropped slightly. Overall, the searches for churches have dropped by 15% since 2010, but searches for porn have increased by 83%.

For Further Thought ?

1. Do these search patterns tell us something about the role of religion and how it is changing in today's society?

2. What interesting research question can you propose that you think could be answered with data on Google searches?

News source: Stephens-Davidowitz, Seth. 2015. "Googling for God." *New York Times,* September 19:SR1.

ENCYCLOPEDIA LINK
Measures of Central Tendency

Variability: The extent to which cases are spread out through the distribution or clustered in just one location.

Skewness: The extent to which cases are clustered more at one or the other end of the distribution of a quantitative variable rather than in a symmetric pattern around its center. Skew can be positive (a right skew), with the number of cases tapering off in the positive direction, or negative (a left skew), with the number of cases tapering off in the negative direction. Skewness does not apply to qualitative variables (those measured at the nominal level).

Mode: The most frequent value in a distribution; also termed the **probability average.**

Bimodal: A distribution that has two nonadjacent categories with about the same number of cases, and these categories have more cases than any others.

Unimodal: A distribution of a variable in which there is only one value that is the most frequent.

Median: The position average, or the point that divides a distribution in half (the 50th percentile).

apart in the distribution (and these are the two most frequent categories). Strictly speaking, the mode would be the one with more cases, even though the other frequent category had only slightly fewer cases. Another potential problem with the mode is that it might happen to fall far from the main clustering of cases in a distribution. It would be misleading in most circumstances to say simply that the variable's central tendency was whatever the modal value was.

You can see this type of problem in the distribution of attitudes toward premarital sex in Exhibit 11.1. The modal value is "always wrong," but the second most common response is "not wrong at all," at the other end of the distribution. By contrast, the modal value of 4, and the adjacent value of 5, clearly represent the highest point in the distribution of Belief That World Is Evil or Good (Exhibit 11.3).

Nevertheless, there are occasions when the mode is very appropriate. Most important, the mode is the only measure of central tendency that can be used to characterize the central tendency of variables measured at the nominal level. We can't say much more about the central tendency of the distribution of marital status in Exhibit 11.7 than that the most common value is married. The mode also is often referred to in descriptions of the shape of a distribution. The terms *unimodal* and *bimodal* appear frequently, as do descriptive statements such as "The typical [most probable] respondent was in her 30s." Of course, when the question is, What is the most probable value?, the mode is the appropriate statistic. Which ethnic group is most common in a given school? The mode provides the answer.

Median

The **median** is the position average—the point that divides the distribution in half (the 50th percentile). The median is inappropriate for variables measured at the nominal level because their values cannot be put in order, and so there is no meaningful middle position. To determine the median, we simply array a distribution's values in numerical order and find the value of the case that has an equal number of cases above and below it. If the median point falls between two cases (which happens if the distribution has an even number of cases), the median is defined as the average of the two middle values and is computed by adding the values of the two middle cases and dividing by 2.

The median in a frequency distribution is determined by identifying the value corresponding to a cumulative percentage of 50. Starting at the top of the years of education distribution in Exhibit 11.4, for example, and adding up the percentages, we find that we have reached 43.5% in the 12 years category and then 70% in the 13–15 years category. The median is therefore 13–15. With most variables, it is preferable to compute the median from ungrouped data so that the result is an exact value for the median, rather than an interval.

Mean

The **mean**, or arithmetic average, considers the values of each case in a distribution—it is a weighted average. The mean is computed by adding up the value of all the cases and dividing by the total number of cases, thereby accounting for the value of each case in the distribution:

$$\text{Mean} = \text{Sum of value of cases/Number of cases}$$

In algebraic notation, the equation is $\bar{Y} = \Sigma Y_i / N$. For example, to calculate the mean of eight (hypothetical) cases, we add the values of all the cases (ΣY_i) and divide by the number of cases (N):

$$(28 + 117 + 42 + 10 + 77 + 51 + 64 + 55)/8 = 444/8 = 55.5$$

Because computing the mean requires adding the values of the cases, it makes sense to compute a mean only if the values of the cases can be treated as actual quantities—that is, if they reflect an interval or ratio level of measurement, or if they are ordinal and we assume that ordinal measures can be treated as interval. It would make no sense to calculate the mean religion. For example, imagine a group of four people in which there were two Protestants, one Catholic, and one Jew. To calculate the mean, you would need to solve the equation (Protestant + Protestant + Catholic + Jew)/4 = ? Even if you decide that Protestant = 1, Catholic = 2, and Jew = 3 for data entry purposes, it still doesn't make sense to add these numbers because they don't represent quantities of religion.

Median or Mean?

Both the median and the mean are used to summarize the central tendency of quantitative variables, but their suitability for a particular application must be assessed carefully. The key issues to be considered in this assessment are the variable's level of measurement, the shape of its distribution, and the purpose of the statistical summary. Consideration of these issues will sometimes result in a decision to use both the median and the mean. But in many other situations, the choice between the mean and the median will be clear-cut as soon as the researcher takes the time to consider these three issues.

Level of measurement is a key concern because, to calculate the mean, we must add the values of all the cases—a procedure that assumes the variable is measured at the interval or ratio level. So even though we know that coding *Agree* as 2 and *Disagree* as 3 does not really mean that *Disagree* is 1 unit more of disagreement than *Agree,* the mean assumes this evaluation to be true. Because calculation of the median requires only that we order the values of cases, we do not have to make this

Photo 11.3 What is the median number of students in each row? Would you also be able to calculate the mean?

assumption. Technically speaking, then, the mean is simply an inappropriate statistic for variables measured at the ordinal level (and you already know that it is completely meaningless for variables measured at the nominal level). In practice, however, many social researchers use the mean to describe the central tendency of variables measured at the ordinal level, for the reasons outlined below.

The shape of a variable's distribution should also be considered when deciding whether to use the median or mean. When a distribution is perfectly symmetric, so that the distribution of values below the median is a mirror image of the distribution of values above the median, the mean and the median will be the same. But the values of the mean and the median are affected differently by skewness, or the presence of cases with extreme values on one side of the distribution but not the other side. Because the median accounts for only the number of cases above and below the median point, not the value of these cases, it is not affected in any way by extreme values. Because the mean is based on adding the value of all the cases, it will be pulled in the direction of exceptionally high (or low) values. When the value of the mean is larger than the value of the median, we know that the distribution is skewed in a positive direction, with proportionately more cases with higher than lower values. When the mean is smaller than the median, the distribution is skewed in a negative direction.

This differential impact of skewness on the median and mean is illustrated in Exhibit 11.10. On the first balance beam, the cases (bags) are spread out equally, and the median and the mean are in the same location. On the second and third balance beams, the median corresponds to the value of the middle case, but the mean is pulled toward the value of the one case with an extremely high value.

Mean: The arithmetic, or weighted, average, computed by adding the value of all the cases and dividing by the total number of cases.

■ EXHIBIT 11.10   **The Mean as a Balance Point**

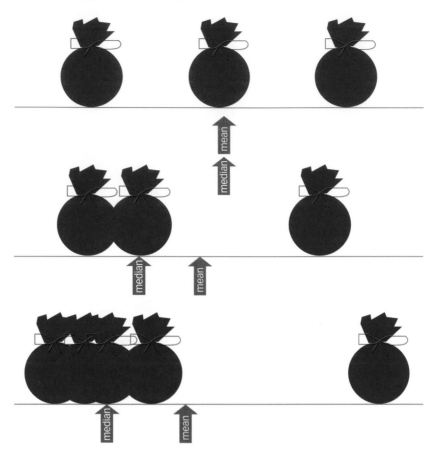

   The single most important influence on the choice of the median or the mean for summarizing the central tendency of quantitative variables should be the purpose of the statistical summary. If the purpose is to report the middle position in one or more distributions, then the median is the appropriate statistic, whether or not the distribution is skewed (Exhibit 11.11). For example, with respect to the age distribution from the GSS, you could report that half the U.S. population is younger than 47 years old, and half the population is older than that. But if the purpose is to show how likely different groups are to have age-related health problems, the measure of central tendency for these groups should account for people's actual ages, not just the number of people who are older and younger than a particular age. For this purpose, the median would be inappropriate because it would not distinguish between two distributions that have the same median but with different numbers of older people. In one distribution, everyone might be between the ages of 35 and 55, with a median of 47. In another distribution with a median of 47, half of the cases could have ages above 60. The mean of the second distribution would be higher, reflecting the fact that it has a greater number of older people.
   It is not appropriate to use either the median or the mean as a measure of central tendency for variables measured at the nominal level because at this level the different attributes of a variable cannot be ordered as higher or lower (as reflected in Exhibit 11.11). Technically speaking, the mode should be used to measure the central tendency of variables measured at the nominal level (and it can also be used with variables measured at the ordinal, interval, and ratio levels). The median is most suited to measure the central tendency of variables measured at the ordinal level (and it can also be used to measure the central tendency of variables measured at the

■ EXHIBIT 11.11   **Selection of Measures of Central Tendency (MCT)**

Level of Measurement	Purpose of MCT	Most Appropriate MCT	Additional Potentially Useful MCT	Definitely Inappropriate MCT
Nominal	Identify most frequent response	Mode	None	Median, mean
Ordinal	Identify middle position	Median	Mean	None
Interval, ratio	Identify arithmetic average	Mean	Median, mode	None

interval and ratio levels). Finally, the mean is unequivocally suited to measure the central tendency for variables measured at only the interval and ratio levels.

It is not entirely legitimate to represent the central tendency of a variable measured at the ordinal level with the mean: Calculation of the mean requires summing the values of all cases, and at the ordinal level, these values indicate only order, not actual numbers. Nonetheless, many social scientists use the mean with ordinal-level variables and find that this is potentially useful for comparisons between variables and as a first step in more complex statistical analyses. The median and the mode can also be useful as measures of central tendency for variables measured at the interval and ratio levels, when the goal is to indicate middle position (the median) or the most frequent value (the mode).

In general, the mean is the most commonly used measure of central tendency for quantitative variables, both because it accounts for the value of all cases in the distribution and because it is the foundation for many more advanced statistics. However, the mean's very popularity results in its use in situations for which it is inappropriate. Keep an eye out for this problem.

Measures of Variation

You already learned that central tendency is only one aspect of the shape of a distribution—the most important aspect for many purposes but still just a piece of the total picture. A summary of distributions based only on their central tendency can be incomplete, even misleading. For example, three towns might have the same median income but still be very different in their social character because of the shape of their income distributions. As illustrated in Exhibit 11.12, Town A is a homogeneous middle-class community; Town B is heterogeneous; and Town C has a polarized, bimodal income distribution, with mostly very poor and very rich people and few in between. However, all three towns have the same median (and mean) income.

The way to capture these differences is with statistical measures of variation. Two popular measures of variation are the range and the standard deviation. The following sections also mention two related but somewhat less popular measures of variation, the interquartile range and the variance, but their calculation is not discussed. To calculate any of these measures of variation, the variable must be at the interval or ratio level (but many would argue that, like the mean, they can be used with ordinal-level measures, too). Statistical measures of variation are seldom used with variables measured at the nominal level, so they are not presented here.

■ EXHIBIT 11.12 **Distributions Differing in Variability but Not Central Tendency**

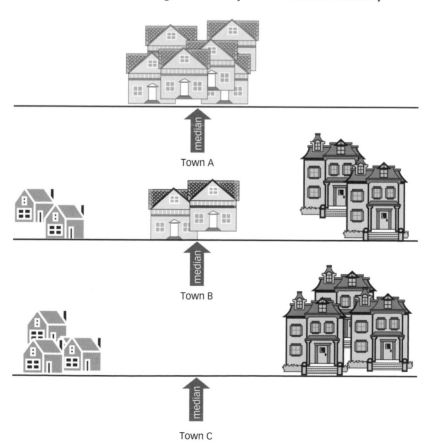

Range

The **range** is a simple measure of variation, calculated as the highest value in a distribution minus the lowest value, plus 1:

$$\text{Range} = \text{Highest value} - \text{Lowest value} + 1$$

It often is important to report the range of a distribution to identify the whole range of possible values that might be encountered. However, because the range can be altered drastically by just one exceptionally high or low value (termed an **outlier**), it does not do an adequate job of summarizing the extent of variability in a distribution.

A version of the range statistic, the **interquartile range**, avoids the problem created by outliers. The interquartile range is the difference between the first **quartile** (the value at which 25% of the cases are included) and the third quartile (the value at which 75% of the cases have been included).

Standard Deviation

The **standard deviation** (σ) is the square root of the average squared deviation of each case from the mean, so it accounts for the amount by which each case differs from the mean.

$$\sigma^2 = \sqrt{\frac{\Sigma(Y_i - \overline{Y})^2}{N}}$$

Symbol key: $\overline{Y}$ = mean; N = number of cases; Σ = sum over all cases; Y_i = value of variable Y for case i; $\surd$ = square root; σ = standard deviation.

Knowing how the standard deviation is calculated will help you to understand what it means. An example of how to calculate the standard deviation appears in Exhibit 11.13. First the mean value is subtracted from the value of each case ($Y - \overline{Y}$). Then each of the resulting quantities is squared and they are all added ($\Sigma = 434.15$). This *sum of squared errors* is then divided by the total number of cases and the square root is taken of the result.

When the standard deviation is calculated from sample data, the denominator is supposed to be $N - 1$, rather than N, an adjustment that has no discernible effect when the number of cases is reasonably large. Also note that the use of *squared* deviations in the formula accentuates the impact of relatively large deviations because squaring a large number makes that number count much more.

The **variance** is another popular measure of variation that is simply the square of the standard deviation. In other words, it is the average squared deviation of each case from the mean without then calculating the square root. The variance is used instead of the standard deviation for some statistical purposes, but this need not concern us here.

The standard deviation has mathematical properties in relation to the **normal distribution** that increase its value for statisticians. As you learned in Chapter 5, a normal distribution is a distribution that results from chance variation around a mean. It is symmetric and tapers off in a characteristic bell shape from its mean. If a variable is normally distributed, 68% of the cases will lie between plus and minus 1 standard deviation from the distribution's mean and 95% of the cases will lie between plus and minus 1.96 standard deviations from the mean (Exhibit 11.14).

So it is these properties of the standard deviation that allow a statistician to make statements about the confidence that can be placed in an estimate of the mean (or other statistics) from sample data, like those in Chapter 5. For example, "Based on the GSS 2012 sample, I can be 95% confident that the true mean age in the population is between 47.4 and 49.0." When you read in media reports about polling results an assertion like the "margin of error was plus or minus 3 points," you'll now know that the pollster was simply providing 95% confidence limits for the statistic.

Range: The highest rounded value minus the lowest rounded value, plus one).

Outlier: An exceptionally high or low value in a distribution.

Interquartile range: The range in a distribution between the end of the first quartile and the beginning of the third quartile.

Quartiles: The points in a distribution corresponding to the first 25% of the cases, the first 50% of the cases, and the first 75% of the cases.

Standard deviation: The square root of the average squared deviation of each case from the mean.

Variance: A statistic that measures the variability of a distribution as the average squared deviation of each case from the mean.

Normal distribution: A symmetric, bell-shaped distribution that results from chance variation around a central value.

Cross-tabulation (crosstab) or contingency table: In the simplest case, a bivariate (two-variable) distribution, showing the distribution of one variable for each category of another variable; can be elaborated using three or more variables.

❖ Crosstabs

Now let's return to the GSS question about premarital sex and see how to determine whether the distribution of attitudes about premarital sex has changed over time. Exhibit 11.15 helps us to answer this question by showing the percentage distributions of responses to this question in 1972, 1993 (the GSS was not conducted in 1992), and 2012. This is now a **cross-tabulation (crosstab)**, rather than a simple frequency distribution. It shows us the relation between two variables: in this case, attitudes about sex before marriage and year. Compare the percentage distribution of responses in

1993 to those in 1972. Was there a change? Now compare the percentage distributions in 1993 and 2012. Was there a change over these two decades? You can see that the percentage responding "always wrong" declined from 35.7 in 1972 to 26.9 in 1993 and then to a low of 21.9 in 2012. Over the same period, the percentage of respondents agreeing that sex before marriage is "not wrong at all" rose from 27.7 in 1972 to 57.5 in 2012. That's a pretty dramatic shift!

You "read the table" by comparing the percentage distributions in each column. With a quantitative variable like "year," you should do this in order, in this case proceeding from the left column (the lowest value) to the column on the right. Can you see why it is helpful to present the distribution with percentages, rather than with the actual number of respondents in each category? By converting the original frequencies into percentages out of 100, we can easily compare the distributions of responses even though a different number of individuals was surveyed in each year. Note that when the total of the percentages does not quite equal 100 due to rounding error, this should be indicated in a footnote.

Cross-tabulation is a useful method for examining the relationship between variables only when they have a limited number of categories. For most analyses, 10 categories is a reasonable upper limit, but even 10 is too many unless you have a pretty large number of cases (more than 100). The values of a variable with many categories, or that varies along a continuum with many values, may be recoded to a smaller number before the variable is used in a crosstab. For example, the values of a 5-point index might be recoded to just *high (representing scores of 3 and 4), medium (3),* and *low (1, 2)*. The numerical values of age might be recoded to 10-year intervals.

Graphs can also help to display the association between two variables. Graphs of an association are particularly useful when one variable has many categories that provide useful information. This is the case if we want to examine the variation in attitudes toward premarital sex across all the years since the GSS began. The graph in Exhibit 11.16 shows at a glance the dramatic increase in acceptance of premarital sex from 1972 to 2012. It is also easy to see in this graph that this increase occurred mostly in the 1970s and after 2000; in the 1980s and 1990s, the percentage of the population believing that premarital sex is "not wrong at all" remained near 40%.

This graph also makes it easy to compare the changes in support for premarital sex with changes in attitudes about other aspects of sexual behavior. Acceptance of same-gender relations also changed dramatically, but in a very different pattern: Acceptance remained just above 10% during the 1970s and 1980s, but then rose quickly in the 1990s, 2000s, and 2010s. By contrast, acceptance of teen sex (14–16 years old) and of extramarital sex remained

■ **EXHIBIT 11.13** **Calculation of the Standard Deviation**

Case #	Score (Y_i)	$Y_i - \bar{Y}$	$(Y_i - \bar{Y})^2$
1	21	−3.27	10.69
2	30	5.73	32.83
3	15	−9.27	85.93
4	18	−6.27	39.31
5	25	0.73	0.53
6	32	7.73	59.75
7	19	−5.27	27.77
8	21	−3.27	10.69
9	23	−1.27	1.61
10	37	12.73	162.05
11	26	1.73	2.99
			Σ=434.15
			$\sqrt{}$=20.84

■ **EXHIBIT 11.14** **The Normal Distribution**

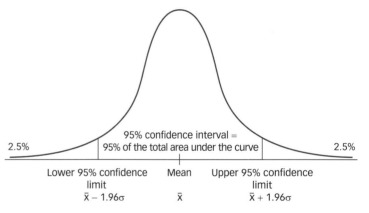

95% confidence interval =
95% of the total area under the curve

2.5%   2.5%

Lower 95% confidence   Mean   Upper 95% confidence
limit   limit
$\bar{x} - 1.96\sigma$ $\bar{x}$ $\bar{x} + 1.96\sigma$

■ **EXHIBIT 11.15** **Attitudes About Sex Before Marriage by Year**

Value	Year		
	1972	**1993***	**2012**
Always wrong	35.7	26.9	21.9%
Almost always wrong	11.4	10.0	5.1
Sometimes wrong	25.2	21.8	15.5
Not wrong at all	27.7	41.4	57.5
Total %**	100%	101%	100.0%
N	(1,533)	(1,054)	(1,267)

*The GSS was not conducted in 1992.

**Percentages may not add to 100 due to rounding error.

Source: Smith, Tom W., and Jaesok Son. 2013. *General Social Survey 2012 Final Report: Trends in Public Attitudes about Sexual Morality*. (Chicago: National Opinion Research Center, University of Chicago, p. 10). (Numbers from report adjusted to remove "don't know" responses from base *N*.)

■ EXHIBIT 11.16 **Attitudes Toward Sex, 1972–2012**

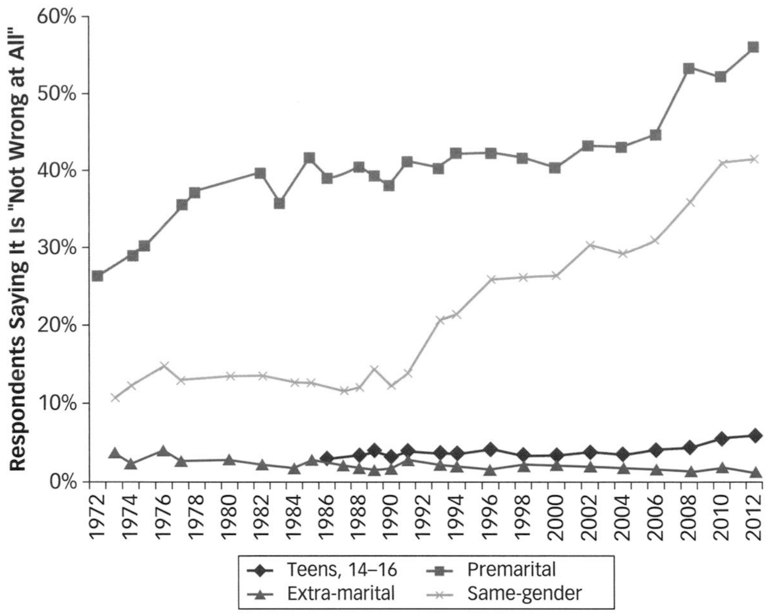

Source: Smith, Tom W., and Jaesok Son. 2013. *General Social Survey 2012 Final Report: Trends in Public Attitudes about Sexual Morality.* (Chicago: National Opinion Research Center, University of Chicago, p. 5). (Numbers from report adjusted to remove "don't know" responses from base *N*.)

low throughout these five decades, with acceptance of sex among teens beginning to increase in the last decade.

Now compare the information presented in Exhibit 11.15 and that in Exhibit 11.16. In the cross-tabulation in Exhibit 11.15, we can see the distribution across each response category, but for only 3 years. In the graph in Exhibit 11.16, however, we see only the percentage in one response category ("not wrong at all"). Why this focus on one response category? It makes it easy to see the changes throughout this 40-year period as well as to compare those changes with the corresponding changes in other attitudes (and this response itself is of interest). This reflects a trade-off between descriptive detail and analytic power that statisticians often make. A statistical analysis can often have more analytic power if the descriptive detail is reduced.

We can use the table in Exhibit 11.17 to learn more about crosstabs. The cells of the table are defined by combinations of row and column values. Each cell represents cases with a unique combination of values of the two variables, corresponding to that particular row and column. The **marginal distributions** of the table are on the right (the *row marginals*) and underneath (the *column marginals*). These are just the frequency distributions for the two variables (in number of cases, percentages, or both), considered separately. (The column marginals in Exhibit 11.17 are for family income; the row marginals are for the distribution of voting.) The independent variable is usually the column variable; the dependent variable then is the row variable.

A crosstab is usually presented as part of a test of a hypothesis that the distribution of the dependent variable will vary in relation to the value of the independent variable. Exhibit 11.15 might have been presented to test the hypothesis that feelings about premarital sex (the dependent variable) were becoming more liberal over time (time being the independent variable). The association in Exhibit 11.15 was consistent with that hypothesis. For Exhibit 11.17, we can imagine a hypothesis having been proposed that likelihood of voting (the dependent variable) increases with income (time being the independent variable) (Manza et al. 2005). Is the pattern in Exhibit 11.17 consistent with this hypothesis? (Remember, read the table by comparing the distribution of percentages in the first column to those in the second column, and so on. When you do this, you can see that the likelihood of having voted increased with income.)

·······

Marginal distribution: The summary distributions in the margins of a cross-tabulation that correspond to the frequency distribution of the row variable and of the column variable.

In the tables in both Exhibits 11.15 and 11.17, the independent variable is the column variable and the dependent variable is the row variable. Read the table by comparing percentages, one column at a time, because the table "is percentaged in the direction of the independent variable"; in other words, the percentages are calculated on the basis of the number of cases in each category of the independent variable (362 with incomes less than $20,000, 382 with incomes between $20,000 and $39,999, etc.). A table should always be percentaged in the direction of the

■ EXHIBIT 11.17 **Cross-Tabulation of Voting in 2008 by Family Income**

Family Income			
Voting	<$20,000	$20,000–$39,999	$40,000–$74,999	$75,000+
Voted	55.8%	70.4%	74.6%	87.1%
Did not vote	44.2	29.6	25.4	12.9
Total	100.0%	100.0%	100.0%	100.0%
Total (*n*)	(362)	(382)	(398)	(472)

Source: General Social Survey (National Opinion Research Center 2013).

independent variable when one variable in a crosstab is treated as independent and the other as dependent.

But the independent variable does not *have* to be the column variable; what is critical is to be consistent within a report or paper. You will find in published articles and research reports some percentage tables in which the independent variable and dependent variable positions are reversed. If the independent variable is the row variable, then the table should be percentaged on the row totals (the *n* in each row), and so the percentages then total 100% across the rows. Let's examine Exhibit 11.18, which is percentaged on the row variable: age. When you read the table in Exhibit 11.18, you find that 56.8% of those in their 20s voted (and 43.2% didn't vote), compared with 66.6% of those in their 30s, 71.9% and 71.8% of those in their 40s and 50s, respectively, and 84% to 90.2% of those ages 60 or older. Of course, this table still adheres to the "percentage in the direction of the independent variable" rule.

■ **EXHIBIT 11.18** **Cross-Tabulation of Voting in 2008 by Age (Row Percentages)**

Age	Voting			
	Yes (%)	No (%)	Total (%)	(*n*)
20–29	56.8%	43.2%	100.0%	(234)
30–39	66.6%	33.4%	100.0%	(359)
40–49	71.9%	28.1%	100.0%	(338)
50–59	71.8%	28.2%	100.0%	(316)
60–69	84.0%	16.0%	100.0%	(282)
70–79	86.0%	14.0%	100.0%	(164)
80 or older	90.2%	9.8%	100.0%	(92)

Source: General Social Survey (National Opinion Research Center 2013).

Inferential statistics are used to decide whether it is likely that an association exists in the larger population from which the sample was drawn. Even when the association between two variables is consistent with the researcher's hypothesis, it is possible that the association was just caused by the vagaries of sampling on a random basis (of course, the problem is even worse if the sample is not random). It is conventional in statistics to avoid concluding that an association exists in the population from which the sample was drawn unless the probability that the association was due to chance is less than 5%. In other words, a statistician typically will not conclude that an association exists between two variables unless he or she can be at least 95% confident that the association was not due to chance. This is the same type of logic that you learned about earlier in this chapter, which introduced the concept of 95% confidence limits for the mean. Estimation of the probability that an association is not due to chance could be based on one of several inferential statistics, but **chi-square** is the one used in most cross-tabular analyses. The probability is customarily reported in a summary form such as $p < .05$, which can be interpreted as "The probability that the association was due to chance is less than 5 out of 100 (5%)."

When the analyst feels reasonably confident (at least 95% confident) that an association was not due to chance, it is said that the association is statistically significant. **Statistical significance** means that an association is not likely to result from chance, according to some criterion set by the analyst. Convention (and the desire to avoid concluding that an association exists in the population when it does not) dictates that the criterion be a probability less than 5%.

But statistical significance is not everything. You may remember from Chapter 5 that sampling error decreases as sample size increases. For this same reason, an association is less likely to appear on the basis of chance in a larger sample than in a smaller sample. In a table with more than 1,000 cases, such as those involving the full 2012 GSS sample, the odds of a chance association are often very low indeed. For example, with our table based on 1,614 cases, the probability that the association between income and voting (Exhibit 11.17) was due to chance is less than 1 in 1,000 ($p < .001$)! The strength of that association was only moderate. Even weak associations can be statistically significant with such a large random sample, which means that the analyst must be careful not to assume that just because a statistically significant association exists, it is important. In a large sample, an association may be statistically significant but still be too weak to be substantively significant; by contrast, in a small sample, an association can be strong but not significantly different from chance.

SAGE JOURNAL ARTICLE
Controlling for a Third Variable: Career Outcomes

SAGE JOURNAL ARTICLE
Controlling for a Third Variable: Guilt and Distress

Controlling for a Third Variable

Cross-tabulation can also be used to study the relationship between two variables while controlling for a third variable, or even more variables. A common reason for introducing a third variable into a bivariate relationship is to see whether that relationship is spurious because of the influence of an extraneous variable—a variable that influences both the independent and dependent variables, creating an association between them that disappears when the extraneous variable is controlled (see Chapter 6). Ruling out possible extraneous variables will help strengthen considerably the conclusion that the relationship between the independent and dependent variables is causal.

One variable that might create a spurious relationship between income and voting is education. You have already seen that the likelihood of voting increases with income. Is it not possible, though, that this association is spurious because of the effect of education? Education, after all, is associated with both income and voting, and we might surmise that it is what students learn in school about civic responsibility that increases voting, not income itself. The trivariate cross-tabulation in

Chi-square: An inferential statistic used to test hypotheses about relationships between two or more variables in a cross-tabulation.

Statistical significance: The mathematical likelihood that an association is due to chance, judged by a criterion set by the analyst (often that the probability is less than 5 out of 100 or $p < .05$).

Subtables: Tables describing the relationship between two variables within the discrete categories of one or more other control variables.

Specification: A type of relationship involving three or more variables in which the association between the independent and dependent variables varies across the categories of one or more other control variables.

Regression analysis: A statistical technique for characterizing the pattern of a relationship between two quantitative variables in terms of a linear equation and for summarizing the strength of this relationship in terms of its deviation from that linear pattern.

Correlational analysis: A statistical technique that summarizes the strength of a relationship between two quantitative variables in terms of its adherence to a linear pattern.

Exhibit 11.19 shows that the relationship between voting and income is not spurious because of the effect of education; if it were, an association between voting and family income would not appear in any of the subtables—somewhat like the first subtable. Subtables describe the relationship between two variables within the discrete categories of one or more other control variables.

The association between family income and voting is higher in the other three subtables in Exhibit 11.19, for respondents with a high school, some college, or a college education. So our hypothesis—that income leads to higher rates of voting—does not appear to be spurious because of the effect of education. Exhibit 11.19 instead illustrates a pattern of specification: Education specifies the conditions for the association between income and likelihood of voting. Those with very little education seem to be so disconnected from the political system that they are unlikely to vote no matter how much they earn, but for those with at least a high school education, more income is associated with a higher likelihood of voting.

❖ Regression Analysis

The goal in introducing you to cross-tabulation has been to help you think about the association between variables and to give you a relatively easy tool for describing association. To read most statistical reports and to conduct more sophisticated analyses of social data, you will have to extend your statistical knowledge. Many statistical reports and articles published in social science journals use a statistical technique called regression analysis or correlational analysis to describe the association between two or more quantitative variables. The terms actually refer to different aspects of the same

■ EXHIBIT 11.19   **Voting in 2008 by Income and Education**

Family Income				
Voting	<$20,000	$20,000–$39,999	$40,000–$74,999	$75,000+
Education = < High school				
Voted	39.8%	38.1%	42.4%	33.3%
Did not vote	60.2	61.9	57.6	66.7
Total	100%	100%	100%	100%
(n)	(113)	(63)	(33)	(12)
Education = High school graduate				
Voted	57.1%	74.4%	73.0%	80.2%
Did not vote	42.9	25.6	27.0	19.8
Total	100%	100%	100%	100%
(n)	(119)	(121)	(122)	(81)
Education = Some college				
Voted	67.0%	75.8%	73.3%	90.4%
Did not vote	33.0	24.2	26.7	9.6
Total	100%	100%	100%	100%
(n)	(91)	(124)	(116)	(104)
Education = College graduate or graduate school				
Voted	71.8%	82.4%	85.8%	90.2%
Did not vote	28.2	17.6	14.2	9.8
Total	100%	100%	100%	100%
(n)	(39)	(74)	(127)	(275)

Source: General Social Survey (National Opinion Research Center 2013).

CAREERS
and Research

CLAIRE WULF WINIAREK, DIRECTOR OF COLLABORATIVE POLICY ENGAGEMENT

Claire Wulf Winiarek didn't set her sights on research methods as an undergraduate in political science and international relations at Baldwin College, nor as a master's student at Old Dominion University; her goal was to make a difference in public affairs. It still is. She is currently director of collaborative policy engagement at a Fortune 50 health insurance company. Her previous positions include working for a member of the U.S. House of Representatives, coordinating grassroots international human rights advocacy for a nonprofit human rights organization, and serving as director of public policy and research at another health insurance company.

Early in her career, Winiarek was surprised by the frequency with which she found herself leveraging research methods. Whether she is analyzing draft legislation and proposed regulations, determining next year's department budget, or estimating potential growth while making the case for a new program, Winiarek's advice for students seeking a career like hers is clear:

The information revolution is impacting all industries and sectors, as well as government and our communities. Research methods will create the critical and analytical foundation to meet the challenge, but internships or special research projects in your career field will inform that foundation with practical experience. Always look for that connection between research and reality.

technique. Statistics based on regression and correlation analysis are used frequently in social science and have many advantages over cross-tabulation—as well as some disadvantages.

Take a look at Exhibit 11.20. It's a plot, termed a *scatterplot,* of the relationship in the GSS 2012 sample between years of education and family income. The values of these variables have not been collapsed into categories, as they were in the preceding cross-tabular analysis. Instead, the scatterplot shows the location of each case in the data in terms of years of education (the horizontal axis) and family income level (the vertical axis).

■ EXHIBIT 11.20   **Scatterplot of Family Income by Highest Year of School Completed**

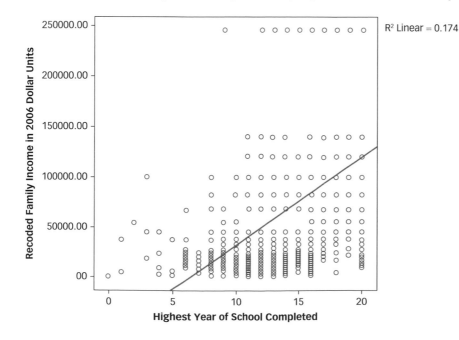

Source: General Social Survey (National Opinion Research Center 2013).

You can see that the data points in the scatterplot tend to run from the lower left to the upper right of the chart, indicating a positive relationship: The more the years of education, the higher the family income. The line drawn through the points is the regression line. The regression line summarizes this positive relationship between years of education, which is the independent variable (often simply termed X in regression analysis), and family income, the dependent variable (often simply termed Y in regression analysis). This regression line is the "best-fitting" straight line for this relationship—it is the line that lies closest to all the points in the chart, according to certain criteria.

ENCYCLEPEDIA LINK
Correlation

VIDEO LINK
Data Visualization

You can easily see that quite a few points are pretty far from the regression line, so we need to ask how well the regression line fits the points. In other words, how close does the regression line come to the points? (Actually, it's the square of the vertical distance, on the y-axis, between the points and the regression line that is used as the criterion.) The **correlation coefficient**, also called *Pearson's r*, or just r, gives one answer to that question. The value of r for this relationship is .42, which indicates a moderately strong positive linear relationship (if it were a negative relationship, r would have a negative sign). The value of r is 0 when there is absolutely no linear relationship between the two variables, and it is 1 or −1 when all the points representing all the cases lie exactly on the regression line (which would mean that the regression line describes the relationship perfectly).

So the correlation coefficient is a summary statistic that tells us about the strength of the association between the two variables. Values of r close to 0 indicate that the relationship is weak; values of r close to ±1 indicate the relationship is strong; in between there is a lot of room for judgment. You will learn in a statistics course that r^2 is often used to describe the strength of a linear relationship instead of r.

You can also use correlation coefficients and regression analysis to study simultaneously the association between three or more variables. In such a *multiple regression analysis,* you could test to see whether several other variables in addition to education are associated simultaneously with family income—that is, whether the variables have independent effects on family income. As an example, Exhibit 11.21 presents the key statistics obtained in a multiple regression analysis with the GSS 2012 data to identify the independent effect on family income of years of schooling, age, sex, and race (dichotomized).

First look at the coefficients listed in the column labeled "Beta Coefficient." Beta coefficients are standardized statistics that indicate how strong the linear association is between the dependent variable (family income, in this case) and each independent variable, while the other independent variables are controlled. Like the correlation coefficient (r), values of beta range from 0, when there is no linear association, to ±1.0, when the association falls exactly on a straight line. You can see in the beta column that education has a moderate positive independent association with family income, whereas sex (being female) and race (being a minority) have a weak association and age has no (linear) association with family income. In the "Significance Level" column, we can see that each of the three effects is statistically significant at the .001 level. We learn from the summary statistic—R^2 (r-squared)—that the four independent variables together explain, or account for, 15.2% of the total variation in family income.

You will need to learn more about the circumstances in which correlation coefficients and regression analysis are appropriate (e.g., both variables have to be quantitative, and the relationship has to be linear). But that's for another time and place (a separate statistics course). For now, this short introduction will enable you to make sense of more of the statistical analyses you find in research articles. You can also learn more about these techniques with the tutorials on the text's study site (edge.sagepub.com/schuttusw).

■ **EXHIBIT 11.21**　**Multiple Regression of Determinants of Family Income**

Variable	Beta Coefficient	Significance Level
Education	.409	$p < .001$
Age	−.015	NS*
Sex (Female)	−.074	$p < .001$
Race (Minority)	−.094	$p < .001$
R^2	.152	
N	1,784	

*****NS:** not [statistically] significant.

Source: General Social Survey (National Opinion Research Center 2013).

❖ Analyzing Data Ethically

Using statistics ethically means first and foremost being honest and open. Findings should be reported honestly, and the researcher should be open about the thinking that guided his or her decision to use particular statistics.

Summary statistics can easily be used unethically, knowingly or not. When we summarize a distribution in a single number, even in two numbers, we are losing much information. Neither central tendency nor variation describes a distribution's overall shape. Taken separately, neither measure tells us about the other characteristic of the distribution (central tendency or variation). So reports using measures of central tendency typically should also include measures of variation so as to avoid giving a misleading impression. And we should inspect the shape of any distribution for which we report summary statistics to ensure that the summary statistic does not mislead us (or anyone else) because the distribution is unusually skewed.

It is possible to mislead those who read statistical reports by choosing statistics that accentuate a particular feature of a distribution. The graph of cocaine usage in Exhibit 11.9 was one example: It made changes seem much more dramatic than the "honest graph" in that exhibit. You can imagine another way to use statistics to create a misleading impression by looking again at Exhibit 11.10.

Correlation coefficient: A summary statistic that varies from 0 to 1 or −1, with 0 indicating the absence of a linear relationship between two quantitative variables and 1 or −1 indicating that the relationship is completely described by the line representing the regression of the dependent variable on the independent variable.

Using the mean to represent the total money on the second and third balance beams would make it seem that the money distributions were the same, when in fact the distribution on the third balance beam is less equal.

When the data analyst begins to examine relationships between variables in some real data, social research becomes most exciting. The moment of truth, it would seem, has arrived. Either the hypotheses are supported or they are not. But this is actually a time to proceed with caution and to evaluate the analyses of others with even more caution. Once large data sets are entered into a computer, it becomes very easy to check out a great many relationships; when relationships are examined between three or more variables at a time, the possibilities become almost endless. If enough crosstabs (or correlation coefficients) are inspected in this way, an association between two variables will certainly turn up and could result in a publication, but it is still likely to be due only to chance. Look for the background story: Was the hypothesis proposed *before* the analysis was conducted?

Photo 11.4 What do you think might motivate some researchers to present misleading data?

©iStockphoto.com/PeopleImages

❖ Conclusions

This chapter has demonstrated how a researcher can describe social phenomena, identify relationships between them, explore the reasons for these relationships, and test hypotheses about them. Statistics provide a remarkably useful tool for developing our understanding of the social world, a tool that we can use both to test our ideas and to generate new ones.

Unfortunately, to the uninitiated, the use of statistics can seem to end debate right there: You can't argue with the numbers! But you now know better than that. The numbers will be worthless if the methods used to generate the data are not valid; and the numbers will be misleading if they are not used appropriately, considering the type of data to which they are applied. Even assuming valid methods and proper use of statistics, the statistics have to be interpreted and reported appropriately in order to be useful. The numbers do not speak for themselves.

AUDIO LINK
Quantitative Studies

VIDEO LINK
Research and Social Problems

Key Terms

REVIEW key terms with eFlashcards.
SAGE edge

Bar chart 175	Histogram 174	Regression analysis 186
Base number (*N*) 173	Interquartile range 182	Skewness 176
Bimodal 177	Marginal distribution 184	Specification 186
Central tendency 176	Mean 179	Standard deviation 182
Chi-square 185	Median 178	Statistical significance 185
Correlation coefficient 188	Mode 177	Subtables 186
Correlational analysis 186	Normal distribution 182	Unimodal 177
Cross-tabulation (crosstab) 182	Outlier 182	Variability 176
Descriptive statistics 172	Percentages 173	Variance 182
Frequency distribution 173	Quartiles 182	
Frequency polygon 175	Range 182	

Highlights

- Frequency distributions display variation in a form that can be easily inspected and described. Values should be grouped in frequency distributions in a way that does not alter the shape of

the distribution. Following several guidelines can reduce the risk of problems.

- Bar charts, histograms, and frequency polygons are useful for describing the shape of distributions. Care must be taken with graphic displays to avoid distorting a distribution's apparent shape.

- Summary statistics often are used to describe the central tendency and variability of distributions. The appropriateness of the mode, mean, and median vary with a variable's level of measurement, the distribution's shape, and the purpose of the summary.

- The variance and standard deviation summarize variability around the mean.

- Cross-tabulations should typically be percentaged within the categories of the independent variable.

- Inferential statistics are used with sample-based data to estimate the confidence that can be placed in a statistical estimate of a population parameter. Estimates of the probability that an association between variables may have occurred on the basis of chance are also based on inferential statistics.

- Regression analysis is a statistical method for characterizing the relationship between two or more quantitative variables with a linear equation and for summarizing the extent to which the linear equation represents that relationship. Correlation coefficients summarize the fit of the relationship to the regression line.

- Honesty and openness are the key ethical principles that should guide data summaries.

Chapter Questions

1. This chapter presented several examples of bivariate and trivariate cross-tabulations involving voting in the 2008 presidential election. What additional influences would you recommend examining to explain voting in elections? Suggest some additional independent variables for bivariate analyses with voting as well as several additional control variables to be used in three-variable crosstabs.

2. Review the frequency distributions and graphs in this chapter. Change one of these data displays so that you are "lying with statistics." (You might consider using the graphic technique discussed by Orcutt and Turner [1993].) How misleading is the resulting display?

3. Consider the relationship between voting and income that is presented in Exhibit 11.17. What third variables do you think should be controlled in the analysis to better understand the basis for this relationship? How might social policies be affected by finding out that this relationship was due to differences in neighborhood of residence rather than to income itself?

TEST your understanding of chapter content. Take the practice quiz. ⑤SAGE edge™

Practice Exercises

1. Test your understanding of basic statistics by visiting the study site (edge.sagepub.com/schuttusw) and completing one set of Interactive Exercises on quantitative data analysis.

2. Search the web for a social science example of statistics. Using the key terms from this chapter, describe the set of statistics you have identified. Which social phenomena does this set of statistics describe? What relationships, if any, do the statistics identify?

3. Do a web search for information on a social science subject in which you are interested. About what fraction of the information you find relies on statistics as a tool for understanding the subject? How do statistics allow researchers to test their ideas about the subject and generate new ideas? Write your findings in a brief report, referring to the websites on which you relied.

STUDENT STUDY SITE

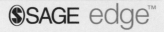
⑤SAGE edge™

The Student Study Site, available at **edge.sagepub.com/schuttusw**, includes useful study materials including eFlashcards, videos, audio resources, journal articles, and encyclopedia articles, many of which are represented by the media links throughout the text.

CHAPTER 12

Qualitative Data Analysis

Learning Objectives

❖ Describe some of the features of qualitative data analysis

❖ Compare and contrast the various approaches to qualitative data analysis

❖ Describe how visual sociologists use photographs to analyze data

❖ Provide examples of systematic data observation

❖ Identify the strengths and weaknesses of participatory action research

❖ Discuss the ways in which computer-aided qualitative data analysis can facilitate research

❖ List at least four ethical issues that should be given special attention in qualitative data analysis

I was at lunch standing in line and he [another male student] came up to my face and started saying stuff and then he pushed me. I said . . . I'm cool with you, I'm your friend and then he push me again and calling me names. I told him to stop pushing me and then he push me hard and said something about my mom. And then he hit me, and I hit him back. After he fell I started kicking him.

—Calvin Morrill et al. (2000:521)

In their qualitative study of youth culture and conflict in high schools, Calvin Morrill, Christine Yalda, and other researchers (2000) analyzed quotes like these to identify common themes and reasons for the eruption of conflict.

❖ Features of Qualitative Data Analysis

The distinctive features of the qualitative data collection methods that you studied in Chapter 8 are also reflected in the methods used to analyze those data. The focus on text—on qualitative data rather than on numbers—is the most important feature of qualitative analysis. The "text" that qualitative researchers analyze is most often transcripts of interviews or notes from participant observation sessions, but pictures or other images can also be a focus.

Qualitative data analyses describe textual data in ways that capture the setting or people who produced this text on their own terms rather than in terms of predefined measures and hypotheses. What this means is that qualitative data analysis tends to be inductive—the analyst identifies important categories in the data, as well as patterns and relationships, through a process of discovery. There are often no predefined measures or hypotheses.

Good qualitative data analyses focus on the interrelated aspects of the setting, group, or person under investigation—the case—rather than breaking the whole into separate parts. The whole is always understood to be greater than the sum of its parts, and so the social context of events, thoughts, and actions becomes essential for interpretation. Within this framework, it doesn't really make sense to focus on two variables out of an interacting set of influences and test the relationship between just those two.

The differences between quantitative and qualitative data analysis reflect the qualitative data analyst's orientation to in-depth, comprehensive understanding in which the analyst is an active participant compared with the quantitative data analyst's role as a dispassionate investigator of specific relationships between discrete variables (Denzin & Lincoln 2000:8–10; Patton 2002:13–14). The focus on meaning and in-depth study also makes qualitative data analysis a valuable supplement to analyses of quantitative data. Qualitative data can provide information about the quality of standardized case records and quantitative survey measures, as well as offer some insight into the meaning of particular fixed responses.

❖ Alternatives in Qualitative Data Analysis

The qualitative data analyst can choose from many interesting alternative approaches. Of course, the research question under investigation should shape the selection of an analytic approach, but the researcher's preferences and experiences also will inevitably have an important influence on the method chosen. The alternative approaches in this section—ethnomethodology, conversation analysis, narrative analysis, grounded theory, case-oriented understanding, and institutional ethnography—give you a good sense of the possibilities (Patton 2002).

Photo 12.1 Qualitative data analysis essentially zooms out to look at the big picture. How is this different from quantitative data analysis?

Ablestock.com/AbleStock.com/Thinkstock

RESEARCH/SOCIAL IMPACT LINK Ethnographic Research

Ethnomethodology

Ethnomethodology focuses on the way that participants construct the social world in which they live—how they "create reality"—rather than on describing the social world itself. Ethnomethodologists do not necessarily believe that we can find an objective reality; rather, the way that participants come to create and sustain a sense of reality is of interest.

Unlike the ethnographic analyst, who seeks to describe the social world as the participants see it, the ethnomethodological analyst seeks to maintain some distance from that world, focusing on how reality is constructed, not on what it is.

Conversation Analysis

Conversation analysis is a specific qualitative method for analyzing the sequential organization and details of conversation. Like ethnomethodology, from which it developed, conversation analysis focuses on how reality is constructed. From this perspective, detailed analysis of conversational interaction is important because

> it is through conversation that we conduct the ordinary affairs of our lives. Our relationships with one another, and our sense of who we are to one another is generated, manifest, maintained, and managed in and through our conversations, whether face-to-face, on the telephone, or even by other electronic means. (Drew 2005:74)

The following excerpt from Elizabeth Stokoe (2006:479–480) is an analysis of a conversation between four first-year British psychology students who must write up a description of some photographs of people (Exhibit 12.1). Stokoe incorporates stills from the video recording of the interaction into her analysis of both the talk and embodied conduct in interaction. In typical conversation analysis style, the text is broken up into brief segments that capture shifts in meaning, changes in the speaker, pauses, nonspeech utterances and nonverbal actions, and emphases.

Can you see how the social interaction reinforces the link of "woman" and "secretary"? Here, in part, is how Stokoe (2006) analyzes this conversation:

> In order to meet the task demands, one member of the group must write down their ideas. Barney's question at the start of the sequence, "is somebody scribing" is taken up after a reformulation: "who's writin' it." Note that, through a variety of strategies, members of the group manage their responses such that they do not have to take on the role of scribe. At line 05, Neil's "Oh yhe:ah." [the colon indicates prolongation of the phrase (Heritage n.d.:30)] treats Barney's turn as a proposal to be agreed with, rather than a request for action, and his subsequent nomination of Kay directs the role away from himself. . . . At line 08, Neil nominates Kay, his pointing gesture working in aggregate with the talk to accomplish the action ("She wants to do it."), whilst also attributing agency to Kay for taking up the role. A gloss [interpretation] might be "Secretaries in general are female, you're female, so you in particular are our secretary." (p. 481)

Ethnomethodology: A qualitative research method focused on the way that participants in a social setting create and sustain a sense of reality.

Conversation analysis: A qualitative method that analyzes the sequence and details of conversational text in order to understand how social reality is constructed.

Narrative Analysis

Narrative methods use interviews and sometimes documents or observations to "follow participants down their trails" (Riessman 2008:24). Unlike conversation analysis, which focuses attention on moment-by-moment interchange, narrative analysis seeks to put together the "big picture" about experiences or events as the participants understand them. **Narrative analysis** focuses on "the story itself" and seeks to preserve the integrity of personal biographies or a series of events that cannot adequately be understood in terms of their discrete elements (Riessman 2002:218). The coding for a narrative analysis is typically of the narratives as a whole, rather than of the different elements within them. The coding strategy revolves around reading the stories and classifying them into general patterns.

SAGE JOURNAL ARTICLE
Sexual Victimization
Qualitative Study

AUDIO LINK
Narrative Analysis

**RESEARCHER
INTERVIEW LINK**
Narrative Analysis

The Sexual Experiences Survey (SES) is used on many college campuses to assess the severity of sexual victimization, but researchers have found that it does not differentiate well between situations of unwanted sexual contact and attempted rape. Jenny Rinehart and Elizabeth Yeater (2011) at the University of New Mexico designed a narrative analysis project to develop "a deeper qualitative understanding of the details of the event, as well as the context surrounding it" (p. 927).

Rinehart and Yeater analyzed written narratives provided by 78 women at a West Coast university who had indicated some experience with sexual victimization on the SES. The authors and an undergraduate research assistant read each of the narratives and identified eight different themes and contexts, such as "relationship with the perpetrator." Next, they developed specific codes to make distinctions within each of the themes and contexts, such as "friend," "boss," or "stranger" within the "relationship" theme.

Here is an incident in one narrative that Rinehart and Yeater (2011) coded as involving unwanted sexual contact with a friend:

> I went out on a date with a guy (he was 24) and we had a good time. He invited me into his apartment after to "hang out" for a little while longer. He tried pressuring me into kissing him at first, even though I didn't want to. Then he wrestled me (playfully to him, but annoyingly and unwanted to me). I repeatedly asked him to get off of me, and eventually he did. I kissed him once. (p. 934)

Narrative analysis can also use documents and observations and focus more attention on how stories are constructed, rather than on the resulting narrative (Hyvärinen 2008:452).

Grounded Theory

Theory development occurs continually in qualitative data analysis (Coffey & Atkinson 1996:23). Many qualitative researchers use a method of developing theory during their analysis that is termed **grounded theory**, which involves building up inductively a systematic theory that is *grounded* in, or based on, the observations. The grounded theorist first summarizes observations into conceptual categories and then tests the coherence of these categories directly in the research setting with more observations. Over time, as the researcher refines and links the conceptual categories, a theory evolves (Glaser & Strauss 1967; Huberman & Miles 1994:436). Exhibit 12.2 diagrams the grounded theory of a chronic illness "trajectory" developed by Anselm Strauss and Juliette Corbin (1990:221). Their notes suggested to them that conceptions of self, biography, and body are reintegrated after a process of grieving.

As observation, interviewing, and reflection continue, grounded theory researchers refine their definitions of problems and concepts and select indicators. They can then check the frequency and distribution of phenomena: How many people made a particular type of comment? How often did social interaction lead to arguments? Social system models may then be developed that specify the relationships between different phenomena. These models are modified as researchers gain experience in the setting. For the final analysis, the researchers check their models carefully against their notes and make a concerted attempt to discover negative evidence that might suggest that the model is incorrect.

Narrative analysis: A form of qualitative analysis in which the analyst focuses on how respondents impose order on the flow of experience in their lives and thus make sense of events and actions in which they have participated.

Grounded theory: Systematic theory developed inductively, based on observations that are summarized into conceptual categories, reevaluated in the research setting, and gradually refined and linked to other conceptual categories.

Heidi Levitt, Rebecca Todd Swanger, and Jenny Butler (2008:435) used a systematic grounded method of analysis to understand the perspective of male perpetrators of violence on female victims. Research participants were recruited from programs the courts used in Memphis, Tennessee, to assess and treat perpetrators who admitted to having physically abused a female intimate partner. All program participants were of low socioeconomic status, but in other respects, Levitt and her colleagues (2008:436) sought to recruit a diverse sample.

The researchers (Levitt et al. 2008:437–438) began the analysis of their interview transcripts by dividing them into "meaning units"—"segments of texts that each contain one main idea"—and labeling these units with terms like those used by participants. The researchers then compared these labels and combined them into larger descriptive categories. This process continued until they had combined all the meaning

■ EXHIBIT 12.1 **Conversation Analysis, Including Pictures**

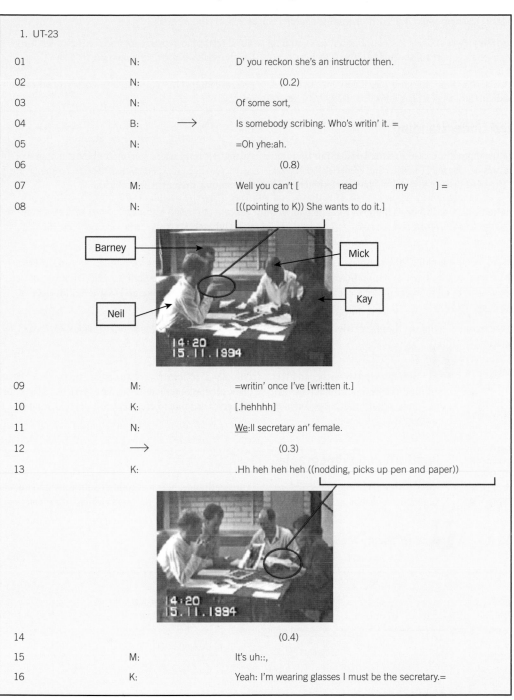

1. UT-23

01	N:		D' you reckon she's an instructor then.
02	N:		(0.2)
03	N:		Of some sort,
04	B:	⟶	Is somebody scribing. Who's writin' it. =
05	N:		=Oh yhe:ah.
06			(0.8)
07	M:		Well you can't [read my] =
08	N:		[((pointing to K)) She wants to do it.]

09   M: =writin' once I've [wri:tten it.]
10   K: [.hehhhh]
11   N: We:ll secretary an' female.
12   ⟶   (0.3)
13   K: .Hh heh heh heh ((nodding, picks up pen and paper))

14   (0.4)
15   M: It's uh::,
16   K: Yeah: I'm wearing glasses I must be the secretary.=

Source: Stokoe, Elizabeth. "On Ethnomethodology, Feminism, and the Analysis of Categorical Reference to Gender in Talk-in-Interaction."
Sociological Review 54:467–494. Copyright © 2006, John Wiley and Sons. Reprinted with permission.

units into seven different clusters. Exhibit 12.3 gives an example of two of their clusters and the four categories of meaning units combined within each (Levitt et al. 2008:439).

Here is how Levitt and her colleagues (2008) discuss the comments that were classified in Cluster 2, Category 3:

Accordingly, when conflicts accumulated that could not be easily resolved, many of the men (5 of 12) thought that ending the relationship was the only way to stop violence from recurring. (p. 440)

"I don't deal with anybody so I don't have any conflicts. . . . It makes me feel bad because I be lonely sometime, but at the same time, it's the best thing going for me right now. I'm trying to rebuild me. I'm trying to put me on a foundation to where I can be a total leader. Like I teach my sons, 'Be leaders instead of followers.'" (p. 440)

Although this interviewee's choice to isolate himself was a strategy to avoid relational dependency and conflict, it left him without interpersonal support and it could be difficult for him to model healthy relationships for his children. (p. 440)

With procedures such as these, the grounded theory approach develops general concepts from careful review of text or other qualitative materials and can then suggest plausible relationships between these concepts.

Case-Oriented Understanding

Like many qualitative approaches, **case-oriented understanding** attempts to understand a phenomenon from the standpoint of the participants. For example, Constance Fischer and Frederick Wertz (2002) constructed such an explanation of the effect of being criminally victimized. They first recounted crime victims' stories and then identified common themes in these stories:

Their explanation began with a description of what they termed the process of "living routinely" *before the crime:* "*he/ she . . . feels that the defended against crime could never happen to him/her.*" "I said, 'nah, you've got to be kidding.'" (pp. 288–289, emphasis in original)

In a second stage, "being disrupted," the victim copes with the discovered crime and fears worse outcomes: "You imagine the worst when it's happening . . . I just kept thinking my baby's upstairs." In a later stage, "reintegrating," the victim begins to assimilate the violation by taking some protective action: "But I clean out my purse now since then and I leave very little of that kind of stuff in there." (p. 289)

Finally, when the victim is "going on," he or she reflects on the changes the crime produced: "I don't think it made me stronger. It made me smarter." (p. 290)

Case-oriented understanding: An understanding of social processes in a group, formal organization, community, or other collectivity that reflects accurately the standpoint of participants.

Institutional ethnography: A commitment to understand, through the social experiences of participants in a setting, the way in which their social world is shaped by larger societal forces.

You can see how Fischer and Wertz (2002:288–290) constructed an explanation of the effect of crime on its victims through this analysis of the process of responding to the experience. This effort to "understand" what happened in these cases gives us a much better sense of why things happened as they did.

Institutional Ethnography

Institutional ethnography adds to traditional ethnographic methods a commitment to understand, through the social experiences of participants in a setting, the way in which their social world

■ EXHIBIT 12.2 **A Grounded Theory Model**

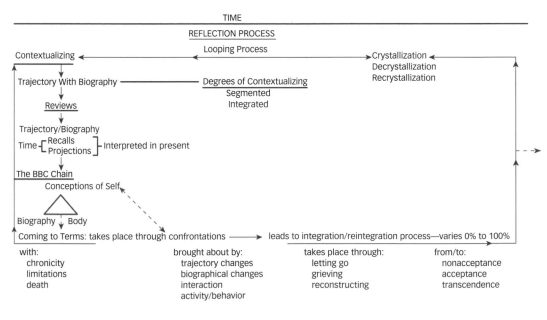

■ EXHIBIT 12.3   **Clusters and Categories in a Grounded Theory Analysis**

Clusters (Endorsement)	Categories (Endorsement)
1. The arrest incident is a hurdle or a test from god that I alone have to deal with, although the responsibility for the abuse was not all my own. (10)	1. If alcohol or drugs had not been in the picture, we wouldn't have come to blows: Substance use is thought to increase the rate of IPV (2) 2. I don't want to get involved in conflict because I don't want to deal with its consequences (9) 3. Joint responsibility in conflict depends on who did more fighting (8) 4. How women cause IPV: Being treated as a child through nagging and being disrespected (5)
2. Passive avoidance and withdrawal from conflict is the best way to prevent aggression and to please god. (10)	1. DV thought to be "cured" by passively attending classes and learning anger management (6) 2. Religious interventions have been vague or guilt producing, we need explicit advice and aren't getting it (9) 3. Intimate partner violence can be stopped by cutting off relationships, but this can be a painful experience (5) 4. Should resolve conflict to create harmony and avoid depression—but conflict may increase as a result (10)

Source: Levitt, H. M., Todd-Swanger, R., & Butler, J. B. "Male Perpetrators' Perspectives on Intimate Partner Violence, Religion, and Masculinity." *Sex Roles: A Journal of Research*, 58, 435–448. Copyright © 2007, Springer Science + Business Media, LLC. Reprinted with permission.

is shaped by larger societal forces (Smith 2005). Drawing on qualitative methods such as participant observation, intensive interviewing, textual analysis, and case-oriented qualitative approaches, institutional ethnographers seek to show how everyday experiences and actions arise from established structures "outside their knowing":

> The conceptual framing of everyday experiences heard or read about, or observed, constitutes one of the distinctive features of an institutional ethnography, another is its political nature. [It involves exploring] how people's lives are bound up in ruling relations that tie individuals into institutional action arising outside their knowing. . . . (Campbell 1998:57)

For example, Megan Welsh's (2015) institutional ethnography of formerly incarcerated women shows how the category into which the state welfare-to-work system places them, "Able-Bodied Adults Without Dependents," obscures constraints imposed by their experiences with securing food and housing, finding jobs, and maintaining appointments with officials and relations with family members. A quote from a recently released California woman Welsh called "Alice" gives an idea of the approach:

Photo 12.2   This is a photo from a visual sociology project. What data do you think could be gleaned from this photo?

> They make you grovel, you know? I had to go apply for [welfare] to have some kind of money. . . . But they asked me what was I in prison for, I told 'em drugs, and they told me I wasn't eligible for food stamps,…if you have certain drug convictions. . . . What has that got to do with you eating? That's what I don't get. What does food stamps have to do with drugs? . . . Now the hard thing for me is the fact that I've been in prison and it's behind me. Looking for a job. And then, every place you go, they're gonna do a background check. So that means that you're still doing time. . . . Like I got a red scarlet letter on my chest. (pp. 64–65)

After categorizing Alice and other interviewees by their welfare aid category and comparing comments about their experiences, Welsh (2015) is able to support a conclusion that "interactions with the welfare system frequently make women's lives more difficult through exclusionary policies" (p. 72).

❖ Visual Sociology

In recent years, the availability of photos and videos has exploded because of the ease of taking them with smartphones; in 2013, 54% of Internet users had posted original photos or videos online (Duggan 2013), and in 2015, one million photos were being uploaded daily at

■ EXHIBIT 12.4   **Interracial Friendships in Wedding Party Photos and in Responses to Survey Questions**

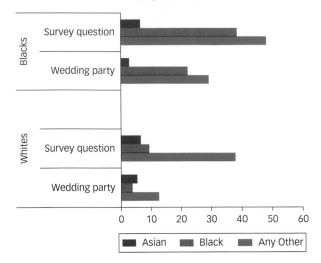

Source: Based on Berry (2006:501, Table 3).

Visual sociology: Sociological research in which the social world is "observed" and interpreted through photographs, films, and other images.

Photo voice: A method in which research participants take pictures of their everyday surroundings with cameras the researcher distributes, and then meet in a group with the researcher to discuss the pictures' meaning.

AUDIO LINK 🌐
Visual Sociology

the photo-sharing site Flickr (Smith 2015). As a result, increasing numbers of social scientists are collecting and analyzing visual representations of social life and **visual sociology** has become a growth industry.

Visual sociologists and other social researchers have been developing methods such as these to learn how others "see" the social world and to create images for further study. Continuous video recordings can help researchers unravel sequences of events and identify nonverbal expressions of feelings (Heath & Luff 2008:501). As in the analysis of written text, however, the visual sociologist must be sensitive to the way in which a photograph or film "constructs" the reality that it depicts.

In an innovative visually based approach to studying interracial friendship patterns, Brent Berry (2006) sampled wedding photos that had been posted on the web. Reasoning that bridesmaids and groomsmen represent whom newlyweds consider to be their best friends, Berry compared the rate of different-race members of wedding parties to the prevalence of different-race friends reported in representative surveys. As you can see in Exhibit 12.4, answers to survey questions create the impression that interracial friendships are considerably more common than is indicated by the actual wedding party photos.

Photo voice is a method of using photography to engage research participants in explaining how they have made sense of their social worlds. Rather than using images from other sources, the researcher directing a photo voice project distributes cameras to research participants and invites them to take pictures of their surroundings or everyday activities. The participants then meet with the researcher to present their pictures and discuss their meaning. In this way, researchers learn more about the participants' social worlds as they see it and react to it. The photo voice method also engages participants as part of the research team themselves, thus enriching the researcher's interpretations of the social world.

Lisa Frohmann (2005) recruited 42 Latina and South Asian women from battered women's support groups in Chicago to participate in research about the meaning of violence in their lives. Frohman used photo voice methodology, so she gave each participant a camera. After they received some preliminary instruction, Frohmann invited participants to take about five to seven pictures weekly for 4 to 5 weeks. The photographs were to capture persons, places, and objects that represent the continuums of comfort–discomfort, happiness–sadness, safety–danger, security–vulnerability, serenity–anxiety, protection–exposure, strength–weakness, and love–hate. Twenty-nine women then returned to discuss the results.

With a simple picture (Photo 12.3), one participant, Jenny, described how family violence affected her feelings:

This is the dining room table and I took this picture because the table is empty and I feel that although I am with my children, I feel that it is empty because there is no family harmony, which I think is the most important thing. (Frohmann 2005:1407)

The image and narrative indirectly represent Jenny's concept of family: a husband and wife who love each other and their children. Food and eating together are important family activities. Part of caring for her family is preparing food. The photo shows that her concept of family is fractured (Frohmann 2005:1407).

❖ Systematic Observation

Observations can be made in a more systematic, quantitative design that allows systematic comparisons and more confident generalizations. A researcher using

Frohmann (2005:1407)

Photo 12.3   This image came from Frohmann's (2005) photo voice project. What stands out to you about the photo?

CAREERS
and Research

LAUREL PERSON MECCA, ASSISTANT DIRECTOR AND SENIOR RESEARCH SPECIALIST, QUALITATIVE DATA ANALYSIS PROGRAM

Laurel Person Mecca was uncertain of the exact career she wanted to pursue during her graduate studies at the University of Pittsburgh. Then she happened upon the University Center for Social & Urban Research (UCSUR). It's hard to imagine a better place to launch a research career involving qualitative data analysis. Founded in 1972, the center has provided services and consultation to investigators in qualitative data analysis since 2005. Mecca used UCSUR to recruit participants for her own research and then made it clear to staff that she would love to work there after finishing her degree. Fourteen years later, she enjoys her work there more than ever.

One of the greatest rewards Mecca has found in her work is the excitement of discovering the unexpected when her preconceived notions about what research participants will tell her turn out to be incorrect. She also finds that her interactions with research participants provide a unique view into peoples' lives, thus providing insights in her own life and a richer understanding of the human condition.

Mecca has some sound advice for students interested in careers that involve conducting research or using research results:

Gain on-the-job experience while in college, even if it is an unpaid internship. Find researchers who are conducting studies that interest you, and inquire about working for them. Persistence pays off! Definitely check out the National Science Foundation's Research Experience for Undergraduates program. Though most of these internships are in the "hard" sciences, there are plenty of openings in social sciences disciplines.

systematic observation develops a standard form on which to record variation within the observed setting in terms of variables of interest. Such variables might include the frequency of some behavior(s), the particular people observed, the weather or other environmental conditions, and the number and state of repair of physical structures. In some systematic observation studies, records will be obtained from a random sample of places or times.

> **VIDEO LINK**
> St. Jean Research

Peter St. Jean (2007) recorded neighborhood physical and social appearances with video cameras mounted in a van that was driven along neighborhood streets. Pictures were then coded for the presence of neighborhood disorder (see Photo 12.4). The systematic observations give us much greater confidence in the measurement of relative neighborhood disorder than we would have from unstructured descriptive reports or from residents' responses to survey questions. Interviews with residents and participant observation helped identify the reasons that offenders chose particular locations when deciding where to commit crimes.

❖ Participatory Action Research

In **participatory action research (PAR)**, also termed *community-based participatory research* (CBPR), the researcher involves as active participants some members of the setting studied. According to Karen Hacker (2013), "The goal of CBPR is to create an effective translational process that will increase bidirectional connections between academics and the communities that they study" (p. 2). Both the members and the researcher are assumed to want to develop valid conclusions, to bring unique insights, and to desire change.

PAR can bring researchers into closer contact with participants in the research setting through groups that discuss and plan research steps and then take steps to implement research findings. For this reason, PAR is "particularly useful for emergent problems for which community partners are in search of solutions but evidence is lacking" (Hacker 2013:8). Stephen Kemmis and Robin McTaggart (2005:563–568) summarize the key steps in the process of conducting a PAR project as creating "a spiral of self-reflecting cycles":

1. Planning a change

2. Acting and observing the process and consequences of the change

Systematic observation: A strategy that increases the reliability of observational data by using explicit rules that standardize coding practices across observers.

Participatory action research (PAR): A type of research in which the researcher involves members of the population to be studied as active participants throughout the research process, from the selection of a research focus to the reporting of research results and efforts to make changes based on the research; also termed *community-based participatory research.*

© Peter K. B. St. Jean. Reprinted with permission.

Photo 12.4 This photo shows one building in St. Jean's (2007) study. What elements of disorder can you discern?

3. Reflecting on these processes and consequences

4. Replanning

5. Acting and observing again

In contrast to the formal reporting of results at the end of a research project, these cycles make research reporting an ongoing part of the research process. According to Hacker (2013), "Community partners can deepen the interpretation process once results are available, as they are intimately familiar with the context and meaning" (p. 8). Community partners may also work with the academic researchers to make changes in the community reflecting the research findings. Publication of results is only part of the process.

❖ Computer-Assisted Qualitative Data Analysis

Software programs designed for qualitative data analysis can speed up the analysis process, make it easier for researchers to experiment with different codes, test different hypotheses about relationships, and facilitate diagrams of emerging theories and preparation of research reports (Coffey & Atkinson 1996; Richards & Richards 1994). The steps involved in **computer-assisted qualitative data analysis** parallel those used traditionally to analyze text such as notes, documents, or interview transcripts: preparation, coding, analysis, and reporting. This section uses one of the most popular programs to illustrate these steps: QSR NVivo.

Text preparation begins with typing or scanning text in a word processor or, with NVivo, directly into the program's rich text editor. Coding the text involves categorizing particular text segments. This is the foundation of much qualitative analysis. You can make up codes as you go through a document and assign codes that you have already developed to text segments. Exhibit 12.5 shows the screen that appears in NVivo at the coding stage, when a particular text is "autocoded" by identifying a word or phrase that should always receive the same code. The program also lets you examine the coded text "in context"—embedded in its place in the original document.

Analysis focuses on reviewing cases or text segments with similar codes and examining relationships between different codes. Codes may be combined into larger concepts. Hypotheses about relationships between codes can be tested and free-form models can be developed (Exhibit 12.6). Reports can include text to illustrate the cases, codes, and relationships that you specify. Counts of code frequencies can also be generated and then imported into a statistical program for quantitative analysis.

❖ Corroboration/Legitimization of Conclusions

No set standards exist for evaluating the validity, or *authenticity,* of conclusions in a qualitative study, but the need to carefully consider the evidence and methods on which conclusions are based is just as great as with other types of research. Individual items of information can be assessed in terms of at least three criteria (Becker 1958:654–656):

- *How credible was the informant?* Were statements made by someone with whom the researcher had a relationship of trust or by someone the researcher had just met? Did the informant have reason to lie? If the statements do not seem to be trustworthy as indicators of actual events, can they at least be used to help understand the informant's perspective?

- *Were statements made in response to the researcher's questions, or were they spontaneous?* Spontaneous statements are more likely to indicate what would have been said had the researcher not been present.

Computer-assisted qualitative data analysis: The use of special computer software to assist qualitative analyses through creating, applying, and refining categories; tracing linkages between concepts; and making comparisons between cases and events.

- *How does the presence or absence of the researcher or the researcher's informant influence the actions and statements of other group members?* Reactivity to being observed can never be ruled out as a possible explanation for some directly observed social phenomenon. However, if the researcher carefully compares what the informant says goes on when the researcher is not present, what the researcher observes directly, and what other group members say about their normal practices, the extent of reactivity can be assessed to some extent.

A qualitative researcher's conclusions should also be assessed by his or her ability to provide a credible explanation for some aspect of social life. That explanation should capture group members' **tacit knowledge** of the social processes that were observed, not just their verbal statements about these processes. Tacit knowledge—"the largely unarticulated, contextual understanding that is often manifested in nods, silences, humor, and naughty nuances"—is reflected in participants' actions as well as their words and in what they fail to state but nonetheless feel deeply and even take for granted (Altheide & Johnson 1994:492–493). These features are evident in William Foote Whyte's (1955) classic analysis of Cornerville social patterns:

> The corner-gang structure arises out of the habitual association of the members over a long period of time. The nuclei of most gangs can be traced back to early boyhood.... Home plays a very small role in the group activities of the corner boy.... The life of the corner boy proceeds along regular and narrowly circumscribed channels.... Out of [social interaction within the group] arises a system of mutual obligations which is fundamental to group cohesion. ... The code of the corner boy requires him to help his friends when he can and to refrain from doing anything to harm them. When life in the group runs smoothly, the obligations binding members to one another are not explicitly recognized. (pp. 255–257)

Confidence in the conclusions from a field research study is also strengthened by an honest and informative account about how the researcher interacted with subjects in the field, what problems he or she encountered, and how these problems were or were not resolved. Such a "natural history" of the development of the evidence enables others to evaluate the findings and reflects the constructivist philosophy that guides many qualitative researchers (see Chapter 1). Such an account is important primarily because of the evolving and variable nature of field research: To an important extent, the researcher "makes up" the method in the context of a particular investigation rather than applying standard procedures that are specified before the investigation begins.

Barrie Thorne (1993) provides a good example of this final element of the analysis:

> Many of my observations concern the workings of gender categories in social life. For example, I trace the evocation of gender in the organization of everyday interactions, and the shift from boys and girls as loose aggregations to "the boys" and "the girls" as self-aware, gender-based groups. In writing about these processes, I discovered that different angles of vision lurk within seemingly simple choices of language. How, for example, should one describe a group of children? A phrase like "six girls and three boys were chasing by the tires" already assumes the relevance of gender. An alternative description of the same event—"nine fourth-graders

■ EXHIBIT 12.5   **NVivo Coding Stage**

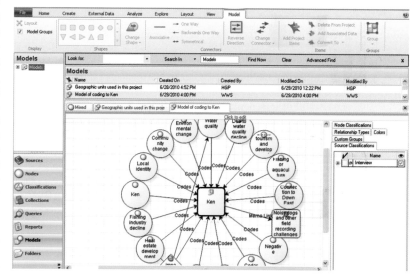

■ EXHIBIT 12.6   **A Free-Form Model in NVivo**

ENCYCLOPEDIA LINK
Reflexivity

Tacit knowledge: In field research, a credible sense of understanding of social processes that reflects the researcher's awareness of participants' actions as well as their words, and of what they fail to state, feel deeply, and take for granted.

RESEARCH

In the News

SECRET PHOTOGRAPHING OF STUDENTS AT HARVARD?

Classes were secretly photographed in spring 2014 as part of a Harvard University research project about classroom attendance. About 2,000 students in 10 lecture halls were included in the photos, although the images were destroyed after they were scanned by a computer program that counted the number of full and empty seats.

Harvard's institutional review board had classified the study as not involving research on human subjects—perhaps because it focused on classroom teaching (given special exemption in federal regulations) and did not retain images of individuals—but that didn't stop an outcry from many students and faculty after the study was revealed in a conference presentation.

For Further Thought **?**
1. Was this an invasion of privacy? Should the instructors and students have been informed in advance? Would the results have differed if there had been disclosure in advance?
2. What policy would you recommend? What do classmates think?

News Source: Rocheleau, Matt. 2014. "Harvard Secretly Photographed Students to Study Attendance." *Boston Globe,* November 5.

were chasing by the tires"—emphasizes age and downplays gender. Although I found no tidy solutions, I have tried to be thoughtful about such choices.... After several months of observing at Oceanside, I realized that my field notes were peppered with the words "child" and "children," but that the children themselves rarely used the term. "What do they call themselves?" I badgered in an entry in my field notes. The answer it turned out, is that children use the same practices as adults. They refer to one another by using given names ("Sally," "Jack") or language specific to a given context ("that guy on first base"). They rarely have occasion to use age-generic terms. But when pressed to locate themselves in an age-based way, my informants used "kids" rather than "children." (pp. 8–9)

Researchers are only human, after all, and must rely on their own senses and process all information through their own minds. By reporting how and why they think they did what they did—by being *reflexive*, they can help others determine whether, or how, the researchers' perspectives influenced their conclusions.

❖ Ethics in Qualitative Data Analysis

The qualitative data analyst is never far from ethical issues and dilemmas. Data collection should not begin unless the researcher has a plan that others see as likely to produce useful knowledge. Relations developed with research participants and other stakeholders to facilitate data collection should also be used to keep these groups informed about research progress and findings. Research participants should be encouraged to speak out about emerging study findings (Lincoln 2009:154–155). Decisions to reproduce photos and other visual materials must be considered in light of privacy and copyright issues. Throughout the analytic process, the analyst must consider how the findings will be used and how participants in the setting will react. The need to minimize harm requires attention even after data collection has concluded.

Qualitative researchers should consider harm that might occur along all points in the research process. Staff who transcribe interview or focus group transcripts may not seem a part of the formal research process—and may even be independent contractors who are contacted only through the Internet—but they may react emotionally to some of the material in particularly charged interviews. In projects where transcripts contain emotionally charged material, those used as transcriptionists should be given advance warning and provided connections to counselors if necessary (Sieber & Tolich 2013:175).

In ethnographic and other participant studies where initial access is negotiated with community leaders or with groups of participants, qualitative researchers should discuss with participants the approach that will be taken to protect privacy and maintain confidentiality. Selected participants should also be asked to review reports or other products before their public release to gauge the extent to which they feel privacy has been appropriately preserved. Research with photographs that identify individuals raises special ethical concerns. Although legal standards are evolving, it is important not to violate an individual's expectations of privacy in any setting and to seek informed consent for the use of images when privacy is expected (Tinkler 2013:196–198).

The following questions also need to be considered when undertaking qualitative data analysis:

- *Intervention and advocacy.* "What do I do when I see harmful, illegal, or wrongful behavior on the part of others during a study? Should I speak for anyone's interests besides my own? If so, whose interests do I advocate?" Maintaining what is called *guilty knowledge* may force the researcher to suppress some parts of the analysis so as not to disclose the wrongful behavior, but presenting "what really happened" in a report may prevent ongoing access and violate understandings with participants. The need for intervention and advocacy is more likely to be anticipated in PAR/CBPR projects because they involve ongoing engagement with community partners who are likely to have an action orientation (Hacker 2013:101–104).

- *Research integrity and quality.* "Is my study being conducted carefully, thoughtfully, and correctly in terms of some reasonable set of standards?" Real analyses have real consequences, so you owe it to yourself and those you study to adhere strictly to the analysis methods that you believe will produce authentic, valid conclusions. Visual images that demean individuals or groups should not be included in publications (Tinkler 2013:197).

- *Ownership of data and conclusions.* "Who owns my field notes and analyses: I, my organization, my funders? And once my reports are written, who controls their diffusion?" Of course, these concerns arise in any social research project, but the intimate involvement of the qualitative researcher with participants in the setting studied makes conflicts of interest between different stakeholders much more difficult to resolve. Working through the issues as they arise is essential. Mitch Duneier (1999:319–330) decided to end *Sidewalk,* his ethnography of New York City sidewalk book vendors, with an afterword by one of his key informants. Such approaches that allow participants access to conclusions in advance and the privilege to comment on them should be considered in relation to qualitative projects. The public availability of visual images on websites does not eliminate concerns about ownership. Copyright law in the United States as well as in the United Kingdom and Australia provides copyright to content on the Internet as soon as it is uploaded, but there are disagreements about the requirement of informed consent before reproducing images from publicly accessible sites (Tinkler 2013:204–205). Researchers leading PAR/CBPR projects must work out data ownership agreements in advance of data collection to ensure there are no misunderstandings about retention of data and maintenance of confidentiality after the project ends (Hacker 2013:99–100).

- *Use and misuse of results.* "Do I have an obligation to help my findings be used appropriately? What if they are used harmfully or wrongly?" It is prudent to develop understandings early in the project with all major stakeholders that specify what actions will be taken to encourage appropriate use of project results and to respond to what is considered misuse of these results. Visual researchers must also consider how participants will feel about their images appearing in publications in the future (Wiles et al. 2012:48).

PAR/CBPR projects are designed to help solve local problems, but harm might also occur if results are not what were expected or if findings cast elements of the community in an unfavorable light. These possibilities should be addressed as the analysis progresses and resolved before they are publicized (Hacker 2013:114–117).

❖ Conclusions

The variety of approaches to qualitative data analysis makes it difficult to provide a consistent set of criteria for interpreting their quality. Norman Denzin's (2002:362–363) "interpretive criteria" are a good place to start. Denzin suggests that at the conclusion of their analyses, qualitative data analysts ask the following questions about the materials they have produced. Reviewing several of them will serve as a fitting summary for your understanding of the qualitative analysis process:

- *Do they illuminate the phenomenon as lived experience?* In other words, do the materials bring the setting alive in terms of the people in that setting?

- *Are they based on thickly contextualized materials?* We should expect thick descriptions that encompass the social setting studied.

- *Are they historically and relationally grounded?* There must be a sense of the passage of time between events and the presence of relationships between social actors.

- *Are they processual and interactional?* The researcher must have described the research process and his or her interactions within the setting.

- *Do they engulf what is known about the phenomenon?* This includes situating the analysis in the context of prior research and acknowledging the researcher's own orientation on first starting the investigation.

When an analysis of qualitative data is judged as successful in terms of these criteria, we can conclude that the goal of authenticity has been achieved.

As a research methodologist, you should be ready to use qualitative techniques, evaluate research findings in terms of these criteria, and mix and match specific analysis methods as required by the research problem to be investigated and the setting in which it is to be studied.

Key Terms

Case-oriented understanding   196
Computer-assisted qualitative
   data analysis   200
Conversation analysis   193
Ethnomethodology   193

Grounded theory   194
Institutional ethnography   196
Narrative analysis   194
Participatory action research
   (PAR)   199

Photo voice   198
Systematic observation   199
Tacit knowledge   201
Visual sociology   198

Highlights

- Narrative analysis attempts to understand a life or a series of events as they unfolded, in a meaningful progression.

- Grounded theory connotes a general explanation that develops in interaction with the data and is continually tested and refined as data collection continues.

- Case-oriented understanding provides a description of how participants viewed their experiences in a setting.

- Visual sociology focuses attention on the record about social life available in photos, videos, or other pictorial displays.

- Systematic observation techniques quantify the observational

process to allow more systematic comparison between cases and greater generalizability.

- Participatory action research (PAR) uses an ongoing collaboration with community participants to define the problem for research, to conduct the research, and to develop research reports.

- Special computer software can be used for the analysis of qualitative, textual, and pictorial data. Users can record their notes, categorize observations, specify links between categories, and count occurrences.

Chapter Questions

1. List the primary components of qualitative data analysis strategies. Compare and contrast each of these components with those relevant to quantitative data analysis. What are the similarities and differences? What differences do these make?

2. Does qualitative data analysis result in trustworthy results—in findings that achieve the goal of authenticity? Why would anyone question its use? What would you reply to the doubters?

3. Participants in social settings often "forget" that an ethnographer is in their midst, planning to record what they say and do, even when the ethnographer has announced his or her role. New participants may not have heard the announcement, and everyone may simply get used to the ethnographer as if he or she was just "one of us." What efforts should ethnographers take to keep people informed about their work in the settings they are studying? Consider settings such as a sports team, a political group, and a book group.

······ **Practice Exercises** ································

1. Write a narrative in class about your first date, car, college course, or something else that you and your classmates agree on. Then collect all the narratives and analyze them in a "committee of the whole." Follow the general procedures discussed in the example of narrative analysis in this chapter.

2. Go forth and take pictures! Conduct a photo voice project with your classmates and write up your own review of the group's discussion of your pictures.

3. Visit the book's study site (edge.sagepub.com/schuttusw) and review one of the articles that used qualitative methods.

Describe the data that were collected, and identify the steps used in the analysis. What type of qualitative data analysis was this? If it is not one of the methods presented in this chapter, describe its similarities to and differences from one of these methods. How confident are you in the conclusions, given the methods of analysis used?

4. *Qualitative Research* is an online journal about qualitative research. Inspect the table of contents for a recent issue at http://qrj.sagepub.com. Read one of the articles and write a brief article review.

STUDENT STUDY SITE

$SAGE edge™

The Student Study Site, available at **edge.sagepub.com/schuttusw**, includes useful study materials including eFlashcards, videos, audio resources, journal articles, and encyclopedia articles, many of which are represented by the media links throughout the text.

CHAPTER 13

Summarizing and Reporting Research

Learning Objectives

❖ Identify unique problems that must be overcome in writing student papers, applied research reports, and journal articles

❖ List the major sections of a research report

❖ Describe the elements that should be considered in writing research reports to ensure adherence to the ethical standard of honesty

❖ Discuss the motivations for plagiarism and how to avoid being suspected of unintentional plagiarism

You learned in Chapter 2 that research is a circular process, so it is appropriate that we end this book where we began. The stage of reporting research results is also the point at which the need for new research is identified. It is the time when, so to speak, "the rubber hits the road"—when research has to make sense to others. For whom is the research report intended? How should the results be presented? Does the report seek to influence public policy or social programs?

The primary goals of this chapter are to orient you to different types of research reports and to highlight the features you may encounter. The chapter concludes by considering some of the ethical issues unique to the reporting process, with special attention to the problem of plagiarism.

❖ Writing Research

The goal of research is not just to discover something but also to communicate that discovery to a larger audience: other social scientists, government officials, the general public—perhaps several of these audiences. Whatever the study's particular outcome, if the intended audience for the research comprehends the results and learns from them, the research can be judged a success. If the intended audience does not learn about the study's results, the research should be judged a failure—no matter how expensive the research or how sophisticated its design.

Successful research reporting requires both good writing and a proper publication outlet. This chapter first reviews guidelines for successful writing before looking at particular types of research publications.

If you must write a research report, even if for a class project, consider the following principles (Booth, Colomb, & Williams 1995:150–151):

- Respect the complexity of the task and don't expect to write a polished draft in a linear fashion. Your thinking will develop as you write, causing you to reorganize and rewrite.

- Leave enough time for dead ends, restarts, revisions, and so on, and accept the fact that you will discard much of what you write.

- Write as fast as you comfortably can. Don't worry about spelling, grammar, and so on until you are polishing things up.

- Ask anyone whom you trust for reactions to what you have written.

- Write as you go along, so that you have notes and report segments drafted even before you focus on writing the report.

It is important to outline a report before writing it, but neither the report's organization nor the first written draft should be considered fixed. As you write, you will get new ideas about how to organize the report. Try them out. As you review the first draft, you will see many ways to improve your writing. Focus particularly on how to shorten and clarify your statements. Make sure that each paragraph concerns only one topic. Remember the golden rule of good writing: Writing is revising!

Most important, leave yourself enough time so that you can revise, several times if possible, and seek others' opinions, before turning in the final draft. See Howard Becker (2007), Lee Cuba (2002), and Kate Turabian (2013) for more suggestions about writing.

The organization of a research report will depend to some extent on the audience for which it is intended and the type of research that has been conducted. Articles that will be submitted to an academic journal will differ from research reports written for a funding agency or for the general public. Research reports based on qualitative research will differ in some ways from those based on quantitative research. Students writing course papers are often required to structure their research reports using the journal article format, and they may be asked to present their results differently if they have used qualitative (or mixed) methods.

SAGE JOURNAL ARTICLE
Writing for Publication

ENCYCLOPEDIA LINK
Writing

AUDIO LINK
Publishing
Controversial Topics

RESEARCHER INTERVIEW LINK
Reporting Research

Journal Articles

Writing for academic journals is perhaps the toughest form of writing because articles are submitted to several experts in your field for careful review—anonymously, with most journals—before acceptance for publication. Perhaps it wouldn't be such an arduous process if so many academic journals did not have rejection rates in excess of 90% and turnaround times for reviews that are usually several months. Even the best articles, in the judgment of the reviewers, are most often given a "revise and resubmit" after the first review and then are evaluated all over again after the revisions are concluded.

But journal article review procedures have some important benefits. Most important is the identification of areas in need of improvement, as the eyes of the author(s) are replaced by those of previously uninvolved subject-matter experts and methodologists. A good journal editor makes sure that he or she has a list of many different types of experts available for reviewing whatever types of articles the journal is likely to receive. There is a parallel benefit for the author(s): It is always beneficial to review criticisms by people who know the field well. The entire field moves forward as researchers continually critique and suggest improvements in each other's research reports.

Photo 13.1 An important part of writing is revising. Creating a schedule and building in time for revising can help writers avoid the pitfall of procrastination.

Exhibit 13.1 presents an outline of the sections in an academic journal article, with some illustrative quotes. A research report should begin with a clear abstract, which summarizes in one paragraph the research question, prior research, study methods and major findings, and key conclusions. Many others who search the literature about the topic will never read the entire article unless they are persuaded by the abstract that the article provides worthwhile and relevant information. The article's introduction highlights the importance of the problem selected—in this case, the relationship between marital disruption (divorce) and depression. The introduction, which in this article includes the literature review, also identifies clearly the gap in the research literature that the article is meant to fill: the untested possibility that depression might cause marital disruption rather than, or in addition to, marital disruption causing depression. Literature reviews in journal articles should be integrated reviews that highlight the major relevant findings and identify key methodological lessons from the prior research as a whole, rather than presenting separate summaries of prior research studies

RESEARCH

In the News

DO SOCIAL SCIENTISTS DO BETTER THAN POLLSTERS?

One of the concerns that emerged from the recent scandal about apparently fictitious data in a published poll about support for same-sex marriage was whether public pollsters are less transparent in their methods than social scientists. Polling organizations are often not fully transparent about their methods and may not release survey data until months after survey findings are publicized. Some observers are concerned also that polling firms "play it safe" by trying to ensure that their own results don't differ too much from the findings of other firms. This practice has been called "herding."

For Further Thought **?**

1. How well do you think the academic peer review process works? Is it sufficient to guard against fraudulent reports?

2. What standards would you recommend for polling firms?

News source: Cohn, Nate. 2015. "Polling's Secrecy Problem." *New York Times,* May 28.

(see Chapter 2). The findings section (titled "Results") begins by presenting the basic association between marital disruption and depression. Then it elaborates on this association by examining sex differences, the impact of prior marital quality, and various mediating and modifying effects. Tables and perhaps graphs are used to present the data corresponding to each of the major findings in an easily accessible format. As indicated in the combined discussion and conclusions section, the analysis shows that marital disruption does indeed increase depression and specifies the time frame (3 years) during which this effect occurs.

These basic article sections present research results well, but many research articles include subsections tailored to the issues and stages in the specific study being reported. Most journals require a short abstract at the beginning, which summarizes the research question and findings. Most research articles include a general methodology section that will include subsections on measurement and sampling. A conclusions section is often used to present the most general conclusions, reflections, and limitations, but some precede that with a general discussion section.

Applied Research Reports

Applied research reports are written for a different audience from the professional social scientists and students who read academic journals. Typically, an applied report is written with a wide audience of potential users in mind and to serve multiple purposes. Often, both the audience and the purpose are established by the agency or other organization that funded the research project on which the report is based. Sometimes, the researcher may use the report to provide a broad descriptive overview of the study findings, which will be presented more succinctly in a subsequent journal article. In either case, an applied report typically provides much more information about a research project than does a journal article and relies primarily on descriptive statistics

▶ **VIDEO LINK**
Publishing Your Research

■ EXHIBIT 13.1   Sections in a Journal Article

Aseltine, Robert H., Jr., and Ronald C. Kessler. 1993. *"Marital Disruption and Depression in a Community Sample."* Journal of Health and Social Behavior 34(September):237–251.

INTRODUCTION
Despite 20 years of empirical research, the extent to which marital disruption causes poor mental health remains uncertain. The reason for this uncertainty is that previous research has consistently overlooked the potentially important problems of selection into and out of marriage on the basis of prior mental health. (p. 237)

SAMPLE AND MEASURES
Sample
Measures

RESULTS
The Basic Association Between Marital Disruption and Depression
Sex Differences
The Impact of Prior Marital Quality
The Mediating Effects of Secondary Changes
The Modifying Effects of Transitions to Secondary Roles

DISCUSSION [includes conclusions]
. . . According to the results, marital disruption does in fact cause a significant increase in depression compared to pre-divorce levels within a period of three years after the divorce. (p. 245)

Source: Aseltine, Robert H., Jr. and Ronald C. Kessler, 1993. "Marital Disruption and Depression in a Community Sample." *Journal of Health and Social Behavior* 34(September):237–251

VIDEO LINK ▶
Applied Research

rather than only those statistics useful for the specific hypothesis tests that are likely to be the primary focus of a journal article. The major difference between an applied research report and a journal article is that a journal article must focus on answering a particular research question, whereas an applied report is likely to have the broader purpose of describing a wide range of study findings and attempting to meet the diverse needs of multiple audiences for the research.

A good example of applied research reporting comes from the Robert Wood Johnson Foundation, which presented an online research report to make widely available the findings from an investigation of the impact of welfare reform (Sunderland 2005). Social scientist P. Lindsay Chase-Lansdale and colleagues (2003) examined the impact of the 1996 federal act mandating changes in welfare requirements—the Personal Responsibility and Work Opportunity Reconciliation Act (PRWORA). Their three-city (Boston, Chicago, and San Antonio) research design sought to test the arguments of reform proponents and opponents about the consequences of the reforms for families and children:

> Proponents of welfare reform argued that . . . moving mothers from welfare to work would benefit children because it would increase their families' income, model disciplined work behavior, and better structure their family routines. Opponents of PRWORA countered that . . . the reforms [would] reduce the time mothers and children spend together, . . . increase parental stress and decrease responsive parenting, and . . . move children into low-quality childcare or unsupervised settings while their parents worked. (p. 1548)

The online report described three different components of the research design during the period of welfare reform: a longitudinal survey of adults and children, a developmental study of a subsample of children, and ethnographic studies of low-income families in each city (Sunderland 2005:4). The report summarized findings and recommendations and concluded with an overview of these findings and acknowledgment of some methodological limitations:

> This study suggests that mothers' welfare and employment transitions during this unprecedented era of welfare reform are not associated with negative outcomes for preschoolers or young adolescents. A few positive associations were tenuously indicated for adolescents. . . . The well-being of preschoolers appeared to be unrelated to their mothers' leaving welfare or entering employment, at least as indexed in measures of cognitive achievement and behavior problems. (Sunderland 2005:6)

Front matter: The section of an applied research report that includes an executive summary, an abstract, and a table of contents.

Back matter: The section of an applied research report that may include appendixes, tables, and the research instrument(s).

Among the limitations they acknowledged was the following:

> Researchers conducted the first two waves of the study during an economic boom that lowered unemployment and increased wages for less skilled workers. Their findings might not be replicated during an extended period with different economic conditions.

The policy brief recommended,

- The intense focus on welfare reform in our country should not impede a general concern and plan of action for all children in poverty, whether on welfare or not. To lessen developmental risks and improve the developmental trajectories of these children, numerous avenues should be pursued for the provision of supportive mental health and educational services.

- State and federal governments should explore options for identifying and reaching out to the most disadvantaged and high-risk families involved in the welfare system—families experiencing welfare sanctions. . . .

What can be termed the **front matter** and the **back matter** of an applied report also are important. Applied reports usually begin with an executive summary: a summary list of the study's main findings, often in bullet fashion. In addition, the front matter typically includes the abstract and a table of contents. Appendixes, the back matter, may present tables containing supporting data that were not discussed in the body of the report. Applied research reports also often append a copy of the research instrument(s).

©iStockphoto.com/Steve Froebe

Photo 13.2 Applied research reports help disseminate research findings to a broader audience and often call attention to social problems.

CAREERS
and Research

RUTH WESTBY, PUBLIC HEALTH RESEARCHER

For Ruth Westby, research— particularly public health research— means the chance to make new discoveries that affect people's lives by improving community health. She has studied how programs for disadvantaged and underserved groups are implemented and whether they have meaningful health impacts.

Westby was inspired to pursue a career in clinical research after her father died from cancer shortly after she received her B.A. from Emory University. After a few years of working with sick individuals on clinical trials, she decided to focus on public health so that she could look toward *preventing* disease. She sought out skill-based research courses and then internships that would help her use those skills as a graduate student. One such internship led to coauthored journal articles and a presentation at a large conference. In this way, Westby was exposed to opportunities that cemented her passion for public health research and provided a job in which every day at work is different and evokes a sense of pride.

Westby's research job also has kept her learning new research methods. She advises current students to take advantage of mentors, faculty members, and anyone who is willing to help you learn:

I've seen first-hand the advantages of getting to know faculty members on a personal level, networking and interning at institutions where I might want to work later, and using new research skills outside of class. Doing all of these things taught me so much more than if I had just attended lectures and read my textbooks. By the time I graduated from graduate school, I felt much more competent and set up for success than after college. In the long run, those relationships and experiences will mean just as much, if not more, than your GPA or course schedule.

Reporting Quantitative and Qualitative Research

The requirements for good research reports are similar in many respects for quantitative and qualitative research projects. Every research report should include good writing; a clear statement of the research question; an integrated literature review; and presentation of key findings with related discussion, conclusions, and limitations. However, the differences between qualitative and quantitative research approaches mean that it is often desirable for research reports based on qualitative research to diverge in some respects from those reflecting quantitative research.

Reports based on qualitative research should be enriched in each section with elements that reflect the more holistic and reflexive approach of qualitative projects. The introduction should include background about the development of the researcher's interest in the topic, whereas the literature review should include some attention to the types of particular qualitative methods used in prior research. The methodology section should describe how the researcher gained access to the setting or individuals studied and the approach used to managing relations with research participants. The presentation of findings in qualitative studies may be organized into sections reflecting different themes identified in interviews or observational sessions. Quotes from participants or from observational notes should be selected to illustrate these themes, although qualitative research reports differ in the extent to which the researcher presents findings in summary form or uses direct quotes to identify key issues. The findings sections in a qualitative report may alternate between presentations of quotes or observations about the research participants, the researcher's interpretations of this material, and some commentary on how the researcher reacted in the setting, although some qualitative researchers will limit their discussion of their reactions to the discussion section.

Reports on mixed-methods projects should include subsections in the methods section that introduce each method, and then distinguish findings from qualitative and quantitative analyses in the findings section. Some mixed-methods research reports may present analyses that use both qualitative and quantitative data in yet another subsection, but others may just discuss implications of analyses of each type for the overall conclusions in the discussions and conclusions sections (Dahlberg, Wittink, & Gallo 2010:785–791). When findings based on each method are presented, it is important to consider explicitly both the ways in which the specific methods influenced findings obtained with those methods and the implications of findings obtained using both methods for the overall study conclusions.

> **SAGE JOURNAL ARTICLE**
> Writing Journal Articles

❖ Ethics, Politics, and Research Reports

The researcher's ethical duty to be honest and open becomes paramount when reporting research results. Here are some guidelines:

- *An honest accounting of how the research was carried out and where the initial research design had to be changed should be reported.* Readers do not have to know about every change in plans, but they should be informed about major changes in hypotheses or research design. If important hypotheses were not supported, this should be acknowledged, rather than conveniently forgotten (Brown & Hedges 2009:383). If a different approach to collecting or analyzing the data could have led to different conclusions, this should be acknowledged in the limitations section (Bergman 2008:588–590).

- *Honest evaluation of the strengths and weaknesses of the research design.* Systematic evaluations suggest that the stronger the research design from the standpoint of establishing internal (causal) validity, the weaker the empirical support that is likely to be found for hypothesized effects (compare Weisburd, Lum, & Petrosino 2001:64). Finding support for a hypothesis tested with a randomized experimental design is stronger evidence than support based on correlations between variables measured in a cross-sectional survey.

- *Findings should be interpreted within the body of literature resulting from that prior research.* The results are only the latest research conducted to investigate a research question that others have studied. Many researchers make the fundamental mistake of presenting their findings as if they are the only empirical information with which to answer the research question (Bergman 2008:599). For example, a systematic evaluation of citation frequency in articles reporting clinical trial results in medical journals found that, on average, just 21% of the available prior research was cited (for trials with at least three prior articles that could have been cited) (Robinson & Goodman 2011:53). The result of such omission is that readers may have no idea whether the new research supports a larger body of evidence or differs from it—and so should be subject to even greater scrutiny.

- *A full record of the research project should be available so that questions can be answered if they arise.* Many details will have to be omitted from all but the most comprehensive reports, but these omissions should not make it impossible to track down answers to specific questions about research procedures that may arise during data analysis or presentation.

- *Report the process of developing the analysis that is presented.* (See Chapter 11 for more on this topic.) There is a more subtle problem that should be avoided: "cherry-picking" the results to present. Although some studies are designed to test only one hypothesis involving variables that each are measured in only one way, many studies collect data that can be used to test many hypotheses, often with alternative measures. If many possible relationships have been examined with the data collected and only those found to yield a statistically significant result are reported, the odds of capitalizing on chance findings are multiplied. This is a major temptation in research practice and has the unfortunate result that most published findings are not replicated or do not stand up to repeated tests over time (Lehrer 2010:57). Every statistical test presented can be adequately understood only in light of the entire body of statistical analyses that led to that particular result.

- *The research sponsors should be acknowledged.* This is important partly so that others can consider whether this sponsorship may have tempted the author(s) to bias results in some way. Whether the research was conducted for a sponsor, or together with members of an underserved community, research participants should have been given an opportunity to comment on findings before they were released to the public, but if this was the case it should be considered as a possible influence on how the findings are presented (Bledsoe & Hopson 2009:392).

Ethical research reporting should not mean ineffective reporting. Every twist and turn in the conceptualization of the research problem or the conduct of the research does not need to be reported. But be suspicious of reports that don't seem to admit to the possibility of any room for improvement. Social science is an ongoing enterprise in which one research report makes its most valuable contribution by laying the groundwork for another, more sophisticated, research project. Important findings should be highlighted in the research report, but it should also point to what are likely to be the most productive directions for future researchers.

RESEARCH/SOCIAL IMPACT LINK
Bad Research

❖ Plagiarism

It may seem depressing to end a book on research methods with a section on **plagiarism**, but it would be irresponsible to avoid the topic. You likely have a course syllabus detailing instructor or university policies about plagiarism and specifying the penalties for violating that policy, so I'm not simply going to repeat that kind of warning. Also, you probably realize that the practice of selling term papers is revoltingly widespread (my search of "term papers" on Google returned 7,600,000 websites on August 27, 2015), so I'm not going to just repeat that academic dishonesty is widespread. Instead, this section reviews the concept of plagiarism and shows how that problem connects to the larger issue of the integrity of social research. When

Plagiarism: Presenting as one's own the ideas or words of another person or persons for academic evaluation without proper acknowledgment.

you understand the dimensions of the problem and the way it affects research, you should be better able to detect plagiarism in other work and to avoid it in your own.

You learned in Chapter 3 that maintaining professional integrity—honesty and openness in research procedures and results—is the foundation for ethical research practice. When it comes to research publications and reports, being honest and open means above all else avoiding plagiarism—that is, presenting as one's own the ideas or words of another person or persons for academic evaluation without proper acknowledgment (Hard, Conway, & Moran 2006:1059).

An increasing body of research suggests that plagiarism is a growing problem on college campuses. Jason Stephen, Michael Young, and Thomas Calabrese (2007:243) found in a web survey of self-selected students at two universities that one quarter acknowledged having plagiarized a few sentences (24.7%) or a complete paper (0.3%) in coursework within the past year (many others admitted to other forms of academic dishonesty, such as copying homework). Hard et al. (2006) conducted an anonymous survey in selected classes in one university, with almost all students participating, and found much higher plagiarism rates: 60.6% reported that they had copied "sentences, phrases, paragraphs, tables, figures, or data directly or in slightly modified form from a book, article, or other academic source without using quotation marks or giving proper acknowledgment to the original author or source" (p. 1069) and 39.4% reported that they had "copied information from Internet websites and submitted it as [their] work" (p. 1069).

So the plagiarism problem is not just about purchasing term papers—although that is really about as bad as it gets (Broskoske 2005:1). Plagiarism is also about how information obtained from a literature review or inspection of research reports is used. And rest assured that this is not only about student papers; it also is about the work of established scholars and social researchers who publish reports that you want to rely on for accurate information. Several noted researchers have been accused of plagiarizing passages that they used in popular books or academic articles; some have admitted to not checking the work of their research assistants, to not keeping track of their sources, or to being unable to retrieve the data they claimed they had analyzed. Whether the cause is cutting corners to meet deadlines or consciously fudging facts, the effect is to undermine the trustworthiness of social research.

Now that you are completing this course in research methods, it's time to think about how to do your part to reduce the prevalence of plagiarism. Of course, the first step is to maintain careful procedures for documenting the sources that you rely on for your own research and papers, but you should also think about how best to reduce temptations among others. After all, what people believe about what others do is a strong influence on their own behavior (Hard et al. 2006:1058).

Sociologists have an obligation to be familiar with their Code of Ethics, other applicable ethics codes, and their application to sociologists' work. Lack of awareness or misunderstanding of an ethical standard is not, in itself, a defense to a charge of unethical conduct.

The American Sociological Association (ASA)'s (1999) *Code of Ethics* includes an explicit prohibition of plagiarism:

14. Plagiarism

(a) In publications, presentations, teaching, practice, and service, sociologists explicitly identify, credit, and reference the author when they take data or material verbatim from another person's written work, whether it is published, unpublished, or electronically available.

(b) In their publications, presentations, teaching, practice, and service, sociologists provide acknowledgment of and reference to the use of others' work, even if the work is not quoted verbatim or paraphrased, and they do not present others' work as their own whether it is published, unpublished, or electronically available. (p. 16)

The next step toward combating the problem and temptation of plagiarism is to keep focused on the goal of social research methods: understanding the social world. If researchers are motivated by a desire to learn about social relations, to understand how people understand society, and to discover why conflicts arise and how they can be prevented, they will be as concerned with the integrity of their research methods as are those, like yourself, who read and use the results of their research. Throughout *Understanding the Social World,* you have been learning how to use research processes and practices that yield valid findings and trustworthy conclusions. Failing to report honestly and openly on the methods used or sources consulted derails progress toward that goal.

> **⊕ AUDIO LINK**
> Ghost Authors

❖ Conclusions

Good critical skills are essential when evaluating research reports, whether your own or those produced by others. There are *always* weak points in any research, even published research. It is an indication of strength, not weakness, to recognize areas where one's own research needs to be, or could have been, improved. And it is really not just a question of sharpening your knife and going for the jugular. You need to be able to weigh the strengths and weaknesses of particular research results and to evaluate a study for its contribution to understanding the social world—not whether it gives a definitive answer for all time.

But this is not to say that anything goes. Too much research has major weaknesses in terms of measurement validity, causal validity, and/or generalizability and contributes more confusion than understanding about the social world. Top journals generally maintain very high standards, partly because they have good critics in the review process and distinguished editors who make the final acceptance decisions. But some daily newspapers do a poor job of screening, and research-reporting standards in many popular magazines, TV shows, and books are often abysmally poor. Keep your standards high and your views critical when reading research reports, but not so high or so critical that you turn away from studies that make tangible contributions to understanding the social world—even if they don't provide definitive answers. And don't be so intimidated by the need to maintain high standards that you shrink from taking advantage of opportunities to conduct research yourself.

The growth of social science methods from their infancy to adolescence, perhaps to young adulthood, ranks as a key intellectual accomplishment of the 20th century. Opinions about the causes and consequences of homelessness no longer need to depend on the scattered impressions of individuals; criminal justice policies can be shaped by systematic evidence of their effectiveness; and changes in the distribution of poverty and wealth in populations can be identified and charted. Employee productivity, neighborhood cohesion, and societal conflict may each be linked to individual psychological processes and to international economic strains.

Of course, social research methods are no more useful than the commitment of researchers to their proper application. Research methods, like all knowledge, can be used poorly or well, for good purposes or bad, when appropriate or not. A claim that a belief is based on social research in itself provides no extra credibility. As you have learned throughout this book, we must first learn which methods were used, how they were applied, and whether interpretations square with the evidence. To understand the social world, we must keep in mind the lessons of research methods. Doing so will help us build a better social world in the 21st century.

Key Terms

Back matter   210

Front matter   210

Plagiarism   212

Highlights

- Research reports should be evaluated systematically, using the review questions introduced in Chapter 2 and detailed in Appendix A.

- Different types of reports typically pose different problems. Authors of student papers must be guided in part by the expectations of their professor. Journal articles must pass a peer review by other social scientists and are often much improved in the process. Applied research reports are constrained by the expectations of the research sponsor; an advisory committee from the applied setting can help avoid problems.

- Research reports should include an introductory statement of the research problem, a literature review, a methodology section, a findings section with pertinent data displays, and a conclusions section that identifies any weaknesses in the research design and points out implications for future research and theorizing. This basic report format should be modified according to the needs of a particular audience and when organizing reports on qualitative projects and when organizing reports on qualitative projects.

- The central ethical concern in research reporting is to be honest. This honesty should include providing a truthful accounting of how the research was carried out, maintaining a full record about the project, using appropriate statistics and graphs, acknowledging the research sponsors, and being sensitive to the perspectives of coauthors.

- Credit must be given where credit is due. The contributions of persons and organizations to a research project must be acknowledged in research reports.

- Plagiarism is a grievous violation of scholarly ethics. All direct quotes or paraphrased material from another author's work must be cited appropriately.

- Social scientists are obligated to evaluate the credibility of information obtained from any source before using it in their research reports.

······· **Chapter Questions** ·····································

1. A good place to start developing your critical skills would be with one of the SAGE research articles available on the study site (edge.sagepub.com/schuttusw). Try reading one, and fill in the answers to the article review questions (see Appendix A). Summarize the strengths and weaknesses of the research design.

2. Rate four journal articles on the study site (edge.sagepub.com/schuttusw) for the overall quality of the research and for the effectiveness of the writing and data displays. Discuss how each could have been improved.

3. Plagiarism is no joke. What are the regulations on plagiarism in class papers at your school? What do you think the ideal policy would be? Should this policy account for cultural differences in teaching practices and learning styles? Do you think this ideal policy is likely to be implemented? Why or why not? Based on your experiences, do you believe that most student plagiarism is the result of misunderstanding about proper citation practices, or is it the result of dishonesty? Do you think that students who plagiarize while in school are less likely to be honest as social researchers?

TEST your understanding of chapter content. Take the practice quiz.
$SAGE edge

······ **Practice Exercises** ·····································

1. Call a local social or health service administrator or a criminal justice official, and arrange for an interview. Ask the official about his or her experience with applied research reports and conclusions about the value of social research and the best techniques for reporting to practitioners.

2. Interview a student who has written an independent paper based on original data. Ask your subject to describe his or her experiences while writing the paper. Review the decisions made in designing the research, and ask about the stages of research design, data collection and analysis, and report writing that proved to be difficult.

3. Complete the Interactive Exercises on reporting research on the study site (edge.sagepub.com/schuttusw).

STUDENT STUDY SITE

$SAGE edge™

The Student Study Site, available at **edge.sagepub.com/schuttusw**, includes useful study materials including eFlashcards, videos, audio resources, journal articles, and encyclopedia articles, many of which are represented by the media links throughout the text.

Appendix A

Questions to Ask About a Research Article

1. What is the basic research question, or problem? Try to state it in just one sentence. (Chapter 2)

2. Is the purpose of the study descriptive, exploratory, explanatory, or evaluative? Did the study have more than one purpose? (Chapter 1)

3. Was a theoretical framework presented? What was it? Did it seem appropriate for the research question addressed? Can you think of a different theoretical perspective that might have been used? What philosophy guides the research? Is this philosophy appropriate to the research question? (Chapters 1, 2)

4. What prior literature was reviewed? Was it relevant to the research problem? Was it relevant to the theoretical framework? Does the literature review appear to be adequate? Are you aware of (or can you locate) any important studies that have been omitted? (Chapter 2)

5. What features identified the study as deductive or inductive? Do you need additional information in any areas to evaluate the study or to replicate it? (Chapters 1, 2)

6. Did the study seem consistent with current ethical standards? Were any trade-offs made between different ethical guidelines? Was an appropriate balance struck between adherence to ethical standards and use of the most rigorous scientific practices? (Chapter 3)

7. Were any hypotheses stated? Were these hypotheses justified adequately in terms of the theoretical framework and in terms of prior research? (Chapter 2)

8. What were the independent and dependent variables in the hypothesis or hypotheses? Did these variables reflect the theoretical concepts as intended? What direction of association was hypothesized? Were any other variables identified as potentially important? (Chapter 2)

9. What were the major concepts in the research? How, and how clearly, were they defined? Were some concepts treated as unidimensional that you think might best be thought of as multidimensional? (Chapter 4)

10. Did the instruments used, the measures of the variables, seem valid and reliable? How did the authors attempt to establish this? Could any more have been done in the study to establish measurement validity? (Chapter 4)

11. Was a sample or the entire population of elements used in the study? What type of sample was selected? Was a probability sampling method used? Did the authors think the sample was generally representative of the population from which it was drawn? Do you? How would you evaluate the likely generalizability of the findings to other populations? (Chapter 5)

12. Was the response rate or participation rate reported? Does it appear likely that those who did not respond or participate were markedly different from those who did participate? Why or why not? Did the author(s) adequately discuss this issue? (Chapter 5)

13. What were the units of analysis? Were they appropriate for the research question? If groups were the units of analysis, were any statements made at any point that are open to the ecological fallacy? If individuals were the units of analysis, were any statements made at any point that suggest reductionist reasoning? (Chapter 6)

14. Was the study design cross-sectional or longitudinal, or did it use both types of data? If the design was longitudinal, what type of longitudinal design was it? Could the longitudinal design have been improved in any way, such as by collecting panel data rather than trend data, or by decreasing the dropout rate in a panel design? If cross-sectional data were used, could the research question have been addressed more effectively with longitudinal data? (Chapter 6)

15. Were any causal assertions made or implied in the hypotheses or in subsequent discussions? What approach was used to demonstrate the existence of causal effects? Were all three criteria and two cautions for establishing causal relationships addressed? What, if any, variables were controlled in the analysis to reduce the risk of spurious relationships? Should any other variables have been measured and controlled? How satisfied are you with the internal validity of the conclusions? What about external validity? (Chapter 6)

16. Which type of research design was used: experimental, survey, participant observation, historical comparative, or some other? How well was this design suited to the research question posed and the specific hypotheses tested, if any? Why do you suppose the author(s) chose this particular design? How was the design modified in response to research constraints? How was it modified to take advantage of research opportunities? (Chapters 6–10)

17. Was this an evaluation research project? If so, which type of evaluation was it? Which design alternatives did it use? (Chapter 10)

18. Was a historical comparative design or a content analysis used? Which type was it? Were problems resulting from using historical or cross-national data addressed? (Chapter 9)

19. Was a secondary data analysis design used? If so, what were the advantages and disadvantages of using data collected in another project? Were Big Data analyzed? If so, did the methods raise any ethical alarms? (Chapter 9)

20. Were mixed methods used? What methods were combined and how can they be distinguished in priority and sequence? In what ways did the combination of qualitative and quantitative data enrich the study's value? (Chapter 10)

21. Was any attention given to social context and subjective meanings? If so, what did this add? If not, would it have improved the study? Explain. (Chapter 12)

22. Summarize the findings. How clearly were statistical or qualitative data presented and discussed? Were the results substantively important? (Chapters 11, 12)

23. Did the author(s) adequately represent the findings in the discussion and/or conclusions sections? Were conclusions well grounded in the findings? Are any other interpretations possible? (Chapter 13)

24. Compare the study to others addressing the same research question. Did the study yield additional insights? In what ways was the study design more or less adequate than the design of previous research? (Chapters 2, 13)

25. What additional research questions and hypotheses are suggested by the study's results? What light did the study shed on the theoretical framework used? On social policy questions? (Chapters 13)

Appendix B

How to Read a Research Article

The discussions of research articles throughout the text may provide all the guidance you need to read and critique research on your own. But reading about an article in bits and pieces to learn about particular methodologies is not quite the same as reading an article in its entirety to learn what the researcher found out. The goal of this appendix is to walk you through an entire research article, answering the review questions introduced in Appendix A. Of course, this is only one article and our "walk" will take different turns than would a review of other articles, but after this review you should feel more confident when reading other research articles on your own.

This example uses an article by Seth Abrutyn and Anna S. Mueller (2014) on suicidal behavior among adolescents, reprinted on pages 222 to 238 of this appendix. It focuses on a topic of great social concern and of key importance in social theory. Moreover, it is a solid piece of research published by a top SAGE journal, the American Sociological Association's *American Sociological Review*.

I have reproduced below each of the article review questions from Appendix A, followed by my answers to them. After each question, I indicate the chapter where the question was discussed and after each answer, I cite the article page or pages that I am referring to. You can also follow my review by reading through the article itself and noting my comments.

1. *What is the basic research question, or problem? Try to state it in just one sentence.* (Chapter 2)

Abrutyn and Mueller present an overall research problem and then four specific research questions. They define their research problem by stating, "We investigate the role suicide suggestion plays in the suicide process, independent of other measures of social integration and psychological well-being" (p. 212). They summarize their research questions as being "the critical questions of how, when, and for whom does suggestion matter?" The four specific research questions highlight

Four major gaps in the literature: (1) whether suicide suggestion is associated with the development of suicidal thoughts among individuals who reported no suicidal thoughts at the time a role model attempted suicide; (2) whether the effects of suicide suggestion fade with time; (3) whether the relationship between the role model and respondent matters; and (4) whether there are differences between boys and girls. (p. 212)

Before this point, the authors focus on this research question by highlighting the apparent paradox that the social integration that Émile Durkheim assumed helped protect individuals from suicide can instead spread suicidality.

2. *Is the purpose of the study descriptive, exploratory, explanatory, or evaluative? Did the study have more than one purpose?* (Chapter 1)

The study's primary purpose is explanatory because the authors conclude each section of their literature review with an expectation for influences on risk of suicidality. For example, the section on "gender differences" concludes with a summary statement that highlights the goal of explanation:

These findings suggest girls may be more susceptible than boys to role models' suicide attempts. (p. 215)

There is also a descriptive element in the authors' framing of the research because they indicate their strategy includes

examining the development of suicidal behaviors in a sample of youth with no suicidal behaviors at Time I. (p. 215)

Of course, the authors also present descriptive statistics for their key variables (Table 1, p. 217).

3. *Was a theoretical framework presented? What was it? Did it seem appropriate for the research question addressed? Can you think of a different theoretical perspective that might have been used? What philosophy guides the research? Is this philosophy appropriate to the research question?* (Chapters 1, 2)

Abrutyn and Mueller's overarching theoretical framework for this research is Durkheim's classic theory of suicide and its emphasis on the protective value of social integration (pp. 212–215). The article begins and ends by discussing Durkheim's theory and it introduces the concept of suicide suggestion as important for sociologists because of the "apparent contradiction" it involves with Durkheim's theory. The literature review is focused on theorizing and research about suicide suggestion and so is very appropriate for the research questions addressed. Some connections are made to identity theory, which provides a somewhat different theoretical perspective that is more appropriate for some of the influences tested. The researchers follow a positivist research philosophy as they seek to understand social processes in the social world, rather than how people make sense of their experiences. In this study, the focus on suicide "suggestion" certainly raises a question about meaning, but their methods use standard measures to identify variation in this phenomenon, rather than intensive interviews or observations to discover how adolescents construct the experience of a friend's suicide. We can conclude that the positivist philosophy guiding the research is appropriate to the research question, while realizing that a researcher guided by a constructivist philosophy could have studied the same phenomenon but with different research methods and a somewhat different research question.

4. *What prior literature was reviewed? Was it relevant to the research problem? Was it relevant to the theoretical framework? Does the literature review appear to be adequate? Are you aware of (or can you locate) any important studies that have been omitted?* (Chapter 2)

Abrutyn and Mueller review literature from the article's first page until the "Methods" section (pp. 212–215). It is all very relevant to the general theoretical framework problem, and there is a section focused on each of the four specific research questions. In the first few paragraphs, several studies are mentioned that draw attention to the importance of suicide suggestion and thus the potential negative effects of social ties on suicidality (pp. 211–212). Subsequent sections in the literature review focus on prior research about suicidality and the effects of media, role models, recency ("temporal limitations"), family versus friends, and gender. The review provides an adequate foundation for expecting these effects. I leave it to you to find out whether any important studies were omitted.

5. *What features identified the study as deductive or inductive? Do you need additional information in any areas to evaluate the study or to replicate it?* (Chapters 1, 2)

The study clearly involves a test of ideas against empirical reality as much as that reality could be measured; it was carried out systematically and with a deductive design. Because the authors used an available data set, others can easily obtain the complete documentation for the study and try to replicate the authors' findings. The authors explicitly note and challenge assumptions made by many other researchers using Durkheim's theory of social integration and suicide (p. 211). They aim clearly to build social theory and encourage others to build on their findings: "this study is not without its limitations" (p. 224). The study thus seems to exemplify adherence to the logic of deductive research and to be very replicable.

6. *Did the study seem consistent with current ethical standards? Were any trade-offs made between different ethical guidelines? Was an appropriate balance struck between adherence to ethical standards and use of the most rigorous scientific practices?* (Chapter 3)

Abrutyn and Mueller use survey data collected by others and so encounter no ethical problems in their treatment of human subjects. The reporting seems honest and open. Although the research should help inform social policy, the authors' explicit focus is on how their research can inform social theory. This is quite appropriate for research reported in a scientific journal, so there are no particular ethical problems raised about the uses to which the research is put. The original survey used by the authors does not appear at all likely to have violated any ethical guidelines concerning the treatment of human subjects, although it would be necessary to inspect the original research report to evaluate this.

7. *Were any hypotheses stated? Were these hypotheses justified adequately in terms of the theoretical framework and in terms of prior research?* (Chapter 2)

Although they do not explicitly label their predictions as hypotheses, Abrutyn and Mueller carefully specify their independent and dependent variables and link them to their four specific research questions. Each one is justified and related to prior research in the "theoretical background" section (pp. 212–215).

8. *What were the independent and dependent variables in the hypothesis or hypotheses? Did these variables reflect the theoretical concepts as intended? What direction of association was hypothesized? Were any other variables identified as potentially important?* (Chapter 2)

Independent and dependent variables are identified explicitly in the measurement section and several control variables are specified as important (pp. 216–218). Independent variables are friend suicide attempt, family suicide attempt, family integration scale, friends care, and religious attendance. Although it is not stated explicitly as an independent variable, the authors identify another independent variable, recency of others' suicide, by distinguishing the survey follow-up wave at which that event occurred and the wave at which the dependent variable is measured. Additional variables controlled as known risk factors for suicide are same-sex attraction and emotional distress. Several demographic and personal characteristics are also used as controls: grade point average, family structure, race/ethnicity, parents' education, and age.

9. *What were the major concepts in the research? How, and how clearly, were they defined? Were some concepts treated as unidimensional that you think might best be thought of as multidimensional?* (Chapter 4)

The key concept in the research is that of "suicide suggestion"; it is defined in the article's second sentence and distinguished from the parallel concept of "social integration" that Durkheim emphasized (p. 211). Two dimensions of this key concept are then distinguished (emotional—suicidality and behavioral—suicides) and the concept of suicidality is discussed at length in a section on the spread of suicide (p. 212). Other important concepts in the research are personal role models, similarity between individuals and role models, type of role model (family versus friends), temporal limits, and gender. They are each elaborated in the separate sections of the literature review. Several related concepts are mentioned in the course of discussing others, including significant others, reality of role model (p. 212), media exposure, depression, social similarity of friends (p. 214), suggestibility and network diffusion (p. 215), family integration and care by others (p. 216), and religious attendance (p. 217).

10. *Did the instruments used, the measures of the variables, seem valid and reliable? How did the authors attempt to establish this? Could any more have been done in the study to establish measurement validity?* (Chapter 4)

The measures of the dependent variables, suicidal ideation and suicide attempts, were based on answers to single questions (p. 216). The wording of these questions is quite straightforward, but no information is provided about their reliability or validity. This can be seen as a weakness of the article, although Abrutyn and Miller do note in the "limitations" section that they do not know how stated thoughts or intentions were related to actual suicidal behavior (p. 225). The same single-question approach was used to measure the independent variables, friend suicide attempt and family suicide attempt (p. 216), again without any information on reliability or validity. The authors report that family integration was measured with a four-item scale, for which they report interitem reliability, and relations with friends, religious attendance, and same-sex attraction were assessed with just single questions (pp. 216–217). Abrutyn and Mueller measured emotional distress with an abridged version of the widely used Center for Epidemiological Studies Depression (CES-D) scale (pp. 217–218). They mention the interitem reliability of the CES-D in their data ("Cronbach's alpha =.873") but do not discuss its validity; because the scale has been used in so many other studies and has been evaluated so many times for its reliability and validity, and because it does not play a central role in this new research, it is reasonable that the authors do not discuss it further. Overall, the study can be described as relatively weak in information provided on measurement reliability and validity.

11. *Was a sample or the entire population of elements used in the study? What type of sample was selected? Was a probability sampling method used? Did the authors think the sample was generally representative of the population from which it was drawn? Do you? How would you evaluate the likely generalizability of the findings to other populations?* (Chapter 5)

The sample was a national random (probability) sample of adolescents at three time points. Called the "Add Health" study, the original researchers used a two-stage cluster sampling design, in which first all schools in the United States containing an 11th grade were sampled, with stratification by region, urbanicity, school type, ethnic composition, and size. A nationally representative subsample of students was then interviewed from these schools ($n = 20,745$). Students (and graduates) from the subsample were then reinterviewed in two more waves, with Wave II 1 to 2 years after Wave I and Wave III another 5 to 6 years after Wave II. A total of 10,828 respondents were interviewed in all three waves (p. 215). Abrutyn and Mueller attempt to determine whether suicidality is influenced among adolescents who have not previously thought of suicide by processes of contagion, so they limit their sample further to those who reported no suicidal thoughts or attempts in Wave I (p. 216). The authors identify their sample explicitly as representative of the national population of adolescents in school in this age range. Do you think the findings could be generalized to adolescents who had dropped out of school, or to other countries with different cultural values about suicide?

12. *Was the response rate or participation rate reported? Does it appear likely that those who did not respond or participate were markedly different from those who did participate? Why or why not? Did the author(s) adequately discuss this issue?* (Chapter 5)

The number of cases is identified at each wave, and the consequences of exclusion criteria applied are specified, but the response rate is not stated. Readers are referred for details to the original research report on the Add Health survey (p. 215). The authors do evaluate the possibility that the exclusion of adolescents who reported suicidal ideation in Wave I could have biased their sample, but they suggest this is unlikely because average levels of emotional distress and demographic variables are similar whether these cases are excluded or not (p. 216). There does not seem to be a serious problem here, but it would have been helpful to have had details about the response rate in the article, instead of just in a separate report (albeit one that is available online). More consideration of possibilities for sample bias could also have led to greater confidence in generalizations from this sample.

13. *What were the units of analysis? Were they appropriate for the research question? If groups were the units of analysis, were any statements made at any point that are open to the ecological fallacy? If individuals were the units of analysis, were any statements made at any point that suggest reductionist reasoning?* (Chapter 4)

The survey sampled adolescents within schools, so individuals were the units of analysis (pp. 215–216). The focus was on the behavior of individuals, so this is certainly appropriate. However, it is possible that the process of suicide contagion could differ between different schools, so the authors could have added a great deal to their study by also using schools as the units of analysis and determining whether there were some distinctive characteristics of schools in which contagion was more likely. Therefore, the individual-level analysis could obscure some group-level processes and thus lead to some reductionist reasoning.

14. *Was the study design cross-sectional or longitudinal, or did it use both types of data? If the design was longitudinal, what type of longitudinal design was it? Could the longitudinal design have been improved in any way, such as by collecting panel data rather than trend data, or by decreasing the dropout rate in a panel design? If cross-sectional data were used, could the research question have been addressed more effectively with longitudinal data?* (Chapter 2)

The study used a longitudinal panel design, although the sample at Wave II was limited to those adolescents who had not already graduated (p. 215). The reduction in the sample size by about half from the first wave to the third follow-up 5 to 6 years later is typical for a panel design; it is not possible to consider whether procedures could have been improved without knowing more about the details contained in the original research report.

15. *Were any causal assertions made or implied in the hypotheses or in subsequent discussions? What approach was used to demonstrate the existence of causal effects? Were all three criteria and two cautions for establishing causal relationships addressed? What, if any, variables were controlled in the analysis to reduce the risk of spurious relationships? Should any other variables have been measured and controlled? How satisfied are you with the internal validity of the conclusions? What about external validity?* (Chapter 6)

Causal assertions are implied in the predictions about "how exposure to suicidal behaviors shapes adolescent suicidality" (p. 215). A nomothetic approach to causation is used and each of the criteria for establishing causal effects is addressed: association (by checking for an association between the independent and dependent variables), time order (by using a longitudinal design that establishes clearly that the precipitating cause occurred before the "contagion"), and nonspuriousness (by controlling for variables that could have created a spurious association). The variables controlled included family integration, closeness to friends, religious attendance, same-sex attraction, and emotional distress, as well as several personal and demographic characteristics. The combination of the longitudinal design and the breadth of the variables controlled increases confidence in the internal validity of the conclusions, but because there was not random assignment to experiencing a friend's or family member's suicide (an ethical and practical impossibility), we cannot be completely confident that adolescents exposed to suicide did not differ from their peers in some unmeasured risk factor. There is little basis for evaluating external validity.

16. *Which type of research design was used: experimental, survey, participant observation, historical comparative, or some other? How well was this design suited to the research question posed and the specific hypotheses tested, if any? Why do you suppose the author(s) chose this particular design? How was the design modified in response to research constraints? How was it modified to take advantage of research opportunities?* (Chapters 6-10)

Survey research was the method used in the Add Health study, which generated the data set used in this secondary data analysis project. Survey research seems appropriate for the research questions posed, although only because Add Health used a longitudinal panel design. The survey design was somewhat modified after the fact for this analysis by eliminating respondents who had already experienced a suicide of a friend or family member at Wave I (p. 215).

17. *Was this an evaluation research project? If so, which type of evaluation was it? Which design alternatives did it use?* (Chapter 10)

This study did not use an evaluation research design. The issues on which it focused might profitably be studied in some evaluations of adolescent suicide prevention programs.

18. *Was a historical comparative design or a content analysis used? Which type was it? Were problems resulting from using historical or cross-national data addressed?* (Chapter 9)

This study did not use any type of historical or comparative design. It is interesting to consider how the findings might have differed if comparisons with other cultures or to earlier times had been made. The authors include in their literature review content analyses of the reporting of suicide as part of investigating media effects on suicide, but they did not take this approach themselves (p. 213).

19. *Was a secondary data analysis design used? If so, what were the advantages and disadvantages of using data collected in another project? Were Big Data analyzed? If so, did the methods raise any ethical alarms?* (Chapter 9)

This article reported a secondary analysis of the Add Health survey data (p. 215). This analysis of the previously collected data allowed the authors to conduct a very careful and fruitful analysis of a research question that had not previously been answered with these data, without having to secure funds for conducting such an ambitious longitudinal survey themselves. However, the result was that they could not include more extensive questions about suicidality and friends' and family members' suicides as they probably would have done if they had designed the primary data collection themselves. This standard survey data set would not qualify as Big Data.

20. *Were mixed methods used? What methods were combined and how can they be distinguished in terms of priority and sequence? In what ways did the combination of qualitative and quantitative data enrich the study's value?* (Chapter 10)

Mixed methods were not used. The analysis is entirely of quantitative data. The original study could have been enriched for the purposes of addressing suicide contagion by adding qualitative interviews of students who had been exposed to a suicide, as the authors note (p. 223).

21. *Was any attention given to social context and subjective meanings? If so, what did this add? If not, would it have improved the study? Explain.* (Chapter 12)

Social context and subjective meanings are really at the heart of the phenomenon of suicide contagion, but the Add Health researchers did not add a qualitative component to their research or adopt a constructivist philosophy to focus more attention on these issues. A participant observation study of suicide contagion in high schools could yield great insights, and a researcher with a constructivist philosophy who focused on how adolescents make sense of others' suicides would add another dimension to understanding this phenomenon.

22. *Summarize the findings. How clearly were statistical or qualitative data presented and discussed? Were the results substantively important?* (Chapters 11, 12, 13)

Statistical data are presented clearly in two tables. The first table describes the sample at each wave in terms of the key variables for the study. The second table presents the results of a multivariate analysis of the data using a technique called "logistic regression." The authors use this technique to test for the associations between their dependent and independent variables over time, while controlling for other variables. The results seem substantively important. In the authors' own words,

> For adolescents, ties do bind, but whether these ties integrate adolescents into society, with positive repercussions for their emotional well-being, or whether they promote feelings of alienation, depends in part on the qualities embedded in those ties. (p. 225)

23. *Did the author(s) adequately represent the findings in the discussion or conclusions sections? Were conclusions well grounded in the findings? Are any other interpretations possible?* (Chapter 13)

The findings are well represented in the discussion and conclusions section, with a limitations section that strikes an appropriate note of caution (pp. 222–225). Interesting conjectures are presented in the discussion of gender differences and differences in the apparent effects of different types of role model. The conclusions section makes explicit connections to the initial questions posed about Durkheim's theorizing. You might want to consider what other interpretations of the findings might be possible. Remember that other interpretations always are possible for particular findings—it is a question of the weight of the evidence, the persuasiveness of the theory used, and the consistency of the findings with other research.

24. *Compare the study to others addressing the same research question. Did the study yield additional insights? In what ways was the study design more or less adequate than the design of previous research?* (Chapters 2, 13)

Summaries of prior research in the literature review suggest that Abrutyn and Mueller have added new insights to the literature on suicide contagion by overcoming limitations in previous research designs. The use of a longitudinal panel design was more adequate than much previous research using cross-sectional designs.

25. *What additional research questions and hypotheses are suggested by the study's results? What light did the study shed on the theoretical framework used? On social policy questions?* (Chapters 2, 13)

Perhaps the most obvious research question suggested by the study's results is that of whether social integration of some type can have protective effects as predicted by Durkheim even at the same time that other social connections heighten the risk of suicide due to a process of social contagion. Research designed to answer this question could lead to an overarching theoretical framework encompassing both the protective benefits of social ties that Durkheim identified and the risk that social ties create a process of social contagion. If the focus is on understanding the process of social contagion, it is clear that Abrutyn and Mueller's research has made an important contribution. The authors highlight some policy implications in their conclusions (p. 225).

Are Suicidal Behaviors Contagious in Adolescence? Using Longitudinal Data to Examine Suicide Suggestion

American Sociological Review
2014, Vol. 79(2) 211–227
© American Sociological
Association 2014
DOI: 10.1177/0003122413519445
http://asr.sagepub.com

Seth Abrutyn[a] and Anna S. Mueller[a]

Abstract

Durkheim argued that strong social relationships protect individuals from suicide. We posit, however, that strong social relationships also have the potential to increase individuals' vulnerability when they expose people to suicidality. Using three waves of data from the National Longitudinal Study of Adolescent Health, we evaluate whether new suicidal thoughts and attempts are in part responses to exposure to role models' suicide attempts, specifically friends and family. We find that role models' suicide attempts do in fact trigger new suicidal thoughts, and in some cases attempts, even after significant controls are introduced. Moreover, we find these effects fade with time, girls are more vulnerable to them than boys, and the relationship to the role model—for teenagers at least—matters. Friends appear to be more salient role models for both boys and girls. Our findings suggest that exposure to suicidal behaviors in significant others may teach individuals new ways to deal with emotional distress, namely by becoming suicidal. This reinforces the idea that the structure—and content—of social networks conditions their role in preventing suicidality. Social ties can be conduits of not just social support, but also antisocial behaviors, like suicidality.

Keywords

suicide, social networks, suicide suggestion, Durkheim, gender, Add Health

Understanding suicide has been essential to the sociological enterprise since Durkheim ([1897] 1951) wrote his famous monograph, arguing that groups that integrated and (morally) regulated their members offered protective benefits against suicide. Durkheimian mechanisms remain highly relevant (cf. Maimon and Kuhl 2008; Pescosolido and Georgianna 1989; Thorlindsson and Bjarnason 1998), but emphasis on *suicide suggestion,* or the effect a role model's suicidal behavior has on an observer's suicidality, has become increasingly essential to the sociological understanding of suicide (e.g., Gould 2001; Phillips 1974; Stack 2003, 2009).

Whereas Durkheim assumed that social integration protected individuals, suicide suggestion demonstrates that suicidality can spread through the very ties that Durkheim theorized as protective. This apparent contradiction is not such a problem for modern interpretations of Durkheim's theory that focus on the structure

[a]The University of Memphis

Corresponding Authors:
Seth Abrutyn and Anna Mueller, Department of Sociology, Clement Hall 231, The University of Memphis, Memphis, TN 38152-3530
E-mail: seth.abrutyn@memphis.edu;
anna.mueller@memphis.edu

of social ties themselves, and how the networks individuals are embedded within produce the protective benefits Durkheim observed (Bearman 1991; Pescosolido 1990; Wray, Colen, and Pescosolido 2011). It is possible to imagine social ties as capable of both social support and social harm (Baller and Richardson 2009; Haynie 2001; Pescosolido 1990). Durkheim was right that collective solidarity is often protective, but we argue that the behaviors, values, and emotions embedded in network ties must be elaborated to truly understand how social relationships shape individuals' life chances.[1] This subtle shift provides an opportunity to integrate two equally important, but often unnecesarrily separate, realms in the sociology of suicide: the literature on suicide suggestion and the literature on social integration.

The existing literature on suicide suggestion demonstrates that concern over the emotions (suicidality) and behaviors (suicides) embedded in social networks is warranted. Suicides often occur in clusters, with spikes in suicide rates following media coverage of suicides (Stack 2003, 2005, 2009), so much so that a group of public health agencies (including the National Institute of Mental Health [NIMH]) issued guidelines for how the media should report on suicides so as to limit their spread (Suicide Prevention Resource Center [SPRC] 2013). Less research has examined how suicides spread through personal role models, but studies show a robust association between a friend's (and sometimes family member's) suicidal behavior and that of the person exposed to it (Bearman and Moody 2004; Bjarnason 1994; Liu 2006; Niederkrotenthaler et al. 2012; Thorlindsson and Bjarnason 1998). However, these studies often fail to address the critical questions of how, when, and for whom does suggestion matter?

With this study, we employ three waves of data from the National Longitudinal Study of Adolescent Health to examine these questions. By using longitudinal data rich in measures of adolescent life, we investigate the role suicide suggestion plays in the suicide process, independent of other measures of social

integration and psychological well-being. We tease out nuances related to the harmful side of social integration by shedding light on four major gaps in the literature: (1) whether suicide suggestion is associated with the development of suicidal thoughts among individuals who reported no suicidal thoughts at the time a role model attempted suicide; (2) whether the effects of suicide suggestion fade with time; (3) whether the relationship between the role model and respondent matters; and (4) whether there are differences between boys and girls.

THEORETICAL BACKGROUND
The Spread of Suicide

Beginning with Phillips's (1974) groundbreaking work, suicide suggestion studies typically examine (1) the association between celebrity suicides and national and local suicide rates (Gould 2001; Stack 2003, 2005), (2) the association between fictionalized media suicides and national and local rates (e.g., Stack 2009), and (3) the apparent geographic and temporal clustering of suicides (e.g., Baller and Richardson 2002; Gould, Wallenstein, and Kleinman 1990). A few studies have also investigated the effect a role model's suicidal behavior has on friends or family members exposed to it. The logic of these studies is predicated on social psychological assumptions. Significant others or persons labeled as members of a reference group with whom we identify are far more likely to influence and shape behavior than are nonsignificant others or outsiders (Turner 2010). Additionally, direct ties infused with socioemotional meanings can act as conduits for the spread of behavioral norms (Goffman 1959) and positive *and* negative affect, which motivate the reproduction of these behavioral norms (Lawler 2006).

Suicide suggestion and the media. In a comprehensive review of the suicide suggestion literature, Stack (2005:121) estimates that about one-third of suicide cases in the

United States involve "suicidal behavior following the dissemination of a suicidal model in the media." Models may be real celebrities like Marilyn Monroe or fictionalized characters such as those found in popular novels or television shows. The length of exposure and the status of the role model appear to matter: on average, publicized celebrity suicides produce a 2.51 percent spike in aggregate rates, whereas Marilyn Monroe's suicide, a high status and highly publicized suicide, was followed by a 13 percent spike in the U.S. suicide rate (Phillips 1974; Stack 2003). The evidence concerning effects of fictionalized suicides, such as those found occasionally in television series (Schmidtke and Hafner 1988), is less consistent (e.g., Niederkrontenthaler and Sonneck 2007), but a recent meta-analysis found youths are particularly at risk of suicide suggestion via fictional suicides (Stack 2009).

Spikes following celebrity suicides are confined geographically to the subpopulation exposed to the suicide—for example, local newspapers should only affect their readership, whereas nationally televised shows should reach more people. Furthermore, research shows that temporal effects of media exposure vary to some degree, typically ranging from two weeks to a month (Phillips 1974; Stack 1987). To date, these studies have had a difficult time determining whether suggestion plays a role above and beyond individuals' personal circumstances: finding an association between media and suicide rates "does not necessarily identify [suggestion] as the underlying mechanism" (Gould et al. 1990:76). If suicide suggestion plays a role in the suicide process, the question is: does it have an effect above and beyond other risk factors for suicide, such as suicidal thoughts or depression prior to exposure to media coverage of a suicide?

Suicide suggestion via personal role models. Like media exposure suggestion studies, studies of personal role models focus on demonstrating a link between a role model's and the exposed individual's suicidal behaviors. The majority of these studies focus on adolescent suicide, perhaps because adolescent suicide has tripled since the 1950s and thus represents a serious public health problem (NIMH 2003). Adolescents may also be particularly vulnerable to suicide suggestion: adolescents are particularly socially conscious—social status and social relationships are a major focus of their daily lives. Moreover, teenagers are greatly influenced by their peers' values and behaviors (Giordano 2003), which may increase their vulnerability to suicide epidemics. Finally, adolescents are unique in that their sense of self is still forming, so they are more malleable than adults (Crosnoe 2000; Crosnoe and Johnson 2011). Any insights into factors contributing to the development of suicidality are thus crucial to teen suicide prevention.

Generally, studies of personal role models show that having a friend or family member exhibit suicidal behavior is positively associated with an exposed adolescent's own suicidality (Bjarnason and Thorlindsson 1994; Bridge, Goldstein, and Brent 2006; Evans, Hawton, and Rodham 2004), even after controlling for other measures of social integration, regulation, and psychological distress (e.g., Bearman and Moody 2004; Bjarnason 1994). A few studies also demonstrate a positive association between exposure to suicidal behavior in role models and an individual's likelihood of attempting suicide (Bearman and Moody 2004). These studies add to our understanding of sociological influences on suicide, but they fail to examine who is most vulnerable to suggestion and how long effects may linger, and they are often limited by the use of cross-sectional data.

Three studies employ longitudinal data and thus shed further light on suicide suggestion within the adolescent suicide process. Brent and colleagues (1989) had the rare opportunity to collect data immediately following a suicide at a high school. Although they were unable to measure students' predispositions to suicide prior to a peer's suicide, their findings suggest that suicide suggestion can spread rapidly and then gradually lose some of its effect. More recently, Niederkrotenthaler and colleagues (2012) found that young children exposed to a parent's suicidal behavior were far more likely to develop suicidal behaviors over time than were their counterparts. This work, however, is primarily epidemiological and fails to control for potentially significant confounding factors, such as social integration. Finally, Thompson and Light (2011) examined which factors are associated with adolescent nonfatal suicide attempts and found that role models' attempts significantly increase adolescents' likelihood of attempting suicide, net of respondents' histories of suicidal thoughts and many other factors. These studies provide insights into exposure to a role model's suicidal behavior, but questions of who is most vulnerable and how long that vulnerability lasts remain open, and the role suggestion plays as an aspect of social integration remains unacknowledged.

Similarity between individuals and role models. A primary limitation in the existing literature on suicide suggestion is its failure to determine whether the similarity between friends' or family members' suicidal behaviors is due to the tendency for individuals to form friendships with people they are similar to. This proverbial "birds of a feather" is often the case for teens, who select friends and peer groups based on how similar potential friends are to themselves (Crosnoe, Frank, and Mueller 2008; Joyner and Kao 2000). Research shows that adolescent friendships tend to be homophilous in terms of depression levels (Schaefer, Kornienko, and Fox 2011) and aggression (Cairns et al. 1988). The effect of suicide suggestion on an adolescent's suicidal behaviors may thus be due to unobserved preexisting similarities between friends. To address this limitation, we focus on the development of suicidal behaviors in a sample of adolescents with no documented history of suicidality, to avoid (to the extent possible with survey data) confounding the observed effect of suicide suggestion with selection into friendships. Answering this crucial question, whether suicide suggestion

contributes to the development of suicidal behaviors, is a central goal of this study.

Temporal limits. In the process of discerning how suggestion shapes adolescent suicidality, it is useful to consider whether effects of suggestion via personal role models linger as time passes, and for whom. Given past research, suggestive effects likely have temporal limitations. Previous studies on effects of media exposure generally find that spikes in suicide rates last between two and four weeks (Phillips 1974; Stack 1987). Significant others tend to have a greater impact on individuals than do nonsignificant others (Turner 2010), so it is reasonable to expect effects of personal role models will last longer than suicides publicized in the media. We thus utilize the Add Health survey to test whether the impact of a role model's suicide attempt is observable after approximately one year and six years.

Family versus friends. Generally, studies of suicide suggestion do not distinguish between effects of a family member's versus a friend's suicide attempt on those exposed. Given that past research demonstrates that "the influence of friends surpasses that of parents" by mid-adolescence (Crosnoe 2000:378), and friends' influence is strongly linked with teen delinquency, health behaviors, and pro-social behaviors (Frank et al. 2008; Giordano 2003; Haynie 2001; Mueller et al. 2010), we would expect to see differences based on an individual's relationship to the role model. It is plausible, given the extant research on adolescents and peer influence, that a friend's suicidal behavior provides a more salient model for imitating than would family. We thus analyze the two types of role models separately.

Gender differences. The final aspect deserving greater attention is potential gender differences in suggestion and suicidality. Little research emphasizes potential gender differences in how adolescents develop suicidal behaviors, despite the fact that key differences exist in suicidal behaviors between adolescent boys and girls (Baca-Garcia et al. 2008); for example, girls are more likely than boys to report nonfatal suicide attempts, whereas boys are more likely to experience fatal suicides. Another important reason to consider how suicide suggestion affects boys and girls stems from differences in boys' and girls' friendships. Girls tend to have fewer, but more intimate, emotionally laden friendships, whereas boys tend to maintain less emotional and more diffuse networks focused around shared activities (Crosnoe 2000). Moreover, girls tend to be more sensitive to others' opinions (Gilligan 1982) and are more easily influenced by peers than are boys (Maccoby 2002). These findings suggest girls may be more susceptible than boys to role models' suicide attempts.

In summary, this study shifts the sociological focus away from the protective nature of social ties toward the potential harm these ties can have on individuals. Specifically, we elaborate how exposure to suicidal behaviors shapes adolescent suicidality by identifying how, when, and for whom suicide suggestion matters. Our strategy includes (1) examining the development of suicidal behaviors in a sample of youth with no suicidal behaviors at Time I; (2) determining how long the effect of suggestion lasts; and if (3) the type of role model or (4) gender makes a difference in the process. Answers to these questions will help us understand how social relationships work in daily life to both protect and, sometimes, put individuals at risk of suicidality, thereby moving us closer to a robust sociological theory of suicide.

METHODS
Data

This study employs data from Waves I, II, and III of the National Longitudinal Study of Adolescent Health (Add Health). Add Health contains a nationally representative sample of U.S. adolescents in grades 7 through 12 in 132 middle and high schools in 80 different communities. From a list of all schools containing an 11th grade in the United States,

Add Health selected a nationally representative sample of schools using a school-based, cluster sampling design, with the sample stratified by region, urbanicity, school type, ethnic composition, and size.

The preliminary in-school survey collected data from all students in all Add Health high schools (n = 90,118 students) in 1994 to 1995; from this sample, a nationally representative subsample was interviewed at Wave I (n = 20,745), shortly after the in-school survey. Wave II followed in 1996 and collected information from 14,738 Wave I participants. Some groups of respondents were generally not followed up at Wave II; the largest of these were Wave I 12th graders, who had generally graduated high school by Wave II. Wave III was collected in 2001 to 2002 and followed up the Wave I in-home respondents (including respondents excluded from Wave II) who were then approximately age 18 to 23 years. Additional information about Add Health can be found in Harris and colleagues (2009).

Sample Selection

We used several sample selection filters to produce analytic samples that allow us to assess suicide suggestion in adolescence. First, we selected respondents with valid sample weights so we could properly account for the complex sampling frame of the Add Health data. Second, we used longitudinal data analysis; as such, we restricted our sample to adolescents who participated in Waves I and II of Add Health for our analyses of Wave II outcomes, and Waves I, II, and III for our analyses of Wave III outcomes. Among respondents, 10,828 had valid sample weights and participated in all three waves of Add Health. Our third selection filter selected only adolescents with no suicidal thoughts or attempts at Wave I, so the time order of events is preserved such that we can determine whether suicide suggestion plays a role above and beyond preexisting vulnerabilities to suicidality. This restriction reduced our analytic sample to 9,309 respondents. With this sample restriction, our models are not estimating the potential for role models to maintain or dissolve an adolescent's suicidal thoughts. Instead, our models estimate whether role models' behaviors at Wave I are associated with the development of previously undocumented suicidal thoughts and attempts at later waves. This also allows us to control for potential unmeasured factors that may shape both who adolescents choose as friends and their vulnerability to suicide (following the logic of classic ANCOVA; cf. Shadish, Campbell, and Cook 2002). Our final selection filter excluded adolescents missing any key independent variables.

These restrictions have the potential to bias our sample, but they also enable our analysis of critical aspects of suicidal behaviors in adolescence. To assess any potential bias, Table 1 presents descriptive statistics for the entire Wave I sample and our Wave II and Wave III analytic samples. The only substantial difference between the Wave I Add Health sample and our analytic sample is the lower incidence of suicidal thoughts and attempts at Waves II and III due to our restricting our analyses to adolescents with no suicidal thoughts at Wave I. Our analytic samples do not vary substantially from the entire Wave I sample in terms of average levels of emotional distress or demographic variables.

Measures

Dependent variables. We analyze two dependent variables: *suicidal ideation* and *suicide attempts* at Wave II and Wave III. *Suicidal ideation* is based on adolescents' responses to the question: "During the past 12 months, did you ever seriously think about committing suicide?" Adolescents who answered "yes" were coded 1 on a dichotomous outcome indicating suicidal ideation. Adolescents who reported having suicidal thoughts were then asked, "During the past 12 months, how many times did you actually attempt suicide?" Answers ranged from 0 (0 times) to four (six or more times). We recoded these responses into a dichotomous variable where 1 indicates a report of at least one suicide

attempt in the past 12 months and 0 indicates no attempts. Adolescents who reported no suicidal thoughts were also coded 0 on *suicide attempts*. These variables were asked at all three waves.

Independent variables. Our first key independent variable, one of two ways we measure suicide suggestion, is *friend suicide attempt* and is based on adolescents' responses to the question: "Have any of your friends tried to kill themselves during the past 12 months?" Adolescents who responded "yes" were coded 1 on a dichotomous variable. This question was asked at all waves. For models predicting suicidal thoughts and attempts at Wave II, we rely on adolescents' responses at Wave I to preserve time order in these data. For models predicting Wave III dependent variables, we use adolescents' responses to this question at Wave II. Our second key independent measure of suicide suggestion is *family suicide attempt*. The treatment of this variable is identical to *friend suicide attempt* and is based on adolescents' responses to the question: "Have any of your family tried to kill themselves during the past 12 months?"

Our models also control for protective factors for suicide suggested by prior research. Following Durkheim's ideas about the importance of social integration as a protective factor for suicide, we measure adolescents' family integration, how close they feel to their friends, and their religious attendance. Our *family integration scale* (Cronbach's alpha = .769) is based on four items that measure how integrated adolescents are in their families (Bjarnason 1994). Adolescents were asked how much they feel their parents care about them, how much people in their family understand them, whether they have fun with their family, and whether their family pays attention to them. Responses were coded so that a higher value on the scale indicates a higher feeling of family caring. Our measure of adolescents' relationships with their friends, *friends care,* is based on adolescents' responses to the question, "How much do you feel that your friends care about you?" Higher

Table 1. Weighted Descriptive Statistics for Key Variables

	Full Wave 1 Sample (mean)		Wave 2 Analytic Sample (mean)		Wave 3 Analytic Sample (mean)	
	Boys	Girls	Boys	Girls	Boys	Girls
Suicide Ideation, W1	.103	.165	.000	.000	.000	.000
Suicide Attempt, W1	.021	.057	.000	.000	.000	.000
Suicide Ideation, W2	.083	.146	.052	.092	.051	.091
Suicide Attempt, W2	.019	.051	.009	.026	.006	.026
Suicide Ideation, W3	.068	.072	.060	.060	.057	.061
Suicide Attempt, W3	.010	.025	.008	.021	.009	.020
Age, W1	15.180	15.370	15.290	15.120	15.130	15.010
	(1.610)	(1.710)	(1.620)	(1.580)	(1.530)	(1.530)
White	.667	.676	.673	.680	.667	.673
African American	.138	.151	.138	.157	.146	.162
Asian American	.044	.038	.040	.036	.039	.035
Hispanic	.118	.109	.115	.105	.115	.108
Other Race/Ethnicity	.033	.025	.034	.022	.033	.021
Parents' Education	2.867	2.853	2.880	2.867	2.935	2.910
	(1.284)	(1.261)	(1.236)	(1.239)	(1.240)	(1.248)
Lives with Two Biological Parents	.581	.571	.594	.588	.590	.602
Same-Sex Attraction, W1	.075	.048	.065	.039	.066	.038
GPA, W1	2.727	2.925	2.751	2.972	2.780	3.001
	(.798)	(.764)	(.766)	(.747)	(.753)	(.740)
Emotional Distress, W1	28.933	30.813	28.110	29.423	27.910	29.110
	(6.868)	(8.137)	(5.910)	(6.990)	(5.830)	(6.800)
N	5,042	5,694	4,301	4,523	3,855	4,075

Note: Standard deviations are in parentheses.
Source: The National Longitudinal Study of Adolescent Health.

values on this measure indicate a higher feeling of caring friends. *Religious attendance* measures how often adolescents attend religious services. Responses range from "never" to "once a week, or more." Items were coded so that a higher value on this measure indicates more frequent religious attendance.

In addition to measures of social integration, we control for several known risk factors for suicide. These include adolescents' reports of *same-sex attraction* (at Wave I) or identity as gay, lesbian, or bisexual (which was only collected at Wave III). At Wave I, adolescents were asked whether they had "ever had a romantic attraction to a female?" or ". . . to a male?" These questions were used to identify adolescents who experienced some

form of same-sex attraction (Pearson, Muller, and Wilkinson 2007). At Wave III, adolescents were asked to choose a description that fit their sexual identity, from 100 percent homosexual to 100 percent heterosexual (with not attracted to males or females as an option). Adolescents who reported being "bisexual," "mostly homosexual (gay), but somewhat attracted to people of the opposite sex," or "100 percent homosexual (gay)" were coded 1. Heterosexual, asexual, and mostly heterosexual adolescents were coded 0.

Because emotional distress may increase an adolescent's likelihood of becoming suicidal, we control for *emotional distress* in all models. *Emotional distress* is measured by a 19-item abridged Center for Epidemiological

Studies-Depression (CESD) scale (Cronbach's alpha = .873). Add Health, at Waves I and II, posed a series of questions asking respondents how often "you didn't feel like eating, your appetite was poor," "you felt that you were just as good as other people," and "you felt depressed." Positive items were reverse coded, so a higher score on every question indicates higher emotional distress. Items were then summed for adolescents who provided a valid answer to every question in the scale.

Finally, all models control for several demographic and personal characteristics, including educational attainment measures, family structure, age, race/ethnicity, and parents' education levels. Overall *grade point average* (GPA) is a self-reported measure and has the standard range of 0 to 4 (indicating the highest possible grade). An indicator for whether the adolescent successfully graduated from high school and if they attended some college is included in the models predicting suicidal behaviors at Wave III. Because of the age range of the sample, some students had not had time to complete a college degree; however, all had an opportunity to begin their college coursework and graduate from high school.

Family structure captures whether respondents lived in a two-biological-parent family, a single-parent family, a family that includes step-parents, or another family type at Wave I. *Race/ethnicity* was coded as five dichotomous variables: Latino/a, Black, Asian American, and other race or ethnicity, with White as the reference category. We took *parents' education* from the parent questionnaire and used the maximum value in the case of two parents. If this information was missing from the parent questionnaire, we used students' reports of their parents' education level. We coded parents' education as (0) never went to school; (1) less than high school graduation; (2) high school diploma or equivalent; (3) some college, but did not graduate; (4) graduated from a college or university; and (5) professional training beyond a four-year college or university.

Analytic Plan

Our goal with these analyses is to investigate whether a role model's suicide attempt is associated with the development of suicidal behaviors at Times II and III in a sample of adolescents with no suicidal behaviors at Time I. We also examine how long the increase in vulnerability lasts after exposure to a role model's suicide attempt, whether the type of role model makes a difference, and if there is variation in these processes by gender. To investigate these questions we estimate a series of nested logistic regression models with a sample of adolescents with no history of suicidal thoughts at Wave I. Because we are interested in (and anticipate based on prior literature) gender differences in what leads adolescents to contemplate suicide, we estimate all models separately by gender. As a first step, we estimate the bivariate relationships between a role model's suicide attempt (at Wave I or II) and an adolescent's likelihood of suicide ideation and attempt (at Waves II and III) to determine whether suicide suggestion is part of the process of developing suicidal behaviors over time. Next, we add a set of demographic, personal, and social characteristics to the model to determine how robust the impact of suicide suggestion is to potentially confounding risk and protective factors.[2]

Because Add Health data were collected using a complex survey design (described earlier), we estimate all models using the SAS SurveyLogistic Procedure (An 2002) to obtain appropriate estimates and standard errors (Bell et al. 2012). The survey logistic procedure is similar to traditional logistic regression, except for the handling of the variance. We estimated variance using a Taylor expansion approximation that computes variances within each stratum and pools estimates together (An 2002). This method accounts for dependencies within the data due to the complex survey design. Our models also include normalized sample weights to compensate for the substantial oversampling of certain populations. These weights render our analyses more representative of the U.S. population than would unweighted analyses that fail to correct for Add Health's oversampled populations.

RESULTS

To begin our investigation of suicide suggestion, we first examine the roles of family members' and friends' suicide attempts in adolescent girls' and boys' suicidal behaviors at Wave II, before turning to boys' and girls' behaviors at Wave III. Among boys, reports of a new suicidal attempt were extremely rare; only 1 percent of boys reported a suicide attempt at Wave II after reporting no suicidal thoughts at Wave 1. For this reason, we focus most heavily on suicidal thoughts and examine suicide attempts only among adolescent girls. The models for boys' suicidal attempts are available from the authors by request.

Suicidal Behaviors at Wave II

Table 2 presents odds ratios from logistic regressions predicting suicide ideation and suicide attempts for girls and boys. As a first step, we estimate the bivariate relationship between family members' suicide attempts (Wave I) and adolescents' suicidal thoughts and attempts a year later (Wave II) (see Models 1, 4, and 7 in Table 2). A family member's attempted suicide (Model 1) significantly increases the likelihood that adolescent girls report suicidal thoughts at Wave II; however, it is not associated with suicide attempts at Wave II (Model 4). On average, girls who reported that a family member attempted suicide at Wave I are 2.994 times more likely to report suicidal thoughts at Wave II than are girls who did not experience a family member's suicide attempt. This pattern is not found among boys. For boys, we find no significant relationship between a family member's suicide attempt and boys' likelihood of reporting suicidal thoughts. This is our first piece of evidence for gender differences in suicide suggestion.

Next we turn to friends as role models for suicide suggestion. For girls, a friend's suicide attempt significantly increases their likelihood of reporting suicidal thoughts (Model 2) and attempts (Model 5). For boys,

experiencing a friend's suicide attempt has a significant and positive relationship to boys' likelihood of reporting suicidal thoughts (Model 8). These significant bivariate relationships indicate that *who* the role model is may condition the likelihood that suicides spread through social relationships in gendered ways. Our next step is to evaluate whether these relationships maintain their significance once potential risk and protective factors are held constant in our models.

Substantively, our findings do not change after the addition of important controls.[3] On average, adolescent girls are 2.129 times more likely to report suicidal *thoughts* after experiencing a family member's attempted suicide, and 1.561 times more likely after experiencing a friend's suicide attempt, net of all other variables (Model 3). Girls' reports of suicide *attempts,* on average, are significantly related to friends' suicide attempts, but not family members' attempts, net of all other variables, confirming in Model 6 the bivariate relationships observed in Models 4 and 5. For girls, the relationship between suicide suggestion, via family or friend role models, is robust to many vital risk and protective factors for suicide.

For boys, the story is similar. The bivariate relationships observed in Models 7 and 8 are robust to the addition of control variables. Boys remain affected by a friend's suicide attempt at Wave I. Specifically, a friend's suicide attempt renders boys 1.649 times more likely to report suicidal thoughts at Wave II. The suicide attempt of a family member remains insignificant (confirming associations found in Model 7).

Overall, these findings suggest that suicide suggestion is associated with the development of suicidal behaviors within a year or so of a role model's suicide attempt, particularly when the role model is a friend. Significant gender differences do emerge: girls appear more sensitive than boys to familial role models.

Suicidal Behaviors at Wave III

In the analyses presented in Table 3, we investigate the impact a role model's suicide attempt at Wave II has on respondents' suicidal thoughts and attempts at Wave III, as

Table 2. Odds Ratios from Models Predicting Suicidal Thoughts and Attempts among Adolescents at Wave II

	Girls						Boys		
	Suicide Ideation			Suicide Attempt			Suicide Ideation		
	Model 1	Model 2	Model 3	Model 4	Model 5	Model 6	Model 7	Model 8	Model 9
Suicide Suggestion									
Family Suicide Attempt	2.994***		2.129**	1.069		.535	1.263		.947
Friend Suicide Attempt		2.054***	1.561**		3.214***	2.577***		1.935**	1.649*
Background									
Age			.733***			.679***			.979
African American			.625*			1.041			.809
Asian American			.966			1.580			.741
Latino\a			.811			1.082			.863
Other Race or Ethnicity			.692			1.332			1.019
Parents' Education Level			.967			.865			1.060
Same-Sex Attraction			1.660			1.281			1.499
GPA			.870			.967			.796
Social Integration									
Religious Attendance			.996			.900			.969
Single-Parent Family			1.499*			1.145			.943
Step-Parent Family			1.295			1.868			.866
Other Family Structure			1.050			1.578			1.817
Family Integration Scale			.877			.681			.770
Friends Care			1.204			1.216			1.404**
Psychological Factors									
Emotional Distress			1.067***			1.067***			1.038**
–2 Log Likelihood	2708.714	2698.139	2499.105	1073.977	1039.891	947.583	1729.374	1717.750	1672.626
Response Profile (n=1/n=0)	351/4172	351/4172	351/4172	100/4423	100/4423	100/4423	222/4079	222/4079	222/4079
N	4,523	4,523	4,523	4,523	4,523	4,523	4,301	4,301	4,301

Note: All independent variables measured at Wave I.
Source: The National Longitudinal Study of Adolescent Health.
*p < .05; **p < .01; ***p < .001 (two-tailed tests).

Table 3. Odds Ratios from Models Predicting Suicidal Thoughts and Attempts among Adolescents at Wave III

| | Girls | | | | | | Boys | | |
| | Suicide Ideation | | | Suicide Attempt | | | Suicide Ideation | | |
	Model 1	Model 2	Model 3	Model 4	Model 5	Model 6	Model 7	Model 8	Model 9
Suicide Suggestion									
Family Suicide Attempt	.725			1.298			1.782		1.572
Friend Suicide Attempt		1.978***	1.546		1.794	1.254		1.665	1.168
Background									
Age			.811***			.824			.861*
African American			.535*			.693			.477*
Asian American			1.286			4.808***			.551
Latino\a			.804			.698			.900
Other Race or Ethnicity			.678			<.001***			.683
Parents' Education Level			1.220*			1.173			1.248*
Gay, Lesbian, Bisexual Identity (W3)			2.879**			2.917			3.042**
GPA			.840			.645			.823
High School Dropout (W3)			1.557			2.688*			1.555
Some College (W3)			1.063			1.264			.881
Social Integration									
Religious Attendance			.845			.883			.964
Single-Parent Family			1.200			2.796*			1.184
Step-Parent Family			.995			2.560*			1.049
Other Family Structure			1.447			1.939			1.894
Not Currently Married or Cohabiting (W3)			1.309			1.173			2.751***
Family Integration Scale			.871			1.015			1.083
Friends Care			1.014			1.481			.799
Psychological Factors									
Emotional Distress			1.041**			1.026			1.055***
−2 Log Likelihood	1841.515	1821.903	1709.455	794.630	789.706	709.774	1660.011	1656.320	1547.991
Response Profile (n=1/n=0)	202/3873	202/3873	202/3873	59/4016	59/4016	59/4016	197/3658	197/3658	197/3658
N	4,075	4,075	4,075	4,075	4,075	4,075	3,855	3,855	3,855

Note: All independent variables measured at Wave II unless otherwise noted.
Source: The National Longitudinal Study of Adolescent Health.
*p < .05; **p < .01; ***p < .001 (two-tailed tests).

respondents are entering early adulthood. These models help us understand the temporality of suicide suggestion, while also allowing us to establish a clear time order between an adolescent's history of suicidal thoughts (Wave I), the experience of a friend's or family member's suicide attempt (Wave II), and subsequent suicidal behaviors (Wave III).

Overall, models presented in Table 3 demonstrate a significantly different pattern from those presented in Table 2. For boys and girls, the impact of a role model's suicide attempt, whether a family member or a friend, appears to fade with time. By Wave III, we find only one significant relationship between a measure of suicide suggestion and suicidal thoughts. Model 2 in Table 3 indicates a significant bivariate relationship between the experience of a friend's suicide attempt at Wave II and girls' reports of suicidal thoughts at Wave III. This finding, however, does not hold in full models, although the odds ratio is in the expected direction (OR = 1.546) and the p-value is very close to the threshold for statistical significance ($p > .055$) (Model 3 in Table 3). We further investigated the change in statistical significance between the bivariate and saturated models in analyses not presented here (but available from the authors by request). We found that adolescent girls' emotional distress at Wave II explains the impact of a friend's suicide attempt on girls' likelihood of reporting suicidal thoughts at Wave III, net of other key controls. The significant effect of a friend's suicide attempt on girls' likelihood of suicidal thoughts remains until emotional distress is included in the model. This suggests that emotional distress may serve as an important mechanism through which suicide suggestion operates, particularly for girls.

Our models from Wave III suggest that the increased risk of suicide suggestion found over the short run (in Table 2) fades with time. Six years later, we find little evidence that experiencing a role model's suicide attempt, whether friend or family member, has a long-term effect, except perhaps for girls for whom it is mediated by emotional distress.

DISCUSSION

Within the sociology of suicide, social integration and regulation are often emphasized as the primary social forces that protect or put individuals at risk of suicide. These Durkheimian mechanisms are undoubtedly important (Bearman 1991; Pescosolido 1990; Pescosolido and Georgianna 1989; Wray et al. 2011), but much research on the spread of health behaviors implicates social ties as not just mechanisms for social support, but also potential conduits for the spread of suicidal behaviors via suicide suggestion, illuminating another side to social integration. We find that suicide attempts of role models—primarily friends—are in fact associated with adolescents' development of suicidal thoughts and, in some cases, attempts. Effects of suicide suggestion appear to fade with time, girls are more vulnerable to suicide suggestion than boys, and the type of role model—for teenagers at least—matters. Our findings suggest that social relationships, contra Durkheim, are not always protective against suicide, at least not when significant others exhibit suicidal tendencies. This reinforces the idea that the structure—and content—of social networks conditions their role in preventing suicidality. Specifically, social ties can be conduits of not just social support but also antisocial behaviors, like suicidality.

Our study has four primary implications for advancing the sociological understanding of suicide. Our most essential contribution to the literature on suicide suggestion via personal role models is the evidence we provide indicating that being aware of a role model's suicide attempt is associated with the development of suicidal thoughts and sometimes attempts. This relationship is robust to many measures of risk and protective factors. Experiencing the suicide attempt of a significant other may serve as a vehicle for learning a way to deal with distressing life events—by becoming suicidal (Jamison 1999). Future research should continue to probe the question of how suicide suggestion contributes to the development of suicidality. Many potential mechanisms—social learning, imitation, and emotional contagion—may underlay the observed association between role models and those exposed to their suicidality. Qualitative research, in particular, may provide valuable insights into which potential mechanisms promote the spread of suicidality via social ties. Understanding how and when suicide suggestion becomes salient to youths' suicidality would greatly help practitioners prevent suicides. Our study provides a first step toward this larger goal.

In addition to providing insights into suicide suggestion as an important mechanism in the adolescent suicide process, our study has implications for understanding the temporality of suicide suggestion via individuals' role models. Previous research on suicide rates and media exposure found effects of suicide suggestion tend to last two to four weeks (Phillips 1974; Stack 1987). Considering the potential differences in connectedness derived from face-to-face relationships and direct contact versus mediated sources, we hypothesized that personal role models would have a stronger, or longer lasting, effect on adolescents exposed to their behavior. In fact, our findings suggest that having a friend attempt suicide has a longer lasting effect than reading about a suicide in the paper or seeing a fictive suicide on television. We find that effects of a friend's or family member's suicide attempt last at least one year, if not more—considerably longer than the effect of exposure via the media documented in prior research. By six years, however, the effect of a friend's or family member's suicide attempt appears to fade in significance. Among adolescent girls, however, a friend's suicide attempt may continue to shape suicidal thoughts even six years later; notably, this effect is explained by girls' emotional distress levels. Future research should examine this pattern in more detail, as this finding suggests an indirect, but potentially important, long-term impact of suicide suggestion via girls' emotional distress.

Perhaps it is not shocking that we do not find strong evidence that effects of role models' suicide attempts last over the long run. Teens who survive the first year (or so) following a friend's suicide attempt may be, or

become, emotionally resilient. By early adulthood, a role model's suicide attempt in adolescence may no longer be central to one's daily life, a life no longer constrained within the bounds of high school. Research on contagion generally focuses on relatively bounded social spaces—like Native American reservations, mental wards, or high schools—and finds these spaces are at higher risk of geographic-temporal suicide clustering (e.g., Gould et al. 1990). Outside of relatively bounded social environments, do effects of role models' suicides spread via social ties? Investigating the role of exposure to suicides inside and out of bounded social contexts would add more depth to our understanding of how suicides—and potentially other behaviors—become socially contagious.

Our third major contribution to the literature comes from our emphasis on the role of gender in the suicide suggestion process. Given that boys and girls experience peer relationships differently (Crosnoe 2000), understanding how a social mechanism, such as suicide suggestion, differs for boys and girls is crucial to arriving at a full understanding of the development of adolescent suicidality. In fact, we find significant gender differences in the role of suicide suggestion: suggestion appears more salient to girls. Among boys, friends are the only relevant personal role models for triggering the development of suicidal thoughts; girls' suicidal behaviors, on the other hand, are influenced by both family and friends. Moreover, among girls, suicidal thoughts *and attempts* are associated with suicide suggestion. Finally, effects of a friend's or family member's suicide attempt may last longer for girls.

Although we found girls were more vulnerable, absent an observed history of suicidal thoughts, boys were not immune to suicide suggestion. Note that Thompson and Light (2011), who analyzed suicide attempts net of prior suicidal thoughts, found that boys and girls responded similarly to a role model's suicide attempt. This suggests the role of gender may change at different points in the suicidal process and that a predisposition toward suicidality may be particularly important for understanding those differences.

Why would girls be more vulnerable than boys to suicide suggestion? A definitive answer to this question is beyond the scope of this article, but we can suggest some theoretical considerations that may help explain this variation and offer paths for future research. Because girls develop and maintain more intense intimate relationships (Crosnoe 2000), they may be more primed to "take the role of the other" and hence may be more vulnerable to suggestive mechanisms, including developing emotional distress that sustains the original suggestive triggers. For boys, having relationships that are far less emotionally anchored may reduce or mitigate the effects of suggestion, which raises vital questions about which mechanisms are more salient in the development of boys' suicidal thoughts. Future research should continue to examine the complex role gender plays in the adolescent suicide process, as this may help determine different strategies for preventing suicides.

Our fourth and final major contribution to the sociology of suicide stems from our examination of how different role models—friends and family members—vary in terms of their importance in the suicide suggestion process. Our findings indicate that peers may be more meaningful than family to adolescents, for both boys and girls. Social psychology has long shown that behavior is more strongly shaped by members of reference groups central to the formation and maintenance of one's identity (Stryker 1980). To be sure, a teen's family consists of similar individuals whom the teen may identify with, but research on adolescents clearly demonstrates that purposive efforts to differentiate oneself from one's family are accompanied by concomitant identification with peers. This is not to say that a family member's suicidal tendencies are not distressing in adolescence. For example, we find that for adolescent girls, over the short run, a family member's suicide attempt increases their likelihood of reporting suicidal thoughts (but not attempts) one year later. Yet taken as a whole, our findings indicate that friends' suicide attempts are more influential than family members' suicide

attempts in adolescents' lives, at least once adolescents' Wave I suicidality is controlled.

Limitations

Although our findings provide new and important insights into the sociology of suicide, this study is not without its limitations. First, and perhaps most obvious, we are limited to analyzing respondents' suicidal behaviors because we have no information on Add Health respondents who commit suicide. Individuals who report suicidal thoughts or have a history of nonfatal suicide attempts are significantly more likely to commit suicide, but fatal suicide attempts are most common among individuals with no history of nonfatal suicide attempts. Generalizing these findings to the spread of suicide deaths should thus be done with caution. Furthermore, there is attrition in the Add Health sample between waves, and given the higher completion rate among male suicide attempters, more boys than girls may be missing from our analyses due to a completed suicide. Additionally, respondents who actually commit suicide may have been the most likely to be affected by suicide suggestion. Unfortunately, we could find no information from Add Health on whether suicide, or even death, played a significant role in sample attrition. Fortunately, the rarity of suicide among adolescents reduces the risk of this substantially biasing our findings. However, this discussion highlights the significance of finding a way to compare the "lethality" of all types of role models, from the personal to the media-based. Future data collection efforts should note this key gap in the literature.

Our second limitation is related. We chose to focus on friends' and family members' suicide attempts, rather than actual suicides, for practical reasons. Very few respondents reported having a friend or family member complete suicide. This fact may affect our findings on the importance of suicide suggestion. The power of suicide suggestion in the case of a suicide may be greater than the power of suggestion based on a nonfatal suicide attempt. If anything, our findings may thus underrepresent the potential salience of suicide suggestion as a social mechanism in suicidal behaviors.

Finally, although we did our best to account for adolescents' vulnerability to suicide, we are limited by available data. Specifically, we analyzed a sample of adolescents who reported no suicidal thoughts at Wave I in an attempt to parse out effects of selection into friendships from the influence those friendships may have on an individual. Some adolescents with a history of suicidality, perhaps prior to Wave I, may have been included in our sample. Our study provides one of the best efforts to date to isolate selection from the effect of suicide suggestion, but further investigation of these issues is needed before we can be confident that suggestion affects the development of suicidality.

CONCLUSIONS

Sociologists commonly turn to Durkheimian measures of social integration and regulation when searching for sociological explanations for suicide, but our findings indicate that suicides, like other behaviors, can spread through social relationships via suicide suggestion. Friends' and family members' suicide attempts may trigger the development of suicidal behaviors, suggesting that exposure to role models is a powerful way that drastic and deviant behaviors, like suicide, become normalized. Notably, the relationship to the role model conditions the experience of suicide suggestion. Furthermore, adolescent girls appear more susceptible than boys to adopting the suicidal behaviors they observe through social relationships. This study provides important information for the evolution of the sociology of suicide, but our findings also have vital policy implications for public health officials attempting to prevent adolescent suicide. Namely, policies and practitioners need to be sensitive to the importance of suicide attempts (and not simply suicides), particularly among peers and for girls. Additionally, the increased risk of suicidality associated with friends' suicide attempts may last a year or more, which is longer than previously thought.

For adolescents, ties do bind, but whether these ties integrate adolescents into society,

with positive repercussions for their emotional well-being, or whether they promote feelings of alienation, depends in part on the qualities embedded in those ties. On the surface, these findings may appear to contradict Durkheim's sociology, given his focus on solidarity through collective effervescence. Yet, Durkheim argued that solidarity was a product of a shared, collective conscience that spreads through ritualized, emotion-laden interaction. Why should we expect deviant behavior like suicide to be precluded from the types of norms that can spread across actors? Instead, we posit that for a full understanding of how social integration works in individuals' lives to shape their life chances, we must consider not only the social support social ties provide, but also the emotions, behaviors, and values that inhere in those social relations.

Acknowledgments

Seth Abrutyn and Anna Mueller contributed equally to this work. This article is a revision of a paper presented at the 2012 annual meetings of the American Sociological Association. The authors would like to thank Marty Levin, Chandra Muller, Ken Frank, Sarah Blanchard, and six anonymous reviewers for their insightful comments and suggestions. The authors acknowledge the helpful research assistance of Cynthia Stockton.

Data and Funding

This research uses data from Add Health (http://www .cpc.unc.edu/addhealth), a program project directed by Kathleen Mullan Harris and designed by J. Richard Udry, Peter S. Bearman, and Kathleen Mullan Harris at the University of North Carolina at Chapel Hill, and funded by grant P01-HD31921 from the Eunice Kennedy Shriver National Institute of Child Health and Human Development, with cooperative funding from 23 other federal agencies and foundations. Special acknowledgment is due Ronald R. Rindfuss and Barbara Entwisle for assistance in the original design. No direct support was received from grant P01-HD31921 for this analysis. Opinions reflect those of the authors and do not necessarily reflect those of the granting agencies.

Notes

1. We are particularly grateful to an anonymous reviewer for suggesting this formulation.
2. The SAS programs used to recode and analyze all data are available from the authors by request.
3. Tables presenting odds ratios and confidence intervals are available from the authors by request.

References

An, Anthony. 2002. "Performing Logistic Regression on Survey Data with the New SURVEYLOGISTIC Procedure." Paper 258-27, pp. 1–9. Proceedings of the 27th Annual SAS Users Group International Conference (SUGI 27), Orlando, FL, April 14–17.

Baca-Garcia, Enrique, M. Mercedes Perez-Rodriguez, J. John Mann, and Maria A. Oquendo. 2008. "Suicidal Behavior in Young Women." *Psychiatric Clinics of North America* 31:317–31.

Baller, Robert D. and Kelly K. Richardson. 2002. "Social Integration, Imitation, and the Geographic Patterning of Suicide." *American Sociological Review* 67:873–88.

Baller, Robert D. and Kelly K. Richardson. 2009. "The 'Dark Side' of the Strength of Weak Ties: The Diffusion of Suicidal Thoughts." *Journal of Health and Social Behavior* 50:261–76.

Bearman, Peter S. 1991. "The Social Structure of Suicide." *Sociological Forum* 6:501–524.

Bearman, Peter S. and James Moody. 2004. "Suicide and Friendships among American Adolescents." *American Journal of Public Health* 94:89–95.

Bell, Bethany A., Anthony J. Onwuegbuzie, John M. Ferron, Qun G. Jiao, Susan T. Hibbard, and Jeffrey D. Kromrey. 2012. "Use of Design Effects and Sample Weights in Complex Health Survey Data: A Review of Published Articles Using Data From 3 Commonly Used Adolescent Health Surveys." *American Journal of Public Health* 102:1399–1405.

Bjarnason, Thoroddur. 1994. "The Influence of Social Support, Suggestion and Depression on Suicidal Behavior among Icelandic Youth." *Acta Sociologica* 37:195–206.

Bjarnason, Thoroddur and Thorolfur Thorlindsson. 1994. "Manifest Predictors of Past Suicide Attempts in a Population of Icelandic Adolescents." *Suicide and Life Threatening Behavior* 24:350–58.

Brent, David A., Mary M. Kerr, Charles Goldstein, James Bozigar, Marty Wartella, and Marjorie J. Allan. 1989. "An Outbreak of Suicide and Suicidal Behavior in a High School." *American Academy of Child and Adolescent Psychiatry* 28:918–24.

Bridge, Jeffrey A., Tina R. Goldstein, and David A. Brent. 2006. "Adolescent Suicide and Suicidal Behavior." *Journal of Child Psychology and Psychiatry* 47:372–94.

Cairns, Robert B., Beverly D. Cairns, Holly J. Neckerman, Scott D. Gest, and Jean-Louis Gariepy. 1988. "Social Networks and Aggressive Behavior: Peer Support or Peer Rejection?" *Developmental Psychology* 61:157–68.

Crosnoe, Robert. 2000. "Friendships in Childhood and Adolescence: The Life Course and New Directions." *Social Psychology Quarterly* 63:377–91.

Crosnoe, Robert, Kenneth Frank, and Anna Strassmann Mueller. 2008. "Gender, Body Size, and Social Relations in American High Schools." *Social Forces* 86:1189–1216.

Crosnoe, Robert and Monica Kirkpatrick Johnson. 2011. "Research on Adolescence in the Twenty-First Century." *Annual Review of Sociology* 37:479–60.

Durkheim, Emile. [1897]1951. *Suicide: A Study in Sociology*. Glencoe, IL: Free Press.

Evans, Emma, Keith Hawton, and Karen Rodham. 2004. "Factors Associated with Suicidal Phenomena in Adolescents: A Systematic Review of Population-Based Studies." *Clinical Psychology Review* 24:957–79.

Frank, Kenneth, Chandra Muller, Catherine Riegle-Crumb, Anna Strassmann Mueller, and Jennifer Pearson. 2008. "The Social Dynamics of Mathematics Coursetaking in High Schools." *American Journal of Sociology* 113:1645–96.

Gilligan, Carol. 1982. *In A Different Voice: Psychological Theory and Women's Development*. Cambridge, MA: Harvard Press.

Giordano, Peggy C. 2003. "Relationships in Adolescence." *Annual Review of Sociology* 29:252–81.

Goffman, Erving. 1959. *The Presentation of Self in Everyday Life*. New York: Anchor Books.

Gould, Madelyn S. 2001. "Suicide and the Media." Pp. 200–224 in *Suicide Prevention: Clinical and Scientific Aspects,* edited by H. Hendin and J. J. Mann. New York: New York Academy of Science.

Gould, Madelyn S., Sylvan Wallenstein, and Marjorie Kleinman. 1990. "Time-Space Clustering of Teenage Suicide." *American Journal of Epidemiology* 131:71–78.

Harris, Kathleen M., C. T. Halpern, E. Whitsel, J. Hussey, J. Tabor, P. Entzel, and J. Richard Udry. 2009. "The National Longitudinal Study of Adolescent Health: Research Design." (http://www.cpc.unc.edu/projects/addhealth/design).

Haynie, Dana L. 2001. "Delinquent Peers Revisited: Does Network Structure Matter?" *American Journal of Sociology* 106:1013–57.

Jamison, Kay Redfield. 1999. *Night Falls Fast: Understanding Suicide*. New York: Vintage Books.

Joyner, Kara and Grace Kao. 2000. "School Racial Composition and Adolescent Racial Homophily." *Social Science Quarterly* 81:810–25.

Lawler, Edward J. 2006. "The Affect Theory of Social Exchange." Pp. 248–67 in *Contemporary Social Psychological Theories,* edited by P. J. Burke. Stanford, CA: Stanford University Press.

Liu, Ruth X. 2006. "Vulnerability to Friends' Suicide Influence: The Moderating Effects of Gender and Adolescent Depression." *Journal of Youth and Adolescence* 35:479–89.

Maccoby, Eleanor E. 2002. "Gender and Group Process: A Developmental Perspective." *Current Directions in Psychological Science* 11:54–58.

Maimon, David and Danielle C. Kuhl. 2008. "Social Control and Youth Suicidality: Situating Durkheim's Ideas in a Multilevel Framework." *American Sociological Review* 73:921–43.

Mueller, Anna S., Jennifer Person, Chandra Muller, Kenneth Frank, and Alan Turner. 2010. "Sizing Up Peers:

Adolescent Girls' Weight Control and Social Comparison in the School Context." *Journal of Health and Social Behavior* 51:64–78.

National Institute of Mental Health (NIMH). 2003. *In Harm's Way: Suicide in America.* U.S. Department of Mental and Human Services. NIH Publication no. 03-4594.

Niederkrotenthaler, Thomas, Brigitta Roderus, Kristina Alexanderson, Finn Rasmussen, and Ellenor Mittendorfer-Rutz. 2012. "Exposure to Parental Mortality and Markers of Morbidity, and the Risks of Attempted and Completed Suicide in Offspring: An Analysis of Sensitive Life Periods." *Journal of Epidemiology and Community Health* 66:232–39.

Niederkrotenthaler, Thomas and Gernot Sonneck. 2007. "Assessing the Impact of Media Guidelines for Reporting Suicides in Austria: Interrupted Time Series Analysis." *Australian and New Zealand Journal of Psychiatry* 41:419–28.

Pearson, Jennifer, Chandra Muller, and Lindsey Wilkinson. 2007. "Adolescent Same-Sex Attraction and Academic Outcomes: The Role of School Attachment and Engagement." *Social Problems* 54:523–42.

Pescosolido, Bernice A. 1990. "The Social Context of Religious Integration and Suicide: Pursuing Network Explanation." *Sociological Quarterly* 31:337–57.

Pescosolido, Bernice and Sharon Georgianna. 1989. "Durkheim, Suicide, and Religion: Toward a Network Theory of Suicide." *American Sociological Review* 54:33–48.

Phillips, David P. 1974. "The Influence of Suggestion on Suicide: Substantive and Theoretical Implications of the Werther Effect." *American Sociological Review* 39:340–54.

Schaefer, David R., Olga Kornienko, and Andrew M. Fox. 2011. "Misery Does Not Love Company: Network Selection Mechanisms and Depression Homophily." *American Sociological Review* 76:764–85.

Schmidtke, Armin and H. Hafner. 1988. "The Werther Effect after Television Films: New Evidence for an Old Hypothesis." *Psychological Medicine* 18:665–76.

Shadish, William R., Donald T. Campbell, and Thomas D. Cook. 2002. *Experimental and Quasi-Experimental Designs for Generalized Causal Inference.* New York: Houghton Mifflin.

Stack, Steven. 1987. "Celebrities and Suicide: A Taxonomy and Analysis, 1948–1983." *American Sociological Review* 52:401–412.

Stack, Steven. 2003. "Media Coverage as a Risk Factor in Suicide." *Journal of Epidemiology and Community Health* 57:238–40.

Stack, Steven. 2005. "Suicide in the Media: A Quantitative Review of Studies Based on Nonfictional

Stories." *Suicide and Life Threatening Behavior* 35:121–33.

Stack, Steven. 2009. "Copycat Effects on Fictional Suicide: A Meta-Analysis." Pp. 231–44 in *Suicide and the Creative Arts,* edited by S. Stack and D. Lester. New York: Nova Science Publishers.

Stryker, Sheldon. 1980. *Symbolic Interactionism: A Social Structural Version.* Menlo Park, CA: The Benjamin Cummings Publishing Company.

Suicide Prevention Resource Center (SPRC). 2013. *Reporting on Suicide: Recommendations for the Media.* Washington, DC: Suicide Prevention Resource Center. Retrieved April 24, 2013 (http://www.sprc.org/sites/sprc.org/files/library/sreporting.pdf).

Thompson, Martie P. and Laney S. Light. 2011. "Examining Gender Differences in Risk Factors for Suicide Attempts Made 1 and 7 Years Later in a Nationally Representative Sample." *Journal of Adolescent Health* 48:391–97.

Thorlindsson, Thorolfur and Thoroddur Bjarnason. 1998. "Modeling Durkheim on the Micro Level: A Study of Youth Suicidality." *American Sociological Review* 63:94–110.

Turner, Jonathan H. 2010. *Theoretical Principles of Sociology.* Vol. 2, *Microdynamics.* New York: Springer.

Wray, Mary, Cynthia Colen, and Bernice Pescosolido. 2011. "The Sociology of Suicide." *Annual Review of Sociology* 37:505–528.

Seth Abrutyn is Assistant Professor of Sociology at the University of Memphis. As a general sociological theorist, he has long been interested in macrosociology and institutions, which has culminated in a recently published book, *Revisiting Institutionalism in Sociology.* Recently, his research interests have moved toward the sociology of suicide, including examining the processes by which suicides can spread as well as how these processes relate to and expand Durkheim's classic thesis.

Anna S. Mueller is Assistant Professor of Sociology at the University of Memphis. Her research examines how peers shape adolescent health and well-being over the transition to adulthood, with a focus on weight-control behaviors, body weight, and suicide. Her research emphasizes why and how behaviors and values spread between individuals generally using insights from social psychology. She recently published a study, with Kenneth A. Frank and Chandra Muller (*American Journal of Sociology* 2013), that investigates how schools shape adolescent friendship formation in ways that have implications for adolescent status hierarchies.

Glossary

Adaptive research design: A research design that develops as the research progresses.

Anomalous findings: Unexpected patterns in data.

Anonymity: Provided by research in which no identifying information is recorded that could be used to link respondents to their responses.

Association: A criterion for establishing a causal relationship between two variables: Variation in one variable is related to variation in another variable.

Authenticity: When the understanding of a social process or social setting is one that reflects fairly the various perspectives of participants in that setting.

Availability sampling: Sampling in which elements are selected on the basis of convenience.

Back matter: The section of an applied research report that may include appendixes, tables, and the research instrument(s).

Bar chart: A graphic for qualitative variables, in which the variable's distribution is displayed with solid bars separated by spaces.

Base number (*N*): The total number of cases in a distribution.

Before-and-after design: A quasi-experimental design consisting of a before-after comparison involving the same variables but no comparison group.

Belmont Report: Guidelines developed by the U.S. National Commission for the Protection of Human Subjects of Biomedical and Behavioral Research in 1979 for the protection of human subjects.

Beneficence: According to the *Belmont Report,* the ethical requirement of minimizing possible harms and maximizing benefits in research involving human subjects.

Big Data: Massive data sets reflecting human activity that are accessible in computer-readable form, available to social scientists, and manageable with today's computers.

Bimodal: A distribution that has two nonadjacent categories with about the same number of cases, and these categories have more cases than any others.

Bipolar response options: Response choices to a survey question that include a middle category and parallel responses with positive and negative valence (can be labeled or unlabeled).

Case study: A setting or group that the analyst treats as an integrated social unit that must be studied holistically and in its particularity.

Case-oriented research: Research that focuses attention on the nation or other unit as a whole.

Case-oriented understanding: An understanding of social processes in a group, formal organization, community, or other collectivity that reflects accurately the standpoint of participants.

Causal effect: When variation in one phenomenon, an independent variable, leads to or results, on average, in variation in another phenomenon, the dependent variable.

Causal explanation: An explanation that identifies common influences on a number of cases or events.

Census: Research in which information is obtained through responses from or information about all available members of an entire population.

Central tendency: The most common value (for variables measured at the nominal level) or the value around which cases tend to center (for a quantitative variable).

Certificate of Confidentiality: A certificate issued to a researcher by the National Institutes of Health that ensures the right to protect information obtained about high-risk populations or behaviors—except child abuse or neglect—from legal subpoenas.

Ceteris paribus: Latin phrase meaning "other things being equal."

Chi-square: An inferential statistic used to test hypotheses about relationships between two or more variables in a cross-tabulation.

Closed-ended (fixed-choice) question: A survey question that provides preformatted response choices for the respondent to circle or check.

Cluster: A naturally occurring, mixed aggregate of elements of the population.

Cluster sampling: Sampling in which elements are selected in two or more stages, with the first stage being the random selection of naturally occurring clusters and the last stage being the random selection of elements within clusters.

Code of Ethics: Professional codes adopted by professional associations of social scientists for the treatment of human subjects by members, employees, and students and designed to comply with federal policy.

Cognitive interview: A technique for evaluating questions in which researchers ask people test questions and then probe with follow-up questions to learn how they understood the question and what their answers mean.

Cohort: Individuals or groups with a common starting point. Examples include a college's class of 1997, people who graduated from high school in the 1980s, General Motors employees who started work between the years 1990 and 2000, and people who were born in the late 1940s or the 1950s (the baby boom generation).

Complete (or covert) participant: A role in field research in which the researcher does not reveal his or her identity as a researcher to those who are observed while participating.

Complete (or overt) observer: A role in participant observation in which the researcher does not participate in group activities and is publicly defined as a researcher.

Computer-assisted personal interview (CAPI): A personal interview in which a laptop computer is used to display interview questions and to process responses that the interviewer types in, as well as to check that these responses fall within allowed ranges.

Computer-assisted qualitative data analysis: The use of special computer software to assist qualitative analyses through creating, applying, and refining categories; tracing linkages between concepts; and making comparisons between cases and events.

Computer-assisted telephone interview (CATI): A phone interview in which a questionnaire is programmed into a computer, along with relevant skip patterns, and only valid entries are allowed; incorporates the tasks of interviewing, data entry, and checking data for invalid responses.

Concept: A mental image that summarizes a set of similar observations, feelings, or ideas.

Conceptualization: The process of specifying what we mean by a term. Conceptualization helps translate portions of an abstract theory into specific variables that can be used in testable hypotheses.

Concurrent validity: The type of validity that exists when scores on a measure are closely related to scores on a criterion measured at the same time.

Confidentiality: Provided by research in which identifying information that could be used to link respondents to their responses is available only to designated research personnel for specific research needs.

Conflict of interest: When a researcher has a significant financial stake in the design or outcome of his or her own research.

Conjunctural research: Research that considers the complex combinations in which causal influences operate.

Constant: A number that has a fixed value in a given situation; a characteristic or value that does not change.

Construct validity: The type of validity that is established by showing that a measure is related to other measures as specified in a theory.

Constructivism: Methodology based on questioning belief in an external reality; emphasizes the importance of exploring the way in which different stakeholders in a social setting construct their beliefs.

Contamination: A source of causal invalidity that occurs when either the experimental or the comparison group is aware of the other group and is influenced in the posttest as a result.

Content analysis: A research method for systematically analyzing and making inferences from recorded human communication, including books, articles, poems, constitutions, speeches, and songs.

Content validity: The type of validity that exists when the full range of a concept's meaning is covered by the measure.

Context: A set of interrelated circumstances that alters a relationship between other variables or social processes.

Context effects: Effects that occur when one or more survey questions influence how subsequent questions are interpreted.

Contingent question: A question that is asked of only a subset of survey respondents.

Continuous measure: A measure with numbers indicating the values of variables as points on a continuum.

Conversation analysis: A qualitative method that analyzes the sequence and details of conversational text in order to understand how social reality is constructed.

Correlation coefficient: A summary statistic that varies from 0 to 1 or −1, with 0 indicating the absence of a linear relationship between two quantitative variables and 1 or −1 indicating that the relationship is completely described by the line representing the regression of the dependent variable on the independent variable.

Correlational analysis: A statistical technique that summarizes the strength of a relationship between two quantitative variables in terms of its adherence to a linear pattern.

Cost-benefit analysis: A type of evaluation research that compares program costs with the economic value of program benefits.

Cover letter: The letter sent with a mailed questionnaire that explains the survey's purpose and auspices and encourages the respondent to participate.

Covert observer: A role in participant observation in which the researcher does not participate in group activities and is not publicly defined as a researcher.

Criterion validity: The type of validity that is established by comparing the scores obtained on the measure being validated with those obtained with a more direct or already validated measure of the same phenomenon (the criterion).

Cross-population generalizability (external validity): When findings about one group, population, or setting hold true for other groups, populations, or settings.

Cross-sectional research design: A study in which data are collected at only one point in time.

Cross-tabulation (crosstab) or contingency table: In the simplest case, a bivariate (two-variable) distribution, showing the distribution of one variable for each category of another variable; can be elaborated using three or more variables.

Debriefing: A researcher's informing subjects after an experiment about the experiment's purposes and methods and evaluating subjects' personal reactions to the experiment.

Deception: Used in social experiments to create more "realistic" treatments in which the true purpose of the research is not disclosed to participants, often within the confines of a laboratory.

Deductive research: The type of research in which a specific expectation is deduced from a general premise and is then tested.

Dependent variable: A variable that is hypothesized to vary depending on, or under the influence of, another variable.

Descriptive research: Research in which social phenomena are defined and described.

Descriptive statistics: Statistics used to describe the distribution of and relationship between variables.

Dichotomy: A variable having only two values.

Differential attrition (mortality): A problem that occurs in experiments when comparison groups become different because subjects are more likely to drop out of one of the groups for various reasons.

Direction of association: A pattern in a relationship between two variables—the values of variables tend to change consistently in relation to change on the other variable; the direction of association can be either positive or negative.

Discrete measure: A measure that classifies cases in distinct categories.

Disproportionate stratified sampling: Sampling in which elements are selected from strata in different proportions from those that appear in the population.

Double negative: A question or statement that contains two negatives, which can muddy the meaning of the question.

Double-barreled question: A single survey question that actually asks two questions but allows only one answer.

Double-blind procedure: An experimental method in which neither the subjects nor the staff delivering experimental treatments know which subjects are getting the treatment and which are receiving a placebo.

Ecological fallacy: An error in reasoning in which incorrect conclusions about individual-level processes are drawn from group-level data.

Elements: The individual members of the population whose characteristics are to be measured.

Embedded mixed-methods design: Qualitative and quantitative methods are used concurrently in the research, but one is given priority.

Empirical generalization: A statement that describes patterns found in data.

Ethnography: The study of a culture or cultures that some group of people shares, using participant observation over an extended period.

Ethnomethodology: A qualitative research method focused on the way that participants in a social setting create and sustain a sense of reality.

Evaluation research: Research that describes or identifies the impact of social policies and programs.

Event-based design (cohort study): A type of longitudinal study in which data are collected at two or more points in time from individuals in a cohort.

Ex post facto control group design: A nonexperimental design in which comparison groups are selected after the treatment, program, or other variation in the independent variable has occurred, but when the participants were able to choose the group in which they participated. Often confused with a quasi-experimental design.

Exhaustive: A question's response choices are exhaustive when they cover all possible responses.

Expectancies of experimental staff: A source of treatment misidentification in experiments and quasi-experiments that occurs when change among experimental subjects results from the positive expectancies of the staff who are delivering the treatment rather than from the treatment itself; also called a *self-fulfilling prophecy.*

Explanatory research: Seeks to identify causes and effects of social phenomena and to predict how one phenomenon will change or vary in response to variation in some other phenomenon.

Exploratory research: Seeks to find out how people get along in the setting under question, what meanings they give to their actions, and what issues concern them.

External validity (cross-population generalizability): When findings about one group, population, or setting hold true for other groups, populations, or settings.

Extraneous variable: A variable that influences both the independent and the dependent variables, creating a spurious association between them that disappears when the extraneous variable is controlled.

Face validity: The type of validity that exists when an inspection of items used to measure a concept suggests that they are appropriate "on their face."

Factorial survey (or survey experiment): A survey in which randomly selected subsets of respondents are asked different questions, or are asked to respond to different vignettes, to determine the causal effect of the variables represented by these differences.

Federal Policy for the Protection of Human Subjects: Specific regulations adopted in 1991 by the U.S. Department of Health and Human Services and the Food and Drug Administration that were based on the principles of the *Belmont Report.*

Feedback: Information about service delivery system outputs, outcomes, or operations that can guide program input.

Fence-sitters: Survey respondents who see themselves as being neutral on an issue and choose a middle (neutral) response that is offered.

Field experiment: A study using an experimental design that is conducted in a real-world setting.

Field notes: Notes that describe what has been observed, heard, or otherwise experienced in a participant observation study. These notes usually are written after the observational session.

Field research: Research in which natural social processes are studied as they happen and left relatively undisturbed.

Field researcher: A researcher who uses qualitative methods to conduct research in the field.

Filter question: A survey question used to identify a subset of respondents who then are asked other questions.

Fixed-sample panel design (panel study): A type of longitudinal study in which data are collected from the same individuals—the panel—at two or more points in time. In another type of panel design, panel members who leave are replaced with new members.

Floaters: Survey respondents who provide an opinion on a topic in response to a closed-ended question that does not include a "don't know" option, but who will choose "don't know" if it is available.

Focus groups: A qualitative method that involves unstructured group interviews in which the focus group leader actively encourages discussion among participants about the topics of interest.

Forced-choice questions: Closed-ended survey questions that do not include "don't know" as an explicit response choice.

Formative evaluation: Process evaluation that is used to shape and refine program operations.

Frequency distribution: Numerical display showing the number of cases, and usually the percentage of cases (the relative frequencies), corresponding to each value or group of values of a variable.

Frequency polygon: A graphic for quantitative variables, in which a continuous line connects data points representing the variable's distribution.

Front matter: The section of an applied research report that includes an executive summary, an abstract, and a table of contents.

Gatekeeper: A person in a field setting who can grant researchers access to the setting.

Generalizability: When a conclusion holds true for the population, group, setting, or event that we say it does, given the conditions that we specify.

Grand tour question: A broad question at the start of an interview that seeks to engage the respondent in the topic of interest.

Grounded theory: Systematic theory developed inductively, based on observations that are summarized into conceptual categories, reevaluated in the research setting, and gradually refined and linked to other conceptual categories.

Group-administered survey: A survey completed by individual respondents who are assembled in a group.

Hawthorne effect: A type of contamination in research designs that occurs when members of the treatment group change relative to the dependent variable because their participation in the study makes them feel special.

Health Insurance Portability and Accountability Act (HIPAA): A congressional act passed in 1996 that creates stringent regulations for the protection of health care data.

Histogram: A graphic for quantitative variables, in which the variable's distribution is displayed with adjacent bars.

History effect: A source of causal invalidity that occurs when events external to the study influence posttest scores; also called an effect of external events.

Holistic research: Research concerned with the context in which events occurred and the interrelations between different events and processes.

Hypothesis: A tentative statement about empirical reality, involving a relationship between two or more variables.

ICPSR (Inter-university Consortium for Political and Social Research): Academic consortium that archives data sets online from major surveys and other social research and makes them available for analysis by others.

Idiosyncratic variation: Variation in responses to questions that is caused by individuals' reactions to particular words or ideas in the question instead of by variation in the concept that the question is intended to measure.

Illogical reasoning: Jumping to conclusions or arguing on the basis of invalid assumptions.

Impact evaluation (or analysis): Analysis of the extent to which a treatment or other service has an effect; also known as **summative evaluation.**

Inaccurate observation: An observation based on faulty perceptions of empirical reality.

Independent variable: A variable that is hypothesized to cause, or lead to, variation in another variable.

Index: The sum or average of responses to a set of questions about a concept.

Indicator: The question or other operation used to indicate the value of cases on a variable.

Inductive research: The type of research in which general conclusions are drawn from specific data.

Inferential statistics: A mathematical tool for estimating how likely it is that a statistical result based on data from a random sample is representative of the population from which the sample is assumed to have been selected.

In-person survey: A survey in which an interviewer questions respondents face-to-face and records their answers.

Inputs: The resources, raw materials, clients, and staff that go into a program.

Institutional ethnography: A commitment to understand, through the social experiences of participants in a setting, the way in which their social world is shaped by larger societal forces.

Institutional review board (IRB): A group of organizational and community representatives required by federal law to review the ethical issues in all proposed research that is federally funded, involves human subjects, or has any potential for harm to human subjects.

Integrated mixed-methods design: Qualitative and quantitative methods are used concurrently, and both are given equal importance.

Intensive (in-depth) interviewing: A qualitative method that involves open-ended, relatively unstructured questioning in which the interviewer seeks in-depth information about the interviewee's feelings, experiences, and perceptions.

Interactive voice response (IVR): A survey in which respondents receive automated calls and answer questions by pressing numbers on their touch-tone phones or speaking numbers that are interpreted by computerized voice recognition software.

Interitem reliability: An approach that calculates reliability based on the correlation among multiple items used to measure a single concept; also known as internal consistency.

Internal validity (causal validity): When a conclusion that A leads to or results in B is correct.

Interobserver reliability: When similar measurements are obtained by different observers rating the same persons, events, or places.

Interpretive questions: Questions included in a questionnaire or interview schedule to help explain answers to other important questions.

Interquartile range: The range in a distribution between the end of the first quartile and the beginning of the third quartile.

Interval/ratio level of measurement: A measurement of a variable in which the numbers indicating a variable's values represent fixed measurement units. They may or may not have an absolute, or fixed, zero point.

Interview schedule: The survey instrument containing the questions asked by the interviewer in an in-person or phone survey.

Jottings: Brief notes written in the field about highlights of an observation period.

Justice: According to the *Belmont Report,* the ethical principle of distributing benefits and risks of research fairly in research involving human subjects.

Key informant: An insider who is willing and able to provide a field researcher with superior access and information, including answers to questions that arise in the course of the research.

Labeled unipolar response options: Response choices for a survey question that use words to identify categories ranging from low to high (or vice versa).

Labeling theory: Labels applied to people can result in behaviors and attitudes consistent with the label, with a particular focus on how labeling a person or group of people as deviant can result in their engaging in deviant behavior.

Level of measurement: The mathematical precision with which the values of a variable can be expressed. The nominal level of measurement, which is qualitative, has no mathematical interpretation; the ordinal level of measurement is less precise mathematically than the interval/ratio level.

Likert item: A statement followed by response choices ranging from "strongly agree" to "strongly disagree."

Longitudinal research design: A study in which data are collected that can be ordered in time; also defined as research in which data are collected at two or more points in time.

Mailed survey: A survey involving a mailed questionnaire to be completed by the respondent.

Marginal distribution: The summary distributions in the margins of a cross-tabulation that correspond to the frequency distribution of the row variable and of the column variable.

Matrix questions: A series of questions that concern a common theme and that have the same response choices.

Mean: The arithmetic, or weighted, average, computed by adding the value of all the cases and dividing by the total number of cases.

Measurement: The process of linking abstract concepts to empirical indicants. Also, the procedures used to identify the empirical variation in a concept of interest.

Measurement validity: When a measure measures what we think it measures.

Mechanism: A discernible process that creates a causal connection between two variables.

Median: The position average, or the point that divides a distribution in half (the 50th percentile).

Mediator: A variable involved in a causal mechanism (intervening variable).

Milgram's obedience experiments: Experiments begun in 1960 at Yale University by psychologist Stanley Milgram to determine the likelihood of people following orders from an authority despite their own sentiments; widely cited as helping to understand the emergence of phenomena such as Nazism and mass cults.

Mixed methods: Research that combines qualitative and quantitative methods in an investigation of the same or related research question(s).

Mixed-mode survey: A survey conducted by more than one method, allowing the strengths of one survey design to compensate for the weaknesses of another and maximizing the likelihood of securing data from different types of respondents; for example, nonrespondents in a mailed survey may be interviewed in person or over the phone.

Mode: The most frequent value in a distribution; also termed the **probability average.**

Moderator: A variable that identifies a context for the effect of other variables.

Mutually exclusive: A question's response choices are mutually exclusive when every case can be classified as having only one attribute (or value).

Narrative analysis: A form of qualitative analysis in which the analyst focuses on how respondents impose order on the flow of experience in their lives and thus make sense of events and actions in which they have participated.

Narrative explanation: A causal explanation that involves developing a narrative of events and processes that indicate a chain of causes and effects.

Needs assessment: A type of evaluation research that attempts to determine the needs of some population that might be met with a social program.

Netnography: The use of ethnographic methods to study online communities; also termed *cyberethnography* and *virtual ethnography.*

Ngrams: Frequency graphs produced by Google's database of all words printed in more than one quarter of the world's books over time (with coverage still expanding).

Nominal level of measurement: Variables whose values have no mathematical interpretation; they vary in kind or quality, but not in amount.

Nonequivalent control group design: A quasi-experimental research design in which experimental and comparison groups are designated before the treatment occurs but are not created by random assignment.

Nonprobability sampling method: A sampling method in which the probability of selection of population elements is unknown.

Nonrespondents: People or other entities who do not participate in a study although they are selected for the sample.

Nonspuriousness: A criterion for establishing a causal relation between two variables; when a relationship between two variables is not caused by variation in a third variable.

Normal distribution: A symmetric, bell-shaped distribution that results from chance variation around a central value.

Nuremberg War Crime Trials: The International Military Tribunal held by the victorious Allies after World War II in Nuremberg, Germany, that exposed the horrific medical experiments conducted by Nazi doctors and others in the name of "science."

Office for Protection From Research Risks, National Institutes of Health: The office in the U.S. Department of Health and Human Services (DHHS) that provides leadership and supervision about the protection of the rights, welfare, and well-being of subjects involved in research conducted or supported by DHHS, including monitoring IRBs.

Omnibus survey: A survey that covers a range of topics of interest to different social scientists.

Open-ended question: A survey question to which the respondent replies in his or her own words, either by writing or by talking.

Operationalization: The process of specifying the measures that will indicate the value of cases on a variable.

Ordinal level of measurement: A measurement of a variable in which the numbers indicating a variable's values specify only the order of the cases, permitting *greater than* and *less than* distinctions.

Outcomes: The impact of the program process on the cases processed.

Outlier: An exceptionally high or low value in a distribution.

Outputs: The services delivered or new products produced by the program process.

Overgeneralization: Concluding unjustifiably that what is true for some cases is true for all cases.

Participant observation: A qualitative method for gathering data that involves developing a sustained relationship with people while they go about their normal activities.

Participant observer (overt participant): A researcher who gathers data through participating and observing in a setting where he or she develops a sustained relationship with people while they go about their normal activities. The term *participant observer* is also used more broadly to refer to a continuum of possible roles, from *complete observer* to *complete participant*.

Participatory action research (PAR): A type of research in which the researcher involves members of the population to be studied as active participants throughout the research process, from the selection of a research focus to the reporting of research results and efforts to make changes based on the research; also termed *community-based participatory research*.

Part-whole question effects: Effects that occur when responses to a general or summary survey

question about a topic are influenced by responses to an earlier, more specific question about that topic.

Percentage: Relative frequency, computed by dividing the frequency of cases in a particular category by the total number of cases and then multiplying by 100.

Periodicity: A sequence of elements (in a list to be sampled) that varies in some regular, periodic pattern.

Phone survey: A survey in which interviewers question respondents over the phone and then record their answers.

Photo voice: A method in which research participants take pictures of their everyday surroundings with cameras the researcher distributes, and then meet in a group with the researcher to discuss the pictures' meaning.

Placebo: A fake "treatment" given to a comparison group to make sure their experience is no different from that of the experimental group except for the actual treatment.

Plagiarism: Presenting as one's own the ideas or words of another person or persons for academic evaluation without proper acknowledgment.

Population: The entire set of individuals or other entities to which study findings are to be generalized.

Population parameter: The value of a statistic, such as a mean, computed using the data for the entire population; a sample statistic is an estimate of a population parameter.

Positivism: The belief, shared by most scientists, that there is a reality that exists quite apart from our own perception of it, that it can be understood through observation, and that it follows general laws.

Posttest: In experimental research, the measurement of an outcome (dependent) variable after an experimental intervention or after a presumed independent variable has changed for some other reason.

Predictive validity: The type of validity that exists when a measure predicts scores on a criterion measured in the future.

Pretest: In experimental research, the measurement of an outcome (dependent) variable before an experimental intervention or change in a presumed independent variable for some other reason. The pretest is exactly the same "test" as the posttest, but it is administered at a different time.

Probability average: See *mode*.

Probability of selection: The likelihood that an element will be selected from the population for inclusion in the sample. In a census of all elements of a population, the probability that any particular element will be selected is 1.0. If half the elements in the population are sampled on the basis of chance (say, by tossing a coin), the probability of selection for each element is one half, or .5. As the size of the sample as a proportion of the population decreases, so does the probability of selection.

Probability sampling method: A sampling method that relies on a random, or chance, selection method so that the probability of selection of population elements is known.

Process consent: An interpretation of the ethical standard of voluntary consent that allows participants to change their decision about participating at any point by requiring that the researcher check with participants at each stage of the project about their willingness to continue in the project.

Process evaluation: Evaluation research that investigates the process of service delivery.

Program process: The complete treatment or service delivered by the program.

Proportionate stratified sampling: Sampling method in which elements are selected from strata in exact proportion to their representation in the population.

Purposive sampling: A nonprobability sampling method in which elements are selected for a purpose, usually because of their unique position.

Qualitative methods: Methods such as participant observation, intensive interviewing, and focus groups that are designed to capture social life as participants experience it rather than in categories predetermined by the researcher. These methods rely on written or spoken words or observations that do not often have a direct numerical interpretation and typically involve exploratory research questions, an orientation to social context and human subjectivity, and the meanings attached by participants to events and to their lives.

Quantitative methods: Methods such as surveys and experiments that record variation in terms of amounts. Data that are treated as quantitative are either numbers or attributes that can be ordered by magnitude.

Quartiles: The points in a distribution corresponding to the first 25% of the cases, the first 50% of the cases, and the first 75% of the cases.

Quasi-experimental design: A research design in which there is a comparison group that is very similar to the experimental group in critical ways, but subjects are not randomly assigned to the comparison and experimental groups.

Questionnaire: The survey instrument containing the questions in a self-administered survey.

Quota sampling: A nonprobability sampling method in which elements are selected to ensure that the sample represents certain characteristics in proportion to their prevalence in the population.

Random assignment: A procedure by which each experimental subject is placed in a group randomly.

Random digit dialing: The random dialing of numbers within designated phone prefixes by a machine, which creates a random sample for phone surveys.

Random number table: A table containing lists of numbers that are ordered solely on the basis of chance; it is used for drawing a random sample.

Random sampling: Sampling that relies on a random, or chance, selection method so that every element of the sampling frame has a known probability of being selected.

Random sampling error (chance sampling error): Differences between the population and the sample that are due only to chance factors (random error), not to systematic sampling error. Random sampling error may or may not result in an unrepresentative sample. The magnitude of sampling error resulting from chance factors can be estimated statistically.

Randomization: The random assignment of cases, as by the toss of a coin.

Randomized comparative change design: The classic true experimental design in which subjects are assigned randomly to two groups; both groups receive a pretest, then one group receives the experimental intervention, and then both groups receive a posttest. Also known as a *pretest-posttest control group design.*

Randomized comparative posttest design: A true experimental design in which subjects are assigned randomly to two groups—one group receives the experimental intervention and both groups receive a posttest; there is no pretest. Also known as a *posttest-only control group design.*

Range: The true upper limit in a distribution minus the true lower limit (or the highest rounded value minus the lowest rounded value, plus one).

Reactive effects: The changes in individual or group behavior that result from being observed or otherwise studied.

Reductionist fallacy (reductionism): An error in reasoning that occurs when incorrect conclusions about group-level processes are based on individual-level data; also known as an individualist fallacy.

Reflexivity: Sensitivity of and adaptation by the researcher to his or her influence in the research setting.

Regression analysis: A statistical technique for characterizing the pattern of a relationship between two quantitative variables in terms of a linear equation and for summarizing the strength of this relationship in terms of its deviation from that linear pattern.

Reliability: A measurement procedure yields consistent scores when the phenomenon being measured is not changing.

Repeated cross-sectional design (trend study): A type of longitudinal study in which data are collected at two or more points in time from different samples of the same population.

Repeated-measures panel design: A quasi-experimental design consisting of several pretest and posttest observations of the same group.

Replications: Repetitions of a study using the same research methods to answer the same research question.

Representative sample: A sample that "looks like" the population from which it was selected in all respects potentially relevant to the study. The distribution of characteristics among the elements of a representative sample is the same as the distribution of those characteristics among the total population. In an unrepresentative sample, some characteristics are overrepresented or underrepresented.

Research circle: A diagram of the elements of the research process, including theories, hypotheses, data collection, and data analysis.

Resistance to change: The reluctance to reevaluate our ideas in light of new information.

Respect for persons: According to the *Belmont Report,* the ethical principle of treating persons as autonomous agents and protecting those with diminished autonomy in research involving human subjects.

Sample: A subset of a population that is used to study the population as a whole.

Sample generalizability: When a conclusion based on a sample, or subset, of a larger population holds true for that population.

Sample statistic: The value of a statistic, such as a mean, computed from sample data.

Sampling error: Any difference between the characteristics of a sample and the characteristics of a population; the larger the sampling error, the less representative the sample.

Sampling frame: A list of all elements or other units containing the elements in a population.

Sampling interval: The number of cases from one sampled case to another in a systematic random sample.

Sampling units: Units listed at each stage of a multistage sampling design.

Saturation point: The point at which subject selection is ended in intensive interviewing, when new interviews seem to yield little additional information.

Science: A set of logical, systematic, documented methods for investigating nature and natural processes; the knowledge produced by these investigations.

Secondary data: Previously collected data that are used in a new analysis.

Secondary data analysis: The method of using preexisting data in a different way or to answer a different research question than intended by those who collected the data.

Selection bias: A source of internal (causal) invalidity that occurs when characteristics of experimental and comparison group subjects differ in any way that influences the outcome.

Selective distribution of benefits: An ethical issue about how much researchers can influence the benefits that subjects receive as part of the treatment being studied in a field experiment.

Selective observation: Choosing to look only at things that are in line with our preferences or beliefs.

Serendipitous findings: Unexpected patterns in data, which stimulate new explanations, insights, or theoretical approaches.

Simple random sampling: Sampling in which every sample element is selected only on the basis of chance, through a random process.

Skewness: The extent to which cases are clustered more at one or the other end of the distribution of a quantitative variable rather than in a symmetric pattern around its center. Skew can be positive (a right skew), with the number of cases tapering off in the positive direction, or negative (a left skew), with the number of cases tapering off in the negative direction. Skewness does not apply to qualitative variables (those measured at the nominal level).

Skip pattern: The unique combination of questions created in a survey by filter questions and contingent questions.

Snowball sampling: Sampling in which sample elements are selected as they are identified by successive informants or interviewees.

Social desirability bias: The tendency to "agree" with a statement just to avoid seeming disagreeable.

Social research question: A question about the social world that is answered through the collection and analysis of firsthand, verifiable, empirical data.

Social science: The use of scientific methods to investigate individuals, societies, and social processes; the knowledge produced by these investigations.

Solomon four-group design: A type of experimental design that combines a randomized pretest–posttest control group design with a randomized posttest-only design, resulting in two experimental groups and two comparison groups.

Specific deterrence theory: Predicts that punishing individuals for crime deters them from further criminal acts, due to their recognition that the costs incurred outweigh the benefits.

Specification: A type of relationship involving three or more variables in which the association between the independent and dependent variables varies across the categories of one or more other control variables.

Spurious relationship: A relationship between two variables that is caused by variation in a third variable.

Staged mixed-methods design: Qualitative and quantitative methods are used in sequence in the research, and one is given priority.

Stakeholders: Individuals and groups who have some basis of concern with the program.

Standard deviation: The square root of the average squared deviation of each case from the mean.

Statistical significance: The mathematical likelihood that an association is due to chance, judged by a criterion set by the analyst (often that the probability is less than 5 out of 100 or $p < .05$).

Stratified random sampling: Sampling in which sample elements are selected separately from population strata that are identified in advance by the researcher.

Subject fatigue: Problems caused by panel members growing weary of repeated interviews and dropping out of a study or becoming so used to answering the standard questions in the survey that they start giving stock or thoughtless answers.

Subtables: Tables describing the relationship between two variables within the discrete categories of one or more other control variables.

Summative evaluation: See *impact evaluation (or analysis)*.

Survey pretest: A method of evaluating survey questions and procedures by testing them on a small sample of individuals like those to be included in the actual survey and then reviewing responses to the questions and reactions to the survey procedures.

Survey research: Research in which information is obtained from a sample of individuals through their responses to questions about themselves or others.

Systematic bias: Overrepresentation or underrepresentation of some population characteristics in a sample resulting from the method used to select the sample; a sample shaped by systematic sampling error is a biased sample.

Systematic observation: A strategy that increases the reliability of observational data by using explicit rules that standardize coding practices across observers.

Systematic random sampling: Sampling in which sample elements are selected from a list or from sequential files, with every *n*th element being selected after the first element is selected randomly within the first interval.

Tacit knowledge: In field research, a credible sense of understanding of social processes that reflects the researcher's awareness of participants' actions as well as their words, and of what they fail to state, feel deeply, and take for granted.

Target population: A set of elements larger than or different from the population sampled and to which the researcher would like to generalize study findings.

Temporal research: Research that accounts for the related series of events that unfold over time.

Test-retest reliability: A measurement showing that measures of a phenomenon at two points in time are highly correlated, if the phenomenon has not changed, or has changed only as much as the measures have changed.

Theoretical sampling: A sampling method recommended for field researchers by Glaser and Strauss (1967). A theoretical sample is drawn in a sequential fashion, with settings or individuals selected for study as earlier observations or interviews indicate that these settings or individuals are influential.

Theory: A logically interrelated set of propositions about empirical reality.

Thick description: A rich description that conveys a sense of what it is like from the standpoint of the natural actors in that setting.

Threat to internal validity: A feature of a research design that creates the potential for an influence on the dependent variable (outcome scores) other than the experimental treatment or stimulus.

Time order: A criterion for establishing a causal relation between two variables; the variation in the presumed cause (the independent variable) must occur before the variation in the presumed effect (the dependent variable).

Time series design: A quasi-experimental design consisting of many observations of the same group before and after an intervention.

Triangulation: The use of multiple methods to study one research question; also used to mean the use of two or more different measures of the same variable.

True experiment: Experiment in which subjects are assigned randomly to an experimental group that receives a treatment or other manipulation of the independent variable and a comparison group that does not receive the treatment or receives some other manipulation; outcomes are measured in a posttest.

Tuskegee Study of Untreated Syphilis in the Negro Male: U.S. Public Health Service study of the "natural" course of syphilis that followed 399 low-income African American men from the 1930s to 1972, without providing them with penicillin, even after the drug was discovered to treat the illness. The study was stopped after it was exposed in 1972, resulting in an out-of-court settlement and then, in 1997, an official public apology by President Bill Clinton.

Unimodal: A distribution of a variable in which there is only one value that is the most frequent.

Units of analysis: The level of social life on which a measure is focused, such as individuals, groups, towns, or nations.

Unlabeled unipolar response options: Response choices for a survey question that use numbers to identify categories ranging from low to high (or vice versa).

Unobtrusive measure: A measurement based on physical traces or other data that are collected without the knowledge or participation of the individuals or groups that generated the data.

Unobtrusive methods: Research methods in which data are collected without the knowledge or participation of the individuals or groups that generated the data.

Validity: When statements or conclusions about empirical reality are correct.

Variability: The extent to which cases are spread out through the distribution or clustered in just one location.

Variable: A characteristic or property that can vary (take on different values or attributes).

Variable-oriented research: Research that focuses attention on variables representing particular aspects of the cases studied and then examines the relations between these variables across sets of cases.

Variance: A statistic that measures the variability of a distribution as the average squared deviation of each case from the mean.

Visual sociology: Sociological research in which the social world is "observed" and interpreted through photographs, films, and other images.

Web survey: A survey accessed and responded to on the World Wide Web.

Zimbardo's prison simulation study: Famous prison simulation study at Stanford University by psychologist Philip Zimbardo designed to investigate the impact of social position on behavior—specifically, the impact of being either a guard or a prisoner in a "total institution"; widely cited as demonstrating the likelihood of emergence of sadistic behavior in guards.

Bibliography

Abbott, Andrew. 1994. "History and Sociology: The Lost Synthesis." Pp. 77–112 in *Engaging the Past: The Uses of History Across the Social Sciences,* edited by Eric H. Monkkonen. Durham, NC: Duke University Press.

Abrams, David. 2007. *The Contributions of Behavioral and Social Science Research to Improving the Health of the Nation: A Prospectus for the Future.* Bethesda, MD: Office of Behavioral and Social Sciences Research, National Institutes of Health.

Abrutyn, Seth, and Anna S. Mueller. 2014. "Are Suicidal Behaviors Contagious in Adolescence? Using Longitudinal Data to Examine Suicide Suggestion." *American Sociological Review* 79:211–227.

Aiden, Erez, and Jean-Baptiste Michel. 2013. *Uncharted: Big Data as a Lens on Human Culture.* New York: Riverhead Books.

Alfred, Randall. 1976. "The Church of Satan." Pp. 180–202 in *The New Religious Consciousness,* edited by Charles Glock and Robert Bellah. Berkeley: University of California Press.

Altheide, David L., and John M. Johnson. 1994. "Criteria for Assessing Interpretive Validity in Qualitative Research." Pp. 485–499 in *Handbook of Qualitative Research,* edited by Norman K. Denzin and Yvonna S. Lincoln. Thousand Oaks, CA: Sage.

Alwin, Duane F., and Jon A. Krosnick. 1991. "The Reliability of Survey Attitude Measurement: The Influence of Question and Respondent Attributes." *Sociological Methods & Research* 20:139–181.

American Association of Universities (AAU). 2013. *Federal Funding for Social and Behavioral Sciences.* Washington, D.C.: American Association of Universities.

American Sociological Association (ASA). 1999. *Code of Ethics and Policies and Procedures of the ASA Committee on Professional Ethics.* Washington, DC: American Sociological Association. Retrieved from www.asanet.org/about/ethics.cfm

Anderson, Elijah. 1999. *Code of the Street: Decency, Violence, and the Moral Life of the Inner City.* New York: Norton.

Archibold, Randal C. 2010. "On Border Violence, Truth Pales Compared to Ideas." *New York Times,* June 19.

Armstrong, Karen. 2008. "Ethnography and Audience." Pp. 54–63 in *The SAGE Handbook of Social Research Methods,* edited by Pertti Alasuutari, Leonard Bickman, and Julia Brannen. Thousand Oaks, CA: Sage.

Arwood, Tracy, and Sangeeta Panicker. 2007. "Assessing Risk in Social and Behavioral Sciences." *Collaborative Institutional Training Initiative.* Retrieved from https://www.citiprogram.org/members/learners

Ayhan, H. Öztaş. 2001. "Gender Bias in Agricultural Surveys Statistics by Gender: Measures to Reduce Gender Bias in Agricultural Surveys." *International Statistical Review* 69:447–460.

Ball, Richard A., and G. David Curry. 1995. "The Logic of Definition in Criminology: Purposes and Methods for Defining 'Gangs.'" *Criminology* 33:225–245.

Bastow, Simon, Patrick Dunleavy, and Jane Tinkler. 2014. *The Impact of the Social Sciences: How Academics and Their Research Make a Difference.* U.S. edition. Thousand Oaks, CA: Sage.

Baumrind, Diana. 1985. "Research Using Intentional Deception: Ethical Issues Revisited." *American Psychologist* 40:165–174.

Becker, Howard S. 1958. "Problems of Inference and Proof in Participant Observation." *American Sociological Review* 23:652–660.

Becker, Howard S. 1963. *The Outsiders: Studies in the Sociology of Deviance.* New York: Free Press.

Becker, Howard S. 2007. *Writing for Social Scientists,* 2nd ed. Chicago: University of Chicago Press.

Bergman, Manfred Max. 2008. "Combining Different Types of Data for Quantitative Analysis." Pp. 585–601 in *The SAGE Handbook of Social Research Methods,* edited by Pertti Alasuutari, Leonard Bickman, and Julia Brannen. Thousand Oaks, CA: Sage.

Berk, Richard A., Alec Campbell, Ruth Klap, and Bruce Western. 1992. "The Deterrent Effect of Arrest: A Bayesian Analysis of Four Field Experiments." *American Sociological Review* 57(October):698–708.

Berman, Greg, and Aubrey Fox. 2009. *Lessons From the Battle Over D.A.R.E.: The Complicated Relationship Between Research and Practice.* Washington, DC: Center for Court Innovation and Bureau of Justice Assistance, U.S. Department of Justice.

Berry, Brent. 2006. "Friends for Better or for Worse: Interracial Friendship in the United States as Seen Through Wedding Party Photos." *Demography* 43:491–510.

Bhutta, Christine Brickman. 2012. "Not by the Book: Facebook as a Sampling Frame." *Sociological Methods & Research* 41:57–88.

Binder, Arnold and James W. Meeker. 1993. "Implications of the Failure to Replicate the Minneapolis Experimental Findings." *American Sociological Review,* 58(December): 886–888.

Bledsoe, Katrina L., and Rodney K. Hopson. 2009. "Conducting Ethical Research and Evaluation in Underserved Communities." Pp. 391–406 in *The Handbook of Social Research Ethics,* edited by Donna M. Mertens and Pauline E. Ginsberg. Thousand Oaks, CA: Sage.

Bloom, Howard S. 2008. "The Core Analytics of Randomized Experiments for Social Research." Pp. 115–133 in *The SAGE Handbook of Social Research Methods,* edited by Pertti Alasuutari, Leonard Bickman, and Julia Brannen. Thousand Oaks, CA: Sage.

Boase, Jeffrey, John B. Horrigan, Barry Wellman, and Lee Rainie. 2006. *The Strength of Internet Ties: The Internet and Email Aid Users in Maintaining Their Social Networks and Provide Pathways to Help When People Face Big Decisions.* Washington, DC: Pew Internet & American Life Project.

Bogdewic, Stephan P. 1999. "Participant Observation." Pp. 47–70 in *Doing Qualitative Research,* 2nd ed., edited by Benjamin F. Crabtree and William L. Miller. Thousand Oaks, CA: Sage.

Bollen, Kenneth A., Barbara Entwisle, and Arthur S. Alderson. 1993. "Macrocomparative Research Methods." *Annual Review of Sociology* 19:321–351.

Bond, Robert M., Christopher J. Fariss, Jason J. Jones, Adam D. I. Kramer, Cameron Marlow, Jaime E. Settle, and James H. Fowler. 2012. "A 61-Million-Person Experiment in Social Influence and Political Mobilization." *Nature* 489:295–298.

Booth, Wayne C., Gregory G. Colomb, and Joseph M. Williams. 1995. *The Craft of Research.* Chicago: University of Chicago Press.

Boruch, Robert F. 1997. *Randomized Experiments for Planning and Evaluation: A Practical Guide.* Thousand Oaks, CA: Sage.

Bosk, Charles L., and Raymond G. De Vries. 2004. "Bureaucracies of Mass Deception: Institutional Review Boards and the Ethics of Ethnographic Research." *Annals of the American Academy of Political and Social Science* 595:249–263.

boyd, danah. 2011. "White Flight in Networked Publics? How Race and Class Shaped American Teen Engagement With MySpace and Facebook." Pp. 203-222 in *Race After the Internet,* edited by Lisa Nakamura and Peter A. Chow-White. New York: Routledge.

boyd, danah. 2015. "Making Sense of Teen Life: Strategies for Capturing Ethnographic Data in a Networked Era." Pp. XXX-XXX in *Digital Research Confidential: The Secrets of Studying Behavior Online,* edited by Eszter Hargittai and Christian Sandvig. Cambridge, MA: MIT Press.

Brewer, John, and Albert Hunter. 1989. *Multimethod Research: A Synthesis of Styles.* Newbury Park, CA: Sage.

Brooks, Clem, and Jeff Manza. 2006. "Social Policy Responsiveness in Developed Democracies." *American Sociological Review* 71:474–494.

Broskoske, Steve. 2005. "How to Prevent Paper Recycling." *The Teaching Professor* 19:1, 4.

Brown, Bruce L., and Dawson Hedges. 2009. "Use and Misuse of Quantitative Methods: Data Collection, Calculation, and Presentation." Pp. 373–386 in *The Handbook of Social Research Ethics,* edited by Donna M. Mertens and Pauline E. Ginsberg. Thousand Oaks, CA: Sage.

Brown, Judith Belle. 1999. "The Use of Focus Groups in Clinical Research." Pp. 109–124 in *Doing Qualitative Research,* 2nd ed., edited by Benjamin F. Crabtree and William L. Miller. Thousand Oaks, CA: Sage.

Bureau of Justice Statistics. 2011. "Key Facts at a Glance: Drug Arrests by Age, 1970–2007." Washington, DC: Bureau of Justice Statistics, U.S. Department of Justice. Retrieved from http://bjs.ojp.usdoj.gov/content/glance/drug.cfm

Burge, Kathleen. 2014. "Overblown Facebook Personas Can Leave Friends Deflated." *Boston Globe,* September 30.

Butler, Declan. 2013. "When Google Got Flu Wrong." *Nature* 494(February 14):155–156.

Butler, Dore, and Florence Geis. 1990. "Nonverbal Affect Responses to Male and Female Leaders: Implications for Leadership Evaluations." *Journal of Personality and Social Psychology* 58(January):48–59.

Buttel, Frederick H. 2000. "World Society, the Nation-State, and Environmental Protection: Comment on Frank, Hironaka, and Schofer." *American Sociological Review* 65:117–121.

Campbell, Donald T., and Julian C. Stanley. 1966. *Experimental and Quasi-Experimental Designs for Research.* Chicago: Rand McNally.

Campbell, Marie L. 1998. "Institutional Ethnography and Experience as Data." *Qualitative Sociology* 21:55-73.

Campbell, Richard T. 1992. "Longitudinal Research." Pp. 1146–1158 in *Encyclopedia of Sociology,* edited by Edgar F. Borgatta and Marie L. Borgatta. New York: Macmillan.

Carey, Benedict, and Pam Belluck. 2015. "Retraction Sought in Study on Views of Gay Marriage." *New York Times,* May 21:A16.

Carmines, Edward G., and Richard A. Zeller. 1979. *Reliability and Validity Assessment,* no. 17, Quantitative Applications in the Social Sciences. Beverly Hills, CA: Sage.

Cava, Anita, Reid Cushman, and Kenneth Goodman. 2007. "HIPAA and Human Subjects Research." *Collaborative Institutional Training Initiative.* Retrieved from https://www.citiprogram.org/members/learners

Center for Survey Research. 2013. *Massachusetts Youth Health Survey.* Boston, MA: Center for Survey Research, University of Massachusetts Boston. Reproduced by permission.

Centers for Disease Control and Prevention (CDC). 2009. "The Tuskegee Timeline." Atlanta, GA: National Center for HIV/AIDS, Viral Hepatitis, STD, and TB Prevention, Centers for Disease Control and Prevention. Retrieved from www.cdc.gov/tuskegee/timeline.htm

Cernat, Alexandru. 2015. "The Impact of Mixing Modes on Reliability in Longitudinal Studies." *Sociological Methods & Research* 44:427-457.

Chase-Dunn, Christopher, and Thomas D. Hall. 1993. "Comparing World-Systems: Concepts and Working Hypotheses." *Social Forces* 71:851–886.

Chatterjee, Arijit, and Donald C. Hambrick. 2007. "It's All About Me: Narcissistic Chief Executive Officers and Their Effects on Company Strategy and Performance." *Administrative Science Quarterly* 52:351-386.

Christian, Leah, Scott Keeter, Kristen Purcell, and Aaron Smith. 2010. "Assessing the Cell Phone Challenge to Survey Research in 2010." Washington, DC: Pew Research Center for the People & the Press and Pew Internet & American Life Project.

Clark, Herbert H., and Michael F. Schober. 1994. "Asking Questions and Influencing Answers." Pp. 15–48 in *Questions About Questions: Inquiries Into the Cognitive Bases of Surveys,* edited by Judith M. Tanur. New York: Russell Sage Foundation.

Coffey, Amanda, and Paul Atkinson. 1996. *Making Sense of Qualitative Data: Complementary Research Strategies.* Thousand Oaks, CA: Sage.

Cohn, Nate. 2015. "Polling's Secrecy Problem." *New York Times,* May 28.

Collins, Randall. 1994. *Four Sociological Traditions.* New York: Oxford University Press.

Cook, Thomas D., and Donald T. Campbell. 1979. *Quasi-Experimentation: Design and Analysis Issues for Field Settings.* Chicago: Rand McNally.

Cook, Thomas D., and Vivian C. Wong. 2008. "Better Quasi-Experimental Practice." Pp. 134–165 in *The SAGE Handbook of Social Research Methods,* edited by Pertti Alasuutari, Leonard Bickman, and Julia Brannen. Thousand Oaks, CA: Sage.

Costner, Herbert L. 1989. "The Validity of Conclusions in Evaluation Research: A Further Development of Chen and Rossi's Theory-Driven Approach." *Evaluation and Program Planning* 12:345–353.

Couper, Mick P. 2000. "Web Surveys: A Review of Issues and Approaches." *Public Opinion Quarterly* 64:464–494.

Couper, Mick P., and Peter V. Miller. 2008. "Web Survey Methods: Introduction." *Public Opinion Quarterly* 72:831–835.

Couper, Mick P., Michael W. Traugott, and Mark J. Lamias. 2001. "Web Survey Design and Administration." *Public Opinion Quarterly* 65:230–253.

Cuba, Lee J. 2002. *A Short Guide to Writing About Social Science,* 4th ed. New York: Addison-Wesley.

Czopp, Alexander M., Margo J. Monteith, and Aimee Y. Mark. 2006. "Standing Up for a Change: Reducing Bias Through Interpersonal Confrontation." *Journal of Personality and Social Psychology* 90:784–803.

Dahlberg, Britt, Marsha N. Wittink, and Joseph J. Gallo. 2010. "Funding and Publishing Integrated Studies: Writing Effective Mixed Methods Manuscripts and Grant Proposals." Pp. 775–802 in *SAGE Handbook of Mixed Methods in Social & Behavioral Research,* 2nd ed., edited by Abbas Tashakkori and Charles Teddlie. Thousand Oaks, CA: Sage.

Dannefer, W. Dale and Russell K. Schutt. 1982. "Race and Juvenile Justice Processing in Court and Police Agencies." *American Journal of Sociology* 87(March): 1113–1132.

D.A.R.E. 2008. *The "New" D.A.R.E. Program.* Retrieved from www.dare.com/newdare.asp

D.A.R.E. 2014. "Drug Abuse Resistance Education." Retrieved from www.dare.org/starting-a-dare-program

Davis, James A., and Tom W. Smith. 1992. *The NORC General Social Survey: A User's Guide.* Newbury Park, CA: Sage.

Davis, Katie, David P. Randall, Anthony Ambrose, and Mania Orand. 2015. "'I Was Bullied Too': Stories of Bullying and Coping in an Online Community." *Information, Communication & Society* 18:357-275.

Davis, Ophera A., and Marie Land. 2007. "Southern Women Survivors Speak About Hurricane Katrina, the Children and What Needs to Happen Next." *Race, Gender & Class* 14:69–86.

de Leeuw, Edith. 2008. "Self-Administered Questionnaires and Standardized Interviews." Pp. 311–327 in *The SAGE Handbook of Social Research Methods,* edited by Pertti Alasuutari, Leonard Bickman, and Julia Brannen. Thousand Oaks, CA: Sage.

de Vaus, David. 2008. "Comparative and Cross-National Designs." Pp. 248–264 in *The SAGE Handbook of Social Research Methods,* edited by Pertti Alasuutari, Leonard Bickman, and Julia Brannen. Thousand Oaks, CA: Sage.

Decker, Scott H., and Barrik Van Winkle. 1996. *Life in the Gang: Family, Friends, and Violence.* Cambridge: Cambridge University Press.

Deegan, Allison. 2012. "Stranger in a Strange Land: The Challenges and Benefits of Online Interviews in the Social Networking Space." Pp. 69–99 in *Cases in Online Interview Research,* edited by Janet Salmons. Thousand Oaks, CA: Sage.

Demos, John. 1998. "History Beyond Data Bits." *New York Times,* December 30, p. A23.

Dentler, Robert A. 2002. *Practicing Sociology: Selected Fields.* Westport, CT: Praeger.

Denzin, Norman K. 2002. "The Interpretive Process." Pp. 349–368 in *The Qualitative Researcher's Companion,* edited by A. Michael Huberman and Matthew B. Miles. Thousand Oaks, CA: Sage.

Denzin, Norman, and Yvonna S. Lincoln. 1994. "Introduction: Entering the Field of Qualitative Research." Pp. 1–28 in *The Handbook of Qualitative Research,* edited by Norman Denzin and Yvonna S. Lincoln. Thousand Oaks, CA: Sage.

Denzin, Norman, and Yvonna S. Lincoln. 2000. "Introduction: The Discipline and Practice of Qualitative Research." Pp. 1–28 in *The Handbook of Qualitative Research,* 2nd ed., edited by Norman Denzin and Yvonna S. Lincoln. Thousand Oaks, CA: Sage.

Denzin, Norman K., and Yvonna S. Lincoln. 2008. *Strategies of Qualitative Inquiry,* 3rd ed. Thousand Oaks, CA: Sage.

Department of Health, Education, and Welfare. 1979. *The Belmont Report: Ethical Principles and Guidelines for the Protection of Human Subjects of Research.* Washington, DC: The National Commission for the Protection of Human Subjects of Biomedical and Behavioral Research, Office of the Secretary, Department of Health, Education, and Welfare. Retrieved from www.hss.gov/ohrp/humansubjects/guidance/belmont.htm

Desilver, Drew. 2013. "For Most Wireless-Only Households, Look South and West." Pew Research Center. Retrieved from http://www.pewresearch.org/fact-tank/2013/12/23/for-most-wireless-only-households-look-south-and-west/

Dewan, Shaila K. 2004a. "As Murders Fall, New Tactics Are Tried Against Remainder." *New York Times,* December 31, pp. A24–A25.

Dewan, Shaila K. 2004b. "New York's Gospel of Policing by Data Spreads Across U.S." *New York Times,* April 26, pp. A1, C16.

Dickson-Swift, Virginia, Erica L. James, Sandra Kippen, and Pranee Liamputtong. 2008. "Risk to Researchers in Qualitative Research on Sensitive Topics: Issues and Strategies." *Qualitative Health Research* 18:133–144.

Dillman, Don A. 1978. *Mail and Telephone Surveys: The Total Design Method.* New York: Wiley.

Dillman, Don A. 2000. *Mail and Internet Surveys: The Tailored Design Method,* 2nd ed. New York: Wiley.

Dillman, Don A. 2007. *Mail and Internet Surveys: The Tailored Design Method,* 2nd ed. Updated With New Internet, Visual, and Mixed-Mode Guide. Hoboken, NJ: Wiley.

Dillman, Don A., and Leah Melani Christian. 2005. "Survey Mode as a Source of Instability in Responses Across Surveys." *Field Methods* 17:30–52.

Doucet, Andrea, and Natasha Mauthner. 2008. "Qualitative Interviewing and Feminist Research." Pp. 328–343 in *The SAGE Handbook of Social Research Methods,* edited by Pertti Alasuutari, Leonard Bickman, and Julia Brannen. Thousand Oaks, CA: Sage.

Drew, Paul. 2005. "Conversation Analysis." Pp. 71–102 in *Handbook of Language and Social Interaction,* edited by Kristine L. Fitch and Robert E. Sanders. Mahwah, NJ: Lawrence Erlbaum.

Duggan, Maeve. 2013. "Photo and Video Sharing Growing Online." Pew Research Center, October 28. Retrieved from http://www.pewinternet.org/files/old-media//Files/Reports/2013/PIP_Photos%20and%20videos%20online_102813.pdf

Duneier, Mitchell. 1999. *Sidewalk.* New York: Farrar, Strauss, and Giroux.

Earle, Paul S., Daniel C. Bowden, and Michelle Guy. 2011. "Twitter Earthquake Detection: Earthquake Monitoring in a Social World." *Annals of Geophysics* 54:708–715.

Eckholm, Erik. 2006. "Report on Impact of Federal Benefits on Curbing Poverty Reignites a Debate." *New York Times,* February 18, p. A8.

Elder, Keith, Sudha Xirasagar, Nancy Miller, Shelly Ann Bowen, Saundra Glover, and Crystal Piper. 2007. "African Americans' Decisions Not to Evacuate New Orleans Before Hurricane Katrina: A Qualitative Study." *American Journal of Public Health* 97(Suppl. 1):S124–S129.

Elliott, Jane, Janet Holland, and Rachel Thomson. 2008. "Longitudinal and Panel Studies." Pp. 228–248 in *The SAGE Handbook of Social Research Methods,* edited by Pertti Alasuutari, Leonard Bickman, and Julia Brannen. Thousand Oaks, CA: Sage.

Ellis, Carolyn. 1995. "Emotional and Ethical Quagmires in Returning to the Field." *Journal of Contemporary Ethnography* 24:68–98.

Emerson, Robert M., Rachel I. Fretz, and Linda L. Shaw. 1995. *Writing Ethnographic Fieldnotes.* Chicago: University of Chicago Press.

Emmons, R. 1984. "Factor Analysis and Construct Validity of the Narcissistic Personality Inventory." *Journal of Personality Assessment* 48:291–300.

Ennett, Susan T., Nancy S. Tobler, Christopher L. Ringwalt, and Robert L. Flewelling. 1994. "How Effective Is Drug Abuse Resistance Education? A Meta-Analysis of Project DARE Outcome Evaluations." *American Journal of Public Health* 84(9):1394–1401.

Erikson, Kai T. 1966. *Wayward Puritans: A Study in the Sociology of Deviance.* New York: Wiley.

Fallon, Kathleen M., Liam Swiss, and Jocelyn Viterna. 2012. "Resolving the Democracy Paradox: Democratization and Women's Legislative Representation in Developing Nations, 1975 to 2009." *American Sociological Review* 77(3):380–408.

Fears, Darryl. 2002. "For Latinos in U.S., Race Not Just Black or White." *Boston Globe,* December 30, p. A3.

Fenton, Steve. 1996. "Counting Ethnicity: Social Groups and Official Categories." Pp. 143–165 in *Interpreting Official Statistics,* edited by Ruth Levitas and Will Guy. New York: Routledge.

File, Thom. 2013. "The Diversifying Electorate—Voting Rates by Race and Hispanic Origin in 2012 (and Other Recent Elections)." *Population Characteristics, Current Population Survey.* Washington, DC: U.S. Census Bureau.

File, Thom, and Camille Ryan. 2014. *Computer and Internet Use in the United States: 2013.*

American Community Survey Reports. Washington, DC: U.S. Census Bureau, U.S. Department of Commerce.

Fink, Arlene. 2005. *Conducting Research Literature Reviews: From the Internet to Paper,* 2nd ed. Thousand Oaks, CA: Sage.

Fischer, Constance T., and Frederick J. Wertz. 2002. "Empirical Phenomenological Analyses of Being Criminally Victimized." Pp. 275–304 in *The Qualitative Researcher's Companion,* edited by A. Michael Huberman and Matthew B. Miles. Thousand Oaks, CA: Sage.

Fisher, Celia B., and Andrea E. Anushko. 2008. "Research Ethics in Social Science." Pp. 94–109 in *The SAGE Handbook of Social Research Methods,* edited by Pertti Alasuutari, Leonard Bickman, and Julia Brannen. Thousand Oaks, CA: Sage.

Forero, Juan. 2000a. "Census Takers Say Supervisors Fostered Filing of False Data." *New York Times,* July 28, p. A21.

Forero, Juan. 2000b. "Census Takers Top '90 Efforts in New York City, With More to Go." *New York Times,* June 12, p. A29.

Fowler, Floyd J. 1995. *Improving Survey Questions: Design and Evaluation.* Thousand Oaks, CA: Sage.

Frank, David John, Ann Hironaka, and Evan Schofer. 2000. "The Nation-State and the Natural Environment Over the Twentieth Century." *American Sociological Review* 65:96–116.

Frohmann, Lisa. 2005. "The Framing Safety Project: Photographs and Narratives by Battered Women." *Violence Against Women* 11:1396–1419.

Frye, Victoria, Mary Haviland, and Valli Rajah. 2007. "Dual Arrest and Other Unintended Consequences of Mandatory Arrest in New York City: A Brief Report." *Journal of Family Violence* 22:397–405.

Gaiser, Ted J., and Anthony E. Schreiner. 2009. *A Guide to Conducting Online Research.* Thousand Oaks, CA: Sage.

Garcia-Moreno, Claudia, Christina Pallitto, Karen Devries, Heidi Stockl, Charlotte Watts, and Naeemah Abrahams. 2013. "Global and Regional Estimates of Violence Against Women: Prevalence and Health Effects of Intimate Partner Violence and Non-Partner Sexual Violence." Geneva, Switzerland: World Health Organization.

Geertz, Clifford. 1973. "Thick Description: Toward an Interpretive Theory of Culture." Pp. 3–30 in *The Interpretation of Cultures,* edited by Clifford Geertz. New York: Basic Books.

Gerth, Matthias A., and Gabriele Siegert. 2012. "Patterns of Consistence and Constriction: How News Media Frame the Coverage of Direct Democratic Campaigns." *American Behavioral Scientist* 56:279–299.

Gilchrist, Valerie J., and Robert L. Williams. 1999. "Key Informant Interviews." Pp. 71–88 in *Doing Qualitative Research,* 2nd ed., edited by Benjamin F. Crabtree and William L. Miller. Thousand Oaks, CA: Sage.

Ginsberg, Jeremy, Matthew H. Mohebbi, Rajan S. Patel, Lynnette Brammer, Mark S. Smolinski, and Larry Brilliant. 2009. "Detecting Influenza Epidemics Using Search Engine Query Data." *Nature* 457(February 19):1012–1015.

Glaser, Barney G., and Anselm L. Strauss. 1967. *The Discovery of Grounded Theory: Strategies for Qualitative Research.* London: Weidenfeld and Nicholson.

Glover, Judith. 1996. "Epistemological and Methodological Considerations in Secondary Analysis." Pp. 28–38 in *Cross-National Research Methods in the Social Sciences,* edited by Linda Hantrais and Steen Mangen. New York: Pinter.

Gobo, Giampietro. 2008. "Re-Conceptualizing Generalization: Old Issues in a New Frame." Pp. 193–213 in *The SAGE Handbook of Social Research Methods,* edited by Pertti Alasuutari, Leonard Bickman, and Julia Brannen. Thousand Oaks, CA: Sage.

Goel, Vindu. 2015. "Study of TV Viewers Backs Twitter's Claims to Be Barometer of Public Mood." *New York Times,* March 8.

Goffman, Erving. 1961. *Asylums: Essays on the Social Situation of Mental Patients and Other Inmates.* Garden City, NY: Doubleday.

González-López, Gloria. 2004. "Fathering Latina Sexualities: Mexican Men and the Virginity of Their Daughters." *Journal of Marriage and Family* 66:1118-1130.

Goodnough, Abby. 2010. "A Wave of Addiction and Crime, With the Medicine Cabinet to Blame." *New York Times,* September 22.

Gordon, Raymond. 1992. *Basic Interviewing Skills.* Itasca, IL: Peacock.

Grady, John. 1996. "The Scope of Visual Sociology." *Visual Sociology* 11:10–24.

Greaves, Colin J., and Lou Farbus. 2006. "Effects of Creative and Social Activity on the Health and Well-Being of Socially Isolated Older People: Outcomes From a Multi-Method Observational Study." *Journal of the Royal Society for the Promotion of Health* 126:134–142.

Grey, Robert J. Jr. 2005. "Jury Service: It's a Privilege." Retrieved from American Bar Association website, www.abanet.org/media/releases/opedjuror2.html

Grieco, Elizabeth M., Yesenia D. Acosta, G. Patricia de la Cruz, Christine Gambino, Thomas Gryn, Luke J. Larsen, Edward N. Trevelyan, and Nathan P. Walters. 2012. *The Foreign-Born Population in the United States: 2010.* Washington, DC: U.S. Census Bureau.

Grissom, Brandi. 2011. "Proposals Could Make It Harder to Leave Prison." *New York Times,* March 12.

Groves, Robert M. 1989. *Survey Errors and Survey Costs.* New York: Wiley.

Groves, Robert M., Eleanor Singer, and Amy Corning. 2000. "Leverage-Salience Theory of Survey Participation: Description and an Illustration." *Public Opinion Quarterly* 64:299–308.

Gubrium, Jaber F., and James A. Holstein. 1997. *The New Language of Qualitative Method.* New York: Oxford University Press.

Guterbock, Thomas M. 2008. *Strategies and Standards for Reaching Respondents in an Age of New Technology.* Presentation to the Harvard Program on Survey Research Spring Conference, New Technologies and Survey Research. Cambridge, MA: Institute of Quantitative Social Science, Harvard University, May 9.

Hacker, Karen. 2013. *Community-Based Participatory Research.* Thousand Oaks, CA: Sage.

Hafner, Katie. 2004. "For Some, the Blogging Never Stops." *New York Times,* May 27, pp. E1, E7.

Hammersley, Martyn. 2008. "Assessing Validity in Social Research." Pp. 42–53 in *The SAGE Handbook of Social Research Methods,* edited by Pertti Alasuutari, Leonard Bickman, and Julia Brannen. Thousand Oaks, CA: Sage.

Hammersley, Martyn, and Anna Traianou. 2012. *Ethics in Qualitative Research: Controversies and Contexts.* Thousand Oaks, CA: Sage.

Hampton, Keith N., Lauren Sessions Goulet, Lee Rainie, and Kristen Purcell. 2011. "Social Networking Sites and Our Lives: How People's Trust, Personal Relationships, and Civic and Political Involvement Are Connected to Their Use of Social Networking Sites and Other Technologies." Washington, DC: Pew Internet & American Life Project. Retrieved from http://pewinternet.org/Reports/2011/Technology-and-social-networks.aspx

Hampton, Keith N., and Neeti Gupta. 2008. "Community and Social Interaction in the Wireless City: Wi-Fi Use in Public and Semi-Public Spaces." *New Media & Society* 10(6):831–850.

Hampton, Keith N., and Barry Wellman. 2000. "Examining Community in the Digital Neighborhood: Early Results From Canada's Wired Suburb." Pp. 475–492 in *Digital Cities: Technologies, Experiences, and Future Perspectives,* edited by Toru Ishida and Katherine Isbister. Berlin, Germany: Springer-Verlag.

Haney, C., C. Banks, and Philip G. Zimbardo. 1973. "Interpersonal Dynamics in a Simulated Prison." *International Journal of Criminology and Penology* 1:69–97.

Hantrais, Linda, and Steen Mangen. 1996. "Method and Management of Cross-National Social Research." Pp. 1–12 in *Cross-National Research Methods in the Social Sciences,* edited by Linda Hantrais and Steen Mangen. New York: Pinter.

Hard, Stephen F., James M. Conway, and Antonia C. Moran. 2006. "Faculty and College Student Beliefs About the Frequency of Student Academic Misconduct." *The Journal of Higher Education* 77:1058–1080.

Hart, Chris. 1998. *Doing a Literature Review: Releasing the Social Science Research Imagination.* London: Sage.

Hawkins, Donald N., Paul R. Amato, and Valarie King. 2007. "Nonresident Father Involvement and Adolescent Well-Being: Father Effects or Child Effects?" *American Sociological Review* 72:990–1010.

Heath, Christian, and Paul Luff. 2008. "Video and the Analysis of Work and Interaction." Pp. 493–505 in *The SAGE Handbook of Social Research Methods,* edited by Pertti Alasuutari, Leonard Bickman, and Julia Brannen. Thousand Oaks, CA: Sage.

Heaton, Janet. 2008. "Secondary Analysis of Qualitative Data." Pp. 506–535 in *The SAGE Handbook of Social Research Methods,* edited by Pertti Alasuutari, Leonard Bickman, and Julia Brannen. Thousand Oaks, CA: Sage.

Hedström, Peter, and Richard Swedberg (Eds.). 1998. *Social Mechanisms: An Analytical Approach to Social Theory.* Cambridge: Cambridge University Press.

Hicks, Lorna. 2013. *The Regulations—SBE.* Miami, FL: Collaborative Institutional Training Initiative at the University of Miami. Retrieved from https://www.citiprogram.org/

Hirschel, David, Eve Buzawa, April Pattavina, and Don Faggiani. 2008. "Domestic Violence and Mandatory Arrest Laws: To What Extent Do They Influence Police Arrest Decisions?" *Journal of Criminal Law & Criminology* 98(1):255–298.

Ho, D. Y. F. 1996. "Filial Piety and Its Psychological Consequences." Pp. 155–165 in *Handbook of Chinese Psychology,* edited by M. H. Bond. Hong Kong: Oxford University Press.

Hoffman, Stephen. 2014. "Zero Benefit: Estimating the Effect of Zero Tolerance Discipline Polices on Racial Disparities in School Discipline." *Educational Policy* 28(1):69–95.

Holbrook, Allyson L., Melanie C. Green, and Jon A. Krosnick. 2003. "Telephone Versus Face-to-Face Interviewing of National Probability Samples With Long Questionnaires: Comparisons of Respondent Satisficing and Social Desirability Response Bias." *Public Opinion Quarterly* 60:58–88.

Howell, James C. 2003. *Preventing and Reducing Juvenile Delinquency: A Comprehensive Framework.* Thousand Oaks, CA: Sage.

Hu, Winnie. 2014. "Severe Cold Moves New York's Homeless to Seek Help." *New York Times,* January 28, p. A19.

Huberman, A. Michael, and Matthew B. Miles. 1994. "Data Management and Analysis Methods." Pp. 428–444 in *Handbook of Qualitative Research,* edited by Norman K. Denzin and Yvonna S. Lincoln. Thousand Oaks, CA: Sage.

Hulbert-Williams, L., R. Hastings, D. M. Owen, L. Burns, and J. Day. 2014. "Exposure to Life Events as a Risk Factor for Psychological Problems in Adults With Intellectual Disabilities: A Longitudinal Design." *Journal of Intellectual Disability Research* 58:48-60.

Humes, Karen R., Nicholas A. Jones, and Roberto R. Ramirez. 2011. *Overview of Race and Hispanic Origin: 2010.* C2010BR-02. Washington, DC: U.S. Census Bureau.

Humphrey, Nicholas. 1992. *A History of the Mind: Evolution and the Birth of Consciousness.* New York: Simon & Schuster.

Humphreys, Laud. 1970. *Tearoom Trade: Impersonal Sex in Public Places.* Chicago: Aldine de Gruyter.

Hunt, Morton. 1985. Profiles of Social Research: The Scientific Study of Human Interactions. New York: Russell Sage Foundation.

Huston, Patricia, and C. David Naylor. 1996. "Health Services Research: Reporting on Studies Using Secondary Data Sources." *Canadian Medical Association Journal* 155:1697–1702.

Hyvärinen, Matti. 2008. "Analyzing Narratives and Story-Telling." Pp. 447–460 in *The SAGE Handbook of Social Research Methods,* edited by Pertti Alasuutari, Leonard Bickman, and Julia Brannen. Thousand Oaks, CA: Sage.

Internet World Statistics. 2012. Retrieved from http://www.internetworldstats.com/stats.htm

Irvine, Leslie. 1998. "Organizational Ethics and Fieldwork Realities: Negotiating Ethical Boundaries in Codependents Anonymous." Pp. 167–183 in *Doing Ethnographic Research: Fieldwork Settings.* Thousand Oaks, CA: Sage.

James, Nalita, and Hugh Busher. 2009. *Online Interviewing.* Thousand Oaks, CA: Sage.

Jarvis, Helen. 1997. "Housing, Labour Markets and Household Structure: Questioning the Role of Secondary Data Analysis in Sustaining the Polarization Debate." *Regional Studies* 31:521–531.

Jervis, Robert. 1996. "Counterfactuals, Causation, and Complexity." Pp. 309–316 in *Counterfactual Thought Experiments in World Politics: Logical, Methodological, and Psychological Perspectives,* edited by Philip E. Tetlock and Aaron Belkin. Princeton, NJ: Princeton University Press.

Jesnadum, Anick. 2000. "Researchers Fear Privacy Breaches With Online Research." *Digital Mass.* Retrieved from www.digitalmass.com/news/daily/09/15/researchers.html

Kagay, Michael R., with Janet Elder. 1992. "Numbers Are No Problem for Pollsters. Words Are." *New York Times,* October 9, p. E5.

Kaplan, Fred. 2002. "NY Continues to See Plunge in Number of Felonies." *Boston Globe,* April 15, p. A3.

Kaufman, Sharon R. 1986. *The Ageless Self: Sources of Meaning in Late Life.* Madison: University of Wisconsin Press.

Keeter, Scott. 2008. *Survey Research and Cell Phones: Is There a Problem?* Presentation to the Harvard Program on Survey Research Spring Conference, New Technologies and Survey Research. Cambridge, MA: Institute of Quantitative Social Science, Harvard University, May 9.

Keeter, Scott. 2015. "Pew Research Will Call More Cellphones in 2015." Pew Research Center, January 7. Retrieved from www.pewresearch.org/fact-tank/2015/01/07/pew-research-will-call-more-cellphones-in-2015/

Keeter, Scott, Michael Dimock, and Leah Christian. 2008. "Cell Phones and the 2008 Vote: An Update." Pew Center for the People & the Press, September 23. Retrieved from www.pewresearch.org/2008/09/23/cell-phones-and-the-2008-vote-an-update-2/

Keeter, Scott, and Rachel Weisel. 2015. "From Telephone to the Web: The Challenge of Mode of Interview Effects in Public Opinion Polls." Pew Research Center, May 13. Retrieved from http://www.pewresearch.org/files/2015/05/2015-05-13_mode-study_REPORT.pdf

Kemmis, Stephen, and Robin McTaggart. 2005. "Participatory Action Research: Communicative Action and the Public Sphere." Pp. 559–603 in *The SAGE Handbook of Qualitative Research,* 3rd ed., edited by Norman K. Denzin and Yvonna S. Lincoln. Thousand Oaks, CA: Sage.

Kenney, Charles. 1987. "They've Got Your Number." *Boston Globe Magazine,* August 30, pp. 12, 46–56, 60.

Kershaw, David, and Jerilyn Fair. 1976. *The New Jersey Income-Maintenance Experiment,* vol. 1. New York: Academic Press.

King, Gary, Robert O. Keohane, and Sidney Verba. 1994. *Scientific Inference in Qualitative Research.* Princeton, NJ: Princeton University Press.

King, Miriam L., and Diana L. Magnuson. 1995. "Perspectives on Historical U.S. Census Undercounts." *Social Science History* 19:455–466.

King, Nigel, and Christine Horrocks. 2010. *Interviews in Qualitative Research.* Thousand Oaks, CA: Sage.

Kitchener, Karen Strohm, and Richard F. Kitchener. 2009. "Social Science Research Ethics: Historical and Philosophical Issues." Pp. 5–22 in *The Handbook of Social Research Ethics,* edited by Donna M. Mertens and Pauline E. Ginsberg. Thousand Oaks, CA: Sage.

Koegel, Paul. 1987. *Ethnographic Perspectives on Homeless and Homeless Mentally Ill Women.* Washington, DC: Alcohol, Drug Abuse, and Mental Health Administration, Public Health Service, U.S. Department of Health and Human Services.

Kohavi, Ron, Randal M. Henne, and Dan Sommerfield. 2007. "Practical Guide to Controlled Experiments on the Web: Listen to Your Customers Not to the HiPPO." Retrieved from http://ai.stanford.edu/~ronnyk/2007GuideControlledExperiments.pdf

Kohavi, Ron, Roger Longbotham, Dan Sommerfield, and Randal M. Henne. 2009. "Controlled Experiments on the Web: Survey and Practical Guide." *Data Mining and Knowledge Discovery* 18:140-181. Retrieved from http://www.exp-platform.com/Pages/hippo_long.aspx

Kohut, Andrew. 1988. "Polling: Does More Information Lead to Better Understanding?" *Boston Globe,* November 7, p. 25.

Kohut, Andrew. 2008. "Getting It Wrong." *New York Times,* January 10, p. A27.

Kohut, Andrew, Scott Keeter, Carroll Doherty, Michael Dimock, and Leah Christian. 2012. *Assessing the Representativeness of Public Opinion Surveys.* Washington, DC: Pew Research Center. Retrieved from www.people-press.org/2012/05/15/assessing-the-representativeness-of-public-opinion-surveys

Korn, James H. 1997. *Illusions of Reality: A History of Deception in Social Psychology.* Albany: State University of New York Press.

Kozinets, Robert V. 2010. *Netnography: Doing Ethnographic Research Online.* Thousand Oaks, CA: Sage.

Kreuter, Frauke, Stanley Presser, and Roger Tourangeau. 2008. "Social Desirability Bias in CATI, IVR, and Web Surveys: The Effects of Mode and Question Sensitivity." *Public Opinion Quarterly* 72:847–865.

Krosnick, Jon A. 1999. "Survey Research." *Annual Review of Psychology* 50:537–567.

Krueger, Richard A., and Mary Anne Casey. 2009. *Focus Groups: A Practical Guide for Applied Research,* 4th ed. Thousand Oaks, CA: Sage.

Kuzel, Anton J. 1999. "Sampling in Qualitative Inquiry." Pp. 33–45 in *Doing Qualitative Research,* 2nd ed., edited by Benjamin F. Crabtree and William L. Miller. Thousand Oaks, CA: Sage.

Kvale, Steinar. 2002. "The Social Construction of Validity." Pp. 299–325 in *The Qualitative Inquiry Reader,* edited by Norman K. Denzin and Yvonna S. Lincoln. Thousand Oaks, CA: Sage.

Labaw, Patricia J. 1980. *Advanced Questionnaire Design.* Cambridge, MA: ABT Books.

Lareau, Annette. 2002. "Invisible Inequality: Social Class and Childrearing in Black Families and White Families." *American Sociological Review* 67:747–776.

Laub, John H. 2012. "Presidential Plenary Address—Strengthening Science to Promote Justice and Public Safety." ACJS Annual Conference, March 15. Retrieved from www.nij.gov/about/speeches/pages/acjs-march-2012.aspx

Lavin, Michael R. 1994. *Understanding the 1990 Census: A Guide for Marketers, Planners, Grant Writers and Other Data Users.* Kenmore, NY: Epoch Books.

Lavrakas, Paul J. 1987. *Telephone Survey Methods: Sampling, Selection, and Supervision.* Newbury Park, CA: Sage.

Layte, Richard, and Christopher T. Whelan. 2003. "Moving In and Out of Poverty: The Impact of Welfare Regimes on Poverty Dynamics in the EU." *European Societies* 5:167–191.

Lehrer, Jonah. 2010. "The Truth Wears Off: Is There Something Wrong With the Scientific Method?" *The New Yorker,* December 13:52–57.

Lempert, Richard. 1989. "Humility Is a Virtue: On the Publicization of Policy-Relevant Research." *Law and Society Review,* 23:146–161.

Lempert, Richard and Joseph Sanders. 1986. *An Invitation to Law and Social Science: Desert, Disputes, and Distribution.* New York: Longman.

Levine, James P. 1976. "The Potential for Crime Overreporting in Criminal Victimization Surveys." *Criminology* 14:307–330.

Levine, Judith. 2015. *Ain't No Trust: How Bosses, Boyfriends, and Bureaucrats Fail Low-Income Mothers and Why It Matters.* Oakland, CA: University of California Press.

Levinson, Martin P. 2010. "Accountability to Research Participants: Unresolved Dilemmas and Unravelling Ethics." *Ethnography and Education* 5:193–207.

Levitt, Heidi M., Rebecca Todd Swanger, and Jenny B. Butler. 2008. "Male Perpetrators' Perspectives on Intimate Partner Violence, Religion, and Masculinity." *Sex Roles* 58:435–448.

Levy, Paul S., and Stanley Lemeshow. 1999. *Sampling of Populations: Methods and Applications,* 3rd ed. New York: Wiley.

Lewis-Beck, Michael S., Alan Bryman, and Tim Futing Liao (Eds.). 2004. *The SAGE Encyclopedia of Social Science Research Methods,* vol. 1. Thousand Oaks, CA: Sage.

Lincoln, Yvonna S. 2009. "Ethical Practices in Qualitative Research." Pp. 150–169 in *The Handbook of Social Research Ethics,* edited by Donna M. Mertens and Pauline E. Ginsberg. Thousand Oaks, CA: Sage.

Locke, Lawrence F., Stephen J. Silverman, and Waneen Wyrick Spirduso. 1998. *Reading and Understanding Research.* Thousand Oaks, CA: Sage.

Lotan, Gilad, Erhard Graeff, Mike Ananny, Devin Gaffney, Ian Pearce, and danah boyd. 2011. "The Revolutions Were Tweeted: Information Flows During the 2011 Tunisian and

Egyptian Revolutions." *International Journal of Communication* 5:1375-1405.

Luxardo, Natalia, Graciela Colombo, and Gabriela Iglesias. 2011. "Methodological and Ethical Dilemmas Encountered During Field Research of Family Violence Experienced by Adolescent Women in Buenos Aires." *The Qualitative Report* 16: 984–1000.

Lynch, Michael and David Bogen. 1997. "Sociology's Asociological 'Core': An Examination of Textbook Sociology in Light of the Sociology of Scientific Knowledge." *American Sociological Review* 62:481–493.

Mabry, Linda. 2008. "Case Study in Social Research." Pp. 214–227 in *The SAGE Handbook of Social Research Methods,* edited by Pertti Alasuutari, Leonard Bickman, and Julia Brannen. Thousand Oaks, CA: Sage.

Madden, Raymond. 2010. *Being Ethnographic: A Guide to the Theory and Practice of Ethnography.* Thousand Oaks, CA: Sage.

Mahfoud, Ziyad, Lilian Ghandour, Blanche Ghandour, Ali H. Mokdad, and Abla M. Sibai. 2014. "Cell Phone and Face-to-Face Interview Responses in Population-Based Surveys: How Do They Compare?" *Field Methods* 27:39-54.

Manza, Jeff, Clem Brooks, and Michael Sauder. 2005. "Money, Participation, and Votes: Social Cleavages and Electoral Politics." Pp. 201–226 in *The Handbook of Political Sociology: States, Civil Societies, and Globalization,* edited by Thomas Janoski, Robert R. Alford, Alexander M. Hicks, and Mildred A. Schwartz. New York: Cambridge University Press.

Mangione, Thomas W. 1995. *Mail Surveys: Improving the Quality.* Thousand Oaks, CA: Sage.

Marchie, Stephen. 2015. "The Epidemic of Facelessness." *New York Times,* February 14.

Marcus, Adam, and Ivan Oransky. 2015. "What's Behind Big Science Frauds?" *New York Times,* May 23:A19.

Marini, Margaret Mooney, and Burton Singer. 1988. "Causality in the Social Sciences." Pp. 347–409 in *Sociological Methodology,* vol. 18, edited by Clifford C. Clogg. Washington, DC: American Sociological Association.

Mark, Melvin M., and Chris Gamble. 2009. "Experiments, Quasi-Experiments, and Ethics." Pp. 198–213 in *The Handbook of Social Research Ethics,* edited by Donna M. Mertens and Pauline E. Ginsberg. Thousand Oaks, CA: Sage.

Markoff, John. 2005. "Transitions to Democracy." Pp. 384–403 in *The Handbook of Political Sociology: States, Civil Societies, and Globalization,* edited by Thomas Janoski, Robert R. Alford, Alexander M. Hicks, and Mildred A. Schwartz. New York: Cambridge University Press.

Martin, Lawrence L., and Peter M. Kettner. 1996. *Measuring the Performance of Human Service Programs.* Thousand Oaks, CA: Sage.

Martin, Linda G., and Kevin Kinsella. 1995. "Research on the Demography of Aging in Developing Countries." Pp. 356–403 in *Demography of Aging,* edited by Linda G. Martin and Samuel H. Preston. Washington, DC: National Academies Press.

Marwick, Alice, and danah boyd. 2011. "The Drama! Teen Conflict, Gossip, and Bullying in Networked Publics." A Decade in Internet time: Symposium on the Dynamics of the Internet and Society. Paper presented at the Oxford Internet Institute, Oxford, UK, September 22, 2011.

Maxwell, Joseph A. 2005. *Qualitative Research Design: An Interactive Approach,* 2nd ed. Thousand Oaks, CA: Sage.

Mayer-Schönberger, Viktor, and Kenneth Cukier. 2013. *Big Data: A Revolution That Will Transform How We Live, Work, and Think.* Boston: Houghton Mifflin Harcourt.

Mayrl, Damon, Ben Moodie, Jon Norman, Jodi Short, Sarah Staveteig, and Cinzia Solari. 2004. "A Theory of Relativity." *Contexts* 3:10.

McCarter, Susan A. 2009. "Legal and Extralegal Factors Affecting Minority Overrepresentation in Virginia's Juvenile Justice System: A Mixed-Method Study." *Child and Adolescent Social Work Journal* 26:533–544.

McGeeney, Kyley and Scott Keeter. 2014. "Pew Research Increases Share of Interviews Conducted by Cellphone." Pew Research Center, January 15. Retrieved July 2, 2014, from www.pewresearch .org/fact-tank/2014/01/15/pew-research-increases-share-of-interviews-conducted-by-cellphone

McPherson, Miller, Lynn Smith-Lovin, and Matthew E. Brashears. 2006. "Social Isolation in America: Changes in Core Discussion Networks Over Two Decades." *American Sociological Review* 71:353–375.

Mertens, Donna M. 2012. "Transformative Mixed Methods: Addressing Inequities." *American Behavioral Scientist* 56:802–813.

Messner, Steven F., Lawrence E. Raffalovich, and Gretchen M. Sutton. 2010. "Poverty, Infant Mortality, and Homicide Rates in Cross-National Perspective: Assessments of Criterion and Construct Validity." *Criminology* 48:509–537.

Mieczkowski, Tom. 1997. "Hair Assays and Urinalysis Results for Juvenile Drug Offenders." *National Institute of Justice Research Preview.* Washington, DC: U.S. Department of Justice.

Milgram, Stanley. 1964. "Issues in the Study of Obedience: A Reply to Baumrind." *American Psychologist* 19:848–852.

Milgram, Stanley. 1992. *The Individual in a Social World: Essays and Experiments,* 2nd ed. New York: McGraw-Hill.

Miller, Arthur G. 1986. *The Obedience Experiments: A Case Study of Controversy in Social Science.* New York: Praeger.

Miller, Delbert C. 1991. *Handbook of Research Design and Social Measurement,* 5th ed. Newbury Park, CA: Sage.

Miller, Delbert C., and Neil J. Salkind. 2002. *Handbook of Research Design and Social Measurement,* 6th ed. Thousand Oaks, CA: Sage.

Miller, William L., and Benjamin F. Crabtree. 1999c. "Depth Interviewing." Pp. 89–107 in *Doing Qualitative Research,* 2nd ed., edited by Benjamin F. Crabtree and William L. Miller. Thousand Oaks, CA: Sage.

Mills, C. Wright. 1959. *The Sociological Imagination.* New York: Oxford University Press.

Mirowsky, John, and Catherine E. Ross. 1999. "Economic Hardship Across the Life Course." *American Sociological Review* 64:548–569.

Mirowsky, John, and Catherine E. Ross. 2001. *Aging, Status, and the Sense of Control (ASOC), 1995, 1998, 2001 [United States] Questionnaire* (ICPSR 3334). Ann Arbor, MI: Inter-University Consortium for Political and Social Research.

Mitchell, Richard G. Jr. 1993. *Secrecy and Fieldwork.* Newbury Park, CA: Sage.

Moe, Angela M. 2007. "Silenced Voices and Structural Survival—Battered Women's Help Seeking." *Violence Against Women* 13(7):676–699.

Mohr, Lawrence B. 1992. *Impact Analysis for Program Evaluation.* Newbury Park, CA: Sage.

Morales, Andrea. 2015. "Visiting Nurses, Helping Mothers on the Margins." *New York Times,* March 8.

Morrill, Calvin, Christine Yalda, Madeleine Adelman, Michael Musheno, and Cindy Bejarano. 2000. "Telling Tales in School: Youth Culture and Conflict Narratives." *Law & Society Review* 34:521–565.

Motel, Seth, and Eileen Patten. 2013. "Statistical Portrait of the Foreign-Born Population in the United States." Pew Research Center, Hispanic Trends, January 29. Retrieved from http://www.pewhispanic.org/2013/01/29/statistical-portrait-of-the-foreign-born-population-in-the-united-states-2011/

Nagourney, Adam. 2002. "Cellphones and Caller ID Are Making It Harder for Pollsters to Pick a Winner." *New York Times,* November 5, p. A20.

Nakonezny, Paul A., Rebecca Reddick, and Joseph Lee Rodgers. 2004. "Did Divorces Decline After the Oklahoma City Bombing?" *Journal of Marriage and Family* 66:90–100.

Narayan, Sowmya, and Jon A. Krosnick. 1996. "Education Moderates Some Response Effects in Attitude Measurement." *Public Opinion Quarterly* 60:58–88.

National Institutes of Health (NIH). n.d. *About Behavioral and Social Sciences Research.* Bethesda, MD: National Institutes of Health.

National Oceanic and Atmospheric Administration (NOAA). 2005. *Hurricane Katrina.* Washington, DC: U.S. Department of Commerce. Retrieved from www.ncdc.noaa.gov/extremeevents/specialreports/Hurricane-Katrina.pdf

National Opinion Research Center (NORC). 2013. Release Notes for the GSS 2012 Merged Data, Release 1. Retrieved from http://publicdata .norc.org/41000/gss/documents//OTHR/Release%20Notes%20for%20the%20GSS%202012%20Merged%20R1.pdf

Neuendorf, Kimberly A. 2002. *The Content Analysis Guidebook.* Thousand Oaks, CA: Sage.

Orcutt, James D., and J. Blake Turner. 1993. "Shocking Numbers and Graphic Accounts: Quantified Images of Drug Problems in the Print Media." *Social Problems* 49(May):190–206.

Orr, Larry L. 1999. *Social Experiments: Evaluating Public Programs With Experimental Methods.* Thousand Oaks, CA: Sage.

Orshansky, Mollie. 1977. "Memorandum for Daniel P. Moynihan. Subject: History of the

Poverty Line." Pp. 232–237 in *The Measure of Poverty. Technical Paper I: Documentation of Background Information and Rationale for Current Poverty Matrix,* edited by Mollie Orshansky. Washington, DC: U.S. Department of Health, Education, and Welfare.

Parker-Pope, Tara. 2010. "As Girls Become Women, Sports Pay Dividends." *New York Times,* February 16, p. D5.

Parks, Kathleen A., Ann M. Pardi, and Clara M. Bradizza. 2006. "Collecting Data on Alcohol Use and Alcohol-Related Victimization: A Comparison of Telephone and Web-Based Survey Methods." *Journal of Studies on Alcohol* 67:318–323.

Pate, Antony M., and Edwin E. Hamilton. 1992. "Formal and Informal Deterrents to Domestic Violence: The Dade County Spouse Assault Experiment." *American Sociological Review* 57(October):691–697.

Paternoster, Raymond, Robert Brame, Ronet Bachman, and Lawrence W. Sherman. 1997. "Do Fair Procedures Matter? The Effect of Procedural Justice on Spouse Assault." *Law & Society Review* 31(1):163–204.

Patton, Michael Quinn. 2002. *Qualitative Research & Evaluation Methods,* 3rd ed. Thousand Oaks, CA: Sage.

Paxton, Pamela. 2002. "Social Capital and Democracy: An Interdependent Relationship." *American Sociological Review* 67:254–277.

Paxton, Pamela. 2005. "Trust in Decline?" *Contexts* 4:40–46.

Perrin, Andrew, and Maeve Duggan. 2015. "American's Internet Access: 2000–2015." Pew Research Center. Retrieved from www.pewinternet.org/2015/06/26/americans-internet-access-2000-2015/

Perry, Gina. 2013. *Behind the Shock Machine: The Untold Story of the Notorious Milgram Psychology Experiments.* New York: New Press.

Peterson, Robert A. 2000. *Constructing Effective Questionnaires.* Thousand Oaks, CA: Sage.

Pew Research Center. 2014. "Mobile Technology Fact Sheet." Retrieved from www.pewinternet.org/fact-sheets/mobile-technology-fact-sheet/

Pew Research Center. 2015. "U.S. Smartphone Use in 2015." Retrieved from www.pewinternet.org/2015/04/01/us-smartphone-use-in-2015/

Piliavin, Jane Allyn, and Irving M. Piliavin. 1972. "Effect of Blood on Reactions to a Victim." *Journal of Personality and Social Psychology* 23:353–361.

Plessy v. Ferguson, 163 U.S. 537 (1896).

Porter, Stephen R., and Michael E. Whitcomb. 2003. "The Impact of Contact Type on Web Survey Response Rates." *Public Opinion Quarterly* 67:579–588.

Posavac, Emil J., and Raymond G. Carey. 1997. *Program Evaluation: Methods and Case Studies,* 5th ed. Upper Saddle River, NJ: Prentice Hall.

Presser, Stanley, Mick P. Couper, Judith T. Lessler, Elizabeth Martin, Jean Martin, Jennifer M. Rothgeb, and Eleanor Singer. 2004. "Methods for Testing and Evaluating Survey Questions." *Public Opinion Quarterly* 68:109–130.

Presley, Cheryl A., Philip W. Meilman, and Rob Lyerla. 1994. "Development of the Core Alcohol and Drug Survey: Initial Findings and Future Directions." *Journal of American College Health* 42: 248–255.

Prewitt, Kenneth, Thomas A. Schwandt, and Miron L. Straf (Eds.). 2012. *Using Science as Evidence in Public Policy.* Washington, DC: National Academies Press.

Price, Richard H., Michelle Van Ryn, and Amiram D. Vinokur. 1992. "Impact of a Preventive Job Search Intervention on the Likelihood of Depression Among the Unemployed." *Journal of Health and Social Behavior* 33 (June):158–167.

Putnam, Israel. 1977. "Poverty Thresholds: Their History and Future Development." Pp. 272–283 in *The Measure of Poverty. Technical Paper I: Documentation of Background Information and Rationale for Current Poverty Matrix,* edited by Mollie Orshansky. Washington, DC: U.S. Department of Health, Education, and Welfare.

Pyrczak, Fred. 2005. *Evaluating Research in Academic Journals: A Practical Guide to Realistic Evaluation,* 3rd ed. Glendale, CA: Pyrczak.

Raento, Mika, Antti Oulasvirta, and Nathan Eagle. 2009. "Smartphones: An Emerging Tool for Social Scientists." *Sociological Methods & Research* 37:426-454.

Ragin, Charles C. 1987. *The Comparative Method: Moving Beyond Qualitative and Quantitative Strategies.* Berkeley: University of California Press.

Ragin, Charles C. 1994. *Constructing Social Research.* Thousand Oaks, CA: Sage.

Ragin, Charles C. 2000. *Fuzzy-Set Social Science.* Chicago: University of Chicago Press.

Rainie, Lee, and John Horrigan. 2005. *A Decade of Adoption: How the Internet Has Woven Itself Into American Life.* Pew Internet & American Life Project. Retrieved from the Pew Internet & American Life Project, www.pewinternet.org/PPF/r/148/report_display.asp (PDF version)

Rainie, Lee, Aaron Smith, and Maeve Duggan. 2013. *Coming and Going on Facebook.* Washington, DC: Pew Internet & American Life Project.

Randall, Ann. 2012. "Beneficial Interview Effects in Virtual Worlds: A Case Study." Pp. 131–149 in *Cases in Online Interview Research,* edited by Janet Salmons. Thousand Oaks, CA: Sage.

Raskin, Robert N., and Calvin S. Hall. 1979. "A Narcissistic Personality Inventory." *Psychological Reports* 45:590.

Revilla, Melanie A., Willem E. Saris, and Jon A. Krosnick. 2013. "Choosing the Number of Categories in Agree-Disagree Scales." *Sociological Methods & Research* 43:73-97.

Rew, Lynn, Deborah Koniak-Griffin, Mary Ann Lewis, Margaret Miles, and Ann O'Sullivan. 2000. "Secondary Data Analysis: New Perspective for Adolescent Research." *Nursing Outlook* 48:223–229.

Reynolds, Paul Davidson. 1979. *Ethical Dilemmas and Social Science Research.* San Francisco: Jossey-Bass.

Richards, Thomas J., and Lyn Richards. 1994. "Using Computers in Qualitative Research." Pp. 445–462 in *Handbook of Qualitative Research,* edited by Norman K. Denzin and Yvonna S. Lincoln. Thousand Oaks, CA: Sage.

Riedel, Marc. 2000. *Research Strategies for Secondary Data: A Perspective for Criminology and Criminal Justice.* Thousand Oaks, CA: Sage.

Riessman, Catherine Kohler. 2008. *Narrative Methods for the Human Sciences.* Thousand Oaks, CA: Sage.

Rinehart, Jenny K., and Elizabeth A. Yeater. 2011. "A Qualitative Analysis of Sexual Victimization Narratives." *Violence Against Women* 17(7):925–943.

Ringwalt, Christopher L., Jody M. Greene, Susan T. Ennett, Ronaldo Iachan, Richard R. Clayton, and Carl G. Leukefeld. 1994. *Past and Future Directions of the D.A.R.E. Program: An Evaluation Review.* Research Triangle, NC: Research Triangle Institute.

Rives, Norfleet W., Jr., and William J. Serow. 1988. *Introduction to Applied Demography: Data Sources and Estimation Techniques.* SAGE University Paper Series on Quantitative Applications in the Social Sciences, series No. 07–039. Thousand Oaks, CA: Sage.

Robinson, Karen A., and Steven N. Goodman. 2011. "A Systematic Examination of the Citation of Prior Research in Reports of Randomized, Controlled Trials." *Annals of Internal Medicine* 154:50–55.

Rocheleau, Carissa M., Paul A. Romitti, Stacey Hockett Sherlock, Wayne T. Sanderson, Erin M. Bell, and Charlotte Druschel. 2012. "Effect of Survey Instrument on Participation in a Follow-Up Study: A Randomization Study of a Mailed Questionnaire Versus a Computer-Assisted Telephone Interview." *BMC Public Health* 12:579.

Rocheleau, Matt. 2014. "Harvard Secretly Photographed Students to Study Attendance." *Boston Globe,* November 5.

Rodríguez, Havidán, Joseph Trainor, and Enrico L. Quarantelli. 2006. "Rising to the Challenges of a Catastrophe: The Emergent and Prosocial Behavior Following Hurricane Katrina." *Annals of the American Academy of Political and Social Science* 604:82–101.

Rosen, Lawrence. 1995. "The Creation of the Uniform Crime Report: The Role of Social Science." *Social Science History* 19:215–238.

Rosenbaum, Dennis P. 2007. "Just Say No to D.A.R.E." *Criminology & Public Policy* 6:815–824.

Rosenbaum, Dennis P., and Gordon S. Hanson.1998. "Assessing the Effects of School-Based Drug Education: A Six-Year Multi-Level Analysis of Project D.A.R.E." *Journal of Research in Crime and Delinquency* 35:381–412.

Rosenthal, Elisabeth. 2000. "Rural Flouting of One-Child Policy Undercuts China's Census." *New York Times,* April 14, p. A10.

Rossi, Peter H., and Howard E. Freeman. 1989. *Evaluation: A Systematic Approach,* 4th ed. Newbury Park, CA: Sage.

Rossman, Gretchen B., and Sharon F. Rallis. 1998. *Learning in the Field: An Introduction to Qualitative Research.* Thousand Oaks, CA: Sage.

Rubin, Herbert J., and Irene S. Rubin. 1995. *Qualitative Interviewing: The Art of Hearing Data.* Thousand Oaks, CA: Sage.

Rueschemeyer, Dietrich, Evelyne Huber Stephens, and John D. Stephens. 1992. *Capitalist Development and Democracy.* Chicago: University of Chicago Press.

Ruggles, Patricia. 1990. *Drawing the Line: Alternative Poverty Measures and Their Implications for Public Policy.* Washington, DC: Urban Institute Press.

Sacks, Stanley, Karen McKendrick, George DeLeon, Michael T. French, and Kathryn E. McCollister. 2002. "Benefit-Cost Analysis of a Modified Therapeutic Community for Mentally Ill Chemical Abusers." *Evaluation and Program Planning* 25:137–148.

Salmons, Janet. 2012. "Designing and Conducting Research With Online Interviews." Pp. 1–35 in *Cases in Online Interview Research,* edited by Janet Salmons. Thousand Oaks, CA: Sage.

Schaeffer, Nora Cate, and Stanley Presser. 2003. "The Science of Asking Questions." *Annual Review of Sociology* 29:65–88.

Schober, Michael F. 1999. "Making Sense of Survey Questions." Pp. 77–94 in *Cognition and Survey Research,* edited by Monroe G. Sirken, Douglas J. Herrmann, Susan Schechter, Norbert Schwartz, Judith M. Tanur, and Roger Tourangeau. New York: Wiley.

Schofield, Janet Ward. 2002. "Increasing the Generalizability of Qualitative Research." Pp. 171–203 in *The Qualitative Researcher's Companion,* edited by A. Michael Huberman and Matthew B. Miles. Thousand Oaks, CA: Sage.

Schuck, Amie M. 2013. "A Life-Course Perspective on Adolescents' Attitudes to Police: DARE, Delinquency, and Residential Segregation." *Journal of Research in Crime and Delinquency* 50(4):579–607.

Schuman, Howard, and Stanley Presser. 1981. *Questions and Answers in Attitude Surveys: Experiments on Question Form, Wording, and Context.* New York: Academic Press.

Schutt, Russell K. 2011. *Homelessness, Housing, and Mental Illness.* Cambridge, MA: Harvard University Press.

Schwarz, Norbert. 2010. "Measurement as Cooperative Communication: What Research Participants Learn From Questionnaires." Pp. 43–59 in *The SAGE Handbook of Measurement,* edited by Geoffrey Walford, Eric Tucker, and Madhu Viswanathan. Thousand Oaks, CA: Sage.

Scull, Andrew T. 1988. "Deviance and Social Control." Pp. 667–693 in *Handbook of Sociology,* edited by Neil J. Smelser. Newbury Park, CA: Sage.

Sechrest, Lee, and Souraya Sidani. 1995. "Quantitative and Qualitative Methods: Is There an Alternative?" *Evaluation and Program Planning* 18:77–87.

Selm, Martine Van, and Nicholas W. Jankowski. 2006. "Conducting Online Surveys." *Quality & Quantity* 40:435–456.

Selwitz, Ada Sue, Norma Epley, and Janelle Erickson. 2013. "Basic Institutional Review Board (IRB): Regulations and Review Process." Miami: Collaborative Institutional Training Initiative at the University of Miami. Retrieved from https://www.citiprogram.org/

Sharma, Divya. 2009. "Research Ethics and Sensitive Behaviors: Underground Economy." Pp. 426–441 in *The Handbook of Social Research Ethics,* edited by Donna M. Mertens and Pauline E. Ginsberg. Thousand Oaks, CA: Sage.

Shepherd, Jane, David Hill, Joel Bristor, and Pat Montalvan. 1996. "Converting an Ongoing Health Study to CAPI: Findings From the

National Health and Nutrition Study." Pp. 159–164 in *Health Survey Research Methods Conference Proceedings,* edited by Richard B. Warnecke. Hyattsville, MD: U.S. Department of Health and Human Services.

Sherman, Lawrence W. 1992. *Policing Domestic Violence: Experiments and Dilemmas.* New York: Free Press.

Sherman, Lawrence W. 1993. "Implications of a Failure to Read the Literature." *American Sociological Review* 58:888–889.

Sherman, Lawrence W., and Richard A. Berk. 1984. "The Specific Deterrent Effects of Arrest for Domestic Assault." *American Sociological Review* 49:261–272.

Sherman, Lawrence W., and Heather M. Harris. 2013. "Increased Homicide Victimization of Suspects Arrested for Domestic Assault: A 23-Year Follow-Up of the Milwaukee Domestic Violence Experiment (MilDVE)." *Journal of Experimental Criminology* 9:491–514.

Sherman, Lawrence W., and Douglas A. Smith, with Janell D. Schmidt and Dennis P. Rogan. 1992. "Crime, Punishment, and Stake in Conformity: Legal and Informal Control of Domestic Violence." *American Sociological Review* 57:680–690.

Sieber, Joan E. 1992. *Planning Ethically Responsible Research: A Guide for Students and Internal Review Boards.* Thousand Oaks, CA: Sage.

Sieber, Joan E., and Martin B. Tolich. 2013. *Planning Ethically Responsible Research,* 2nd ed. Thousand Oaks, CA: Sage.

Simpson, Brent. 2006. "The Poverty of Trust in the Southern United States." *Social Forces* 84:1625-1638.

Sjoberg, Gideon (Ed.). 1967. *Ethics, Politics, and Social Research.* Cambridge, MA: Schenkman.

Skinner, Harvey A., and Wen-Jenn Sheu. 1982. "Reliability of Alcohol Use Indices: The Lifetime Drinking History and the MAST." *Journal of Studies on Alcohol* 43(11):1157–1170.

Skocpol, Theda. 1984. "Emerging Agendas and Recurrent Strategies in Historical Sociology." Pp. 356–391 in *Vision and Method in Historical Sociology,* edited by Theda Skocpol. New York: Cambridge University Press.

Sloboda, Zili, Richard C. Stephens, Peggy C. Stephens, Scott F. Grey, Brent Teasdale, Richard D. Hawthorne, Joseph Williams, and Jesse F. Marquette. 2009. "The Adolescent Substance Abuse Prevention Study: A Randomized Field Trial of a Universal Substance Abuse Prevention Program." *Drug and Alcohol Dependence* 102(1–3):1–10.

Smith, Craig. 2015. "By the Numbers: 14 Interesting Flikr Stats." DMR, August 10. Retrieved from http://expandedramblings.com/index.php/flickr-stats/

Smith, D. E. 2005. *Institutional Ethnography: A Sociology for People.* Toronto: AltaMira Press.

Smith, Erica L., and Alexia Cooper. 2013. *Homicide in the U.S. Known to Law Enforcement, 2011.* Washington, DC: Bureau of Justice Statistics, U.S. Department of Justice.

Smithson, Janet. 2008. "Focus Groups." Pp. 357–370 in *The SAGE Handbook of Social Research Methods,* edited by Pertti Alasuutari, Leonard Bickman, and Julia Brannen. Thousand Oaks, CA: Sage.

Snipp, C. Matthew. 2003. "Racial Measurement in the American Census: Past Practices and Implications for the Future." *Annual Review of Sociology* 29:563–588.

Speiglman, Richard, and Patricia Spear. 2009. "The Role of Institutional Review Boards: Ethics: Now You See Them, Now You Don't." Pp. 121–134 in *The Handbook of Social Research Ethics,* edited by Donna M. Mertens and Pauline E. Ginsberg. Thousand Oaks, CA: Sage.

St. Jean, Peter K. B. 2007. *Pockets of Crime: Broken Windows, Collective Efficacy, and the Criminal Point of View.* Chicago: University of Chicago Press.

Stake, Robert, and Fazal Rizvi. 2009. "Research Ethics in Transnational Spaces." Pp. 521–536 in *The Handbook of Social Research Ethics,* edited by Donna M. Mertens and Pauline E. Ginsberg. Thousand Oaks, CA: Sage.

Statista. 2015. "Number of Monthly Active Facebook Users Worldwide as of 2nd Quarter 2015 (in Millions)." Retrieved from http://www.statista.com/statistics/264810/number-of-monthly-active-facebook-users-worldwide/

Statistic Brain. 2013. "Social Networking Statistics." Retrieved from www.statisticbrain.com/social-networking-statistics/

Stephen, Jason M., Michael F. Young, and Thomas Calabrese. 2007. "Does Moral Judgment Go Offline When Students Are Online? A Comparative Analysis of Undergraduates' Beliefs and Behaviors Related to Conventional and Digital Cheating." *Ethics & Behavior* 17:233–254.

Stephens-Davidowitz, Seth. 2015. "Googling for God." *New York Times,* September 19:SR1.

Stewart, David W., and Michael A. Kamins. 1993. *Secondary Research: Information Sources and Methods,* 2nd ed. Newbury Park, CA: Sage.

Stewart, James K. 2011. "John Laub and Robert Sampson Awarded Stockholm Prize." Retrieved from www.nij.gov/about/director/Pages/stockholm-prize.aspx

Stokoe, Elizabeth. 2006. "On Ethnomethodology, Feminism, and the Analysis of Categorical Reference to Gender in Talk-in-Interaction." *Sociological Review* 54:467–494.

Strauss, Anselm L., and Juliette Corbin. 1990. *The Basics of Qualitative Research: Grounded Theory Procedures and Techniques.* Newbury Park, CA: Sage.

Sudman, Seymour. 1976. *Applied Sampling.* New York: Academic Press.

Sue, Valerie M., and Lois A. Ritter. 2012. *Conducting Online Surveys,* 2nd ed. Thousand Oaks, CA: Sage.

Sunderland, Antonia. 2005. *Children, Families and Welfare Reform: A Three-City Study.* Princeton, NJ: The Robert Wood Johnson Foundation. Retrieved from www.rwjf.org/reports/grr/037218.htm

Testa, Maria, Jennifer A. Livingston, and Carol VanZile-Tamsen. 2011. "Advancing the Study of Violence Against Women Using Mixed Methods: Integrating Qualitative Methods Into a Quantitative Research Program." *Violence Against Women* 17(2): 236–250.

Thorne, Barrie. 1993. *Gender Play: Girls and Boys in School.* New Brunswick, NJ: Rutgers University Press.

Tigges, Beth Baldwin. 2003. "Parental Consent and Adolescent Risk Behavior Research." *Journal of Nursing Scholarship* 35:283–289.

Tinkler, Penny. 2013. *Using Photographs in Social and Historical Research.* Thousand Oaks, CA: Sage.

Tjaden, Patricia and Nancy Thoennes. 2000. Extent, Nature, and Consequences of Intimate Partner Violence: Findings From the National Violence Against Women Survey, NCJ 181867. Washington, DC: Office of Justice Programs, National Institute of Justice and the Centers for Disease Control and Prevention.

Toppo, Greg. 2002. "Antidrug Program Backed by Study." *Boston Globe,* October 29, p. A10.

Tourangeau, Roger. 1999. "Context Effects." Pp. 111–132 in *Cognition and Survey Research,* edited by Monroe G. Sirken, Douglas J. Herrmann, Susan Schechter, Norbert Schwartz, Judith M. Tanur, and Roger Tourangeau. New York: Wiley.

Tourangeau, Roger. 2004. "Survey Research and Societal Change." *Annual Review of Psychology* 55:775–801.

Tourangeau, Roger, Frederick G. Conrad, and Mick P. Couper. 2012. *The Science of Web Surveys.* Oxford, UK: Oxford University Press.

Tufte, Edward R. 1983. *The Visual Display of Quantitative Information.* Cheshire, CT: Graphics Press.

Turabian, Kate L. 2013. *A Manual for Writers of Research Papers, Theses, and Dissertations,* 8th ed. Chicago: University of Chicago Press.

Turner, Charles F., and Elizabeth Martin (Eds.). 1984. *Surveying Subjective Phenomena,* vols. 1 and 2. New York: Russell Sage Foundation.

Tuskegee University. 2015. "About the USPHS Syphilis Study." Retrieved from www.tuskegee.edu/about_us/centers_of_excellence/bioethics_center/about_the_usphs_syphilis_study.aspx

UCLA Center for Communication Policy. 2003. *The UCLA Internet Report: Surveying the Digital Future, Year Three.* Los Angeles: UCLA Center for Communication Policy. Retrieved from www.digitalcenter.org/pdf/InternetReportYearThree.pdf

U.S. Census Bureau. 1981. *Section 1, Vital Statistics. Statistical Abstract of the United States, 1981,* 102nd ed. Washington, DC: U.S. Department of Commerce, Census Bureau.

U.S. Census Bureau. 1994. *Census Catalog and Guide, 1994.* Washington, DC: U.S. Bureau of the Census.

U.S. Census Bureau. 2013. "U.S. and World Population Clock." Retrieved from www.census.gov/popclock

Van Hoye, Greet, and Filip Lievens. 2003. "The Effects of Sexual Orientation on Hirability Ratings: An Experimental Study." *Journal of Business and Psychology* 18:15–30.

Van Maanen, John. 1995. "An End to Innocence: The Ethnography of Ethnography." Pp. 1–35 in *Representation in Ethnography,* edited by John Van Maanen. Thousand Oaks, CA: Sage.

Vega, Tanzina. 2014. "To Measure More Diverse America, Solution May Be in Census Questions." *New York Times,* July 2, pp. A12, A16.

Venkatesh, Sudhir. 2008. Gang Leader for a Day: *A Rogue Sociologist Takes to the Streets.* New York: Penguin.

Vincus, Amy A., Chris Ringwalt, Melissa S. Harris, and Stephen R. Shamblen. 2010. "A Short-Term, Quasi-Experimental Evaluation of D.A.R.E.'s Revised Elementary School Curriculum." *Journal of Drug Education* 40:37–49.

Walker, Robert, Mark Tomlinson, and Glenn Williams. 2010. "The Problem With Poverty: Definition, Measurement and Interpretation." Pp. 353–376 in *The SAGE Handbook of Measurement,* edited by Geoffrey Walford, Eric Tucker, and Madhu Viswanathan. Thousand Oaks, CA: Sage.

Wallgren, Anders, Britt Wallgren, Rolf Persson, Ulf Jorner, and Jan-Aage Haaland. 1996. *Graphing Statistics and Data: Creating Better Charts.* Thousand Oaks, CA: Sage.

Walters, Pamela Barnhouse, David R. James, and Holly J. McCammon. 1997. "Citizenship and Public Schools: Accounting for Racial Inequality in Education for the Pre- and Post-Disfranchisement South." *American Sociological Review* 62:34–52.

Ward, Jane. 2000. "A New Kind of AIDS: Adapting to the Success of Protease Inhibitors in an AIDS Care Organization." *Qualitative Sociology* 23:247-265.

Ward, Jane. 2003. "Producing 'Pride' in West Hollywood: A Queer Cultural Capital for Queers With Cultural Capital." *Sexualities* 6:65-94.

Warner, Barbara D. 2014. "Neighborhood Factors Related to the Likelihood of Successful Informal Control." *Journal of Criminal Justice* 42:421-430.

Washington, Harriet A. 2006. *Medical Apartheid: The Dark History of Medical Experimentation on Black Americans from Colonial Times to the Present.* New York: Doubleday.

Webb, Eugene J., Donald T. Campbell, Richard D. Schwartz, and Lee Sechrest. 2000. *Unobtrusive Measures,* rev. ed. Thousand Oaks, CA: Sage.

Weber, Robert Philip. 1990. *Basic Content Analysis,* 2nd ed. Newbury Park, CA: Sage.

Weinberg, Darin. 2000. "'Out There': The Ecology of Addiction in Drug Abuse Treatment Discourse." *Social Problems* 47:606–621.

Weisburd, David, Cynthia M. Lum, and Anthony Petrosino. 2001. "Does Research Design Affect Study Outcomes in Criminal Justice?" *Annals of the American Academy of Political and Social Science* 578:50–70.

Wellman, Barry, Anabel Quan Haase, James Witte, and Keith Hampton. 2001. "Does the Internet Increase, Decrease, or Supplement Social Capital? Social Networks, Participation, and Community Commitment." *American Behavioral Scientist,* 45:436–455.

Wellman, Barry, and Keith Hampton. 1999. "Living Networked in a Wired World." *Comparative Sociology* 28:1–12.

Welsh, Megan. 2015. "Categories of Exclusion: The Transformation of Formerly Incarcerated Women Into 'Able-Bodied Adults Without Dependents' in Welfare Processing." *Journal of Sociology and Social Welfare* 42:55-77.

West, Steven L., and Ken K. O'Neal. 2004. "Project D.A.R.E. Outcome Effectiveness Revisited." *American Journal of Public Health* 94:1027–1029.

Whyte, William Foote. 1955. *Street Corner Society,* 2nd ed. Chicago: University of Chicago Press.

Wiles, Rose, Amanda Coffey, Judy Robinson, and Sue Heath. 2012. "Anonymisation and Visual Images: Issues of Respect, 'Voice' and Protection." *International Journal of Social Research Methodology* 15:41–53.

Willer, David, and Henry A. Walker. 2007. *Building Experiments: Testing Social Theory.* Stanford, CA: Stanford University Press.

Witkin, Belle Ruth, and James W. Altschuld. 1995. *Planning and Conducting Needs Assessments: A Practical Guide.* Thousand Oaks, CA: Sage.

Wolcott, Harry F. 1995. *The Art of Fieldwork.* Walnut Creek, CA: AltaMira Press.

Wolf, Amanda, David Turner, and Kathleen Toms. 2009. "Ethical Perspectives in Program Evaluation." Pp. 170–184 in *The Handbook of Social Research Ethics,* edited by Donna M. Mertens and Pauline E. Ginsberg. Thousand Oaks, CA: Sage.

Zacks, Jeffrey. 2015. "Why Movie 'Facts' Prevail." *New York Times,* March 8.

Zaret, David. 1996. "Petitions and the 'Invention' of Public Opinion in the English Revolution." *American Journal of Sociology* 101:1497–1555.

Zeoli, April M., Echo A. Ribera, Cris M. Sullivan, and Sheryl Kubiak. 2013. "Post-Separation Abuse of Women and Their Children: Boundary-Setting and Family Court Utilization Among Victimized Mothers." *Journal of Family Violence* 9:491-514.

Zhong, Juan, and Jeffrey J. Arnett. 2014. "Conceptions of Adulthood Among Migrant Women Workers in China." *International Journal of Behavioral Development* 38:255–265.

Zimbardo, Philip. 2007. *The Lucifer Effect: Understanding How Good People Turn Evil.* New York: Random House.

Index

Exhibits and photos are indicated by e or p following the page number.